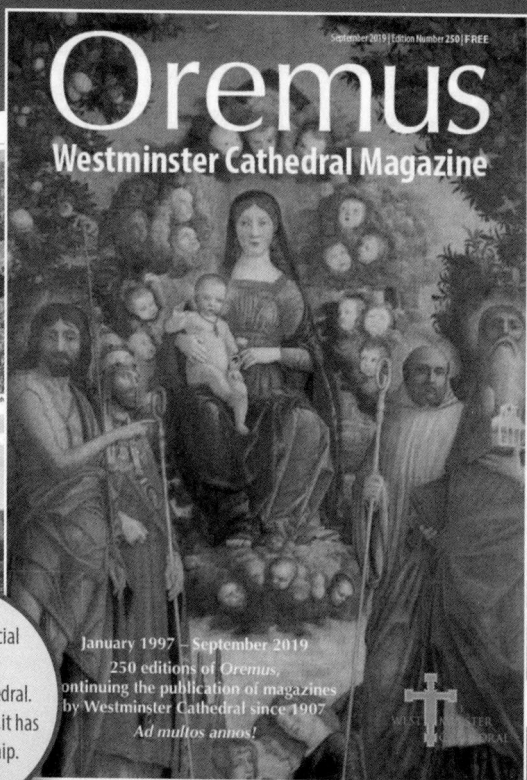

THE SODALITY OF THE BLESSED SACRAMENT

A Confraternity dedicated to Jesus Christ, Truly Present in the Most Holy Sacrament of the Eucharist

Solemn Sung Mass, Adoration & Benediction every month with a different guest preacher at the *Diocesan Shrine of the Blessed Sacrament*

Members receive a monthly newsletter and a Sodality lapel badge.

Monthly Mass offered for the intentions of members around the world. Music by the *Schola Corpus Christi.*

SODALITY 2020 MASSES

9th January
6th February
5th March
2nd April
7th May
4th June
2nd July
3rd September
1st October
5th November
3rd December

All at 6:30pm

SOLEMNITY OF CORPUS CHRISTI 2020 ANNUAL QUARANT'ORE AT THE SHRINE

Thursday 11th June, 7pm
Extraordinary Form Mass, opening *Quarant'Ore.*
Exposition until Midnight

Friday 12th June, 7am – Midnight
Exposition and continuation of Forty Hours

Satruday 13th June, 7am – 6pm
Exposition and continuation of Forty Hours
6pm – Solemn Mass closing *Quarant'Ore*

Sunday 14th June, 11am
Solemn Mass, followed by Procession of the Blessed Sacrament around Covent Garden

JOIN TODAY!

sodality.co.uk
facebook.com/blessedsacramentsodality

CORPUS CHRISTI SHRINE, MAIDEN LANE, LONDON, WC2E 7NB | 0207 836 4700

Corpus Christi is part of the Westminster Roman Catholic Diocesan Trust.
Registered Charity Number 233699

Westminster Year Book 2020

68th Edition

Patrons of the Diocese

Our Blessed Lady Immaculate, 8 December;
St Joseph, 19 March; St Peter, Prince of the Apostles, 29 June;
and St Edward the Confessor, 13 October.
Consecration to the Sacred Heart of Jesus 17 June 1873.

The Westminster Year Book
Archbishop's House, Ambrosden Avenue
London SW1P 1QJ
Editor: Fr John Scott
Tel: 020 7798 9370
Email: wyb@rcdow.org.uk

Published with authority by Westminster Roman Catholic Diocese Trustee © WRCDT
Compilation completed 31 October 2019. Information is correct at the time of going to print.

The Diocese of Westminster
comprises the London Boroughs
north of the River Thames
and west of Waltham Forest and Newham,
the Borough of Spelthorne, and the County of Hertfordshire

Unless stated otherwise,
all email addresses in this publication
are formed as follows:
Individuals: firstname+surname@rcdow.org.uk,
e.g. francesmurphy@rcdow.org.uk
Parishes: parish@rcdow.org.uk,
e.g. abbotslangley@rcdow.org.uk

Front cover:
On Sunday 13 October at Mass in St Peter's Square,
Pope Francis canonised St John Henry Newman
and four other saints in front of a large crowd
including many from the diocese,
both clergy and laity
© Photo: Marcin Mazur

Perfect-bound ISBN 978-0-9956262-5-6
Ring-bound ISBN 978-0-9956262-6-3

CONTENTS

Printed on paper
from responsible sources

Dear Brothers and Sisters in Christ

As we prepare for the year 2020, the great treasure we bring is the newly-canonised St John Henry Newman. Not only was the Canonisation Mass so filled with joy, but that joy continues, to encourage and enliven us. Reflection on his life and ministry has highlighted again how apt was the motto he chose at his creation as a Cardinal. The phrase 'Heart speaks unto heart' goes to the very essence of his ministry, which was often based on friendship and always on sensitivity to matters of the heart. His constant self-reflection was not at all a self-absorption, but rather a search for how God was at work in his life and for the pathway along which God was calling him.

That way was often difficult; his days were marked by weariness and misunderstanding. There were times of public criticism and condemnation, but he persevered, confident that the quiet presence of God was the firmest of foundation. In this we do well to follow him.

2020 is also the 10th anniversary of the Papal Visit of Pope Benedict XVI to our countries. Two themes from his words remain in my thoughts. In the Beatification homily, he quoted from a discourse of John Henry Newman, who insisted that the ministry of priests is, in some ways, superior to that of the angels. Newman said: 'Had Angels been your priests, they could not have condoled with you, sympathised with you, have had compassion on you, felt tenderly for you, and made allowances for you, as we can; they could not have been your patterns and guides, and have led you on from your old selves into a new life, as they can who come from the midst of you.' In this, too, we do well to follow him.

The second theme comes from Pope Benedict's speech in Westminster Hall in which he addressed the political culture which we still face today, particularly the need for constructive and respectful dialogue. In the year ahead we must always be offering prayer for the harmony of action which such respectful dialogue can help to engender. Our countries need a fresh vision of the values for which we stand and which should draw us all together in common causes, to be centred round the God-given dignity of every person. Therefore among them are the scourge of knife crime, the tragedy of human trafficking, the protection of the most vulnerable and our care for the created world.

May St John Henry Newman inspire our ministry and support us by his prayers.

✠ Vincent Nichols

Section 1

FRANCIS

BISHOP OF ROME, VICAR OF JESUS CHRIST
Successor of St Peter (Prince of the Apostles), Supreme Pastor of the Universal Church, Primate of Italy, Archbishop and Metropolitan of the Province of Rome, Sovereign of the State of the Vatican City, Servant of the Servants of God

His Holiness Pope Francis (Jorge Mario Bergoglio SJ)

Born in Buenos Aires, Argentina 17 December 1936.

Ordained Priest 13 December 1969.

Ordained Titular Bishop of Auca and Auxiliary Bishop of Buenos Aires 27 June 1992.

Appointed Co-adjutor Archbishop of Buenos Aires 3 June 1997.

Installed as Archbishop of Buenos Aires 28 February 1998.

Created Cardinal Priest of San Roberto Bellarmino 21 February 2001.

Elected Pope 13 March 2013.

Inaugurated 19 March 2013.

© Photo: Alexander Balzanella

Keep Faith Alight

This girl from Syria is one of millions of Christians worldwide suffering today — amidst war, famine and persecution. Please can you help them to keep faith alight?

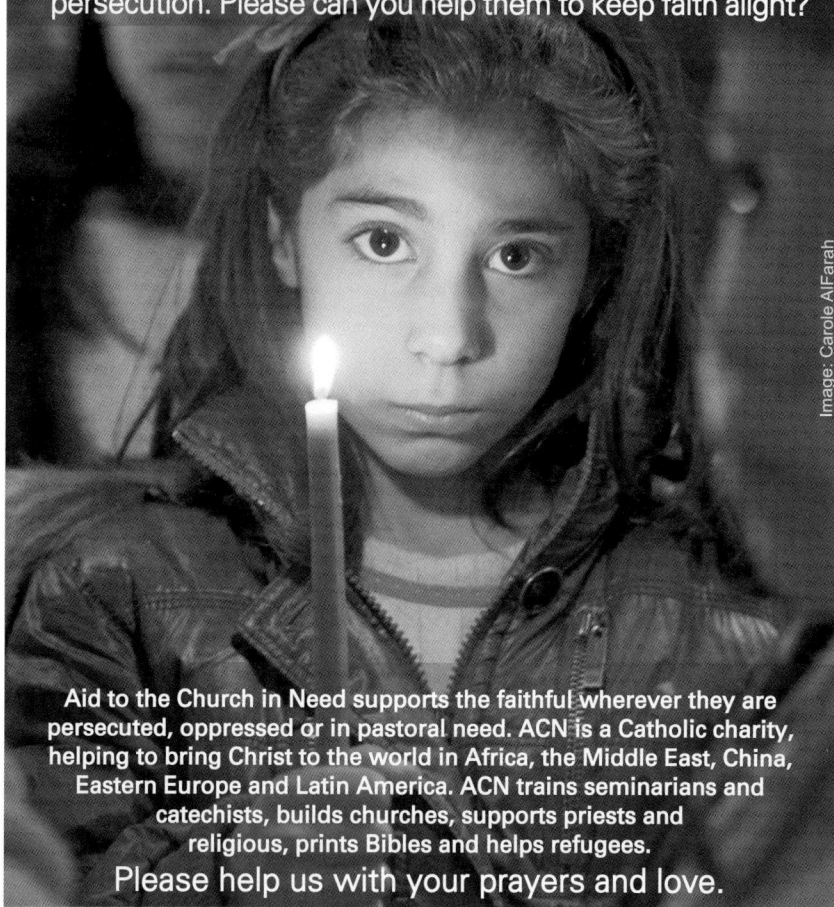

Image: Carole AlFarah

Aid to the Church in Need supports the faithful wherever they are persecuted, oppressed or in pastoral need. ACN is a Catholic charity, helping to bring Christ to the world in Africa, the Middle East, China, Eastern Europe and Latin America. ACN trains seminarians and catechists, builds churches, supports priests and religious, prints Bibles and helps refugees.

Please help us with your prayers and love.

Aid to the
Church in Need

ACN UNITED KINGDOM

12-14 Benhill Avenue, Sutton, Surrey SM1 4DA

A registered charity in England and Wales (1097984) and Scotland (SC040748)

www.acnuk.org Email: acn@acnuk.org Tel: 020 8642 8668

THE HIERARCHY IN ENGLAND AND WALES

Dates shown below are of Episcopal Ordination and Translation.
The Cardinal is addressed as **His Eminence**; Archbishops as **The Most Reverend**; and Bishops as **The Right Reverend**.

THE PROVINCE OF WESTMINSTER

WESTMINSTER Cardinal Vincent Nichols (1992; 2009)
Archbishop's House, Ambrosden Avenue SW1P 1QJ
Auxiliary Bishops John Sherrington (2011), Nicholas Hudson (2014), Paul McAleenan (2016)
BRENTWOOD Alan Williams SM (2014)
Cathedral House, Ingrave Road, Brentwood, Essex CM15 8AT
Bishop Emeritus Thomas McMahon (1980)
EAST ANGLIA Alan Hopes (2003; 2013)
The White House, 21 Upgate, Poringland, Norwich NR14 7SH
NORTHAMPTON Peter Doyle (2005)
Bishop's House, Marriott Street, Northampton NN2 6AW
Bishop Emeritus Leo McCartie (1977; 1990)
NOTTINGHAM Patrick McKinney (2015)
Bishop's House, 27 Cavendish Road East, The Park, Nottingham NG7 1BB

THE PROVINCE OF BIRMINGHAM

BIRMINGHAM Bernard Longley (2003; 2009)
Archbishop's House, 8 Shadwell Street, Birmingham B4 6EY
Auxiliary Bishops David McGough (2005), William Kenney CP (1987; 2006)
Retired Auxiliary Bishop Philip Pargeter (1990)
CLIFTON Declan Lang (2001)
St Ambrose, North Road, Leigh Woods, Bristol BS8 3PW
SHREWSBURY Mark Davies (2010; 2011)
Bishop's House, Laburnum Cottage, 97 Barnston Road, Barnston, Wirral L61 1BW

THE PROVINCE OF CARDIFF

CARDIFF George Stack (2001; 2011)
Archbishop's House, 43 Cathedral Road, Cardiff CF1 9HD
MENEVIA George Stack (2001; 2011) *Apostolic Administrator*
Convent Street, Swansea SA1 2BX
Bishops Emeriti Daniel J Mullins (1970; 1987), Mark Jabalé OSB (2000; 2001), Tom M Burns SM (2002; 2008)
WREXHAM Peter Brignall (2012)
Bishop's House, Sontley Road, Wrexham, Clwyd LL13 7EW
Bishop Emeritus Edwin Regan (1994)

THE PROVINCE OF LIVERPOOL

LIVERPOOL Malcolm McMahon OP (2000, 2014)

Archbishop's House, 19 Salisbury Road, Cressington Park, Liverpool L19 0PQ

Archbishop Emeritus Patrick Kelly (1984; 1986)

Auxiliary Bishop Tom Williams (2003)

Retired Auxiliary Bishop Vincent Malone (1989)

HALLAM Ralph Heskett CSsR (2010; 2014)

75 Norfolk Road, Sheffield S2 2SZ

Bishop Emeritus John Rawsthorne (1981; 1997)

HEXHAM & NEWCASTLE Robert Byrne (2014; 2019)

Bishop's House, East Denton Hall, 800 West Road, Newcastle-upon-Tyne NE25 2BJ

Bishop Emeritus Seamus Cunningham (2009)

LANCASTER Paul Swarbrick (2018)

Cathedral House, Balmoral Road, Lancaster LA13BT

Bishops Emeriti Patrick O'Donoghue (1993; 2001), Michael Campbell OSA (2008)

LEEDS Marcus Stock (2014)

Bishop's House, 13 North Grange Road, Leeds LS6 2BR

Bishop Emeritus Arthur Roche (2001; 2004), Archbishop *ad personam*

MIDDLESBROUGH Terry Drainey (2008)

Bishop's House, 16 Cambridge Road, Middlesbrough, Cleveland TS5 5NN

Bishop Emeritus John Crowley (1992)

SALFORD John Arnold (2006; 2014)

Wardley Hall, Worsley, Manchester M28 5ND

Bishop Emeritus Terence Brain (1991; 1997)

THE PROVINCE OF SOUTHWARK

SOUTHWARK John Wilson (2016; 2019)

Archbishop's House, 150 St George's Road SE1 6HX

Archbishops Emeriti Kevin McDonald (2001; 2003), Peter Smith (1995; 2010)

Auxiliary Bishops Paul Hendricks (2006), Patrick Lynch SS.CC (2006)

Retired Auxiliary Bishops Howard Tripp (1980), John Hine (2001)

ARUNDEL & BRIGHTON Richard Moth (2009; 2015)

High Oaks, Old Brighton Road North, Pease Pottage, West Sussex RH11 9AJ

PLYMOUTH Mark O'Toole (2014)

Bishop's House, 31 Wyndham Street West, Plymouth, Devon PL1 5RZ

Bishop Emeritus Christopher Budd (1986)

PORTSMOUTH Philip Egan (2012)

Bishop's House, Bishop Crispian Way, Portsmouth PO1 3HG

Bishop Emeritus Crispian Hollis (1987; 1988)

THE BISHOPRIC OF THE FORCES

BISHOP OF THE FORCES Paul Mason (2016; 2018)

Wellington House, St Omer Barracks, Thornhill Road, Aldershot, Hants GU11 2BG

THE APOSTOLIC NUNCIATURE

APOSTOLIC NUNCIO His Excellency Archbishop Edward Adams, Titular Archbishop of Scala (1996, 2017)
54 Parkside SW19 5NE Tel: 020 8944 7189 Fax: 020 8947 2494

THE BISHOPS' CONFERENCE OF ENGLAND AND WALES

General Secretary Fr Christopher Thomas
Catholic Bishops' Conference of England and Wales, 39 Eccleston Square SW1V 1BX
Tel: 020 7901 4815 Fax: 020 7901 4819 Email: christopher.thomas@cbcew.org.uk
Web: www.cbcew.org.uk
Registered in England and Wales
Company Number: 4734592 Registered Charity Number: 109748239
The Secretariat of the Conference consists of the office of the General Secretary and a number of departments whose work focuses on the work of the Bishops of England and Wales. These are Christian Life and Worship, Christian Responsibility and Citizenship, Catholic Education and Formation, Dialogue and Unity, Evangelisation and Catechesis, and International Affairs. Further information on their work, and contact details, can be found on the website.

The Bishops' Conference also has a number of agencies and offices, for which entries can be found in Section 6, under Catholic Societies and Organisations, and Other Useful Addresses:
Catholic Agency for Overseas Development
Catholic Association for Racial Justice
Catholic Communications Network
Catholic Education Service
Catholic Safeguarding Advisory Service
Catholic Social Action Network
National Office for Vocation
Stella Maris (Apostleship of the Sea)

They have been there for us...
Let's be there for them...

'Even in your old age...
I will care for you'
– Isaiah 46.4

Your generosity to the Sick &
Retired Clergy Fund ensures
our elderly priests receive the
best care and support when
they retire or fall ill.

Diocese of Westminster

Registered charity no. 233699

To find out how to become a regular supporter, or make a
one-off donation, please contact our Supporter Care Manager
on **020 7798 9025** or you can donate online at
www.rcdow.org.uk/donations

Section 2

PATRONS, SAINTS AND BLESSED

Here are listed the Diocesan Patrons and other Saints and Blessed associated with Westminster. The Liturgical Calendar can be found on page 299.

PATRONS

19 March
St Joseph
On 10 December 1898, at the request of Cardinal Vaughan, St Joseph was added as a patron of the diocese. Blessed Pius IX had already declared him to be Patron of the Universal Church (1870) and Cardinal Vaughan himself had a great devotion to him. As a young priest he had founded St Joseph's Society for the Foreign Missions and established a National Shrine of St Joseph at Mill Hill (now at St Michael's Abbey, Farnborough). This patronage of St Joseph was thought appropriate since, as Vaughan noted, 'the Church itself is the expansion of the Holy Family'.

29 June
St Peter, Prince of the Apostles
The inclusion of St Peter among our diocesan patrons testifies to the age-old devotion shown by English men and women to the 'Prince of the Apostles'. From an early date English pilgrims flocked to Rome to visit his tomb and it was King Ine of Wessex who is thought to have initiated the Peter's Pence collection to support the papacy. Many churches were dedicated to the chief of the apostles, including Westminster Abbey. On 29 June 1893 England was re-consecrated to St Peter.

13 October
St Edward the Confessor, King (1003-66)
King of England from 1042, St Edward was famed for his piety, alms-giving and the building of Westminster Abbey. He died on 5 January 1066 and the resulting Norman and Saxon claims to the succession were fought out on the battlefield of Hastings. Canonised in 1161, St Edward's incorrupt body was translated to a new shrine on 13 October 1163 (the origin of his present feast day). His cult flourished in the Middle Ages and he was considered one of the patrons of England. Pope Benedict XVI prayed before his shrine on 17 September 2010, alongside the Archbishop of Canterbury, and called St Edward 'a model of Christian witness and an example of that true grandeur to which the Lord summons his disciples'.

8 December
Our Blessed Lady Immaculate
Our Blessed Lady Immaculate was the original primary patron of the diocese. There are several local Marian shrines within the diocese, including Our Lady of Graces at Tower Hill, Our Lady of Muswell Hill, Our Lady of Warwick Street and Our Lady of Westminster. Our Lady of Willesden in particular was an important Marian shrine for Londoners on the eve of the Protestant Reformation. Although the statue of Our Lady was destroyed in 1538, the shrine was restored in 1892. Since then, Our Lady of Willesden has become the focus of Marian devotion in the diocese and during the Marian Year Rally at Wembley Stadium on 3 October 1954 Cardinal Griffin solemnly crowned the statue before a crowd of over 90,000. Moreover, the shrine is unusual in having been visited by two canonised saints: St Thomas More and (in the 1950s) St Josemaria Escriva, the founder of Opus Dei.

SAINTS

15 February
St Claude de la Colombière, Priest (1641-82)

St Claude was a Jesuit chaplain to Mary of Modena, then Duchess of York and wife of the future James II, at St James' Palace between 1676 and 1679. Before coming to London he was the spiritual director of St Margaret Mary at Paray-le-Monial. He became a great proponent of modern devotion to the Sacred Heart of Jesus and the Catholics of London were one of the first to receive it. Nearly two hundred years later, on 17 June 1873, the diocese was consecrated to the Sacred Heart. St Claude was banished to France at the time of the 'Popish Plot' and died on 15 February 1682. He was canonised by St John Paul II on 31 May 1992.

19 April
St Alphege, Bishop & Martyr (c.953-1012)

St Alphege started life as a monk in Gloucestershire and Somerset, but despite trying to live a solitary life his talents were soon recognised and he became successively Abbot of Bath, Bishop of Winchester and (in 1005) Archbishop of Canterbury. In 1011 he was captured and imprisoned by the Danish invaders ('Vikings'). When he refused to let his ransom be paid, he was killed at Greenwich; according to tradition, the Danes threw bones at him from their table during a banquet and then one of them struck him on the head with an axe. He was buried at St Paul's Cathedral, where his shrine was visited by many pilgrims, before being moved to Canterbury in 1023. St Thomas Becket prayed to St Alphege just before his own martyrdom in Canterbury Cathedral.

24 April
St Erconwald, Bishop (d. 693)

Born to a rich family, St Erconwald founded the Abbeys of Chertsey (where he was Abbot) and Barking (where his sister, St Ethelburga, was Abbess). In 675 he became Bishop of London - a medieval hymn calls him *Lux Lundoniae* ('light of London'). His final years were plagued by poor health, but he was transported around his diocese in a wooden litter or cart. He was buried at St Paul's Cathedral. In the present diocesan calendar, St Erconwald is kept with the first Bishop of London, St Mellitus, on 24 April.

24 April
St Mellitus, Bishop (d. 624)

St Mellitus was sent to England by St Gregory the Great in 601 to assist the mission of St Augustine. In 604 he was consecrated first Bishop of London. However, he was expelled under St Ethelbert's pagan son, King Saeberht, and eventually became third Archbishop of Canterbury (619). He died on 24 April 624 and was buried at Canterbury. In the present diocesan calendar, St Mellitus is kept with St Erconwald on 24 April.

22 June (celebrated 20 June)
St Alban, Protomartyr (d. *circa* 209)
St Alban is the earliest British Christian whom we know by name. He was a prominent citizen of Verulamium (a town later renamed St Albans), who hid a priest fleeing from persecution. So impressed was he by the priest's example that he took instruction and was baptised. When the soldiers came to search for the priest, Alban put on the fugitive's cloak and was arrested and beheaded – the punishment reserved for Roman citizens. A cult quickly grew up around the martyr – St Germanus, Bishop of Auxerre, visited his shrine in 429 and spread his cult on the continent. Pilgrims visited his shrine in St Albans Abbey until the Reformation. Perhaps the most astonishing thing about St Alban is that he may have suffered as early as 209, testifying to the early existence of Christianity in Britain.

9 October
St John Henry Newman, Priest (1801-90)
Cardinal Newman is normally associated with the West Midlands but it is often forgotten that he was born a Londoner. He was born at 88 Old Broad Street (in the City) on 21 February 1801 and moved the following year to 17 Southampton Street (now Southampton Place). The Newman family lived there until 1816. St John Henry went to school in Ealing before entering Trinity College, Oxford as an undergraduate. Newman was a leading force in the Oxford Movement within the Church of England until his search for truth led him to the Catholic Church. He was received into the Church by Blessed Dominic Barberi at Littlemore on 9 October 1845. He set up the Oratory of St Philip Neri in England and spent most of the remainder of his life in Birmingham. After many disappointments and trials, he was created a Cardinal by Leo XIII in 1879 in recognition of his theological work and personal witness. Newman died on 11 August 1890.

16 November
St Edmund of Abingdon, Bishop (c.1175-1240)
Educated at Oxford and Paris, St Edmund started off as an academic and pioneer of scholasticism. In 1222 he became Treasurer of Salisbury and, in 1233, Archbishop of Canterbury. As Metropolitan, he became known as a defender of the Church's rights, which often brought him into conflict with the king. He died on his way to see the Pope on 16 November 1240 and was buried at Pontigny. He is the patron of St Edmund's College, Ware, which was for many years the location of the diocesan seminary. Several other Archbishops of Canterbury are remembered in our diocesan calendar – Ss Laurence (d.619), Dunstan (909-88) and Theodore (d.690) (3 February) – stressing the links between Canterbury and Westminster. Indeed, the arms of the See of Westminster are similar to those of Canterbury, although there is a red instead of blue background (or 'field') and there is no cross above the pallium.

29 December
St Thomas of Canterbury, Bishop and Martyr (1118-70)
St Thomas Becket was born in Cheapside and entered the service of the Archbishop of Canterbury. He was soon noticed by Henry II, who became a close friend and appointed him Chancellor (1155). St Thomas lived a worldly life, like many in his station, until becoming Archbishop of Canterbury in 1162 when, in the saint's own words, he went from being 'a patron of play-actors and a follower of hounds to being a shepherd of souls'. Taking his responsibilities seriously and living an austere life, he was careful to defend the rights and prerogatives of the Church. Inevitably his relationship with the king began to suffer and for six years he lived as an exile in the French towns of Pontigny and Sens. Returning to England at the end of 1170, he was murdered in his own Cathedral by four of Henry's knights on 29 December (his feast day). The king did penance and Canterbury soon became one of the most popular shrines in Europe. St Thomas was quickly canonised by Alexander III in 1173 and, in more recent times, was proclaimed Patron of the English Secular Clergy.

THE MARTYRS OF THE SIXTEENTH AND SEVENTEENTH CENTURIES

Many of these men and women had London connections – some ministered in the diocese, others were brought to the capital for trial and execution. Among the sites of martyrdom in London are Tyburn, Clerkenwell, Fleet Street, Gray's Inn, Isleworth, Lincoln's Inn Fields, Mile End Green, St Paul's Churchyard, Shoreditch, Smithfield and Tower Hill. Of special importance are the following martyrs:

4 May
St Richard Reynolds (c.1492-1535)
Born in Devon and educated at Cambridge, St Richard joined the Bridgettine community at Syon Abbey, Isleworth in 1513. Famed for his holiness and learning, Ss Thomas More and John Fisher consulted him over Henry VIII's divorce. He was arrested in the spring of 1535 and, refusing to take the Oath of Supremacy, was taken to the Tower together with the three Carthusian Priors. He suffered with them at Tyburn on 4 May.

11 May
The Carthusian Martyrs (1535)
The London Charterhouse (founded 1371) was one of the great religious houses of pre-Reformation London. At the break with Rome, the monks remained loyal to the Pope. The three English Carthusian Priors (including St John Houghton of London) suffered on 4 May 1535. Some other members of the Charterhouse (Bl Sebastian Newdigate, Humphrey Middlemore and William Exmew) were martyred on 25 May; others died in prison. Traditionally the diocese kept their feast on 11 May.

27 June
St John Southworth (d.1654)

St John Southworth's significance for our diocese lies in the discovery of his body at Douai in 1927 and his subsequent translation to Westminster Cathedral in 1930. He acts as a representative figure for the many priests who courageously worked in London in the sixteenth and seventeenth centuries, at the risk of imprisonment and execution. Southworth was trained at Douai and worked in Lancashire and London. Together with the Jesuit St Henry Morse (1595-1645), Southworth cared for the victims of the 1636 plague at great personal risk. Spending many years in prison, he was finally hung, drawn and quartered at Tyburn on 28 June 1654, together with two counterfeiters. Westminster has traditionally kept his feast on 27 June because 28 June (the day of his martyrdom) is already occupied by St Irenaeus and the Vigil of Ss Peter and Paul.

6 July (celebrated 22 June)
St Thomas More (1478-1535)

Born in Milk Street in Cheapside (near the birthplace of St Thomas Becket), he studied at Oxford and Lincoln's Inn and followed a successful career as lawyer, politician and humanist scholar. Henry VIII appointed him Lord Chancellor in 1529 but More resigned three years later as pressure was put on him to support the king's divorce. His refusal to take the Oath of Supremacy led to his imprisonment and execution on Tower Hill on 6 July 1535, a few weeks after the martyrdom of his friend St John Fisher, Bishop of Rochester. He was a devoted family man, twice-married and father of four. His beloved 'great house' in Chelsea was situated near Allen Hall. St Thomas More was canonised by Pius XI in 1935 and has since been proclaimed Patron of Politicians.

BLESSED

29 October
The Blessed Martyrs of Douai College (1577-1679)

Cardinal Allen founded the English College, Douai, in 1568 to train new recruits for the priesthood. This was crucial to the survival of English Catholicism. Over 160 of the priests trained at Douai are now recognised as martyrs, led by the proto-martyr, St Cuthbert Mayne (1577). This is of special significance to the diocese, since St Edmund's, Ware and Allen Hall claim continuity with Douai.

PATRONS, SAINTS AND BLESSED

'I was in prison and you visited me'

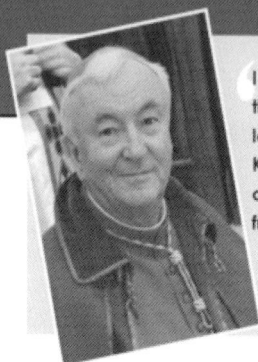

Pact
Prisoners · Families · Communities
A Fresh Start Together

> I pray that we may never forget all people, whoever they are and whatever they may have done, are loved by God and called to be sharers in His Kingdom. I commend to you the work of Pact, who do so much to support those in need of hope and a fresh start.

Cardinal Vincent Nichols, President of Pact

Pact is the national Catholic charity that supports prisoners, people with convictions, their children and families. We keep families together; we reduce crime; we make a real difference.

We have been supporting people affected by imprisonment for over 120 years and we continue to innovate and deliver our services through out staff, volunteers and supporters. We extend you an invitation to join us. Whether you are a priest, deacon, parishioner, member of a religious community; whether you've been coming to church your whole life or are recently discovering what life as a faithful Catholic means, then this invitation is for you.

Our work is inspired by Catholic Social Teaching, giving hope to women and men in prison, to their loved ones in our communities and to their children.

- We urgently need volunteers for our children and family services across the Diocese of Westminster. You don't need experience, just a few spare hours and a willing heart.
- We need toys and children's books, and other items for our family centres.
- We need 'Parish Champions', people who will share about our work in your parish, in the deanery and the diocese.
- And of course, we need funds, to help us carry on with our life-changing work. Consider setting up a regular donation with us or find out about leaving us a legacy or memorial donation.

HOW TO CONTACT US

Please support the work of Pact, the Catholic charity for prisoners and their families.

Contact us at **parish.action@prisonadvice.org.uk** or call us on **0207 735 9535.**

www.prisonadvice.org.uk

THE ARCHBISHOP

His Eminence Cardinal Vincent Nichols
Born Crosby, Liverpool 8 November 1945. Ordained
Priest in Rome on 21 December 1969 for the
Archdiocese of Liverpool. Appointed assistant priest in St
Mary's Parish, Wigan and chaplain to the Sixth Form
College and St Peter's High School in 1971. Ordained
Bishop of the titular see of Othona and Auxiliary Bishop
of Westminster on 24 January 1992. Translated to
Birmingham as Archbishop on 29 March 2000, and to
Westminster on 21 May 2009. Created Cardinal Priest
of the Most Holy Redeemer and St Alphonsus Liguori
on 22 February 2014.

Archbishop's House, Ambrosden Avenue SW1P 1QJ
Tel: 020 7798 9033 Fax: 020 7798 9077
Email: cardinalnichols@rcdow.org.uk Web: www.rcdow.org.uk/cardinal

Private Office of the Cardinal Archbishop

Private Secretary to the Cardinal Fr Alexander Master
Tel: 020 7798 9041 Email: privatesecretary@rcdow.org.uk

PA to the Cardinal's Private Office (Correspondence) Ellen Dunleavy
Tel: 020 7798 9039 Email: ellendunleavy@rcdow.org.uk

PA to the Cardinal's Private Office (Diary) Maura McBride
Tel: 020 7931 6007 Email: mauramcbride@rcdow.org.uk

Press Enquiries

Press Secretary to the Cardinal Alexander DesForges
Tel: 020 7798 9045 Email: alexander.desforges@cbcew.org.uk

Archbishop's House Reception

Tel: 020 7798 9033 Email: abhreception@rcdow.org.uk
Gillian Reid Email: gillianreid@rcdow.org.uk,
Michael Holmes

Sisters responsible for the Cardinal's Household

La Sagesse
Tel: 020 7798 9398

THE AUXILIARY BISHOPS, EPISCOPAL VICARS AND VICAR GENERAL

The Right Rev John Sherrington Titular Bishop of Hilta
Born Leicester 5 January 1958. Ordained Priest 13 June 1987.
Ordained Bishop 14 September 2011 by Archbishop Vincent Nichols.
Archbishop's House, Ambrosden Avenue SW1P 1QJ Tel: **020 7798 9060**
PA Virginia Utley Tel: **020 7798 9075** Email: virginiautley@rcdow.org.uk

The Right Rev Nicholas Hudson Titular Bishop of St Germans
Born Hammersmith 14 February 1959. Ordained Priest 19 July 1986.
Ordained Bishop 4 June 2014 by Cardinal Vincent Nichols.
Archbishop's House, Ambrosden Avenue SW1P 1QJ Tel: **020 7931 6061**
PA Julie McMahon Tel: **020 7798 9381** Email: juliemcmahon@rcdow.org.uk

The Right Rev Paul McAleenan Titular Bishop of Mercia
Born Belfast 15 July 1951. Ordained Priest 8 June 1985.
Ordained Bishop 25 January 2016 by Cardinal Vincent Nichols.
Archbishop's House, Ambrosden Avenue SW1P 1QJ Tel: **020 7931 6062**
PA Oliver Delargy Tel: **020 7798 9061** Email: oliverdelargy@rcdow.org.uk

Fr Duncan Adamson Episcopal Vicar
73 Pembroke Road, Ruislip HA4 8NN
Tel: **01895 632739** Email: duncanadamson@rcdow.org.uk
PA Rebecca Goode Tel: **020 7798 9023**
Email: rebeccagoode@rcdow.org.uk

Canon Paschal Ryan Episcopal Vicar
7 Cheyne Row SW3 5HS
Tel: **020 7352 0777** Email: paschalryan@rcdow.org.uk
PA Rebecca Goode Tel: **020 7798 9023**
Email: rebeccagoode@rcdow.org.uk

Mgr Martin Hayes
Vicar General
Archbishop's House, Ambrosden Avenue SW1P 1QJ
Tel: **020 7931 6076** Email: martinhayes@rcdow.org.uk
PA Paola Greco Tel: **020 7798 9151** Email: pgreco@rcdow.org.uk

THE DIOCESE OF WESTMINSTER AND CATHEDRAL CHAPTER

ARCHBISHOP'S COUNCIL

The Cardinal Archbishop, Auxiliary Bishops, Vicar General, Judicial Vicar, Chair of the Council of Priests, Private Secretary, Chief Operating Officer/Financial Secretary (attends for non-clergy matters).

THE WESTMINSTER ROMAN CATHOLIC DIOCESAN TRUST is the charitable trust through which the activities of the Diocese are conducted. Established by a trust deed dated 1 November 1940, it is registered under the Charities Act 2011 with Charity Registration Number 233699. The Trustees are also the **FINANCE COMMITTEE** (Canon 492, CIC) **Trustees** The Cardinal Archbishop and Auxiliary Bishops; Mgr Séamus O'Boyle; Mgr Martin Hayes; Dame Colette Bowe; Miss Leslie Ferrar; Mr Kevin Ingram; Mrs Ruth Kelly; Mr Christopher Kembell; and Mr Andrew Ndoca. **Secretary** Mr Paolo Camoletto.

FINANCE BOARD (with responsibilities delegated from the Trustees) **Chair** Bishop John Sherrington; Bishop Nicholas Hudson; Bishop Paul McAleenan; Mgr Martin Hayes; Mr John Gibney; Mr Andrew Ndoca. **In attendance** Mr Paolo Camoletto; Mrs Marta Luiz.

METROPOLITAN CATHEDRAL CHAPTER (est. 19 June 1852) (Canons 377, 463, 503-10, CIC) The Chapter assembles at Archbishop's House for a meeting once a month, generally on the first Tuesday, after which Vespers and Capitular Mass are celebrated in the Cathedral for the intentions of the Diocese.

Provost Canon Michael Brockie; **Secretary** Canon Patrick Browne; **Treasurer** Canon Colin Davies; **Theologian** Canon John O'Leary; **Penitentiary** Canon Anthony Dwyer; **M.C.** Canon Daniel Cronin; Canon Michael Munnelly; Mgr Canon Paul McGinn; Canon Robert Plourde; Canon Stuart Wilson; Canon Christopher Tuckwell; Canon Paschal Ryan; Canon Peter Newby; Canon Shaun Lennard; Canon Terence Phipps; Canon Roger Taylor; Canon Alexander Sherbrooke; Canon Gerard King.

Provost Emeritus Mgr Canon Frederick Miles; **Canons Emeriti** Canon Philip Cross; Canon Bernard Scholes; Canon Edward Matthews; Canon Vincent Berry; Mgr Canon Henry Turner; Mgr Canon Thomas Egan.

SECTION 2

CONSULTATIVE BODIES

COLLEGE OF CONSULTORS (Canon 502, CIC)
Functions are entrusted to the Cathedral Chapter.

COUNCIL OF DEANS
Chair The Cardinal Archbishop; Auxiliary Bishops; Vicar General; Deans; Chair of Council of Priests; Private Secretary

COUNCIL OF PRIESTS (Canons 495-501, CIC)
President The Cardinal Archbishop
Chair Mgr James Curry **Secretary** Fr Daniel Humphreys

HISTORIC CHURCHES COMMITTEE
Particular Pastoral Responsibility Mgre James Curry

Under the Ecclesiastical Exemption provision of the Town and Country Planning Act, listed churches are exempt from the requirement to obtain from their local authority Listed Building Consent for works of repair and refurbishment, providing they obtain approval from the local Historic Churches Committee. These regulations have been confirmed by the Bishops' Conference of England and Wales in its 1999 'Directory on the Ecclesiastical Exemption from Listed Building Control'.

Chair Fr Peter Harris **St Joseph's, 3 Windhill, Bishop's Stortford CM23 2ND**
Tel: 01279 654063
Secretary Chris Fanning **Historic Churches Committee, c/o Property Services Office, St Joseph's Grove NW4 4TY Tel: 020 8457 6540 / 07885 768889**
Administrative Secretary Lesley McNealis **Tel: 020 8457 6532**
Committee Members
Fr Peter Harris (Chair), Mgr James Curry (Vice-Chair), Fr Andrew Cameron-Mowat SJ, Paolo Camoletto, Andrew Derrick, Clive Horscroft, Bruce Kirk, Paul Moynihan, Canon Peter Newby, Mark Price, Paul Velluet, Chris Fanning (Secretary), Lesley McNealis (Administrative Secretary)

LITURGY COMMISSION
Particular Pastoral Responsibility Mgr James Curry

The Commission is charged by the Cardinal Archbishop to assist him in promoting liturgical renewal and on-going liturgical formation in the Diocese. It is to establish policy for the ordering of churches and to approve such. It also has oversight of principal diocesan liturgies.
Chair Fr Allen Morris **Email: allenmorris@rcdow.org.uk Web: www.rcdow.org.uk/liturgy**
Chair of Art and Architecture Committee Canon Peter Newby **Tel: 020 8892 3902**

MASTER OF CEREMONIES for the Cardinal Archbishop Paul Moynihan

MASTERS OF CEREMONIES for the Diocese Fr Agustin Conesa; Fr Michael Dunne; Fr James Neal; Fr David Reilly; Fr Antonio Ritaccio; Fr Gerard Skinner; Fr Sławomir Witoń; Rev Gordon Nunn

AGENCY FOR EVANGELISATION

Particular Pastoral Responsibility Bishop Nicholas Hudson

Working under the banner of 'Proclaim: Forming Missionary Disciples, Building Missionary Parishes', the Agency for Evangelisation provides assistance to parish communities in developing local evangelising initiatives and programmes of Adult Faith Formation, Sacramental Catechesis, the Rite of Christian Initiation of Adults (RCIA), Parish Religious Education for Children and support for Marriage and Family Life at all stages.

Director Fr Christopher Vipers **Tel: 020 7798 9157 Email: chrisvipers@rcdow.org.uk**
Vaughan House, 46 Francis Street SW1P 1QN
Administrative Assistant Warren Brown **General Enquiries Tel: 020 7798 9152**
Email: evangelisation@rcdow.org.uk Web: www.rcdow.org.uk/evangelisation

Evangelisation
Evangelisation Co-ordinator Rev Adrian Cullen
Tel: 020 7798 9150 Email: adriancullen@rcdow.org.uk

Catechesis
The Catechesis Support Team oversees the provision of formation, resources, training and the certification of parish catechists in all parishes of the Diocese for Baptism Preparation, First Reconciliation, Holy Communion, Confirmation, RCIA, Parish-based Religious Education for Children, Children's Liturgy, and initial and ongoing training and formation of parish catechists.
Email: catadmin@rcdow.org.uk
Catechesis Advisers for Deaneries and Parishes
Mary Crowley **Tel: 020 7931 6090 Email: marycrowley@rcdow.org.uk**
Anna Dupelycz **Tel: 020 7798 9026 Email: annadupelycz@rcdow.org.uk**

Adult Faith Formation and Faith Sharing Resources
Adult Faith Formation Advisor Ausra Cane **Tel: 020 7931 6078**
Email: ausracane@rcdow.org.uk / smallgroups@rcdow.org.uk

Learn From Me
'Learn From Me' is a formation programme for all involved in parish ministry, offering Certificates in Catechesis, Parish Mission and Ministry, and A Catechesis on Marriage and Family in partnership with Maryvale Institute.
Anna Dupelycz **Tel: 020 7798 9026 Email: annadupelycz@rcdow.org.uk**

Marriage and Family Life
Our role is to work alongside existing groups, to promote a renewed culture of the Gospel of Life within parishes, schools and the wider community. We help the single, married couples and families to deepen their understanding of the beauty of Catholic teaching on marriage and the family. We provide guidance and resources on the preparation of couples for marriage, the provision of on-going enrichment, healing and counselling, and help for the divorced and separated. We arrange the Annual Mass of Thanksgiving for Matrimony, a

diocesan-wide celebration of this great vocation. We help families to grow in their awareness that God is present in the everyday events of family life and that they are 'the domestic church', where the Word of God is first proclaimed, received, studied and experienced. We have produced a resource, Made4Love, for schools, which includes a couple witness testimony on married life, and is designed to enable young people to discuss and explore long-term, positive, healthy relationships within the context of marriage and Catholic teaching.

Co-ordinator Rev Roger Carr-Jones **Tel: 020 7798 9363**
Email: rogercarrjones@rcdow.org.uk
Administrative Assistant Charlotte McNerlin **Tel: 020 7931 6064**
Email: charlottemcnerlin@rcdow.org.uk / family@rcdow.org.uk

The Year of the Word

Through 2020, which is designated as *'The God Who Speaks': The Year of the Word*, the Agency will be rolling out a programme of information, activities and events to encourage Catholics to become more familiar with the Scriptures, day-to-day. The year also marks the 10th Anniversary of *Verbum Domini*, the Exhortation of Pope Benedict XVI on The Word of the Lord, and the 1,600th anniversary of the death of St Jerome. He translated the Bible into Latin, and declared that: 'Ignorance of the Scriptures is ignorance of Christ'. This year, therefore, is an opportunity to support Catholics in coming closer to God, through becoming closer to his Word.

ARCHIVES

Particular Pastoral Responsibility Bishop John Sherrington

Archivist Fr Nicholas Schofield (Uxbridge)
Administrative Archivist Susannah Rayner
Archives Assistant Judi McGinley
16a Abingdon Road W8 6AF
Tel: 020 7938 3580 Email: archivist@rcdow.org.uk
Open by appointment (Mon, Tue, 10-12.30pm, 1.30-5pm)

CARITAS WESTMINSTER

Particular Pastoral Responsibility Bishop Paul McAleenan

CARITAS COMMITTEE Awaiting appointment

Caritas Westminster is the diocesan social action and engagement agency. We seek to bring about a society where everyone lives a life of dignity and worth by enabling Catholic communities to identify and respond to all forms of poverty and social exclusion. We run three of our own projects for some of the most marginalised people in our society, and offer grants for individuals in crisis and for social action projects in the Diocese of Westminster.

Vaughan House, 46 Francis Street SW1P 1QN   **Tel: 020 7931 6077**
Email: caritaswestminster@rcdow.org.uk Web: www.caritaswestminster.org.uk

Director	John Coleby	Tel: 020 7798 9357
Assistant Director	Awaiting appointment	Tel: 020 7798 9078
Administrator	Caitlin Boyle	Tel: 020 7931 6077
Communications Assistant	Louise Cook	Tel: 07522 229438
Volunteer Co-ordinator	Elke Springett	Tel: 07738 183833
West London Development Worker		
	Silvana Dallanegra	Tel: 07921 471506
South West London Development Worker		
	Joseph Kilsby	Tel: 07801 572434
North London Development Worker		
	Rosa Lewis	Tel: 07719 563125
East London Development Worker		
	Minet Masho	Tel: 07525 812513
South Hertfordshire Development Worker		
	Ines Ignasse	Tel: 07525 812511
Central London Development Worker		
	Finola Ryan	Tel: 07525 812518
North Hertfordshire Development Worker		
	Elizabeth Wills	Tel: 07877 902313

SECTION 2

THE ST JOHN SOUTHWORTH CARITAS FUND

Through the Fund, Caritas Westminster provides grants to individuals in crisis and to social action projects in the Diocese.

Vaughan House, 46 Francis Street SW1P 1QN Tel: 020 7798 9063

Administrator Awaiting appointment

Email: caritasgrants@rcdow.org.uk Web: www.caritaswestminster.org.uk/grants

CARITAS BAKHITA HOUSE

Accommodation and support for women escaping human trafficking and modern slavery.

Email: bakhitahouse@rcdow.org.uk

Web: www.caritaswestminster.org.uk/bakhitahouse

Service Manager	Karen Anstiss	Tel: 020 7931 6045

CARITAS DEAF SERVICE

Working with Deaf, Deafblind and Hard of Hearing people of all ages to enable them to participate fully in the life of the Church and share their gifts.

St Joseph's Pastoral Centre, St Joseph's Grove NW4 4TY

Textphone: 020 8732 8340 SMS: 07779 341 136 Fax: 020 8203 9745 Email: michelleroca@rcdow.org.uk

Web: www.caritaswestminster.org.uk/deafservice

Director	Shell (Michelle) Roca	Tel: 020 8457 6536
Assistant	Sarah Metcalfe	Tel: 020 8457 6535

Signs of Hope – Deaf Counselling Service
Offers counselling to Deaf and Hard of Hearing people and their relatives in sign language or English. Mini-loop system available.
Tel/SMS: 07534 570 429 Email: signsofhope@rcdow.org.uk

CARITAS FOOD COLLECTIVE

Tackling the problem of food poverty and insecurity in the Diocese of Westminster.
Email: cfc@rcdow.org.uk

Co-ordinator	Anna Gavurin	Tel: 07525 812508
Administrator	Caitlin Boyle	Tel: 020 7931 6077

CARITAS ST JOSEPH'S

Supporting people with intellectual disabilities, their families and friends.
St Joseph's Pastoral Centre, St Joseph's Grove NW4 4TY
Email: enquiries@stjoseph.org.uk Web: www.stjoseph.org.uk

Centre Manager	Gail Williams	Tel: 020 8202 3999

SEIDS Social Innovation and Enterprise Hub

The Hub is a social enterprise community centre offering a unique ecosystem of resources, ispiration and collaboration opportunities for those who have a credible enterprise idea.
SEIDS Hub, Empire Way, Wembley HA9 0RJ
Email: hello@seids.org.uk Web: www.seids.org.uk

Hub Manager	Elena Bologna	Tel: 020 3026 2502
Engagement Manager	Kathy Margerison	Tel: 020 3026 2502
Administrative Assistant	Marta da Silva	Tel: 020 3026 2504 / 020 3026 2530

SEIDS Property Services

SEIDS Property Services provides high-quality painting and decorating, and general maintenance services at an affordable price across the Diocese of Westminster.
Email: pawelszkolnik@rcdow.org.uk Web: seids.org.uk

Manager	Pawel Szkolnik

CHANCERY

Archbishop's House, Ambrosden Avenue SW1P 1QJ
For *Celebrets* please email: celebret@rcdow.org.uk

Chancellor Fr Jeremy Trood MA, JCL
Email: jeremytrood@rcdow.org.uk
Vice-Chancellor Brenda Roberts MA (Canon Law)
Tel: 020 7798 9037 Email: brendaroberts@rcdow.org.uk
Chancery Adminstrator Laura Dale BA (Hons), MTh
Tel: 020 7931 6042 Email: lauradale@rcdow.org.uk

CLERGY AND CONSECRATED LIFE

ALLEN HALL SEMINARY (Douai 1568; Old Hall Green 1793; Chelsea 1975)
Particular Pastoral Responsibility Bishop John Sherrington

28 Beaufort Street SW3 5AA Tel: 020 7349 5600 Fax: 020 7349 5601
PA to the Rector Mrs Helena Duckett Tel: 020 7349 5786
Email: allenhall@rcdow.org.uk Web: www. allenhall.org.uk

Formation Staff:

Rector (resident)	Canon Roger Taylor	Tel: 020 7349 5627
Vice-rector / Dean of Studies (resident)	Canon John O'Leary	Tel: 020 7349 5608
Formation Advisor	Fr Lorenzo Andreini	Tel: 020 7724 8643
Formation Advisor	Sr Helen Costigane SHCJ	
		Tel: 020 7349 5786
Formation Advisor (resident)	Rev Dr Michael Doyle	Tel: 020 7349 5610
Formation Advisor (resident)	Fr John Hemer MHM	Tel: 020 7349 5618
Formation Advisor	Sr Bernadette Hunston SCSJA	
		Tel: 020 7349 5786
Pastoral Director / Formation Advisor (resident)	Fr William Nicol	Tel: 020 7349 5617
Spiritual Director	Awaiting appointment	

See pages 191/2 for a list of those currently training for priesthood in the Diocese of Westminster.

COMMITTEE FOR THE WELFARE OF SICK AND RETIRED PRIESTS
Particular Pastoral Responsibility Bishop Paul McAleenan

Chair Canon Gerard King
Healthcare Visitor Sr Clement Doran RGN, RMN Tel: 020 7798 9154 / 07817 143353

DECEASED CLERGY ASSOCIATION
Vaughan House, 46 Francis Street SW1P 1QN
Registrar Mgr John Conneely Tel: 020 7798 9003

EASTERN CATHOLIC CHURCHES
Episcopal Vicar Mgr John Conneely Tel: 020 7798 9003

ETHNIC CHAPLAINCIES
Particular Pastoral Responsibility Bishop Paul McAleenan

Episcopal Vicar Fr David Irwin Tel: 07786 769392 (Co-ordinator for Westminster, Brentwood and Southwark)

ONGOING FORMATION OF CLERGY
Episcopal Vicar for Ongoing Formation of Clergy Canon Peter Newby
Ongoing Formation of Junior Clergy Fr Gerard Skinner

PASTORAL CARE FOR CHAPLAINCIES See relevant entries in Section 3 for details

PERMANENT DIACONATE
Particular Pastoral Responsibility Bishop Paul McAleenan

Vaughan House, 46 Francis Street SW1P 1QN Tel: 020 7798 9360
Director of Diaconate Programme
Rev Anthony Clark   Tel: 020 8455 9822 Email: anthonyclark@rcdow.org.uk
Assistant Directors
Rev Adrian Cullen   Tel: 01920 462140   Email: adriancullen@rcdow.org.uk
Rev Tony Barter   Tel: 07711 894244   Email: tonybarter@rcdow.org.uk

VICAR FOR RELIGIOUS
Episcopal Vicar Fr Tom O'Brien a.a. 16 Nightingale Road, Hitchin SG5 1QS
Tel: 01462 459126 Email: vfr@rcdow.org.uk
Team members Sr Brigid Collins RSM, Sr Rachel Harrington SND, Sr Monica O'Brien SM,
Sr Margaret Barrett DC

VOCATION TO PRIESTHOOD IN THE DIOCESE OF WESTMINSTER
See page 39 below for full information and contact details.

COUNCIL OF CENSORSHIP

Secretary Fr Terry Tastard **38 Mulberry Court Bedford Road N2 9DZ**
Email: terrytastard@rcdow.org.uk
For applications and information concerning the *Nihil obstat* and *Imprimatur.*
Please allow two months for examination of proofs.

DIOCESAN CURIA

Moderator of the Curia Bishop John Sherrington
Chief Operating Officer Paolo Camoletto

Based in ARCHBISHOP'S HOUSE
Ambrosden Avenue SW1P 1QJ Tel: 020 7798 9033

PRINT ROOM
Email: printroom@rcdow.org.uk
Manager   Rochelle Fernandes   Tel: 020 7798 9380
Assistant   Rudy Rodrigues (Tue-Thu)   Tel: 020 7798 9380

Based in VAUGHAN HOUSE
46 Francis Street SW1P 1QN Tel: 020 7798 9009
Receptionists Warren Brown (am) Ronita Fernandes (pm)

COMMUNICATIONS
Communications Officer   Marie Saba   Tel: 020 7798 9031
Content Writer / Editor   Anna Dixon   Tel: 020 7798 9178
Communications Assistant   Simeon Elderfield   Tel: 020 7798 9030
Diocesan Website   Tel: 020 7798 9030
Email: communications@rcdow.org.uk

Westminster Information (published in the middle of each month, except in August)
Editor — Fr Jeremy Trood

Westminster Record (Diocesan newspaper, published five times annually)

Editor	Mgr Mark Langham	
Advertising in the Record	Andrea Black	Tel: 0161 820 5722
Email: andrea.black@thecatholicuniverse.com		
Distribution queries	Michelle Jones	Tel: 0161 820 5722
Email: michelle.jones@thecatholicuniverse.com		
Westminster Year Book	Fr John Scott	Tel: 020 7798 9370
Email: wyb@rcdow.org.uk		

DATA PROTECTION OFFICER — Mathew D'Souza — Tel: 020 7798 9015
Email: dpo@rcdow.org.uk

FINANCIAL SECRETARY and
CHIEF OPERATING OFFICER — Paolo Camoletto — Tel: 020 7798 9036
Executive Assistant — Nicola Atkinson — Tel: 020 7798 9160

FINANCE

Director of Finance	Marta Luiz	Tel: 020 7798 9174
PA	Mary Ann D'Cruz	Tel: 020 7798 9170
Deputy Director of Finance	Nicholas Seed	Tel: 020 7931 6031
Head of Financial Systems		
Transformation	Ksenija Glover	Tel: 020 7931 6096
Financial Controller	Jolanta Stalmach	Tel: 020 7798 9360
Management Accountant	Abiola Seweje	Tel: 020 7798 9169
Management Accountant	Santhi Kurup	Tel: 020 7931 6006
(covering maternity leave for	Gabriela Szkolnik)	
Financial Accounting Manager	Gisele Mantsounga	Tel: 020 7798 9161
Purchase Ledger Clerk	Kanchan Merai	Tel: 020 7798 9089
Accounts Assistant	Anita Lobo	Tel: 020 7798 9171
Accounts Assistant (12 months)	Eimear Keegan	Tel: 020 7798 9163
Accounts Assistant (6 months)	Maribel Alfabeto	Tel: 020 7798 9388
Parish Finance Officer	Margaret Brady	Tel: 020 7798 9197
School Building Project Manager	Marisa Borgerth	Tel: 020 7798 9176
School Building Project Assistant	Loan Tran	Tel: 020 7798 9016

FUNDRAISING AND STEWARDSHIP

Director of Development	Matt Parkes	Tel: 020 7798 9375
Assistant Director		
of Development (Appeals)	Helen Bright	Tel: 020 7798 9353
Development Manager (Trusts and		
Foundations, Gifts in Wills)	Alison Smith	Tel: 020 7798 9087
Fundraising Officer (Parishes)	João Tavares	Tel: 020 7798 9159

Supporter Care Manager	Eszter Croitor-Tifan	Tel: 020 7798 9025

supportercare@rcdow.org.uk
(Secretary to Stewardship Committee)

Supporter Care Officer (Gift Aid) Francisca Yawson — Tel: 020 7798 9351
giftaid@rcdow.org.uk

Supporter Care Officer — Matthew Taylor — Tel: 020 7798 9088

HUMAN RESOURCES
Director of Human Resources	Robert Walker *ad interim*	Tel: 020 7798 9166
Senior Human Resources Adviser	Julie Dauncey	Tel: 020 7798 9167
Payroll Officer	Awaiting appointment	Tel: 020 7798 9172
Pensions Administrator	Anthony Williams	Tel: 020 7798 9162
Administrative Assistant	Madelayne Lang	Tel: 020 7798 9158

SECTION 2

INFORMATION & COMMUNICATION TECHNOLOGY
Head of ICT	Rod de Silva	Tel: 020 7798 9165
Systems Administrator	Daniel Prasanna	Tel: 020 7798 9164
ICT Support / Help Desk	Andrew Baptista	Tel: 020 7798 9050

Email: ictsupportdesk@rcdow.org.uk

PARISH SUPPORT TEAM - Parish Finance and Gift Aid Support, Internal Auditors
Team Manager Marie Ryan Tel: 07889 537138 Email: marieryan@rcdow.org.uk

Alison Gartlan Tel: 07736 293640 Email: alisongartlan@rcdow.org.uk
Barnet, Brent, Hillingdon and Hounslow Deaneries
Boguslawa Psiuch Tel: 07736 272832 Email: boguslawapsiuch@rcdow.org.uk
Chaplaincies, Hackney, Haringey and Tower Hamlets Deaneries
Pascal Kwo Tel: 07808 362937 Email: pascalkwo@rcdow.org.uk
Lea Valley and St Albans Deaneries
Beverley Meakes Tel: 07736 272830 Email: beverleymeakes@rcdow.org.uk
Enfield, Islington, Stevenage and Watford Deaneries
Richard Robinson Tel: 07790 472716 Email: richardrobinson@rcdow.org.uk
Hammersmith & Fulham, Harrow, Kensington & Chelsea and Upper Thames Deaneries
Elizabeth Wills Tel: 07877 902313 Email: elizabethwills@rcdow.org.uk
Marylebone, North Kensington and Westminster Deaneries
Margaret Wilson Tel: 07825 519080 Email: margaretwilson@rcdow.org.uk
Camden and Ealing Deaneries

SCHOOL BUILDING FUNDRAISING
Manager	John Lee	Tel: 020 7798 9168

Based in ST JOSEPH'S, HENDON
St Joseph's Centre, St Joseph's Grove NW4 4TY

PROPERTY

Director	Clive Horscroft	Tel: 020 8457 6538
Estates Surveyor	Carol Haigh	Tel: 020 8457 6534
Estates Surveyor	Sarah Nagle	Tel: 020 8457 6533
Estates Building Surveyor	James Keegan	Tel: 020 8457 6542
Estates Building Surveyor	Awaiting appointment	Tel: 020 8457 6542
Health and Safety Officer	Awaiting appointment	Tel: 020 8457 6532
Technical Administrator	Anthony Williams	Tel: 020 8457 6541

Senior Parish Buildings Surveyor and
Secretary, Historic Churches Committee

	Chris Fanning	Tel: 020 8457 6540 / 07885 768889
Secretary / PA to Chris Fanning	Roz Freedland	Tel: 020 8457 6539
Property Secretary / HCC Admin / Property Archives		
	Lesley McNealis	Tel: 020 8457 6532

ECUMENISM

Particular Pastoral Responsibility Awaiting appointment

Ecumenical activity in the Diocese is very much rooted at the local level, with numerous clergy and laity involved in a variety of ecumenical bodies and projects that are too many to list here. In addition to this local ecumenical engagement:
Cardinal Vincent Nichols attends London Church Leaders;
Bishop John Sherrington (North London), **Bishop Nicholas Hudson** (Central and East London), **Bishop Paul McAleenan** (Hertfordshire) and **Fr Duncan Adamson** (West London) all support the Church Leaders' groups in their areas.
Mgr Canon Henry Turner is Ecumenical Chaplain at St. Albans Abbey.

EDUCATION AND FORMATION

Particular Pastoral Responsibility Bishop John Sherrington *ad interim*

THE DIOCESAN EDUCATION COMMISSION

is appointed by the Cardinal Archbishop as a decision-making body which acts in his name. It is responsible to him in all areas relating to education in schools and colleges set out in Canon law and English law. It is responsible to the Diocesan Trustees for the financial aspects of providing and maintaining Catholic education in the Diocese. Through its Chair, the Education Commission liaises with the Cardinal Archbishop, his Auxiliary Bishops and the Diocesan Trustees. It liaises with schools and colleges mainly through the Director of Education and the staff of the Education Service.

Members of the Commission
Chair Fr Michael Dunne, Mr John Asgian, Mrs Lisa Barton, Mr Edward Conway, Mrs Kate Griffin, Mrs Juliette Jackson, Mrs Pamela Singh OBE
In attendance Director of Education, Chief Operating Officer   **Secretary** Linette Blackmore

THE EDUCATION SERVICE
works to the Diocesan Education Commission in providing professional support for Catholic Schools and Colleges, Head Teachers, Principals and Governing Bodies.

Vaughan House, 46 Francis Street SW1P 1QN
Tel: 020 7798 9005 Fax: 020 7798 9013
Email: education@rcdow.org.uk Web: https://education.rcdow.org.uk

Director of Education (Diocesan Schools Commissioner)	John Paul Morrison	Tel: 020 7798 9005
Deputy Director of Education	Amanda Crowley	Tel: 020 7798 9005
Chief Inspector	Jane Goring	Tel: 020 7798 9005
Assistant Director (Strategic Operations)	Mike Pittendreigh	Tel: 020 7798 9005
Assistant Director (Capital Strategy and Pupil Placement)	Nigel Spears	Tel: 020 7798 9005
Education Officer (Legal & Policy)	Mary Ryan	Tel: 020 7798 9005
Advisers for Catholic Education (Primary)	Elaine Arundell	Tel: 020 7798 9005
	Tony Gorton	Tel: 020 7798 9005
	Patrick Murphy	Tel: 020 7798 9005
	Theresa O'Sullivan	Tel: 020 7798 9005
	Diana Roberts	Tel: 020 7798 9005
Advisers for Catholic Education (Secondary)	Trisha Hedley	Tel: 020 7798 9005
	Claire O'Neill	Tel: 020 7798 9005
Office Manager & PA to the Director	Linette Blackmore	Tel: 020 7798 9193
Office Administrator	Greeny Longville-Ancel	Tel: 020 7798 9187
Governance Co-ordinator	Carol Campbell	Tel: 020 7931 6050
Events & Marketing Co-ordinator	Diwura Olayinka	Tel: 020 7798 9189
Co-ordinator of School Chaplains	Fr David Reilly	Tel: 020 7798 9005

INTERFAITH

Particular Pastoral Responsibility Bishop Nicholas Hudson

Vaughan House, 46 Francis Street SW1P 1QN Tel: 020 7931 6028
Email: westminsterinterfaith@rcdow.org.uk
Director Rev Jon Dal Din
Tel: 07889 536957 / 07527 758729 Email: jondaldin@rcdow.org.uk

SECTION 2

Co-ordinator for North London Sr Elizabeth O'Donohoe HC
Tel: 020 7272 8048 Email: eodonohoe@btinternet.com

JUSTICE AND PEACE

Particular Pastoral Responsibility Bishop Nicholas Hudson

JUSTICE & PEACE COMMISSION

The Commission exists to promote action and reflection on peace and social justice in parishes, in the light of the Gospel and Catholic Social Teaching.

4 Vincent Road N15 3QH Tel: 020 8888 4222 Fax: 020 8888 4333
Email: justiceandpeace@rcdow.org.uk   Web: www.rcdow.org.uk/justiceandpeace
Chair Fr Dominic Robinson SJ
Co-ordinator Awaiting appointment
Commission Members Maggie Beirne, Barbara Kentish, Lauri Clarke, Santana Luis, Fr Tom O'Brien AA, Sr Elizabeth O'Donohoe HC, Tony Sheen, Edmund Tierney, Dr David Toorawa.
Parish Contacts for details of parish Justice and Peace contacts, see pages 167/8

METROPOLITAN TRIBUNAL

Vaughan House, 46 Francis Street SW1P 1QN Tel: 020 7798 9003

Judicial Vicar Mgr John Conneely JCL
Assistant Judicial Vicar Canon Michael Brockie JCL
Canonical Assistant Alicia Sloan JCL
Judges Canon Vincent Berry, Sr Rachel Harrington SND JCD, Fr Gerard Quinn STL, Alicia Sloan JCL
Defenders of the Bond Fr Dominic Byrne JCD, Sr Isabel MacPherson SND JCD, Paul Robbins JCL, Diana Sliwka JCL
Advocates Fr Noel Barber SJ, Dr Francesca Bugliani-Knox
Tribunal Assistant Matthew Gillespie
Auditors Mr Nathan Paine-Davey, Mrs Margaret Dixon, Mrs Jo O'Neill, Fr Dennis F P Touw Tempelmans-Plat

PILGRIMAGES

HOLY LAND
Director Fr Paul McDermott
The Presbytery, St Mellitus Church, Tollington Park N4 3AG Tel: 020 7272 3415

LOURDES
Director Fr Dennis F P Touw Tempelmans-Plat
60 Rylston Road SW6 7HW Tel: 020 7835 4040 Email: lourdes@rcdow.org.uk
For volunteer helpers aged 16+ interested in the diocesan pilgrimage to Lourdes
contact Katrina Lavery, Youth Director Tel: 07921 409402

SECTION 2

WALSINGHAM
DIRECTOR Fr John McKenna
82 Union Street, Barnet EN5 4HZ Tel: 020 8449 3338

Pilgrimage Co-ordinator Elizabeth Uwalaka **Vaughan House, 46 Francis Street SW1P 1QN** Tel: 020 7798 9173 Email: elizabethuwalaka@rcdow.org.uk

SAFEGUARDING SERVICE

Vaughan House, 46 Francis Street SW1P 1QN Email: safeguarding@rcdow.org.uk

Episcopal Vicar for Safeguarding Mgr Séamus O'Boyle
Tel: 020 7226 3277 Email: seamusoboyle@rcdow.org.uk
Safeguarding Co-ordinator Geraldine Allen
Tel: 020 7798 9350 Email: geraldineallen@rcdow.org.uk
PA, Team Administrator and Commission Secretary Gabriele Sedda
Tel: 020 7798 9356 Email: gabrielesedda@rcdow.org.uk
Safeguarding Officer Natalie Creswick
Tel: 020 7798 9359 Email: nataliecreswick@rcdow.org.uk
Safeguarding Support Officer Arianna Sommariva
Tel: 0207 798 9358 Email: ariannasommariva@rcdow.org.uk
DBS Administrator Jackie Krobo
Tel: 020 7798 9352 Email: jackiekrobo@rcdow.org.uk

Westminster Safeguarding Commission Chair Peter Houghton
Email: peterhoughton@rcdow.org.uk

VOCATION TO PRIESTHOOD IN THE DIOCESE OF WESTMINSTER

Particular Pastoral Responsibility Bishop John Sherrington

GENERAL CONTACT INFORMATION ABOUT VOCATIONS
Web: www.rcdow.org.uk/vocations
Twitter: @WestminsterVoca Facebook: WestminsterVocations
All initial enquiries about the call to priesthood should be made to Canon Stuart Wilson, the Vocations Promoter:

VOCATIONS PROMOTER
Canon Stuart Wilson **22 George Street W1U 3QY** Tel: 020 7935 0943 / 07515 065696
Email: vocationspromoter@rcdow.org.uk

ASSISTANT VOCATIONS PROMOTER
Fr Michael Maguire **247 High Road W4 4PU** Tel: 020 8994 2877
Email: vocations@rcdow.org.uk

VOCATIONS DIRECTOR
Fr Stephen Wang **Newman House, 111 Gower Street WC1E 6AR**
Tel: 020 7387 6370 Email: vocationsdirector@rcdow.org.uk
The Vocations Director is responsible for helping men in the later stages of discernment, as they consider applying to the Diocese and as they prepare for the selection conference.

PRIESTS' TRAINING FUND (PTF)

Chair Bishop John Sherrington

The Fund **(Registration No 233699-13, formerly 312528)** supports the work of vocations to the priesthood, formation of priests and on-going clergy formation.

WESTMINSTER YOUTH MINISTRY

Particular Pastoral Responsibility Bishop Nicholas Hudson

Director of Youth Ministry
Andrzej Wdowiak — Tel: 020 3757 2502 Email: andrzejwdowiak@rcdow.org.uk
Diocesan Youth Chaplain
Fr Mark Walker — Tel: 020 3757 2519 Email: markwalker@rcdow.org.uk
Communications and Events
James Kelliher — Tel: 020 3757 2517 Email: jameskelliher@rcdow.org.uk

1. Westminster Youth Ministry Outreach, Waxwell House, 125 Waxwell Lane, Pinner HA5 3EP Tel: 020 3757 2516 Email: youth@rcdow.org.uk Web: http://dowym.com

Manager
Phoebe Prendergast — Tel: 020 3757 2516 Email: phoebeprendergast@rcdow.org.uk
Senior Development Worker
Holly Cook — Tel: 020 3757 2517 Email: hollycook@rcdow.org.uk
Development Worker
Salvatore La Barbera — Tel: 020 3757 2517 Email: salvatorelabarbera@rcdow.org.uk

2. SPEC Retreat Centre, Waxwell House, 125 Waxwell Lane, Pinner HA5 3EP
Tel: 020 3757 2500 Email: spec@rcdow.org.uk Web: http://dowym.com/spec
SPEC is the diocesan day and residential retreat centre for young people in our parishes and schools.

Centre Manager
Maria West — Tel: 020 3757 2507 Email: mariawest@rcdow.org.uk
Retreats and Formation Manager
JJ Hussem — Tel: 020 3757 2503 Email: jjhussem@rcdow.org.uk
Administration and Operations Manager
Angie Cook — Tel: 020 3757 2500 Email: angiecook@rcdow.org.uk
Enquiries and Bookings — Tel: 020 3757 2500 Email: spec@rcdow.org.uk

DIOCESE OF
WESTMINSTER
YOUTH MINISTRY

Residential Retreats for young people at
SPEC Retreat Centre

We welcome groups of young people for primary and secondary school retreats and from parishes for pre- and post-sacramental retreats; they can be themed or bespoke. All residential retreats include Holy Mass, Exposition of the Blessed Sacrament, the Sacrament of Reconciliation and group activities. Set in beautiful and tranquil surroundings, SPEC is located in Pinner and is easily accessible from all parts of the Diocese of Westminster and is well served by public transport.

For bookings or planning a retreat visit **dowym.com/spec/bookings**
Contact us at: **020 3757 2500** or e-mail: **spec@rcdow.org.uk**

Waxwell House, 125 Waxwell Lane, Pinner, London, HA5 3EP

CATHOLIC CHILDRENS SOCIETY (CRUSADE OF RESCUE, FOUNDED 1859)

73 St Charles Square W10 6EJ Tel:020 8969 5305 Fax: 020 8960 1464
Email: info@cathchild.org.uk Web: www.cathchild.org.uk
Chief Executive Officer Rosemary Keenan BA, DSA, DASS, CQSW, MA, PhD

The Catholic Children's Society (CCS) works across the Diocese to support disadvantaged children and families. Services include:

SCHOOL COUNSELLING & THERAPY
CCS's ConnectEd counselling and therapy service supports the mental health and emotional wellbeing of thousands of children each year. Qualified and experienced counsellors/therapists work on-site in over 70 primary, secondary and special schools.
Contact Greg Brister **Head of Service Development & Communications**
Email: gregb@cathchild.org.uk

MENTAL HEALTH TRAINING
Expert training delivered to school staff, clergy and other members of the children's workforce, helping enhance their skills to identify and support children experiencing mental health issues. Examples of topics covered include: mental health awareness and promoting positive mental health; introduction to attachment theory; working with challenging and hard-to-reach children. Bespoke training is also available.
Contact Jo Trickett **Mental Health Trainer** Email: joannet@cathchild.org.uk

RAINBOWS BEREAVEMENT SUPPORT PROGRAMME
Training for school staff so they can deliver support groups for pupils who have experienced separation, bereavement and loss.
Contact Katrina Avery **Rainbows Registered Director** Email: katrinaa@cathchild.org.uk

CRISIS FUND
A special fund providing emergency financial assistance for families in immediate need. Applications can be made by Headteachers and Parish Priests.
Contact Duty Manager **Email:** reception@cathchild.org.uk

GRENFELL CRISIS FUND
A fund to deliver material and therapeutic help to all those affected by the Grenfell Tower fire. Applications can be made by Headteachers and Parish Priests.
Contact Duty Manager **Email:** reception@cathchild.org.uk

FAMILY CENTRE BASED SERVICES
Qualified Early Years staff operate in two centres to help disadvantaged families. Services include an Ofsted-rated 'Outstanding' nursery, drop-in, after school groups, holiday play-schemes and trips, a toy library, welfare advice and information.
St Francis Family Centre 34 Wades Place E14 0DE

Contact Margaret Wilkinson **Centre Co-ordinator**
Tel: 020 7987 8257 Email: margaretw@cathchild.org.uk

St Mark's Stay & Play, St Mark's Road W10 6BZ
Contact Sandra Mullings **Drop-in Worker** Tel: 020 8960 2970 (Noon – 4pm)

POST ADOPTION & AFTERCARE

Although no longer an adoption agency, we offer support, counselling and advice to former adoptees, their adopters and birth families. We also provide information to those formerly in our care.
Contact Irena Lyczkowska **Post-Adoption Manager** Email: irenal@cathchild.org.uk

OTHER RESOURCES

MINISTRY TO ALIENATED CATHOLICS

The purpose of the apostolate is to be a practical sign that the Church is reaching out to alienated Catholics and to allow them to voice any hurt or grievance.
Fr Francis Wahle **Tel: 020 7487 5956 Email: franciswahle@yahoo.com**

PARLIAMENTARY ROMAN CATHOLIC DUTY PRIEST

Canon Pat Browne is, by kind permission of the Speaker, available for the celebration of the Sacraments and pastoral care of Peers, MPs and Staff of the Palace of Westminster.
Holy Apostles Church, 47 Cumberland Street SW1V 4LY
Tel: 07988 441691 Email: patbrowne@rcdow.org.uk

JOIN US TO CONTINUE CARDINAL BASIL HUME'S LEGACY AND HELP YOUNG PEOPLE AND FAMILIES AVOID HOMELESSNESS AND POVERTY

For over 30 years the Cardinal Hume Centre charity has continued Basil Hume's vision of helping those in the most need, here in Westminster Diocese.

Inspired by Catholic Social Teaching. we believe that each person is created in the image of God, and *"Each person matters; no human life is ever redundant".*

HOW CAN WE SUPPORT YOU?

We can visit your primary or secondary school to talk about youth homelessness and family poverty, and how our work aligns with CST. We also regularly visit parishes across the Diocese to speak after Mass, or we can help you run a Confirmation class.

CAN YOU HELP US?

We depend on funding from parish collections, Confirmation group donations and school fundraising events. You can also make a donation on-line at:
cardinalhumecentre.org.uk/donate-now
We rely on over 100 regular volunteers, and often have new volunteering opportunities.

www. CardinalHumeCentre.org.uk
Cardinal Hume Centre, 3 Arneway Street, Westminster,
London, SW1P 2BG. Phone - 020 7222 1602.
Email - StephenCurrid@cardinalhumecentre.org.uk.
Charity number - 1090836

Cardinal Hume
Centre
Turning Lives Around

CARDINAL HUME CENTRE

The Centre welcomes homeless young people, individuals and families in need from all backgrounds. Our teams help them access the support, and gain the skills they need, to overcome poverty and possible homelessness. A range of specialist services are on-site: advice and assessment; family and young people's services; housing and welfare rights advice and advocacy; learning and employment services; immigration advice and representation; and residential services for homeless young people. There is also a GP surgery and a charity shop in Horseferry Road. The Centre is supported by regular volunteers who work in different roles and play an integral part in all that we do. Opportunities include teaching English, digital inclusion support, working in the shop and supportive roles in various clubs for families and children. Vacancies and role descriptions are listed on the website.
Chair of Trustees Robert Arnott **Chief Executive** George O'Neill **Community Fundraiser** Stephen Currid **Volunteer Co-ordinators** Flora Swartland / Emily Hynes
Partnership Manager Hilary Nightingale **Surgery** Sr Dr Mary Hickey MBE
3-7 Arneway Street SW1P 2BG Tel: 020 7222 1602
Email: info@cardinalhumecentre.org.uk Web: www.cardinalhumecentre.org.uk

PROVIDENCE ROW

For homeless or vulnerably housed people, finding employment and housing opportunities can feel like an uphill battle, even more so if affected by health, mental health or substance misuse issues. Providence Row works with more than 1,600 people a year in East London, offering an integrated service of crisis support, advice, recovery and learning and training programmes. It helps those who are so often excluded from mainstream services gain the support and opportunities they need to help create a safer, healthier life off the streets.
Chief Executive Tom O'Connor **The Dellow Centre, 82 Wentworth Street E1 7SA**
Tel: 020 7375 0020 Email: info@providencerow.org.uk
Web: www.providencerow.org.uk

THE PASSAGE

We provide resources which encourage, inspire and challenge homeless people to transform their lives, and undertake street outreach work, including the area around the Cathedral and Victoria stations, which has the UK's highest incidence of people sleeping outside. The Resource Centre provides food, showers, laundry and clothing store facilities, as well as addressing health, education, employment, housing and welfare rights issues. The hostels help give people additional support when they first move from the streets, including some of the longest-term rough sleepers. The Passage's Home for Good project enables volunteers to support former rough sleepers across London. In summary, the Passage helps people to stop living on the streets and supports them as they move into places of their own, and helps many to return to employment. We welcome support from parishes and schools and are happy to deliver talks and provide information about our work.
Chief Executive Mick Clarke **Community Fundraiser** Andrew Hollingsworth
St Vincent's, Carlisle Place SW1P 1NL Tel: 020 7592 1850 Fax: 020 7592 1870
Email: info@passage.org.uk Web: www.passage.org.uk

Section 3

DEANERIES

The name of the Auxiliary Bishop or Episcopal Vicar with particular pastoral responsibility is given in brackets.

1. BARNET (Bishop John Sherrington)
Barnet, Burnt Oak, Cricklewood, Edgware, Finchley Church End, Finchley East, Finchley North, Golders Green, Grahame Park, Hendon, Hendon West, Mill Hill, New Barnet, Whetstone
Dean Fr John McKenna **(Barnet)**   Tel: 020 8449 3338

2. BRENT (Bishop John Sherrington)
Dollis Hill, Kensal Rise, Kingsbury Green, Neasden, Stonebridge, Wembley 1, Wembley 2, Wembley 3, Willesden, Willesden Green
Dean Fr Stephen Willis **(Willesden)**   Tel: 020 8965 4935

3. CAMDEN (Bishop Nicholas Hudson)
Camden Town, Hampstead, Haverstock Hill, Kentish Town, Kilburn, Kilburn West, Lebanese Church, Somers Town, Swiss Cottage
Dean Awaiting appointment **()**   Tel:

4. EALING (Fr Duncan Adamson)
Acton, Acton East, Acton West, Ealing, Greenford, Hanwell, Northfields, Perivale, Polish Church 3, Southall
Dean Fr Jim Duffy **(Northfields)**   Tel: 020 8567 5421

5. ENFIELD (Bishop John Sherrington)
Cockfosters, Cuffley, Edmonton, Enfield, New Southgate, Palmers Green, Ponders End, Potters Bar
Dean Fr David Reilly **(New Southgate)**   Tel: 020 8368 1638

6. HACKNEY (Bishop Nicholas Hudson)
Clapton, Clapton Park, Hackney, Homerton, Hoxton, Kingsland, Manor House, Stoke Newington
Dean Fr David Evans **(Hackney)**   Tel: 020 8985 2496

7. HAMMERSMITH & FULHAM (Canon Paschal Ryan)
Brook Green, Fulham1, Fulham 2, Hammersmith, Parsons Green, Polish Church 2, Shepherd's Bush, White City
Dean Fr Richard Andrew **(Brook Green)**   Tel: 020 7603 3832

8. HARINGEY (Bishop John Sherrington)
Muswell Hill, Stamford Hill, Stroud Green, Tottenham, West Green, Wood Green
Dean Fr Mark Anwyll **(Muswell Hill)**   Tel: 020 8883 5607

SECTION 3

9. HARROW (Bishop John Sherrington)
Harrow-on-the-Hill, Harrow North, Harrow South & Northolt, Headstone Lane, Kenton, Pinner, Stanmore, Sudbury, Wealdstone
Dean Canon Michael Munnelly **(Stanmore)**   Tel: 020 8954 1299

10. HILLINGDON (Fr Duncan Adamson)
Eastcote, Harefield, Hayes, Hillingdon, Northwood, Ruislip, Ruislip South, Uxbridge, West Drayton, Yeading
Dean Fr Nicholas Schofield **(Uxbridge)**   Tel: 01895 233193

11. HOUNSLOW (Fr Duncan Adamson)
Brentford, Chiswick, Cranford, Feltham, Grove Park, Heathrow Airport, Heston, Hounslow, Isleworth, Osterley
Dean Fr Gerard Quinn **(Brentford)**   Tel: 020 8560 1671

12. ISLINGTON (Bishop Nicholas Hudson)
Archway, Bunhill Row, Clerkenwell, Copenhagen Street, Highbury, Highgate, Holloway, Islington, Polish Church 1, Tollington Park
Dean Mgr Séamus O'Boyle **(Islington)**   Tel: 020 7226 3277

13. KENSINGTON AND CHELSEA (Canon Paschal Ryan)
Chelsea 1, Chelsea 2, Fulham Road, Kensington 1, Kensington 2, Oratory
Dean Fr Patrick Ryall OSM **(Fulham Road)**   Tel: 020 7352 6965

14. LEA VALLEY (Bishop Paul McAleenan)
Bishop's Stortford, Buntingford, Cheshunt, Hertford, Hoddesdon, Old Hall Green & Puckeridge, Waltham Cross, Ware
Dean Fr Peter Harris **(Bishop's Stortford)**   Tel: 01279 654063

15. MARYLEBONE (Bishop Nicholas Hudson)
Farm Street, Marylebone, Ogle Street, St John's Wood, Spanish Place, Ukrainian Cathedral, University Chaplaincy
Dean Fr Stephen Wang **(University Chaplaincy)**   Tel: 020 7387 6370

16. NORTH KENSINGTON (Canon Paschal Ryan)
Bayswater, Harrow Road, Kensal New Town, Notting Hill, Paddington, Queensway, St Charles Square
Dean Fr Gerard Skinner **(Notting Hill)**   Tel: 020 7727 7968

17. ST ALBANS (Bishop Paul McAleenan)
Berkhamsted, Borehamwood, Borehamwood North, Harpenden, Hemel Hempstead Boxmoor, Hemel Hempstead East, Hemel Hempstead North, Hemel Hempstead West, London Colney, Radlett, Redbourn, St Albans, St Albans South, Shenley, Tring, Wheathampstead
Dean Canon Anthony Dwyer (Harpenden)   Tel: 01582 712245

18. STEVENAGE (Bishop Paul McAleenan)
Baldock, Hatfield, Hatfield South, Hitchin, Knebworth, Letchworth, Royston, Stevenage Bedwell, Stevenage Old Town, Stevenage Shephall, Welwyn Garden City, Welwyn Garden City Digswell and Welwyn Garden City East
Dean Fr Norbert Fernandes (Welwyn Garden City) Tel: 01707 323234

19. TOWER HAMLETS (Bishop Nicholas Hudson)
Bethnal Green, Bow, Bow Common, Commercial Road, German Church, Limehouse, Lithuanian Church, Mile End, Millwall, Poplar, Tower Hill, Underwood Road, Wapping
Dean Fr William Skehan (Commercial Road)   Tel: 020 7790 5911

20. UPPER THAMES (Canon Paschal Ryan)
Ashford, Hampton Hill, Hampton-on-Thames, St Margarets-on-Thames, Shepperton, Staines-upon-Thames, Stanwell, Sunbury-on-Thames, Teddington, Twickenham, Whitton
Dean Fr Philip Dyer-Perry (Staines-upon-Thames)   Tel: 01784 452381

21. WATFORD (Bishop Paul McAleenan)
Abbots Langley, Bushey, Carpenders Park, Chipperfield, Chorleywood, Croxley Green, Garston, Mill End & Maple Cross, Rickmansworth, Watford, Watford North
Dean Fr Shaun Church (Rickmansworth)   Tel: 01923 773387

22. WESTMINSTER (Bishop Nicholas Hudson)
(City) Ely Place, Italian Church, Lincoln's Inn Fields, Moorfields;
(West End) Cathedral, Covent Garden, French Church, Pimlico, Soho Square, Warwick Street
Dean Canon Alexander Sherbrooke (Soho Square) Tel: 020 7437 2010

23. ETHNIC CHAPLAINCIES (Fr David Irwin)
Dean Fr Petras Tverijonas (Lithuanian Church)   Tel: 020 7739 8735

SECTION 3

PARISH MAP

The diocesan website features an
interactive map-based search facility
on which you can search for
Catholic parishes and schools, and
explore the geography of the
Diocese on Google Maps.

Please visit
www.rcdow.org.uk/virtual

Royston

Baldock
Letchworth
Hitchin

Buntingford

Stevenage
Shephall
Bedwell

Puckeridge

Knebworth
Old Hall Green

Bishops
Stortford

(Much Hadham)

Harpenden
Welwyn Garden
City Digswell

Tring
Wheathampstead

Redbourn
Welwyn Garden
City (East)
Welwyn Garden
City
Ware
(Sawbridgeworth)

Berkhamsted
Hertford

Hemel Hempstead N.
St. Albans
Hemel Hempstead West/Boxmoor
Hatfield
Hemel Hempstead E.
St. Albans S.
Hatfield S.
Hoddesdon
Abbots Langley
London Colney

Chipperfield

Radlett
Cuffley

Garston
Shenley
Cheshunt
Watford N.
Potters Bar
Chorleywood
Croxley
Watford
Borehamwood
Waltham Cross
Green
(North)
Barnet
Bushey
Ponders End
Rickmansworth
Carpenders
Borehamwood
Enfield
Mill End
Park
New
Cockfosters
Barnet

Harefield
Northwood
Stanmore

Pinner
Headstone Lane
Eastcote
Wealdstone

Uxbridge
Harrow N.
Kenton
SEE
Ruislip
INSET
Northolt
Harrow S.
Harrow
MAPS

S. Ruislip
Sudbury

Hillingdon
Yeading
Perivale
CENTRAL
West Drayton
Cranford
Greenford
LONDON
Heathrow
Polish Church 3
Ealing
Hayes
Southall
Hanwell
Northfields
Stanwell
Heston
Brentford
River Thames
Hounslow
Osterley
Staines-upon-Thames
Isleworth
Whitton
St. Margarets
Ashford
Feltham
Twickenham
Sunbury-on-Thames
Hampton
MILES
Hampton
Shepperton
Hill
Teddington
0   5   10   15
Hampton-on-Thames

Parishes in the Diocese of Westminster

Mill Hill
Whetstone
Edmonton
Finchley N.
Palmers Green
Edgware
Finchley Church End
Grahame Park
New Southgate
Tottenham
Burnt Oak
Wood Green
Finchley E.
West Green
Kingsbury Geen
Muswell Hill
Stroud Green
Hendon W.
Hendon
Archway
Stamford Hill
Wembley 2
Golders Green
Tollington Park
Wembley 3
Dollis Hill
Highgate
Clapton
Wembley 1
Cricklewood
Holloway
Stoke Newington
Neasden
Hampstead
Homerton
Willesden Green
Swiss Cottage
Haverstock Hill
Clapton Park
Stonebridge
Highbury
Manor House
Hackney
Willesden
Kentish Town
Islington
Kingsland
Bow
Kensal Rise
Kilburn
Bow Common
Mile End
St Charles' Square
Harrow Rd.
W. Kilburn
St Johns Wood
Poplar
Acton W.
Acton E.
White City
Kensal New Town
Paddington
CENTRAL LONDON
Limehouse
Acton
Notting Hill
Bayswater
Westminster Cathedral
Shepherds Bush
Kensington 2
Brook Gn.
Queensway
Pimlico
Westminster
Polish Church 2
Kensington 1
Oratory
Chelsea 1
Millwall
Gunnersbury
Chiswick
Hammersmith
Chelsea 2
River Thames
Grove Park
Fulham
Fulham, Rd
Stephendale Rd.
Parsons Green

MILES

0   1   2   3   4   5

Parishes in London

Camden Town
Copenhagen St.
Somers Town
Polish Ch. 1
Lithuanian Ch.
University Chaplaincy
Hoxton
Clerkenwell
Bunhill Row
Bethnal Grn.
Italian Ch.
Marylebone Rd.
Underwood Rd.
Spanish Pl.
Ogle St.
Ely Pl.
German Ch.
Ukrainian Ch.
Soho Sq.
Lincoln's Inn Fields
Moorfields
Commercial Rd.
Warwick St.
French Ch.
River Thames
Tower Hill
Covent Garden
Wapping
Farm St.

Parishes in Central London

SECTION 3

PARISH DIRECTORY

1. Within the Diocese the parishes are grouped in deaneries. The deaneries, with their component parishes, are listed on the preceding pages.

2. + Indicates a church registered for marriages.

3. Each parish entry gives the name of the parish, the title of the church, the postal address, telephone number, email address and website, the road in which it is situated, and its deanery reference (*in italic bold type*). Dates in parentheses refer to its founding, the building of the church and its consecration. London postal addresses indicate the name of the road and postcode. Hertfordshire and Middlesex addresses include the name of the nearest town. Details of all parishes can be found at **parish.rcdow.org.uk/parishname**.

4. The name highlighted in red is that of the Parish Priest. Priests are listed by name only; degrees etc. can be found in the alphabetical list of clergy in Section 4.

5. Diocesan email addresses are formed thus: **firstname+surname@rcdow.org.uk**.

6. The first Mass of Sunday celebrated on Saturday evening, or the first Mass of a Holy Day celebrated on the evening of the preceding day, is indicated thus:
Sunday Mass (Sat 6pm), 8, 9, ... **Holy Day Mass** (Vigil 8pm), 10, 11 .....
Different timetables will apply at Christmas, Easter and on Public Holidays; enquire at the church.

7. Times of services shown are a.m. (i.e. 11.15), unless specifically indicated as p.m. (i.e. 6pm).

8. For Ecumenical or Justice and Peace contacts, ring the parish office. A list of Justice and Peace contacts is also given at the end of this Section.

9. Parish details are followed by relevant mission institutions, houses of female and male religious, then other public institutions (e.g. hospitals). These are served by priests of the parish unless otherwise stated.

10. Facilities for physically disabled and/or hearing impaired people are indicated after the name of the church by the following symbols:

   A   Access only (ramps, etc)
   ♿   Full facilities (access, plus disabled access lavatory)
   ♪   Loop System for hearing-aid users
   S   Mass celebrated regularly in Word and Sign, and/or Confession in Sign Language; enquire for details and times.

WESTMINSTER CATHEDRAL + METROPOLITAN CATHEDRAL OF THE MOST PRECIOUS BLOOD

Sunday Mass (6pm Sung) 8, 9, 10.30 (Choir), 12noon (Sung), 5.30pm (Sung), 7pm;
Holy Day Mass (Vigil 5.30pm, Choir), 7, 8, 10.30 (Latin), 12.30pm, 1.05pm, 5.30pm
(Choir); **Weekday Mass** Mon-Fri 7, 8, 10.30 (Latin), 12.30pm, 1.05pm, 5.30pm (Choir);
Saturday Mass 8, 9, 10.30 (Latin, Choir), 12.30pm; **Public Holidays** Mass 10.30, 12.30pm,
5pm

Divine Office: Morning Prayer Sun 10, Mon-Fri 7.40, Sat 10; **Vespers** Sun 3.30pm with
Benediction (Choir), Mon-Fri 5pm (Choir, except Tue), Sat 5.30pm; **Public Holidays**
Morning Prayer 10; *No Vespers*

Confession Sat 10.30-6.30pm, Sun 11-1pm, 4.30pm-7pm, Mon-Fri 11.30-6pm, **Public
Holidays** 11-12.30pm

Opening times Mon-Fri 7-7pm; Sat 8-7pm, Sun 7-7.45pm; **Public Holidays** 8-5.30pm

Victoria Street SW1P 1LT; Clergy House is at 42 Francis Street SW1P 1QW
Clergy House Reception open Mon-Fri 8-7pm, Sat, Sun 10-1pm
Enquiries Tel: 020 7798 9055; Times of services Tel: 020 7798 9097
Email: chreception@rcdow.org.uk Web: www.westminstercathedral.org.uk
Victoria Station (BR/TfL)
Westminster Deanery (1903; cons 28 June 1910)

Administrator Canon Christopher Tuckwell Tel: 020 7798 9374
PA Elizabeth Arnot Tel: 020 7798 9062

Cathedral Chaplains:
Fr Daniel Humphreys **(Sub-Administrator)** Tel: 020 7798 9180
Fr Julio Albornoz Tel: 020 7931 6097
Fr Michael Donaghy Tel: 020 7798 9048
Fr Andrew Gallagher **(Precentor)** Tel: 020 7798 9098
Fr Rajiv Michael Tel: 020 7798 9055
Fr John Scott **(Registrar)** Tel: 020 7931 6041

Sub-Administrator's Assistant James Coeur-de-Lion Tel: 020 7798 9179
Design Service Manager Lorcán Keller Tel: 020 7798 9058

Music Department:
Email: music@westminstercathedral.org.uk
Master of Music Martin Baker Tel: 020 7798 9066
Assistant Master of Music Peter Stevens Obl OSB Tel: 020 7931 6091
Organ Scholar Callum Alger Tel: 020 7798 9378
Music Administrator Madeline Smith (Mon, Wed-Fri) Tel: 020 7798 9057
Email: musicadmin@rcdow.org.uk
Cathedral Choir School, Ambrosden Avenue SW1P 1QH Tel: 020 7798 9081

SECTION 3

Head Neil McLaughlan **Acting Chaplain** Fr Daniel Humphreys

Cathedral Manager Peter McNulty **Tel:** 020 7798 9064
Retail and Procurement Manager Glynn McNiven **Tel:** 020 7798 9389
Head of Security Andrew Grange **Tel:** 020 7798 9014 / 07801 572433
Works Manager Neil Fairbairn **Tel:** 020 7798 9054
Works Assistant Caroline Keogh **Tel:** 020 7798 9053

Franciscan Sisters of Our Lady of Victories, Cathedral Clergy House **Tel:** 020 7798 9067

Friends of Westminster Cathedral
Director Christina White **Tel:** 020 7798 9059

Oremus, **the Magazine of Westminster Cathedral**
Editor Fr John Scott **Tel:** 020 7798 9052

Registry **Tel:** 020 7798 9376 **Email:** registrar@rcdow.org.uk

Sacred Heart Church, Horseferry Road SW1P 2EF (Parochial Chapel of Ease)
Enquiries Fr John Scott **Tel:** 020 7931 6041
Sunday Mass 11, 4pm (Croatian); **Weekday Mass** Thu 12.30pm

• **Daughters of Charity, St Vincent's, Carlisle Place SW1P 1NL**
Tel: 020 7834 4004 **Fax:** 020 7630 5467
Email: carlisleplace@btconnect.com **Web:** www.daughtersofcharity.org.uk
also **94a Horseferry Road SW1P 2EE** **Tel:** 020 7222 6485
Email: horseferryroaddc@gmail.com
• **Vincentian Care Plus** (Care of Elderly in Own Home)
• **Cardinal Hume Centre, 3-7 Arneway Street SW1P 2BG** **Tel:** 020 7222 1602
Web: www.cardinalhumecentre.org.uk
Director George O'Neill
• **The Passage, St Vincent's, Carlisle Place SW1P 1NL** **Tel:** 020 7592 1850
Web: www.passage.org.uk
Chief Executive Mick Clarke
• **The Gordon Hospital** **Tel:** 020 8746 8733
• **St Paul's Bookshop Managing Director** Fr Francy Kochupaliathil SSP
Morpeth Terrace SW1P 1EP **Tel:** 020 7828 5582 **Fax:** 020 7828 3329

ABBOTS LANGLEY + ST SAVIOUR

Sunday Mass (Sat 5pm), 8.30, 11.30; **Holy Day Mass** 10, 7pm; **Weekday Mass** Mon-Fri 10; **Exposition** *Ist Fri only* 10.30-12noon; **Holy Hour** and **Benediction** *Ist Sunday only* 4 pm, with **Confession** available; **Confession** Sat 4.15-4.45pm & on request

Salvatorians (SDS) Fr Richard Mway-Zeng, Fr Christopher Luoga (clergy also serve Chipperfield)
The Presbytery, 96 The Crescent, Abbots Langley, Watford WD5 0DS
Tel: 01923 266177 (Presbytery)
Email: abbotslangley@rcdow.org.uk Web: parish.rcdow.org.uk/abbotslangley
Watford Deanery (1928; 1963)

ACTON + OUR LADY OF LOURDES

Sunday Mass (Sat 7pm), 9, 10.30, 12noon, 6pm; **Holy Day Mass** 10, 7pm; **Weekday Mass** Mon-Sat 10, Fri 10, 7pm; **Confession** Sat 10.30, 6-7pm & on request

Congregation of the Sacred Hearts of Jesus and Mary (SS.CC) Fr Fergal Maguire (resident at 85 Old Oak Common Lane W3 7DD), Fr Fintan Crotty, Fr Pearse Mullen; Rev Tito Pereira (Deacon)
5 Berrymead Gardens W3 8AA Tel: 020 8992 2014
Email: acton@rcdow.org.uk Web: parish.rcdow.org.uk/acton
On High Street, between Town Hall and Horn Lane.
Ealing Deanery (1878; 1902; cons 17 May 1961)

• Medical Mission Sisters (Generalate) (SCMM), 41 Chatsworth Gardens W3 9LP
Tel: 020 8992 6444 Email: generalate@medicalmissionsisters.org.uk
Web: www.medicalmissionsisters.org.uk
• Religious Sisters of Charity, Caritas, 4 Buxton Gardens W3 9LQ Tel: 020 8992 8550
also 9 Rosemont Road W3 9LU Tel: 020 8992 4461
Email: rsocacton@gmail.com Web: www.religioussistersofcharity.org
• Damien Centre (Acton Homeless Concern), 3-5 Church Road W3 8BU
Tel: 020 8993 6096
• Emmaus House (Acton Homeless Concern), 1 Berrymead Gardens W3 8AA
Tel: 020 8992 5768

ACTON EAST + ST AIDAN OF LINDISFARNE

Sunday Mass (Sat 6.30pm), 9, 11 (Sung), 1pm (Gheez Rite); **Holy Day Mass** 10, 7.30pm; **Weekday Mass** 10, also Wed 6.30 pm; **Exposition** Sat 5.30-6.15pm, with **Benediction** 6.15pm; **Confession** Sat 5.30-6.15pm

Congregation of the Sacred Hearts of Jesus and Mary (SS.CC) Fr Fergal Maguire, Fr Christopher McAneny (resident at 372 Uxbridge Road W5 3LH)
85 Old Oak Common Lane W3 7DD Tel: 020 8743 5732
Email: actoneast@rcdow.org.uk Web: parish.rcdow.org.uk/actoneast
On Old Oak Common Lane just off Western Avenue (A40) at Savoy Circus, 1 min East Acton Stn
Ealing Deanery (1922; 1961; cons 31 October 1972)

SECTION 3

Parish Office Mon, Wed, Fri 10.30-12noon
Head Server Donald Allwright **Tel: 020 8992 7616**
Music Co-ordinator Amy Cotton **Tel: 020 8743 5732**

• Infant Jesus Sisters, 16 East Acton Lane W3 7EG **Tel: 020 8248 9458**,
also at **30 Sunningdale Avenue W3 7NS Tel: 020 8743 0116**
• HMP Wormwood Scrubs Chaplain Fr Chima Ibekwe **(See HM Prison Service)**
• **Hammersmith, Queen Charlotte's & Chelsea Hospitals**
Sunday Mass 11.30; Weekday Mass Tue 12.30pm
Chaplains Fr Giles Pinnock, Fr Blaise Amadi CM **Tel 020 3313 4574**

ACTON WEST + THE HOLY FAMILY

Sunday Mass (Sat 6pm), 8.45, 10 (Polish), 11.15, 12.45pm (Iraqi, Chaldean Rite); **Holy Day Mass** 10, 7.30pm; **Weekday Mass** as announced; **Exposition** and **Benediction** *First Fri only* after 10 Mass; **Rosary** *in May and October only* after weekday Mass; **Confession** Sat 9.45-10, 5.30-5.45pm

Fr Neil Reynolds
The Presbytery, Vale Lane W3 0DY Tel: 020 8992 1308
Email: actonwest@rcdow.org.uk Web: parish.rcdow.org.uk/actonwest
Closest Stns: North Ealing or West Acton
Ealing Deanery (1967; cons 1 April 2017)

• IBVM, 21 Twyford Avenue W3 9PY Tel: 020 8993 6931
Email: magdalenibvm@gmail.com
• Congregation of the Sacred Hearts of Jesus and Mary (SS.CC), 372 Uxbridge Road W5 3LH Tel: 020 8992 5941 Web: www. ssccpicpus.com
Frs Kenneth Barnes, Chris McAneny
• Focolare Movement, 57 Twyford Avenue W3 9PZ

ARCHWAY + ST GABRIEL OF OUR LADY OF SORROWS   A

Sunday Mass (Sat 6.30pm), 9, 11.30 (with Children's Liturgy), 6.30pm; **Meditative Rosary** precedes each Sunday Mass, with **Exposition** Sun 10.30-11.30; **Holy Day Mass** 12noon, 7pm; **Weekday Mass** Mon-Sat 12noon; **Healing Mass, Holy Hour** and **Benediction** *First Fri only* 12 noon; **Confession** Sat 11.30, 6pm & on request

Spiritans (CSSp) Fr Ugo Ikwuka, Fr David Sandambongo, Fr Oliver Ugwu (in residence, Hospital Chaplain)
15 St John's Villas N19 3EE Tel: 020 7272 8195
Email: archway@rcdow.org.uk Web: parish.rcdow.org.uk/archway
Between Upper Holloway Stn (BR) and Archway Stn (TfL)
Islington Deanery (1928; cons 1967)

• Marist Sisters, 17 St John's Villas N19 3EE Tel: 020 7272 1079
Email: marist.sisters@btinternet.com
• Ugandan Martyrs Catholic Community
Mass *Last Sunday of the month* 3pm

ARNOS GROVE, N11: *SEE NEW SOUTHGATE*

ASHFORD + ST MICHAEL   S

Sunday Mass (Sat 6pm), 9.15, 11, 6pm; **Holy Day Mass** 9.15, 7pm; **Weekday Mass** Mon, Tue, Wed, Fri, Sat 9.15; **Exposition** Sat 9.45-10.15; **Confession** Sat 10.15-10.45

Sons of Divine Providence **(FDP)** Fr Sidon Sagar, Fr Carlo Mazzotta (clergy also serve Stanwell)
112 Clarendon Road, Ashford TW15 2QD Tel: 01784 252230
Email: ashford@rcdow.org.uk Web: parish.rcdow.org.uk/ashford
Corner of Fordbridge Road & Clarendon Road, close to the War Memorial
Upper Thames Deanery (1906; 1928; cons 19 November 2006)

• HMP Bronzefield **Chaplain** Karen Connaughton **(See HM Prison Service)**

BALDOCK + HOLY TRINITY AND ST AUGUSTINE OF CANTERBURY   A

Sunday Mass (Sat 6.30pm), 8.30, 10.30 (Sung), 3pm (Extraordinary Form, *First Sun only)*; **Holy Day Mass** 10, 7.30pm; **Weekday Mass** Mon-Thu 10; **Holy Hour** Sat 5.15-6.15pm; **Confession** Sat 5.45-6.15pm

Fr Denis Sarsfield
Holy Trinity Church, London Road, Baldock SG7 6LQ Tel: 01462 893127
Email: baldock@rcdow.org.uk Web: parish.rcdow.org.uk/baldock
Stevenage Deanery (1913; 1926; cons 17 December 1977)

BARNET + MARY IMMACULATE AND ST GREGORY THE GREAT   A

Sunday Mass (Sat 6.30pm), 8, 9.30, 11.15, 6.30pm; **Holy Day Mass** 10, 7.30pm; **Weekday Mass** Mon-Sat 10; **Mass for Healing** *First Fri only* 7.30pm, *Third Sun only* 6.30pm; **Confession** Sat 5.45-6.15pm

Fr John McKenna
82 Union Street, Barnet EN5 4HZ Tel: 020 8449 3338
Email: barnet@rcdow.org.uk Web: parish/rcdow.org.uk/barnet
Barnet Deanery (1849; 1860; cons 15 December 1931; new church cons 8 December 1977; renewed church cons 3 September 2017)
Pastoral Assistant Anita Hammond
Parish Administrator Janet Nestor
Evangelisation Co-ordinator Jonathan Stephens

• Barnet Hospital
Chaplain Awaiting appointment Tel: 0845 111 4000
• Poor Clares, Poor Clare Monastery, 102 Galley Lane, Arkley, Barnet EN5 4AN
Tel: 020 8449 8815 Email: stclaresarkley@yahoo.co.uk
Web: www.arkleypoorclares.weebly.com
Chaplain Awaiting appointment
• Sisters of Christian Instruction, Summerhill, Leecroft Road, Barnet EN5 2TH
Tel: 020 8440 1853 Email: stgildasbarnet@yahoo.co.uk

SECTION 3

BAYSWATER + ST MARY OF THE ANGELS A

Sunday Mass (Sat 6pm), 9.30 (Family), 11 (Portuguese), 12.30pm, 6pm; *Summer Sunday Mass* (Sat 6pm), 11, 6pm; **Holy Day Mass** 10, 7pm; **Weekday Mass** 10 and **Exposition** Mon-Sat 9-9.50; **Confession** Sat 10.30-11, 5.30-6pm & on request

Mgr Keith Barltrop, Fr Richard Price (in residence)
The Presbytery, Moorhouse Road W2 5DJ Tel: 020 7229 0487 Fax: 020 7229 3223
Email: bayswater@rcdow.org.uk Web: www.humilitas.org
West of junction of Westbourne Grove & Chepstow Road, via Artesian Road
North Kensington Deanery (1857; cons 4 November 2007)

• Convent of the Assumption, St Catherine's, 7 Pembridge Square W2 4EQ
Tel: 020 7792 0623 Email: Shafto38@hotmail.com
• Sisters of Our Lady of Sion, 34 Chepstow Villas W11 2QZ
Tel: 020 7229 6266 Email: sionbayswater@gmail.com
Sion Centre for Dialogue and Encounter, Conference Centre and Jewish/Christian
Library Study Days and Reading/Library Resources Tel: 020 7313 8286
Email: sioncentrefordialogue@gmail.com Web: sioncentre.org
• Comboni Missionaries (MCCJ), 16 Dawson Place W2 4TJ
Tel: 020 7229 7059 Email: benitodemarchi@hotmail.com, anzioli47@hotmail.com
Web: www.comboni.org.uk
Frs Angelo Anzioli (Superior), Carmine Curci, Benito De Marchi, Pasquino Panato
• Pembridge House, 29 Pembridge Square W2 4DS Tel: 020 7221 0588
Pastoral care entrusted to the Prelature of Opus Dei
• **Courage** Support group for those experiencing same-sex attraction and who wish to live
a chaste life in accordance with the Church's teaching. **Contact** the **Parish Priest** or
london.courage@gmail.com

BERKHAMSTED + SACRED HEART CHURCH

Sunday Mass 8.30, 10.15; **Holy Day Mass** as announced; **Weekday Mass** Tue, Fri, Sat 10;
Liturgy of the Word with **Holy Communion** Wed 10; **Holy Hour** with **Exposition** and
Benediction follows Sat Mass; **Confession** Sat 10.30-11.15

Fr David Burke (also serves Tring)
Sacred Heart Church, Park Street, Berkhamsted HP4 1HX Tel: 01442 863845
Email: berkhamsted@rcdow.org.uk Web: parish.rcdow.org.uk/berkhamsted
Off Berkhamsted High Street (north side)
St Albans Deanery (1909; 1967)

BETHNAL GREEN + OUR LADY OF THE ASSUMPTION

Sunday Mass (Sat 6.30pm), 9.30, 11.30 (all with Children's Liturgy), 2.15pm (Chinese), 5pm
(Tagalog, *4th Sun only*); **Holy Day Mass** 7.30 (Priory Chapel), 12.15pm, 6.30pm; **Weekday
Mass** Mon-Fri 12.15pm; Sat 9.30; **Exposition** Wed 11-12noon; **Confession** Sat 5.45-
6.15pm

Assumptionists (a.a.) Fr Justin Kasereka, Fr Antigon Claude Bahati; Br Joseph Quoc Cuong Tran;
Fr Joseph Liang (in residence, Chinese Chaplain)
Assumption Priory, Victoria Park Square E2 9PB Tel: 020 8980 1968
Email: bethnalgreen@rcdow.org.uk Web: parish.rcdow.org.uk/bethnalgreen
Just off main road, close to Bethnal Green Stn (TfL)
Tower Hamlets Deanery (1901; 1912)

• Sisters of La Sainte Union, 36 Gawber Street E2 0JH
• Chinese Community Fr Joseph Liang Tel: 020 8709 5281 / 07753 471611
Email: josephliang1998@gmail.com; Amy Lou (Mandarin & Cantonese-speaking)
Tel: 07878 582111 Email: amyfclou@hotmail.com

BISHOP'S STORTFORD + ST JOSEPH AND THE ENGLISH MARTYRS

Bishop's Stortford, + St Joseph and the English Martyrs: **Sunday Mass** (Sat 6pm), 9, 11, 6pm; **Holy Day Mass** 9.30, 7.30pm; **Weekday Mass** Mon-Fri 9.30, **Confession** (also **Exposition**) Sat 5.15-5.45pm
Much Hadham, + Shared Church of St Andrew and Holy Cross: **Sunday Mass** 11.15
Sawbridgeworth, Most Holy Redeemer: **Sunday Mass** 9
Live streaming from St Joseph's at www.churchservices.tv/bishopsstortford

Fr Peter Harris, Fr Carlos Quito
St Joseph's, 3 Windhill, Bishop's Stortford CM23 2ND Tel: 01279 654063
Email: bishopsstortford@rcdow.org.uk Web: parish.rcdow.org.uk/bishopsstortford
St Andrew and Holy Cross, Church Lane, Much Hadham SG10 6DH; Most Holy Redeemer, Sayesbury Road, Sawbridgeworth CM21 0ED
Lea Valley Deanery (St Joseph's: 1900; 1906; cons 19 June 1906; Much Hadham 1939; Sawbridgeworth 1940)
Parish Administrator Debbie Jackson

• Daughters of the Cross of Liège, St Elizabeth's Centre, South End, Much Hadham SG10 6EW Tel: 01279 843451 Email: enquiries@stelizabeths.org.uk
Web: www.stelizabeths.org.uk
52 week residential Special School, FE College and Adult Residential Care Home for those with severe epilepsy, autism and other complex medical needs. St Elizabeth's also has a 5-bedded Respite Care Unit for people aged 18+ with epilepsy.
Sunday Mass 11; **Holy Day Mass** 5.30pm; **Weekday Mass** Mon, Wed, Fri 8, Tue, Thu 5.30pm
Chaplain Fr Paul Arnold Tel: 01279 842145
• Herts and Essex Community Hospital
• Rivers Hospital

BOREHAMWOOD + ST TERESA OF THE CHILD JESUS

Sunday Mass (Sat 6pm), 10; **Holy Day Mass** 7, 9.15; **Weekday Mass** Mon, Tue, Thu, Fri 9.15; **Rosary** Thu after 9.15 Mass, Fri 6.30pm; **Confession** Sat 11-11.30 and 5-5.40pm
Live streaming from St Teresa's at www.churchservices.tv/borehamwood

Fr Dominic McKenna, Fr Antonio Pineda (clergy also serve Borehamwood North)
291 Shenley Road, Borehamwood WD6 1TG Tel: 020 8953 1294
Email: borehamwood@rcdow.org.uk
Web: www.catholicparishesofborehamwood.org
Opposite Hertsmere Civic Offices
St Albans Deanery (1925; 1962; cons 27 September 1978)
Parish Administrator Sue Partington

BOREHAMWOOD NORTH + SS JOHN FISHER AND THOMAS MORE

Sunday Mass 8.30, 12noon; **Holy Day Mass** 7.30pm; **Weekday Mass** and **Confession** see times for St Teresa's

Fr Dominic McKenna, Fr Antonio Pineda (clergy resident at **291 Shenley Road,**
Borehamwood WD6 1TG Tel: 020 8953 1294),
28 Rossington Avenue, Borehamwood WD6 4LA
Email: borehamwood@rcdow.org.uk
Web: www.catholicparishesofborehamwood.org
St Albans Deanery (1955; 1958; cons 27 October 1992)

• Daughters of Divine Love, Villa Scalabrini, Green Street, Shenley WD7 9BB
• Scalabrini Fathers, Villa Scalabrini, Green Street, Shenley WD7 9BB
Tel: **020 8207 5713** Fr Alberto Vico CS

BOW + OUR LADY REFUGE OF SINNERS AND ST CATHERINE OF SIENA A

Sunday Mass (Sat 6pm), 9.30 (Sung), 11.30 (Family), 6pm; **Holy Day Mass** 10, 7pm; **Weekday Mass** Mon 10, Tue 10 (but 7 in term time), Wed 10, Fri 12noon; **Exposition** 11, with **Benediction** 11.45 *on First Fri only*; **Confession** and **Exposition** Sat 5-5.30pm, with **Rosary** 5.30pm and **Benediction** 5.45pm

Fr F Javier Ruiz-Ortiz
177 Bow Road E3 2SG Tel/Fax: 020 8980 3961
Email: bow@rcdow.org.uk Web: https://www.stcatherinebow.church/
Tower Hamlets Deanery (1869; 1870)

• Columban Sisters, 6/8 Ridgdale Street E3 2TW
Tel: 020 8980 3017 Web: www.columbansisters.org

BOW COMMON + THE HOLY NAME AND OUR LADY OF THE SACRED HEART

English: **Sunday Mass** 9.15; **Holy Day Mass** as announced; **Weekday Mass** Thu 9.15;
Vietnamese: **Sunday Mass** 12noon; **Holy Day Mass** as announced; **Weekday Mass** Mon, Tue 10, Thu, Fri 8pm, Sat 10; **Confession** before Mass or by arrangement

Fr Simon Thang Duc Nguyen
117 Bow Common Lane E3 4AU Tel: 020 7987 3477
Email: bowcommon@rcdow.org.uk Web: parish.rcdow.org.uk/bowcommon
Tower Hamlets Deanery (1892; 1894; cons 30 June 1894)

• Vietnamese Chaplaincy **Tel: 020 7987 3477 Chaplains** Fr Simon Thang Duc Nguyen (**Tel: 07920 044275**), Fr Tam Huu Nguyen, Fr Van Dien Nguyen, Rev Paul Song Trong Ly (Deacon)

BOXMOOR: *SEE HEMEL HEMPSTEAD WEST*

BRENTFORD + ST JOHN THE EVANGELIST   A

Sunday Mass (Sat 6.30pm), 9.30, 11.30; **Holy Day Mass** 9, 7.30pm; **Weekday Mass** as announced; **Confession** and **Exposition** Sat 5.30-6.15pm

Fr Gerard Quinn
44 Boston Park Road, Brentford TW8 9JF Tel: 020 8560 1671
Email: brentford@rcdow.org.uk Web: parish.rcdow.org.uk/brentford
North side of Great West Road (A4); approach via Windmill Road
Hounslow Deanery (1856; cons 1866)

• Poor Servants of the Mother of God, St Mary's Convent, 10 The Butts, Brentford
TW8 8BQ Tel: 020 8847 4800 Email: kathleen.coleman@psmgs.org.uk
Chaplain Fr Hilary Crewe
Maryville Care Home Tel: 020 8560 7124
• Missionaries of Africa (MAfr) (White Fathers), 64 Little Ealing Lane W5 4XF
Tel: 020 8799 5010 Email: lelsuperior@mafrgb.org.uk
Frs Richard Calcutt, Joseph Cummins, Thomas Cummins, Peter Kelly, Francis Nolan, Aylward
Shorter, Peter Smith, Denis Starkey (Treasurer **Tel: 020 8799 5011**), Gerry Stones,
Christopher Wallbank (Superior **Tel: 020 8799 5037**), Edward Woo; Br Patrick O'Reilly
• Hungarian Chaplaincy, 62 Little Ealing Lane W5 4EA Tel: 020 8566 0271
Fr János Csicsó
• Clayponds Hospital

BROOK GREEN + HOLY TRINITY

Sunday Mass (Sat 6pm), 8.30, 10, (Family), 11.30 (Solemn), 1pm (Syriac Rite), 6pm; **Holy Day Mass** 9.30, 12.30pm, 6pm; **Weekday Mass** 9.30, followed by **Divine Mercy Prayers**, 6pm, followed by **Rosary** Mon-Fri; **Exposition** *First Fri only* 6.30-7.30pm, Sat 5-6pm; **Confession** Sat 10-10.30, 5.15-5.45pm

Fr Richard Andrew, Fr Mark Dunglinson
41 Brook Green W6 7BL Tel: 020 7603 3832
Email: brookgreen@rcdow.org.uk Web: www.holytrinityw6.org
Off Hammersmith Road (north side) between Hammersmith Broadway & Olympia.
Hammersmith & Fulham Deanery (1851;1853; cons 2 June 1866)
Catechetical Co-ordinator Sr Jenefer Glencross OSU
Parish Administrator Mrs Anja Huynh

• Sisters of Nazareth, Nazareth House, 169-175 Hammersmith Road W6 8DB
Tel: 020 8600 6841 Web: www.sistersofnazareth.com
Chaplain Awaiting appointment

SECTION 3

• Society of the Holy Child Jesus, 42 Batoum Gardens W6 7QD Tel: 020 7602 9265
• Society of the Sacred Heart (Paris), 3 Bute Gardens W6 7DR (Provincial House)
Tel: 020 8748 9353 Email: sshprovincial@btopenworld.com
Web: www.societysacredheart.org.uk
11 Bute Gardens W6 7DR Tel: 020 8748 9887 Web: societysacredheart.org.uk
• St Joseph's House, 42 Brook Green W6 7BW Tel: 020 7603 9817

BUNHILL ROW + ST JOSEPH

Sunday Mass 11.30; **Holy Day Mass** 12.05pm, 7pm; **Weekday Mass** Wed 12.05pm; **Confession** Sun 11.15-11.30

Moorfields: **Sunday Mass** 9.30; **Holy Day Mass** (Vigil 7pm) 8.05, 12noon, 12.30 pm, 1.05pm, 5.30pm; **Weekday Mass** Mon-Fri 8.05, 1.05pm; **Exposition** as announced; **Confession** Mon-Fri 12.30-12.50pm, 1.30-1.50pm

Priest in Charge Fr Christopher Vipers (also serves Moorfields and is resident at **4/5** Eldon Street EC2M 7LS Tel: 020 7247 8390)
15 Lamb's Passage, off Bunhill Row EC1Y 8LE
Email: bunhillrow@rcdow.org.uk Web: parish.rcdow.org.uk/bunhillrow
In small street linking Bunhill Row to Errol Street; 3 mins from entrance to Barbican Centre, beside City University Business School; nearest TfL Stns Barbican, Moorgate, Old Street
Islington Deanery (1856; 1901)
Quiet Garden Mon-Fri 8-6pm (Open Easter-Sept)

• Moorfields Eye Hospital

BUNTINGFORD + ST RICHARD OF CHICHESTER

Sunday Mass 9.15 (with term time Children's Liturgy, *2nd & 4th Sun only*) ; **Holy Day Mass** 7pm; **Weekday Mass** Tue, Thu 9.30, Fri 10.30, with **Exposition** and **Benediction** 11-11.30, Sat 9.30; **Confession** Sat 10-11

Old Hall Green and Puckeridge **Sunday Mass** (Sat 6pm, Puckeridge); 11.30 (Old Hall Green); **Holy Day Mass** 10.30 (Puckeridge); **Weekday Mass** Wed 10.30 (Puckeridge); **Confession** Sat 5.15-5.45pm (Puckeridge)

Fr Cyril Chiaha (also serves Old Hall Green and Puckeridge)
3 Station Road, Buntingford SG9 9HT Tel: 01763 271471
Email: buntingford@rcdow.org.uk Web: parish.rcdow.org.uk/buntingford
Lea Valley Deanery (1912; 1914; cons 5 June 1940)

BURNT OAK + THE ANNUNCIATION A

Sunday Mass (Sat 6.30pm), 9, 10.30, 12noon; **Holy Day Mass** 9, 2pm (Annunciation Junior School), 7.30pm; **Weekday Mass** Mon 7.30, Tue-Fri 9, Sat 10, with **Morning Prayer** 20 mins before Mass and **Rosary** after; **Exposition** Wed 9.30-10.30; **Novena** Tue 7pm; **Confession** Sat 10.30-11, 5.30-6.15pm

Canon Colin Davies
4 Thirleby Road, Burnt Oak, Edgware HA8 0HQ Tel: 020 8959 1971

Email: burntoak@rcdow.org.uk Web: parish.rcdow.org.uk/burntoak
Off Gervase Road, close to Burnt Oak Stn (TfL)
Barnet Deanery (1928)

• Edgware Community Hospital
Chaplain Awaiting appointment **Tel: 020 8952 2381**

BUSHEY AND OXHEY + SACRED HEART OF JESUS AND ST JOHN THE EVANGELIST A

Sunday Mass (Sat 6pm), 8.30, 10.30 (Sung), 6pm; **Holy Day Mass** 9, 7.30pm; **Weekday Mass** Mon (**Eucharistic Service**) 9.15, Tue 7.30pm, Wed-Fri 9.15; **Confession** Sat 11-11.30, 5-5.30pm & on request

Fr James McNicholas
Sacred Heart Presbytery, London Road, Bushey WD23 1BA Tel: 020 8950 2077
Email: busheyandoxhey@rcdow.org.uk Web: parish.rcdow.org.uk/bushey/.
Ten minutes walk up Chalk Hill from Bushey BR Stn
Watford Deanery (1863; 1959; cons 20 September 1977)
Sacred Heart Parish Centre Tel: 07925 979414

• Dominican Sisters' Generalate, Rosary Priory, 93 Elstree Road, Bushey Heath WD23 4EE
Tel: 020 8950 1148 (Convent) 020 8950 6065 (Generalate) 07746 707 247 (Niland Conference Centre) Email: congsecretary@rosarypriory.co.uk / sisters@dominicansisters.co.uk Web: www.dominicansisters.co.uk / www.nilandconferencecentre.co.uk
• Heath House, Birchville Court

CAMDEN TOWN + OUR LADY OF HAL

Sunday Mass (Sat 6pm), 8.30, 10 (Family), 12noon (Solemn), 5pm (Portuguese); **Holy Day Mass** 9.30, 12noon, 7pm; **Weekday Mass** Mon-Sat 12noon; **Holy Hour and Benediction** Fri 12.30-1.30pm; **Confession** Fri 12.45-1.15pm, Sat 11-11.30, 5.15-5.45pm

Fr John Hai Pham, Fr Christopher Connor (in residence, School Chaplain), Fr Sebastian Chamakala John (in residence, Syro-Malabar Chaplaincy), Fr Colin McLean (in residence, retired)
165 Arlington Road NW1 7EX Tel: 020 7485 2727
Email: camdentown@rcdow.org.uk Web: www.ourladyofhal.org.uk
Camden Deanery (1933; cons 1984)
Parish Administrator Judith Murphy

CANARY WHARF CATHOLIC CHAPLAINCY: *SEE MILLWALL*

CARPENDERS PARK AND SOUTH OXHEY + ST JOSEPH A

Sunday Mass (Sat 6pm), 8.30, 10.30; **Weekday Mass** Tue (**Healing Mass**) 6pm, Wed-Fri 9.15; **Confession** Sat 5.30pm, Tue 6.30pm

SECTION 3

Priest in Charge Fr Stephen Hewitt
St Joseph's Church, Oxhey Drive, South Oxhey, Watford WD19 7SW
Tel: 020 8428 2774
Email: carpenderspark@rcdow.org.uk Web: parish.rcdow.org.uk/carpenderspark
Off Prestwick Road, close to Carpenders Park Stn - on South Oxhey side of railway line
Watford Deanery (1952; 1960; cons 1981)
Pastoral Associate Jacqueline Faria
Children & Family Worker Donna Osborne

• The Fairways Care Home, Pinewood Lodge Care Home

CHELSEA 1 + ST MARY CADOGAN STREET A

Sunday Mass (Sat 6.30pm), 10, 11.30, 6.30pm; **Holy Day Mass** 12noon, 7pm; **Weekday Mass** Mon 10.30 (Royal Hospital), Tue, Thu, Fri 12noon; **Exposition** Fri 11-11.45; **Confession** Sat 5.45-6.15pm

Fr Shaun Middleton, Mgr Martin Hayes, Vicar General (in residence)
Presbytery & Communication address: St Mary's Rectory, Draycott Terrace SW3 2BG
Tel: 020 7589 5487
(Church address: Cadogan Street SW3 2QR)
Email: chelsea1@rcdow.org.uk Web: parish.rcdow.org.uk/chelseastmary
Corner of Cadogan Street and Draycott Terrace
Kensington & Chelsea Deanery (1798; 1811; 1879; cons 12 June 1882)
Administrator and Lead Catechist Muriel Akahi
Royal Hospital Chelsea, Royal Hospital Road SW3 4SR

• Daughters of the Cross, St Wilfrid's Convent, 29 Tite Street SW3 4JX
Tel: 020 7351 5339 (Convent) 020 7351 2117 (Provincialate)
Email: maureen.obrien@stwilfridssw3.org.uk Web: www.daughtersofthe cross.org.uk
Chaplain Fr William Wilby Tel: 020 7351 5339 ext 381
• Dawliffe Hall, 2 Chelsea Embankment SW3 4LG Tel: 020 7351 0719
Pastoral care entrusted to the prelature of Opus Dei
• Lister Hospital
• Royal Hospital, Chelsea

CHELSEA 2 + OUR MOST HOLY REDEEMER AND ST THOMAS MORE

Sunday Mass (Sat 6.30pm), 10 (Family), 11 (Sung Latin), 12.15pm, 6.30pm; **Holy Day Mass** 8, 6.30pm; **Weekday Mass** Mon-Fri 8, Sat and Public Holidays 10; **Morning Prayer** Mon-Fri 7.45, Sat and Sun 9.30; **Evening Prayer** Sat and Sun 6pm; **Confession** Sat 10.30-11, 5.30-6pm

Canon Paschal Ryan
7 Cheyne Row SW3 5HS Tel: 020 7352 0777 Fax: 020 7352 4223
Email: chelsea2@rcdow.org.uk Web: www.holyredeemerchelsea.com

North of Albert Bridge, off Oakley Street
Kensington & Chelsea Deanery (1892; 1895; cons 21 June 1905)

• **Diocesan Seminary:** see entry for Allen Hall in Section 2
• **Chelsea Court Place Residential and Day Memory Care**

CHESHUNT + ST PAUL A

Sunday Mass (Sat 5pm) 9, 11; **Holy Day Mass** 9.30, 8pm; **Weekday Mass** Mon-Wed, Fri 9.30 ; **Mass for parents bereaved of children** 9.30 *17th of every month;* **Mass for Carers** 9.30 *First Fri;* **Exposition** Fri 9; **Confession** Sat 4.15-4.45pm

Priest in Charge Fr Clement Nyarko
17 Churchfield Path, off Church Lane, Cheshunt EN8 9EG Tel: 01992 629878
Email: cheshunt@rcdow.org.uk Web: parish.rcdow.org.uk/cheshunt
Lea Valley Deanery (1998)

CHIPPERFIELD + OUR LADY MOTHER OF THE SAVIOUR A

Sunday Mass (Sat 6.30pm), 10; **Holy Day Mass** 12 noon; **Weekday Mass** Tue, Fri 10 (subject to change); **Confession** before any Mass & on request

Salvatorians (SDS) Fr Richard Mway-Zeng, Fr Christopher Luoga (clergy also serve Abbots Langley, Bovingdon and Sarratt)
Catholic Church, Dunny Lane, Chipperfield WD4 9DB (Clergy resident at **The Presbytery, 96 The Crescent, Abbots Langley, Watford WD5 0DS Tel: 01923 266177**)
Email: chipperfield@rcdow.org.uk Web: parish.rcdow.org.uk/chipperfield
Watford Deanery (1978; 1988; cons 15 July 2018)

• **Bovingdon, HM Prison The Mount Chaplain** Kim Davey **(See HM Prison Service)**

CHISWICK + OUR LADY OF GRACE AND ST EDWARD

Our Lady of Grace and St Edward: Sunday Mass (Sat 6.30pm), 8.30, 9.45 (Family), 11 (Sung), 12.15pm, 6.30pm; **Holy Day Mass** 10, 12.30pm, 7.30pm, **Weekday Mass** 10, 12.30pm (as announced); **Exposition** Mon-Fri 3-4pm, Sat 5-6pm; **Benediction** Mon-Fri 4pm, Sat 6pm; **Confession** Sat 11-12noon, 5-6pm & on request
St Dunstan: Sunday Mass 10; **Weekday Mass** Tue, Thu 9.30 or as announced; **Confession** as announced

Fr Michael Dunne, Fr Michael Maguire
247 High Road W4 4PU Tel: 020 8994 2877 Fax: 020 8987 8332
Email: chiswick@rcdow.org.uk Web: www.ourladyofgracechiswick.org
Hounslow Deanery
Administrator Sharon Bowden

+ Our Lady of Grace and St Edward
247 High Road W4 4PU
Main road, corner of Chiswick High Road and Duke's Avenue
(1852; 1886; cons 10 October 1904)

+ St Dunstan
141 Gunnersbury Avenue W3 8LE
On North Circular Road (A406), 300 yards north of Chiswick roundabout
(1931)

• Comboni Missionary Sisters (Community), 2 Chiswick Lane W4 2JF
Tel: 020 8994 0449 Email: trinircastellano@gmail.com
Comboni Centre for Spirituality and Mission, 2 Chiswick Lane W4 2JF
Tel: 020 8994 1220 Email: combonicentre16@gmail.com
• Little Company of Mary (Provincialate), 93 Gunnersbury Avenue W5 4LR
Tel: 020 8993 6129
• Missionary Sisters of the Immaculate (PIME), Regina Pacis Convent, 10 Chiswick Lane
W4 2JE Tel: 020 8994 2053 Email: msilondon@aol.com Web: www.mdipime.org
• Westpark, 1 Leopold Road W5 3PB Tel: 020 8992 3954
Pastoral care entrusted to the Prelature of Opus Dei Fr Bernard Marsh
• Woodlands, 12 Gunnersbury Avenue W5 3NJ Tel: 020 8992 4025
Pastoral care entrusted to the Prelature of Opus Dei

CHORLEYWOOD + ST JOHN FISHER

Sunday Mass (Sat 6pm), 9; **Holy Day Mass** as announced; **Weekday Mass** Tue, Fri 9.30;
Confession on request & by appointment

Mill End: **Sunday Mass** (Sat 6pm), 10.30; **Holy Day Mass** as announced; **Weekday Mass**
Mon, Wed 9.30; **Exposition** Sat 5.30-5.55pm; **Confession** on request & by appointment

Rickmansworth: **Sunday Mass** 8.30, 11, 6pm; **Holy Day Mass** 9.30, 8pm; **Weekday Mass**
Mon, Tue, Thu, Fri 9.30, Sat 10; **Exposition** and **Confession** Sat 10.30-11.30

Fr Shaun Church, Fr Damian Ryan (clergy also serve Mill End and Rickmansworth and are
resident at 5 Park Road, Rickmansworth WD3 1HU Tel: 01923 773387)
Hill Cottage, Shire Lane, Chorleywood, Rickmansworth WD3 5NH
Email: rickmansworth@rcdow.org.uk Web: parish.rcdow.org.uk/chorleywood
Close to shopping centre & Stn
Watford Deanery (1955)

CLAPTON + ST SCHOLASTICA A

Sunday Mass (Sat 6pm), 10, 11.45, 6pm; **Holy Day Mass** 9.05, 7pm; **Weekday Mass** Mon-Fri
9.05, preceded by **Exposition** 8-9; Fri 6.05pm, preceded by **Exposition** 5-6pm; Sat 10.05,
preceded by **Exposition** 9-10; **Confession** Fri 5-6pm, Sat 9-10, 5-5.45pm

Fr Thevakingsley Arulananthem, Rev Kingsley Izundu (Deacon)
17 Kenninghall Road E5 8BS Tel: 020 8985 2178
Email: clapton@rcdow.org.uk Web: parish.rcdow.org.uk/clapton
Hackney Deanery (1862; 1962; cons 15 February 1987)

• Servite Sisters, 12 Cleveleys Road E5 9JN Tel: 020 8880 0257
• Servite Sisters Generalate, 1 Brownsea Court, 160 Clarence Road E5 8EF
Tel: 020 8533 6628 Web: www.servites.org

CLAPTON PARK + ST JUDE

Sunday Mass (Sat 6pm), 9.30 (Sung), 11.30 (Sung); **Holy Day Mass** 9.30; **Weekday Mass** Tue-Sat 9.30; **Legion of Mary** Thu 5.30pm; **Prayer Group** Thu 7-8pm, **Confession** Sat 5.30-5.45pm and on request

Priest in Charge Fr Neil Hannigan
131 Glenarm Road E5 0NB (Church is at 76 Blurton Road E5 0NH)
Tel: 020 8525 1929
Email: claptonpark@rcdow.org.uk Web: parish.rcdow.org.uk/claptonpark
Off Chatsworth Road
Hackney Deanery (1964)

• Sisters of Mercy, 4 Hilsea Street E5 0SG Tel: 020 8986 3196
• Homerton University Hospital NHS Trust Tel: 020 8510 5555
Chaplain Awaiting appointment Tel: 020 8510 5555
Sunday Mass 11

CLERKENWELL + ST PETER AND ST PAUL A

Sunday Mass (Sat 6.30pm) 9.45 (Sung), 12noon (Sung); **Holy Day Mass** 12.30pm; **Weekday Mass** Mon 12:30pm, Tue, Wed 8, Fri 12.30pm; **Confession** Sat 5.45pm & on request

Fr Ivano Millico
5 Amwell Street EC1R 1UL Tel: 020 7837 2094 Fax: 020 7837 2724
Email: clerkenwell@rcdow.org.uk Web: parish.rcdow.org.uk/clerkenwell
Islington Deanery (1842; 1847)
Secretary Helen Lebab

• Pallottine Missionary Sisters, 35 Wilmington Square WC1X 0EG Tel: 020 7837 3010
Email: bohr@talktalk.net Web: www.pallottinesisters-tanzania.org
• Royal National Throat, Nose & Ear Hospital

CLERKENWELL + ST PETER'S: *SEE ITALIAN CHURCH*

COCKFOSTERS + CHRIST THE KING

Sunday Mass (Sat 5.30pm), 9, 11; **Holy Day Mass** 11; **Weekday Mass** 11
Ecumenical Prayer Group Mon 8pm, Thu 11.30; **Confession** Sat 11.30, 5pm

Chemin Neuf (CCN) Fr Christophe Brunet, Fr Sebastian Ostrynski
29 Bramley Road N14 4HE Tel: 020 8449 6648
Email: cockfosters@rcdow.org.uk Web: parish.rcdow.org.uk/cockfosters
On main road, a few yards west of Oakwood Stn (TfL), junction with Peace Close
Enfield Deanery (1936; 1940)
Community Frs Christophe Brunet, Sebastian Ostrynski; Mme Hélène Guilbault

- Net for God Prayer Group Tue 8pm
- Cockfosters Centre for Spirituality Tel: 020 8449 6648
Web: www.cockfosterscs.org.uk
- Sisters of St Louis, Flat 8, 34 Green Road N14 4AU Tel: 020 8441 2858
- Homes for Aged: Servite House, Sir Thomas Lipton's, The Chine, Elizabeth Lodge

COMMERCIAL ROAD + ST MARY AND ST MICHAEL

Sunday Mass (Sat 6pm), 9, 11; **Holy Day Mass** 9.30, & as announced; **Weekday Mass** Mon-Wed, Fri, 9.30; **Confession** Sat 5-5.30pm

Fr William Skehan, Fr James McMahon OSB (in residence, Hospital Chaplaincy), Fr Julien Matondo Mboko (in residence, Congolese Chaplaincy, contact details below), Fr Aidan Sharratt (in residence, contact details below)
2 Lukin Street E1 0AA Tel: 020 7790 5911
Email: commercialroad@rcdow.org.uk Web: parish.rcdow.org.uk/commercialroad
200 yards east of Watney Market
Tower Hamlets Deanery (1856; cons 4 December 1929)
(Fr Aidan Sharratt **Tel: 020 7790 0383**) (Congolese Chaplaincy **Tel: 020 7790 2211 / 07452 772111** Email julienmboko@rcdow.org.uk / julienmboko@hotmail.fr)

- Sisters of Mercy, 88 Hardinge Street E1 0EB Tel: 020 7790 1459
Mass Thu, Sat 9.30
- Royal London Hospital (Whitechapel) Tel: 020 3416 5000
Chaplains Fr Rory Murphy IVD, Fr James McMahon OSB **Tel: 020 3594 2070** Sr Andrena Mulligan SM
Emails: Rory.Murphy3@nhs.net, James.McMahon2@nhs.net

COPENHAGEN STREET + THE BLESSED SACRAMENT A

Sunday Mass 8.30, 11 (Family, Sung); **Holy Day Mass** 10.30, 7.30pm; **Weekday Mass** Mon-Wed, Sat 10.30; **Confession** Sun 8-8.25, 10.30-10.55

Islington: **Sunday Mass** (Sat 6pm), 9, 10.30 (Sung, with Children's Liturgy), 12noon (Sung), 6pm; **Holy Day Mass** 10, 12.30pm, 7.30pm; **Weekday Mass** 10; **Exposition** Sat 10.30-11.30; **Confession** Sat 10.30-11, 5.15-5.45pm

Mgr Séamus O'Boyle, Fr Allan Alvarado Gil, Fr Lawrence Milby (clergy also serve Islington and are resident at **39 Duncan Terrace N1 8AL Tel: 020 7226 3277)**
157 Copenhagen Street N1 0SR
Email: copenhagenstreet@rcdow.org.uk Web: parish.rcdow.org.uk/copenhagenstreet
Off Caledonian Road, half mile north of Kings Cross Stn (BR/TfL)
Islington Deanery (1916)

- School Sisters of Notre Dame, 41 Havelock Street N1 0DA Tel: 020 7837 8378
Email: ssnd27@yahoo.co.uk Web: www.ssnd.org and www.gerhardinger.org

COVENT GARDEN (MAIDEN LANE) + CORPUS CHRISTI A

The Church is the Diocesan Shrine of the Most Blessed Sacrament (2018)
Sunday Mass (Sat 6pm), 9.30, 11.30; Holy Day Mass 8 (Extraordinary Form), 12.05pm, 1.05pm; Weekday Mass Mon-Fri 1.05pm, also Mon 6.30pm (Extraordinary Form), Bank Holidays 10; Sodality of the Blessed Sacrament First Thu 6.30pm; Eucharistic Prayer Group Wed 7pm; Exposition Mon, Wed-Fri 12-1pm; Confession 30 mins before each Mass & on request

Fr Alan Robinson

Corpus Christi Presbytery, Maiden Lane WC2E 7NB Tel: 020 7836 4700
Email: coventgarden@rcdow.org.uk   Web: www.corpuschristimaidenlane.org.uk
Off Southampton Street, north of Strand; near Covent Garden
Westminster Deanery (1873; cons 18 October 1956)

CRANFORD + OUR LADY AND ST CHRISTOPHER

Sunday Mass (Sat 6pm), 8.30, 10.30, 1pm (Portuguese); Holy Day Mass as announced; Weekday Mass Mon, Tue, Thu-Sat 9.30, Wed 9; Exposition Sat 10-11; Confession Sat 10-10.45, 5.15-5.45pm & on request
Ethnic Chaplaincy Masses: Portuguese Sun 1pm, Konkani (Goan) *4th Sun* 5pm

Fr Bernard Akoeso

32 High Street, Cranford, Hounslow TW5 9RG Tel: 020 8759 9136
Email: cranford@rcdow.org.uk Web: parish.rcdow.org.uk/cranford
Next to Holy Angels Church, opposite The Avenue
Hounslow Deanery (1967; 1970, cons 1979)

CRICKLEWOOD + ST AGNES

Sunday Mass (Sat 6.30pm), 9, 10.30, 12noon, 6.30pm; Holy Day Mass as announced; Weekday Mass Mon-Fri 9.15, Sat 10; Confession Sat 10.30-11, 5.30-6pm & on request

Fr John Buckley

35 Cricklewood Lane NW2 1HR Tel: 020 8452 2475
Email: cricklewood@rcdow.org.uk Web: parish.rcdow.org.uk/cricklewood
On A407, midway between A41 and Cricklewood Broadway (A5)
Barnet Deanery (1883; 1930)
Pastoral Assistant Elizabeth Sayer

• Dominican Sisters (St Rose's Convent, St Rose's Chapel, Prayer Garden and Poustinia), 160 Anson Road NW2 6BH Tel: 020 8830 7465 Email: raymundaop72@gmail.com
• Sisters of Mercy, 149 Walm Lane NW2 3AU Tel: 020 8450 7472
• Sisters of St Joseph of Peace, 157 Walm Lane NW2 3AY Tel: 020 8450 8859
Web: www.csjp.org

SECTION 3

CROXLEY GREEN + ST BEDE A

Sunday Mass (Sat 6pm), 10, 6pm; **Holy Day Mass** 10, 7.30pm; **Weekday Mass** 10; **Confession** Sat 10.30

Fr John Wiley
185 Baldwins Lane, Croxley Green, Rickmansworth WD3 3LL Tel: 01923 231969
Email: croxleygreen@rcdow.org.uk Web: parish.rcdow.org.uk/croxleygreen
Watford Deanery (1958; cons 1975)

CUFFLEY + ST MARTIN DE PORRES A

Sunday Mass (Sat 5.30pm) 9, 11; **Holy Day Mass** 9.30, 8pm; **Weekday Mass** as announced; **Confession** Sat 10.30

Priest in Charge Fr Patrick Carroll
4 Church Close, Cuffley EN6 4LS Tel: 01707 873308
Email: cuffley@rcdow.org.uk Web: parish.rcdow.org.uk/cuffley
Enfield Deanery

DOLLIS HILL + ST MARY AND ST ANDREW

Sunday Mass (Sat 7pm), 8.30, 10.30 (Family), 12noon (Sung); (*in August* (7pm), 9, 11); **Holy Day Mass** as announced; **Weekday Mass** Mon-Thu 9.30; **Confession** Sat 12.30pm & on request

Fr Michael O'Doherty
216 Dollis Hill Lane NW2 6HE Tel: 020 8452 6158
Email: dollishill@rcdow.org.uk   Web: parish.rcdow.org.uk/dollishill
Brent Deanery (1915; 1933)

EALING + ABBEY CHURCH OF ST BENEDICT

Sunday Mass (Sat 6pm, 8.30pm with Neocatechumenate Community in Chapel), 8, 9, 10.15 (Family, in Parish Centre), 10.30 (Sung), 12noon, 7pm; **Holy Day Mass** 7, 9.15, 6pm, 8pm; **Weekday Mass** 7, 9.15, 6pm; **Exposition** Thu 8.15-9pm, Fri 9.45-12.30pm; **Rosary** Mon-Sat 9.40; **Confession** Sat 10-11, 4-5pm, 7-7.30pm, Thu 8-8.30pm.
Divine Office: Matins 6, but Sat 6.30, (Sun Vigil on Sat 7.30pm); **Lauds** 7.35; **Conventual Mass** 7 (Sat 9.15, Sun 10.30); **Vespers** 6.35pm (Sat 5.30pm; Sun 6pm, with **Exposition**); **Compline** 8pm (except Sat and Sun)

Benedictines of the English Congregation (OSB) Dom Ambrose McCambridge, Dom Timothy Gorham (Sub Prior);
Rev Alex Burke (Deacon), Rev Ian Edwards (Deacon), Rev Gordon Nunn (Deacon)
Ealing Abbey, Charlbury Grove W5 2DY
Parish Tel: 020 8862 2160 Parish Fax: 020 8862 2166
Email: ealingabbey@rcdow.org.uk Web: www.ealingabbeyparish.org.uk
1/4 mile north of station and shops; local bus via Eaton Rise to Marchwood Crescent
Ealing Deanery (1897; 1899)
Monastery Tel: 020 8862 2100 Fax: 020 8862 2206
Email: ealingmonk@ealingabbey.org.uk

Other priests OSB in the community: Abbot Dominic Taylor, Dom Alexander Bevan (Prior), Abbot Francis Rossiter, Abbot Martin Shipperlee, Doms Peter Burns, Gregory Chillman, Andrew Hughes, James Leachman, Alban Nunn, Thomas Stapleford

• The Benedictine Institute, 74 Castlebar Road W5 2DD
Tel: 020 8862 2156 Fax: 020 8862 2133 Email: info@benedictine-institute.org
• Capitanio Sisters, Nile Lodge, Queen's Walk W5 1TJ
Tel: 020 8997 3933 Email: stbc.sisters@gmail.com
• Little Company of Mary, Flat 10, Berkeley Court, 33 Gordon Road W5 2AE
Tel: 020 8810 4432 Email: jbugeja@aol.com
• Medical Missionaries of Mary, 2 Denbigh Road W13 8PX Tel: 020 8998 1725
Email: mmmealing37@yahoo.co.uk Web: www.mmmworldwide.org
• Missionary Sisters of Our Lady of Africa, Flat 13 Montpelier Court, Montpelier Road W5
2QN Tel: 020 8998 6731 (Office), 020 8997 3166, 020 8810 7619
Regional Superior Email: ukmsolareg@btinternet.com Web: www.msolafrica.org
• Sisters of Charity of St Jeanne Antide, 6/8 Woodfield Road W5 1SJ
Tel: 020 8998 9549 Email: srstrion16@btinternet.com
• Sisters of the Holy Cross, 82 The Avenue W13 8LB Tel: 020 8997 2858
Email: holycross@hcengland.co.uk Web: www.holycrossengland.org.uk
• Sisters of the Resurrection, 18 Carlton Road W5 2AW
Tel: 020 8810 6241 Email: csr.englishregion@yahoo.co.uk
also 84 Gordon Road W5 2AR Tel: 020 8998 8954
• Columban Fathers (SSC), 12 Blakesley Avenue W5 2DW
Tel: 020 8997 0587 Fax: 020 3581 9676 Email: columbanlondon12@gmail.com
Web: www.columbans.co.uk
Frs Gerard Markey, Aodh O'Halpin , Daniel O'Malley (Superior), Thomas Ryan
• Congregation of Marian Fathers, Divine Mercy Apostolate, 1 Courtfield Gardens W13 0EY
Tel: 020 8998 0925 Email: info@divinemercy.org.uk
Web: www.divinemercyapostolate.co.uk
Sunday Mass (Polish) 10; Daily Mass and Divine Mercy Chaplet (English) Mon-Fri 2.30pm
except first Fri
Community Fr Andrzej Gowkielewicz, Fr Dariusz Mazewski
• Missionaries of Africa (White Fathers) (MAfr), 15 Corfton Road W5 2HP
Tel: 020 8601 7900 Email: corftonsuperior@mafrgb.org.uk
Frs John Gerrard (Superior), Michael Heap, Agustin Sawadogo, Edward Wildsmith; Br
Nicholas Murphy

EASTCOTE + ST THOMAS MORE

Sunday Mass (Sat 6.30pm), 9.30 (Family), 11.30; Holy Day Mass 9.30, 7.30pm; Weekday
Mass 9.30 (or Liturgy of the Word with Holy Communion as advised); Confession
with Exposition Sat 10-10.30

Fr Martin Plunkett
32 Field End Road, Eastcote, Pinner HA5 2QT Tel: 020 8866 6581 Fax: 020 8429 2346
Email: eastcote@rcdow.org.uk Web: parish.rcdow.org.uk/eastcote

SECTION 3

On main road, north of station and shops, just beyond Bridle Road junction
Hillingdon Deanery (1935; 1977; cons 6 February 1978)

• St Vincent's Nursing Home, Wiltshire Lane, Eastcote HA5 2NB
Tel: 020 8872 4900 Web: www. svnh.co.uk
Chaplain Fr Bernard Boylan **Tel: 020 8429 4778**

EDGWARE + ST ANTHONY OF PADUA

Sunday Mass (Sat 6.30pm), 10, 12noon, 6pm; **Holy Day Mass** 9, 7.30pm; **Weekday Mass** Mon-Fri 9, Tue 7.30pm (followed by **Devotions to St Anthony** and **Benediction**), Sat 10; **Exposition** Mon-Sat 8(am)-10pm, Sun 8-9.30, 7-10pm; **Confession** Sat 9.30-9.50, 5.30-6pm

Fr Robert Pachuta
5 Garratt Road, Edgware HA8 9AN Tel: 020 8952 0663 Office: 020 8951 5769
Email: edgware@rcdow.org.uk Web: parish.rcdow.org.uk/edgware
Off the A5 mid-way between the junctions with Station Road and Deansbrook Road
Barnet Deanery (1913;1931;1958)

• Daughters of Mary, Mother of Mercy, 16 St Margaret's Road, Edgware HA8 9UP
Tel: 020 8958 8316
• Dominican Sisters of St Catherine of Siena, St Albert's, 267 Hale Lane, Edgware HA8 8NW Tel: 020 8958 5622

EDMONTON + THE MOST PRECIOUS BLOOD AND ST EDMUND, KM

Sunday Mass (Sat 7pm), 8, 9.15, 10.30, 12noon, 2pm *in Igbo, 2nd Sun only*, 6.30pm; **Holy Day Mass** 9.15, 12noon, 7pm; **Weekday Mass** 9.15 preceded by **Morning Prayer** 8.55, 12noon; **Exposition** Mon-Thu 10-12noon (*except 2nd Tue*), Fri, Sat 11-12noon; **Confession** Sat 11-11.45, 6-6.45pm

Missionary Society of St Paul (MSP) Fr Emmanuel Ogunnaike, Fr Anthony Umoren
115 Hertford Road N9 7EN Tel: 020 8803 6631 Fax: 020 8345 6495
Email: edmonton@rcdow.org.uk Web: www.stedmundsedmonton.co.uk
Corner of Croyland Road, 1/4 mile north of Edmonton Green
Enfield Deanery (1903; cons 17 May 1907)
Catechetical Co-ordinator Mike Boggis
Parish Secretary Susan Phagoo

• Handmaids of the Holy Child Jesus, Trinity House, 48 Cavendish Road N18 2LS
Tel: 020 8803 3839 Email: trinityconventhouse@yahoo.com
and Ancilla Convent, 4 Woodstock Crescent N9 7LY 020 8804 4070
• North Middlesex Hospital

ELY PLACE + ST ETHELDREDA

Sunday Mass 9, 11 (Sung Latin); **Holy Day Mass** 1pm; **Weekday Mass** Mon-Fri 1pm; **Confession** Weekdays 1.20pm and on request

Institute of Charity (IC) **Fr Tom Deidun,** Fr Tom Thomas (in residence)
14 Ely Place EC1N 6RY Tel: 020 7405 1061 Fax: 020 7405 7440
Email: elyplace@rcdow.org.uk Web: www.stetheldreda.com
Westminster Deanery (1252-1290; 1297; crypt re-opened 1876; upper church re-opened 1879)

ENFIELD + OUR LADY OF MOUNT CARMEL AND ST GEORGE   S

Our Lady of Mount Carmel and St George: Sunday Mass (Sat 6pm, 7.30pm with Neo-
Catechumenate), 8, 9 (with Children's Liturgy), 10.30, 12noon, 6pm; **Holy Day Mass** 12noon,
7pm; **Weekday Mass** Mon-Fri 12noon, Sat 9.30; **Exposition** Sat 10-11, 5-5.45pm and *First Fri
only* 9.30-6.30pm; **Rosary** Mon-Fri 11.30; **Confession** Sat 10-11, 5.15-5.45pm
Chapel of Ease: Sunday Mass 10
Holy Family Convent: Sunday Mass (Sat 6pm, Polish), 9 (Polish), 10.30 (Maronite);
Weekday Mass Mon, Tue 7.30; **Exposition** Tue 7-8pm, Wed 8-9pm, Thu 4.45pm-5.45pm

Fr Sławomir Witoń, Fr Chinedu Udo
45 London Road, Enfield EN2 6DS Tel: 020 8363 2569 Fax: 020 8342 0159
Email: enfield@rcdow.org.uk Web: www.catholicenfield.org
Main road, near Enfield Town Stn (Overground)
Enfield Deanery (1862; 1958; cons 16 July 1967)
Chapel of Ease: Our Lady of Walsingham and the English Martyrs, Holtwhites Hill, Enfield
EN2 8HG
Catechetical Co-ordinator Sybil Lee **Email:** sybillee@rcdow.org.uk
Parish Secretary Susi Thompson (Mon-Thu)

• Holy Family Convent Chapel, 52 London Road, Enfield EN2 6EN
Fr Maciej Michałek (Polish Chaplain) **c/o Holy Family Convent** Email: jeszuam@interia.pl
Email: enfield@pcmew.org Web: www.parafiaenfield.org
• Sisters of the Holy Family of Nazareth, 52 London Road, Enfield EN2 6EN
Tel: 020 8363 4483 Web: www.nazarethfamily.org
• Chase Farm Hospital, Enfield Community Care Centre at St Michael's Hospital, BMI
Cavell Hospital, BMI King's Oak Hospital

EUSTON, NW1: *SEE SOMERS TOWN*

FARM STREET + THE IMMACULATE CONCEPTION A

Sunday Mass (Sat 6pm), 8, 9.30 (Family), 11 (Sung Latin), 12.30pm, 5.30pm, Young Adults
Mass 7pm; **Holy Day Mass** (Vigil 6pm), 8, 1.05pm, 6pm; **Weekday Mass** Mon-Fri 8,
1.05pm, 6pm, Sat 8 only, Bank Holiday 1.05pm only; **Exposition** Mon-Fri 12.30-1pm;
Confession Mon-Sat 10 mins before Mass, Sun 10 mins before each Mass

Society of Jesus (SJ) **Fr Dominic Robinson,** Fr Chris Pedley
114 Mount Street W1K 3AH Tel: 020 7493 7811 Fax: 020 7495 6685
Email: farmstreet@rcdow.org.uk Web: www.farmstreet.org.uk
Opposite Carlos Place (south side, Grosvenor Square); and at Farm Street (off Berkeley Square)
Marylebone Deanery (1849, cons 1993)
Parish Administrator George McCombe

Jesuits (SJ) Provincial Curia, 114 Mount Street W1K 3AH
Tel: 020 7499 0285 Fax: 020 7408 7111
Other members of Community: Frs Brendan Carmody, Damian Howard (Provincial),
Patrick Hume, Michael Beattie, Paul Nicholson (Superior), Adrian Porter

• **LGBT Catholics Westminster** meet on the 2nd and 4th Sunday evenings at Farm Street
Church; email: lgbtcatholicswestminster@gmail.com, or Mgr Keith Barltrop (**Chaplain;** *see
Bayswater* entry).

FELTHAM + ST LAWRENCE

Sunday Mass (Sat 6pm), 9, 11, 1pm Polish, 6pm; **Holy Day Mass** 9.30, 12.15pm, 7.30pm;
Weekday Mass Mon-Fri 9.30, Sat 12noon; **Confession** Sat 11-11.45, 5-5.45pm
Ethnic & Eastern Catholic Chaplaincy Masses: Polish Sun 1pm; **Ukrainian Liturgy** 7pm
4th Sat only, 3pm *2nd Sun only;* Malayalam 3pm *3rd Sun only;* Filipino 3pm *4th Sat only;*
African Liturgy 2.30pm *4th Sun only*

Fr John Byrne, Fr John Tabor, Rev Colin Macken (Deacon)
St Lawrence's Presbytery, The Green, Feltham TW13 4AF Tel: 020 8890 2367 / 07879
058732
Email: feltham@rcdow.org.uk   Web: www.saintlawrences.org.uk
Set back on east side of High Street, not far from Feltham Stn
Hounslow Deanery (1910; 1934)
Pastoral Assistant Dr Jordan Pullicino

• Sisters of Mercy, 35 Ruscombe Way, Feltham TW14 9NY Tel: 020 8751 0862
• **HMYOI and Remand Centre Chaplains** Barry Phillips-Devaney, Bridget Brinkley **(See
HM Prison Service)**

FINCHLEY CHURCH END + ST PHILIP THE APOSTLE

Sunday Mass (Sat 6.30pm), 9.30 (Sung), 11.30 (Family), 6.30pm (Polish); **Holy Day Mass**
10, 7.30pm; **Weekday Mass** Mon, Tue, Thu-Sat 10; **Exposition** Sat 10.30-11; **Confession**
Sat 10.30-11, 5.45-6.15pm

Fr John P. Dermody, Fr Marek Gałuszka (in residence)
Priests House, Gravel Hill N3 3RJ Tel: 020 8346 2459
Email: finchleychurchend@rcdow.org.uk   Web: www.stphilipsfinchley.org.uk
Regent's Park Road near Finchley Central Stn, junction with Gravel Hill
Barnet Deanery (1918; 1933; cons 3 May 1975)

• Consolata Fathers (IMC), 3 Salisbury Avenue N3 3AJ
Tel: 020 8346 5498 Email: consolatafathers.uk@consolata.net
Frs Luis Tomas (Superior), Carlo Bonelli
• Finchley Memorial Hospital, Dell Field Court Nursing Home

FINCHLEY EAST + ST MARY

Sunday Mass (Sat 6pm), 8.30, 10 (Family), 12noon; **Holy Day Mass** 10, 7.30pm; **Weekday Mass** 10, with **Morning Prayer** 9.45; **Exposition** Thu 10.30-11, Sat 5.30-6pm; **Confession** Sat 10.30-11, 5.30-6pm

Fr Peter-Michael Scott

279 High Road N2 8HG Tel: 020 8883 4234
Email: finchleyeast@rcdow.org.uk Web: www.stmaryseastfinchley.org
10 minutes walk from East Finchley Stn (TfL), heading north
Barnet Deanery (1898; 1953)
Administrator Astrid Viegas Email: finchleyeastsec@rcdow.org.uk
Director of Christian Education and Youth Holly Graham
Email: finchleyeastcatechist@rcdow.org.uk

• Sisters of Nazareth, Nazareth House, 162 East End Road N2 0RU
Tel: 020 8883 1104 Fax: 020 8444 3691 Email: superior.finchleyuk@nazarethcare.com
Larmenier Centre, Nazareth Care (Regional Office)
Chaplain Fr John Boland

FINCHLEY NORTH + ST ALBAN

Sunday Mass (Sat 6pm), 8.45, 10.15 (Family Mass with Children's Liturgy), 12noon (with Music); **Holy Day Mass** as announced; **Weekday Mass** 9.30 with **Morning Prayer** preceding, followed by **Rosary** until 10.30; **Exposition** *First Fri only* 10.30-11.30, each Sat after morning Mass; **Confession** Sat 10-10.30, 5.15-5.45pm

Fr Dermot O'Neill

51 Nether Street N12 7NN Tel: 020 8446 0224 Fax: 020 8343 7400
Email: finchleynorth@rcdow.org.uk Web: parish.rcdow.org.uk/finchleynorth
200 yds from Tally Ho Corner
Barnet Deanery (1903; 1909; cons 24 February 1995)
Key Catechist Ursula Morrissey

• Belarusian Catholic Mission: see under *Eastern Catholic Churches* at the end of this Section
• Care and Nursing Homes:
Abbeyfield, Acacia Lodge, Ashfield House, Barnet Temporary Unhoused, Clovelly House, Catherine Lodge, Elmhurst, Fernbank, Dr French Memorial, Grace House, The Grange, Hilton Lodge, Kenwood House, The Limes, Meadowside Home, Safestart Foundation, Torrington, Wimbush House, Woodlands
• North London Hospice

FRENCH CHURCH + NOTRE DAME DE FRANCE A

Sunday Mass - *all French* - (Sat 6pm), 11, 6pm *Summer Sunday Mass* (Sat 6pm), 11; **Holy Day Mass** 12.15pm *English*, 6pm *English*, 7.30pm *French*; **Weekday Mass** 12.15pm except Tue, 6pm; **Confession** before & after Mass & by arrangement

SECTION 3

Marists (SM) Fr Pascal Boidin
5 Leicester Place WC2H 7BX Tel: 020 7437 9363 Fax: 020 7440 2645
Email: frenchchurch@rcdow.org.uk   Web: www.ndfchurch.org
Off north side of Leicester Square
Westminster Deanery (1865; 1868; 1955)
Community: Frs Pascal Boidin, Hubert Bonnet-Eymard, (Superior), Damien Diouf, Kevin Duffy; Br Ivan Vodopivec
Parish Administrator Philippine de Beauregard **Tel: 020 7440 2642**

• Missionary Sisters of the Society of Mary SMSM, 34 Lisle Street WC2H 7BD
Tel: 020 3659 7836
• Chaplaincy to the French Schools, 23 Cromwell Mews SW7 2JY
Florence Blagburn **Tel: 020 7584 3006**

FULHAM 1 + ST THOMAS OF CANTERBURY

Sunday Mass (Sat 5.30pm), 9, 10.30 (Family), 12noonSung) 3pm (Portuguese), 6pm; **Holy Day Mass** 9.30, 8pm; **Weekday Mass** Mon-Fri 9.30, Sat 10; **Exposition** Sat 10.30-11.30; **Confession** Sat 10.30-11.30, 6.15-6.45pm

Fr Dennis F P Touw Tempelmans-Plat, Fr Linferd Fernandes, Rev Wayne O'Reilly (Deacon)
60 Rylston Road SW6 7HW Tel: 020 7385 4040
Email: fulham@rcdow.org.uk Web: www.stocf.wordpress.com
Hammersmith & Fulham Deanery (1847; cons 5 December 1969; recons 2006)

FULHAM 2 STEPHENDALE ROAD + OUR LADY OF PERPETUAL HELP A

Sunday Mass (Sat 6.30pm), 9, 11; **Holy Day Mass** as announced; **Weekday Mass**, **Exposition** and **Confession** as announced in newsletter & on the website

Fr Bill Bowder
Parish House, 2 Tynemouth Street SW6 2QT Tel: 020 7736 4864 / 07598 878599
Email: stephendaleroad@rcdow.org.uk Web: parish.rcdow.org.uk/stephendaleroad
Sand's End: east of Wandsworth Bridge Road, south of New King's Road, southwest of Imperial Wharf
Hammersmith & Fulham Deanery (1922)
Parish Administrator Susan Keogh **Catechetical Co-ordinator** Jackie Charles

FULHAM: *SEE ALSO PARSONS GREEN*

FULHAM ROAD + OUR LADY OF DOLOURS A

Sunday Mass (Sat 6.30pm), 8.30, 10 (Family), 11.15 (Spanish), 12.15pm, 7pm; **Holy Day Mass** (Vigil 6.30pm), 10, 6.30pm; **Weekday Mass** 10, 6.30pm; **Exposition** Mon-Fri 10.30-11.15; **Rosary** Wed 10.30-10.45; **Legion of Mary** Tue 7.15pm; **Confession** daily 6.15-6.30pm & on request, Sat 10.45-11.15, 6-6.30pm

Servites (OSM) Fr Patrick Ryall
St Mary's Priory, 264 Fulham Road SW10 9EL Tel: 020 7352 6965 Fax: 020 7351 9749
Email: fulhamroad@rcdow.org.uk   Web: www.servitechurch.org

In Fulham Road, east of Redcliffe Gardens/Edith Grove traffic lights
Kensington & Chelsea Deanery (1864; 1875; cons 4 November 1953)
Community: Frs Patrick Ryall (Prior and Parish Priest), Paul Addison, Chris O'Brien
(Formation Master), Patrick O'Connell, Allan Satur
Parish Sister Sr Clementina Wasike

• Sisters of the Cross and Passion (CP), 7 Stadium Street SW10 0PU
Tel: 020 7352 6013 Email: ritamcahill@yahoo.co.uk
• Sisters Hospitallers of the Sacred Heart (Spanish), St Teresa's Residential Care Home
40-46 Roland Gardens SW7 3PW Tel: 020 7373 5820, Provincialate Tel: 020 7373 3054
Email: provincial@hsc-uk.org Web: www.sisterhospitallers.org
• Chelsea & Westminster Hospital

GARSTON + OUR LADY AND ST MICHAEL

Sunday Mass (Sat 6pm), 8.30, 10, 12noon; **Holy Day Mass** 9.30, 7pm; **Weekday Mass**
Mon-Wed, Fri 9.30; **Confession** Sat 5-5.30pm & on request

Fr Fortunato Pantisano, Rev Paul Quinn (Deacon)
Catholic Church, Crown Rise, Garston, Watford WD25 0NE Tel: 01923 673239
Email: garston@rcdow.org.uk Web: parish.rcdow.org.uk/garston
On A405 North Orbital Road, just south of St Albans Road junction
Watford Deanery (1954)
Parish Administrator Veronika Clark   Tel: 01923 673239 (Mon, Wed, Fri 9.30-1pm)

• Langley House, Tenterden House, Allington Court

GERMAN CHURCH + ST BONIFACE

Sunday Mass (Sat 5pm, 1st & 3rd Sun), 11 (2nd, 4th & 5th Sun); **Confession** (German)
by appointment

Fr Andreas Blum
47 Adler Street E1 1EE Tel: 020 7247 9529
Email: germanchurch@rcdow.org.uk Web: parish.rcdow.org.uk/germanchurch
Tower Hamlets Deanery (1809; 1875; cons 4 October 1925; recons 2 October 1960)

• Wynfrid House, 20 Mulberry Street E1 1EH
Tel: 020 7247 6110 Email: info@wynfridhouse.com
German Community Centre and Youth Hostel
Manager Anthony Perera
• St Boniface Secular Institute (English Region) & Lioba House German Hostel for Young
People 42-44 Exeter Road NW2 4SB Tel: 020 8438 9628
Email: hostel@institut-st-bonifatius.de Web: www.hostel-lioba-house.de
(see also *Willesden Green* entry)

SECTION 3

GOLDERS GREEN + ST EDWARD THE CONFESSOR

Sunday Mass under review, see parish website www.stedwardgg.uk; Holy Day Mass (Vigil 7pm), 10, 7pm; Weekday Mass as announced; Confession Sat 10.30-11, 5.30-6pm & on request before & after Mass as available

Fr Antony Convery, Rev Anthony Clark (Deacon, non-resident,
Email: anthonyclark@rcdow.org.uk)
700 Finchley Road NW11 7NE Tel: 020 8455 1300
Email: goldersgreen@rcdow.org.uk Web: www.stedwardgg.uk
On main road just north of Golders Green Stn (TfL)
Barnet Deanery (1909; 1915; cons 30 September 1931)

GRAHAME PARK + ST MARGARET CLITHEROW A

Sunday Mass (Sat 6.30pm), 9, 12noon; Holy Day Mass 9.15, 7pm; Weekday Mass Mon, Fri 7pm, Tue, Wed, Thu 9.15, Sat 12noon; Exposition Sat 5-6pm; Novena Mon after Mass; Confession Sat 10-12noon, 5-6pm

Fr Brian Griffiths

The Presbytery, Everglade Strand NW9 5PX Tel: 020 8205 6830
Email: grahamepark@rcdow.org.uk Web: parish.rcdow.org.uk/grahamepark
Off Great Strand (near RAF Museum)
Barnet Deanery (1970; 1973; cons 14 November 1998)

• Metropolitan Police Training School

GREENFORD + OUR LADY OF THE VISITATION

Sunday Mass (Sat 7pm), 8, 9, 10.30, 12noon, 7pm; Holy Day Mass 8.30, 12noon, 7.30pm; Weekday Mass Mon-Sat 12noon; Confession Sat 11-12noon, 6.15-6.45pm

Pallottine Fathers (SAC) Fr Eugene Lynch, Fr Thomas Daly, Fr Joseph McLoughlin, Fr Liam O'Donovan,
358 Greenford Road, Greenford UB6 9AN Tel: 020 8578 1363 Fax: 020 8813 2230
Email: greenford@rcdow.org.uk Web: parish.rcdow.org.uk/greenford
Main Road (A4127) south of Ruislip Road junction
Ealing Deanery (1928; 1937)
Catechetical Co-ordinator Henry Chichon

GROVE PARK + ST JOSEPH

Sunday Mass (Sat 6.30pm), 9, 11; Holy Day Mass (Vigil 7.30pm), 10, 7.30pm; Weekday Mass as announced; Confession Sat 11-11.30
Fr John Seabrook
1 Bolton Road W4 3TE Tel: 020 8994 6861
Email: grovepark@rcdow.org.uk Web: parish.rcdow.org.uk/grovepark
South A4, close to Chiswick Stn (BR), corner of Devonshire Gardens
Hounslow Deanery (1964; cons 23 February 1973)

HACKNEY + ST JOHN THE BAPTIST

Sunday Mass (Sat 6pm), 9.30, 11.30; **Holy Day Mass** 9.30, 5.30pm (Latin), 7pm;
Weekday Mass Mon 12noon (Hospice), Tue-Fri 12noon, Sat 10; **Confession** Sat 10.30

Fr David Evans

3 King Edward's Road E9 7SF Tel: 020 8985 2496
Email: hackney@rcdow.org.uk Web: parish.rcdow.org.uk/hackney
King Edward's Road, off Mare Street, north of St Joseph's Hospice
Hackney Deanery (1847; 1956; cons 14 June 1972)

• Religious Sisters of Charity, St Joseph's Convent, 36 Mare Street E8 4AD
Tel: 020 8525 4242 Email: rschackney@yahoo.co.uk Web: www.religioussistersofcharity.org
• Sisters of Charity of St Paul, 28 Warneford Street E9 7NG
Tel: 020 8986 2346 Email: b.devine@btinternet.com
• St Joseph's Hospice
Chaplain Fr Gerard O'Brien **Tel: 020 8525 3032**

HAMMERSMITH + ST AUGUSTINE

Sunday Mass (Sat 6pm), 9, 10.30, 12.15pm, 6.30pm; **Holy Day Mass** 8, 12.15pm, 7pm;
Weekday Mass 8 (not Sat), 12.15pm; **Exposition** Sat 10.30-12noon; **Confession** Sat
10.30-11.30; 5-5.45pm

Augustinians (OSA) Fr Barry Clifford

55 Fulham Palace Road W6 8AU Tel: 020 8748 3788
Email: hammersmith@rcdow.org.uk Web: www.saintaugustineshammersmith.org
South Hammersmith Broadway, just beyond flyover
Hammersmith & Fulham Deanery (1903; 1916; cons 1933)
Community Bishop Michael G Campbell (in residence); Frs Mark Minihane (Prior), Barry
Clifford (Parish Priest), Thomas Banayag, Gladson Dabre; Br David Tan
Discernment Community for men Fr Gladson Dabre
Email: Vocations@theaugustinians.org Web: www.theaugustians.org
Parish Administrator Claudette Foley

• St Augustine's Centre
Venue Manager Helen Murphy **Hall hire enquiries** Tel: 020 8748 3254
Email: helen@austin-forum.org
Order of St Augustine Communication Officer Marie Marin La Meslée
Email: marie@austin-forum.org
• Charing Cross Hospital, Chapel of the Holy Cross
Sunday Mass 10; **Weekday Mass** Mon 1pm
Chaplains Fr Giles Pinnock, Fr Blaise Amadi CM **Tel 020 3311 1056**

HAMPSTEAD + ST MARY

Sunday Mass (Sat 6.30pm), 8.30, 10, 11.30, 6.30pm; **Holy Day Mass** 10, 7.30pm;
Weekday Mass as announced; **Confession** Sat 6-6.30pm & on request

Mgr Phelim Rowland
4 Holly Place NW3 6QU Tel: 020 7435 6678 Fax: 020 7435 8436
Email: hampstead@rcdow.org.uk Web: parish.rcdow.org.uk/hampstead
Near Hampstead Stn (TfL); via Church Row, lower end of Heath Street
Camden Deanery (1796; 1816; cons 1977)
Parish Administrator / Pastoral Assistant Mary Stanier Email: marystanier@rcdow.org.uk

• Sisters of St Dorothy 99 Frognal NW3 6XR
International Students' Residence Tel: 020 7794 6893
Email: stdorothylondon@gmail.com Web: www.st.dorothys.talktalk.net
• Sisters of St Marcellina, Hampstead Towers, 6 Ellerdale Road NW3 6BD
Tel: 020 7435 0181 Email: sisters@stmarcellina.org.uk Web: stmarcellina.org.uk

HAMPTON HILL (AND UPPER TEDDINGTON) + ST FRANCIS DE SALES

Sunday Mass (Sat 6pm), 9, 11; **Holy Day Mass** (Vigil 7.30pm), 9.30; **Weekday Mass** as announced; **Confession** Sat 10-11 & before weekday Masses

Society of Christ (SChr) Fr Wojciech Stachyra
16 Wellington Road, Hampton Hill TW12 1JR Tel: 020 8977 1415
Email: hamptonhill@rcdow.org.uk Web: http://stfrancisdesales.co.uk/.
Upper Thames Deanery (1920; 1928; 1966; cons 18 December 1976)
Parish Secretary Mrs Annie D'Souza (Wed all day, Fri pm only)

• Laurel Dene Care Home, Hampton

HAMPTON-ON-THAMES + ST THEODORE OF CANTERBURY

Sunday Mass (Sat 6.30pm), 8.30, 10.30; **Holy Day Mass** 9.30, 7.30pm; **Weekday Mass** as announced; **Confession** Sat 5.45-6.15pm & on request

Fr Dominic Byrne
110 Station Road, Hampton-on-Thames TW12 2AS Tel: 020 8979 3596
Email: hamptononthames@rcdow.org.uk Web: parish.rcdow.org.uk/hamptononthames
Upper Thames Deanery (1927; 1986; cons 22 March 1987)
Parish Secretary Paul Danon (Thu, Fri) Email: pauldanon@rcdow.org.uk

• Poor Servants of the Mother of God (PSMG), 112 Station Road, Hampton-on-Thames
TW12 2AS Tel: 020 8255 1106

HANWELL + OUR LADY AND ST JOSEPH A

Sunday Mass (Sat 6pm), 8, 10 (Sung Family), 12noon; **Holy Day Mass** 10, 7pm; **Weekday Mass** Mon-Wed, Fri 10; **Exposition** Sat 5-6pm; **Confession** Sat 5-5.30pm & on request

Fr Cristiano Braz
52 Uxbridge Road W7 3SU Tel: 020 8567 4056
Email: hanwell@rcdow.org.uk Web: parish.rcdow.org.uk/hanwell
On main road, corner of St George's Road (traffic lights)
Ealing Deanery (1853; 1967)

Parish Administrators Pamela Sheridan, Marlene Wakim
Catechetical Co-ordinator Awaiting appointment

• Medical Mission Sisters, 8 Springfield Road W7 3JP
Email: mmsspringfield@gmail.com Web: www.medicalmissionsisters-uk.org
• Sisters of St Joseph of Peace, St Mary's Convent, 50 Uxbridge Road W7 3PP
Tel: 020 8567 8635
• Ealing Hospital, Southall: General Wing
Mass Wed 2pm
St Bernard's Wing

HAREFIELD + ST PAUL, MERLE AVENUE A

Sunday Mass (Sat 6.30pm), 9, 11, 5pm *2nd Sun only, Syro-Malabar Rite*; **Holy Day Mass** 9.15, 7pm; **Weekday Mass** Mon-Sat 9.15; **Confession** Sat after morning Mass & 6pm

Fr James Mulligan
St Paul's House, 2 Merle Avenue, Harefield UB9 6DG Tel: 01895 822365
Email: harefield@rcdow.org.uk Web: parish.rcdow.org.uk/harefield
Bus 331 Uxbridge, U9 Northwood; church in Merle Avenue off High Street at south end of shopping parade
Hillingdon Deanery (1963; 1965; ext 1983)

• Harefield Hospital, Courtfield, Rylstone, Bardom Court, Harefield Nursing Home, Cedar House, Coppermill Care Home

HARPENDEN + OUR LADY OF LOURDES

Sunday Mass (Sat 6pm), 8.30, 9.45 (Family), 11.30 (sung); **Holy Day Mass** 9.15, 6pm; **Weekday Mass** Mon, Tue, Wed, 9.15, Thu 11, Fri Liturgy of the Word & Holy Communion 9.15, Sat 10; **Novena** after Wed Mass; **Exposition** Sat 5-5.45pm; **Confession** Sat 10.30-11, 5–5.30pm

Canon Anthony Dwyer
1 Kirkwick Avenue, Harpenden AL5 2QH Tel: 01582 712245
Email: harpenden@rcdow.org.uk Web: parish.rcdow.org.uk/harpenden
Rothamsted Avenue; off High Street, up from Church Green
St Albans Deanery (1905; 1929; cons 28 May 1936)
Office Administrator Melanie Armitage Mon-Thu 9.30-12.30pm **Tel: 01582 712245**
Email: harpenden@rcdow.org.uk
Parish Safeguarding Rep Brigid Brennan

• Dominican Sisters, 18 Kirkdale Road, Harpenden AL5 2PT Tel: 01582 712814
• Spire Hospital

HARROW NORTH + ST JOHN FISHER A

Sunday Mass (Sat 6pm), 8.30, 10, 11.30; **Holy Day Mass** 9.30, 7pm; **Weekday Mass** Mon, Tue 9.30, Thu (see newsletter), Fri, Sat 9.30; **Exposition** Mon 8.15-9.15, *First Fri only*, with **Benediction** 10-11; Sat 10-10.30 **Confession** Sat 10-10.30, 5.15-5.45pm & by appointment

Fr Graham Stokes

80 Imperial Close, Harrow HA2 7LW Tel: 020 8868 7531
Email: harrownorth@rcdow.org.uk Web: www.stjohnfisheronline.org.uk
Between North Harrow & Rayners Lane Stns, just south of The Ridgeway junction
Harrow Deanery (1939; cons 2014)
Parish Administrator Awaiting appointment
Catechist Kay O'Connor **Email:** kayoconnor@rcdow.org.uk

HARROW-ON-THE-HILL + OUR LADY AND ST THOMAS OF CANTERBURY

Sunday Mass (Sat 6pm), 8.30, 9.45 (Family), 11.15 (Sung), 6.30pm; **Holy Day Mass** 9.30, 8pm; **Weekday Mass** Mon 9.30, Tue 9.30 (Eucharistic Service), Wed 7pm, Thu, Fri 9.30; **Exposition** Sat 11.30-12noon; **Confession** Sat 11.30-12noon

Fr Guy Sawyer

22 Roxborough Park, Harrow-on-the-Hill HA1 3BE
Tel: 020 8422 2513 Fax: 020 8869 6896
Email: harrowonthehill@rcdow.org.uk Web: parish.rcdow.org.uk/harrowonthehill
Harrow Deanery (1873; 1894)
Parish Safeguarding Officer Desmond Gaynor **Tel:** 01923 778987
Parish Secretary Anna Byrne **Mon-Fri 9.30-12.30pm**
Pastoral Assistant Awaiting appointment **Tel:** 07724 362853

• Sisters of St Mary of Namur, 1 Grafton Road, Harrow HA1 4QS Tel: 020 8424 8185

HARROW SOUTH + ST GABRIEL & NORTHOLT + ST BERNARD

St Gabriel: Sunday Mass (Sat 6pm), 8.30, 10, 12noon; **Holy Day Mass** 10; **Weekday Mass** Mon, Wed, Thu 10; **Exposition** Thu 10.30-11; **Confession** Sat 5.15-5.45pm
St Bernard: Sunday Mass 9, 11, 5pm (Polish); **Holy Day Mass** 7.30pm; **Weekday Mass** Tue, Fri 10, Sat 9.30; **Exposition** Sat 10-11; **Confession** Sat 10.15-10.45

Fr James Neal (resident at St Bernard's), Fr Tom Montgomery (resident at St Gabriel's)

The Presbytery, 17 Mandeville Road, Northolt UB5 5HE
Parish Office: 390b Northolt Road, South Harrow HA2 8EX Tel: 020 8864 5455
Email: harrowsouth@rcdow.org.uk Web: parish.rcdow.org.uk/harrowsouth

+ St Gabriel's Church
390b Northolt Road, South Harrow HA2 8EX
On main road, south of South Harrow Stn, near junction with Park Lane
Harrow Deanery (1933; 2002; cons 2003)

+ St Bernard's Church
17 Mandeville Road, Northolt UB5 5HE
On main road, between Target Roundabout & Northolt Stn
Harrow Deanery (1965; cons 2010)

• Sisters of St Louis, 67 Parkfield Road, South Harrow HA2 8LA Tel: 020 8248 3838

HARROW ROAD + OUR LADY OF LOURDES AND ST VINCENT DE PAUL

Sunday Mass (Sat 6pm), 11.30; **Holy Day Mass** as Weekday Mass, also 7pm; **Weekday Mass** Mon, Fri 10 (Tue, Thu 10 at Paddington); **Exposition** and **Benediction** Mon, Fri 9-10, Sat 5-6pm; **Confession** Sat 5-6pm

Fr Michael Jarmulowicz (also serves Paddington)
337 Harrow Road W9 3RB Tel: 020 7286 2170
Email: harrowroad@rcdow.org.uk Web: parish.rcdow.org.uk/harrowroad
East of Great Western Road junction; near Westbourne Park Stn
North Kensington Deanery (1876; 1912; 1975)
Parish Administrator Mrs Jennifer Ellis **Mon, Fri 9-3pm**

HARROW WEALD: *SEE WEALDSTONE*

HATCH END: *SEE HEADSTONE LANE*

HATFIELD + MARYCHURCH A

Sunday Mass (Sat 6pm), 11 (with Children's Liturgy); **Holy Day Mass** 9.30, 7.30pm; **Weekday Mass** Mon, Tue 9.30, Wed 7.30pm, Thu, Fri 9.30; **Divine Office** 20 mins before Weekday Mass; **Novenas** Tue: after Mass - Our Lady of Perpetual Succour, Thu after Mass - Most Sacred Heart of Jesus; **Exposition** Fri after Mass; **Confession** Sat 5.15-5.45pm

Missionary Society of St Paul (MSP) Fr Livinus Onyebuchi, Fr Julius Otoaye (clergy also serve Hatfield South and are resident at **St Peter's Presbytery, Bishop's Rise, Hatfield AL10 9HN Tel: 01707 262121**)
26 Salisbury Square, Hatfield AL9 5JD Tel: 01707 262 439
Email: hatfield@rcdow.org.uk Web: parish.rcdow.org.uk/hatfield
Just off Great North Road (A1000), near BR Stn & Hatfield House
Stevenage Deanery (1930, 1971)

Chapel of Ease: St Thomas More, Station Road, Welham Green
Sunday Mass 9.30; **Holy Day Mass** (Vigil 7.30pm)

HATFIELD SOUTH + ST PETER

Sunday Mass 9.15, 11 (with Children's Liturgy), Student Mass 6pm; **Holy Day Mass** 9.30, 7pm; **Weekday Mass** Mon, Tue, Wed, Fri 9.30, preceded by **Morning Prayer** 9.10, Thu 7pm, Sat 10.30; **Exposition** Sat 11-12noon, with **Benediction** 12noon; **Novenas** Tue after Mass - Our Lady of Perpetual Help, Fri after Mass - Most Sacred Heart of Jesus; **Rosary** Wed after Mass; **Confession** Sat 11-12noon, 5-5.30pm

Missionary Society of St Paul (MSP) Fr Livinus Onyebuchi, Fr Julius Otoaye (also Chaplain to University of Hertfordshire) (clergy also serve Hatfield Marychurch)
St Peter's Presbytery, Bishop's Rise, Hatfield AL10 9HN Tel: 01707 262121
Email: hatfieldsouth@rcdow.org.uk Web: www.stpetershatfield.org
Half-mile from Comet Roundabout, via Cavendish Way
Stevenage Deanery (1959; 1961)

HAVERSTOCK HILL + OUR LADY OF THE ROSARY AND ST DOMINIC A

The Church is the Diocesan Shrine of the Most Holy Rosary (2016)
Sunday Mass (Sat 6pm), 8.30, 10 (Family), 12noon (Solemn Shrine Mass), 6pm; **Holy Day Mass** (Vigil 6pm), 7.30, 10, 6pm; **Weekday Mass** Mon-Fri 7.30, 6pm (Thu 6pm with Vespers), Sat 7.30, 10; **Morning Prayer** Mon-Fri 7, Sat, Sun 8; **Evening Prayer** Mon, Tu, Fri 6.45pm, Sun 5.30pm; **Exposition** Mon-Fri 5-5.45pm, also **Benediction** Thu 5.45pm, **Exposition** and **Rosary Procession** Sat 10.30; **Confession** Sat 10.30-11, 5.30-6.15pm, Sun 9.45-10.15, 11.45-12.15pm

Dominicans (OP) Fr Oliver Keenan (Tel: 020 7482 9224)
St Dominic's Priory, Southampton Road NW5 4LB
Tel: 020 7482 9210 Fax: 020 7482 9239
Email: haverstockhill@rcdow.org.uk Web: www.rosaryshrine.co.uk
Top of Malden Road, nearest TfL Stns Chalk Farm & Belsize Park.
Camden Deanery (1867; 1874; cons 1 August 1923)
Community: Frs Michael Dunn, Leo Edgar, Martin Ganeri (Provincial **Email:** provincial@english.op.org), Peter Harries, Oliver Keenan, Lawrence Lew, Rudolf Löwenstein, Thomas Skeats

• Hospital Chaplain to UCLH NHS Trust Fr Peter Harries OP **Tel: 020 7482 9216**
(Elizabeth Garrett Anderson Wing, Heart, National for Neurology & Neurosurgery and University College Hospitals)
Sunday Mass 9.45
• Royal Free Hospital
Tel: 020 7794 0500 Chaplain Fr John McCarthy **Tel: 020 7830 2742**

HAYES + THE IMMACULATE HEART OF MARY A

Sunday Mass (Sat 6.30pm), 8.30, 10, 12noon, 8.30pm; **Holy Day Mass** 9.30, 12.15pm, 7.30pm; **Weekday Mass** Mon, Tue, Thu 8.15, Mon-Sat 12.15pm, Wed, Fri 7.30pm; **Bank Holidays** 10; **Confession** (Spanish, Polish available) Sat 10.30-11.30, 5.45-6.15pm & by appointment

Claretian Missionaries (CMF) Fr Paul Smyth
Botwell House, Botwell Lane, Hayes UB3 2AB Tel: 020 8573 2544
Email: hayes@rcdow.org.uk Web: www.botwell.org.uk
In town centre, just off Coldharbour Lane/Station Road; near Hayes and Harlington Stn (BR)
Hillingdon Deanery (1912; 1954; 1961; cons 24 October 1972)
Community: Frs Joseph Katthula, Chris Newman, John O'Byrne, Paul Smyth (Major Superior), Krzysztof Stawicki
Pastoral Assistant Daniel Ortiz **Administrator** Jackie Morris **General Parish Assistant** Bridget Fahy **Tel: 020 8573 2544**
Claretian Pastoral Centre, Botwell House, Botwell Lane, Hayes UB3 2AB
Tel: 020 8573 2544

• Hayes Cottage Nursing Home

HEADSTONE LANE + ST THERESA OF THE CHILD JESUS

Sunday Mass (Sat 5pm), 10, 6pm; **Holy Day Mass** 9.30, 7.30pm; **Weekday Mass** Mon-Thu 9.30, Fri, Sat 10; **Exposition** and **Benediction** *First Fri only* 8.50-9.45; **Confession** Sat 10.30, with **Exposition** and **Benediction** 4-4.30pm

Fr Richard Parsons (Tel: 020 8864 8021)
22 Boniface Walk, Harrow HA3 6PU Tel: 020 8428 3260
Email: headstonelane@rcdow.org.uk Web: parish.rcdow.org.uk/headstonelane
Uxbridge Road, Hatch End, junction Headstone Lane; near Headstone Lane/Hatch End Stns
Harrow Deanery (1953)

HEATHROW AIRPORT + ST GEORGE'S CHAPEL

Sunday Mass 12.30pm - Chapel of St George; **Weekday Mass** Mon, Wed, Fri 12.30pm

Chaplain Fr Daniel Adayi CSSp Tel: **020 8745 4261** (in residence at Hounslow Parish, 94 Bath Road, Hounslow TW3 3EH Tel: **020 8570 1693 ext 6**), Rev Robert Levett (Deacon) Tel: 07882 491127
Chapel of St George, Heathrow Airport, Central Terminal Area, Hounslow TW6 1BP
Tel: 020 8745 4261 Email: heathrowairport@rcdow.org.uk
Web: parish.rcdow.org.uk/heathrow
Hounslow Deanery (1968)
Pastoral Assistants Susan Badua, Helen Baly, Hertiberto Demelo, Fiona Gonsalves, Shaun Loader, Elisangela Rivera
The Chapel is located in the central area of Heathrow Airport. It can be accessed by the Piccadilly Line Underground (Terminals 1, 2, 3); the train from Paddington (Terminals 2, 3) and the Central Bus Station. From any point, go towards the Central Bus Station. The way to Chapel is designated along all the pathways leading to the bus and train stations. It is about three minutes from the Central Bus Station. Contact the Chapel office for details of services during the week. Priests and groups who wish to celebrate Mass at the airport should contact the Chaplain directly. Multi-faith prayer rooms are to be found in all the Terminals, either airside or landside, and are available for prayer and quiet times.

HEMEL HEMPSTEAD EAST A

+ *Our Lady, Queen of All Creation (Rant Meadow):* **Sunday Mass** (Sat 5pm), 10.30, 12noon; **Holy Day Mass** as announced; **Weekday Mass** Mon, Tue 10, Fri 6.30pm, Sat 10; **Exposition** Sat 10.30-11; **Confession** Sat 10.30-11

+ *The Resurrection (Grovehill):* **Sunday Mass** 9; **Holy Day Mass** as announced; **Weekday Mass** Thu 10; **Confession** before Mass

Two churches, one parish; for Weekday Mass times, please check the parish newsletter at www.hemelcatholic.org

Fr Kim Addison
The Presbytery, Rant Meadow, Hemel Hempstead HP3 8PG Tel: 01442 210610

SECTION 3

+ Our Lady, Queen of All Creation
The Presbytery, Rant Meadow, Hemel Hempstead HP3 8PG Tel: 01442 210610
Email: hemeleast@rcdow.org.uk Web: www.hemelcatholic.org
On dual carriageway A414 between M1 (exit 8) & town centre
St Albans Deanery (1955; 1987; cons 13 November 1987)

+ The Church of the Resurrection
9 Henry Wells Square, Grovehill, Hemel Hempstead HP2 6BJ (Postal address:
The Presbytery, Rant Meadow, Hemel Hempstead HP3 8PG) Tel: 01442 210610
Email: hemel@rcdow.org.uk Web: www.hemelcatholic.org
Access from Washington Avenue into Turnpike Green
St Albans Deanery (Shared church, 1977)

HEMEL HEMPSTEAD WEST   A

+ *Ss Mary and Joseph (Boxmoor):* **Sunday Mass** (Sat 6pm), 8.45, 11.45; **Holy Day Mass** as
announced; **Weekday Mass** Wed, Fri 10; **Exposition** *1st Fri only* 10.30-11; **Confession** Sat
5.15-5.45pm
+ *St Mark (Warners End):* **Sunday Mass** 8.45 (Ordinariate Rite), 10.15; **Holy Day Mass** as
announced; **Weekday Mass** Wed 7.45pm (Ordinariate Rite); **Confession** before Mass
Two churches, one parish; for Weekday Mass times, please check the parish newsletter at
www.hemelcatholic.org

Fr Brian McMahon, Rev Simon Wright (Deacon)
186 St John's Road, Boxmoor HP1 1NR Tel: 01442 391759

+ Ss Mary and Joseph
186 St John's Road, Boxmoor HP1 1NR Tel: 01422 391759
Email: hemel@rcdow.org.uk Web: www.hemelcatholic.org
St Albans Deanery (1890; 1938; 1951)

+ St Mark
Hollybush Lane, Warners End, in the grounds of John F Kennedy Catholic School, Hemel
Hempstead HP1 2PH
(Postal address: 186 St John's Road, Boxmoor HP1 1NR)
Email: hemel@rcdow.org.uk Web: www.hemelcatholic.org
St Albans Deanery (1977)

HENDON + OUR LADY OF DOLOURS   A

Sunday Mass (Sat 6pm), 10, 12noon; **Holy Day Mass** as announced; **Weekday Mass**
Mon-Wed 10 (Wed at Hendon West), Thu 7.30, Fri 10, Sat 9; **Exposition**, then
Benediction Sat 9.30-10; **Confession** Sat 9.30-10, 5.15-5.45pm and on request

Fr Tim Edgar
4 Egerton Gardens NW4 4BA Tel: 020 8202 0560
Email: hendon@rcdow.org.uk Web: www.ourladyofdolours.org.uk

Off The Burroughs (opp. Town Hall), close to Watford Way (A41) & Hendon Central Stn (TfL)
Barnet Deanery (1849; 1863; cons 1927; recons 25 March 1966)

• Poor Handmaids of Jesus Christ, St Joseph's Convent, Westminster House, Watford Way NW4 4TY Tel: 020 8202 7626 Email: winifred.orourke@btinternet.com
Web: www.poorhandmaidsofjesuschrist.org.uk
• Hendon Hospital

HENDON WEST + ST PATRICK

Sunday Mass 9.30, 6pm; Holy Day Mass as announced; Weekday Mass Mon 7pm, Wed 10 (other weekday Masses at Hendon)

Fr Tim Edgar (resident at 4 Egerton Gardens NW4 4BA Tel: 020 8202 0560), Fr Bartosz Rajewski (in residence)
167 West Hendon Broadway NW9 7EB Tel: 020 8202 5143
Email: hendonwest@rcdow.org.uk Web: parish.rcdow.org.uk/hendonwest
Hendon Broadway on main road (A5), 800 yds north of Staples Corner
Barnet Deanery (1964)

HERTFORD + THE IMMACULATE CONCEPTION AND ST JOSEPH

Sunday Mass (Sat 6pm), 8.30, 10.30 (Sung), 6pm; Holy Day Mass 7.30, 10 (at school in term time), 8pm; Weekday Mass Mon, Wed, 10, Tue, Fri, 12.15pm, Thu 7.30; Exposition Sat 5-5.45pm (*Stations of the Cross replace Exposition on Saturdays in Lent*); Confession Sat 10-10.30, 5-5.40pm

Canon Terence Phipps
23 St John's Street, Hertford SG14 1RX Tel: 01992 582109
Email: hertford@rcdow.org.uk Web: parish.rcdow.org.uk/hertford
Off Railway Sreet, close to Hertford East Stn (BR)
Lea Valley Deanery (Priory 1087-1539; 1848; 1858; cons 16 October 1866)

HESTON + OUR LADY QUEEN OF APOSTLES

Sunday Mass (Sat 7pm), 8, 9.30, 11.30, 3pm (Polish), 5.30pm; Holy Day Mass (Vigil 7pm), 9, 7pm; Weekday Mass 9, 7pm; Exposition Sat 9.30-10; Novena during Wed 7pm Mass; Confession Sat 9.30-10, 6.15-6.45pm & on request

Society of Divine Vocations (SDV) Fr Luigi Morrone, Fr Vipin James;
Fr Paul Rout OFM (in residence)
15 The Green, Heston Road, Heston TW5 0RL Tel: 020 8570 1818 Fax 020 8572 7861
Email: heston@rcdow.org.uk Web: parish.rcdow.org.uk/heston
Set back from main road, just south of motorway bridge
Hounslow Deanery (1928; 1929; 1964; cons 19 May 1974)
Fr Colin Whatling (retired) 2B Eton Avenue, Heston TW5 0HB Tel: 020 8606 9544
Heston Catholic Social Club (Pope John Centre) Tel: 020 8574 5411
Parish Halls (Parish Secretary) Tel: 020 8570 1818

SECTION 3

HIGHBURY + ST JOAN OF ARC A

Sunday Mass (Sat 6pm), 9, 11, 2pm (Congolese Community); **Holy Day Mass** 9.15, 7.30pm; **Weekday Mass** Mon-Fri 9.15, Sat 10; **Confession** Sat 5.15-5.45pm

Canon Gerard King

60 Highbury Park N5 2XH Tel: 020 7226 0257
Email: highbury@rcdow.org.uk Web: www.stjoanofarcparish.co.uk
Islington Deanery (1920; 1962; cons 14 June 2001)

• Our Lady of Mercy Sisters, 40 Aberdeen Road N5 2XD Tel: 020 7359 3897
• Sisters of St Paul de Chartres, 30 Aberdeen Park N5 2BL Tel: 020 7359 1712
Email: ndf_2003@yahoo.fr

HIGHGATE + ST JOSEPH

Sunday Mass (Sat 7pm), 8, 10, 12noon, 1.30pm (Polish), 7pm; **Holy Day Mass** (Vigil 6.30pm), 9.30, 6.30pm; **Weekday Mass** Mon-Fri 9.30, 6.30pm, Sat & Bank Holidays 9.30; **Confession** Sat 10-10.30, 6.30-6.45pm

Passionists (CP) Fr George Koloth

St Joseph's Retreat, Highgate Hill N19 5NE Tel: 020 7272 2320
Email: highgate@rcdow.org.uk Web: www.stjosephshighgate.org.uk
Corner Dartmouth Park Hill; Archway Stn (TfL)
Islington Deanery (1858; 1888; cons 28 April 1932)
Community: Frs Tiernan Doherty (Rector), George Koloth, Benedict Lodge, Thomas Rockey
St Joseph's Parish Centre, Highgate Hill N19 5NE Tel: 020 7272 4571

• Whittington Hospital & Hornsey Central Hospital
Chaplain Fr Oliver Ugwu Tel: 020 7288 5337

HILLINGDON + ST BERNADETTE

Sunday Mass (Sat 6pm), 9 (with Children's Liturgy), 11, 5.30pm; **Holy Day Mass** 10, 7pm; **Weekday Mass** Mon, Wed-Sat 10; **Exposition** with **Benediction** Fri after Mass, also Fri 7.30pm; **Rosary** after weekday Mass; **Confession** Sat 10.30-11 & on request

Fr Matthew J Heslin, Rev Reg Abrahams (Deacon)
160 Long Lane, Hillingdon UB10 0EH Tel: 01895 234577
Email: hillingdon@rcdow.org.uk Web: parish.rcdow.org.uk/hillingdon
South Long Lane (half mile up from Uxbridge Road)
Hillingdon Deanery (1937; 1961; cons 7 October 1978)

• Sisters of Mercy, St Raphael's Convent, Court Drive, Hillingdon UB10 0BW
Tel: 01895 233771
• Hillingdon Hospital
Sunday and **Holy Day Mass** 4pm

HITCHIN + OUR LADY IMMACULATE AND ST ANDREW

Sunday Mass (Sat 6pm) 8.30, 10.30, 5pm; **Holy Day Mass** 7.30, 10, 7.30pm; **Weekday Mass** 10; **Confession** (French available) with **Exposition** and **Benediction** Sat 10.30-11.15

Assumptionists (a.a.) Fr Tom O'Brien, Fr Euloge Katsuva Kasine, Fr Andrew O'Dell (in residence)

16 Nightingale Road, Hitchin SG5 1QS Tel: 01462 459126

Email: hitchin@rcdow.org.uk Web: parish.rcdow.org.uk/hitchin

Junction with Grove Road, opposite Bancroft Recreation Ground

Stevenage Deanery (1890; 1902; cons 18 December 1977)

Assistant Trish Bonnett (Pastoral) Email: hitchinpastoral@rcdow.org.uk

Administrator Cheryl Saunders (Mon-Thu)

• Cheshire Home

HODDESDON + ST AUGUSTINE

Sunday Mass (Sat 4pm (Italian), 6.30pm), 9.15 (with Children's Liturgy), 11.15, *First Sun only* 5pm (Latin); **Holy Day Mass** 9.30, 12noon, 8pm; **Weekday Mass** Mon, Tue, Wed 9.15 (preceded by **Morning Prayer** 9), Fri 12noon (preceded by **Exposition** 11), Sat 10; **Holy Hour** *3rd Sun only* 5pm; **Confession** Sat 10.30-11, 5.30-6.15pm, Sun 8.30-9

Fr Philip Miller, Fr Joshy Philip (in residence, Knanaya Chaplaincy)

The Presbytery, Esdaile Lane, Hoddesdon EN11 8DS

Tel: 01992 440986 Fax: 01992 440244

Email: hoddesdon@rcdow.org.uk Web: parish.rcdow.org.uk/hoddesdon

Junction of High Street with Charlton Way

Lea Valley Deanery (1932; 1962; cons 1971)

HOLBORN (CIRCUS), EC1: *SEE ELY PLACE*; (HIGH), WC1: *SEE LINCOLN'S INN FIELDS*

HOLLOWAY + SACRED HEART OF JESUS A

Sunday Mass (Sat 6pm), 8.30, 11 (Sung, with choir); **Holy Day Mass** 10; **Weekday Mass** (**Morning Prayer** precedes by 15 mins) Mon, Wed, Thu, Fri 9.15, Public Holidays 10; **Confession** Sat 11-12noon & on request

Fr Gideon Wagay, Fr Henry Mobela (in residence, Zambian Chaplaincy, contact details below), Fr Bogdan Velyanyk (in residence)

62 Eden Grove N7 8EN Tel: 020 7607 3594 Fax: 020 7607 1867

Email: holloway@rcdow.org.uk Web: www.sacredheartchurchholloway.org.uk

Off Holloway Road, opposite Metropolitan University and Emirates (Arsenal FC) Stadium

Islington Deanery (1855; 1870; cons 29 May 1928)

(Fr Henry Mobela Tel: 07495 866069 Email: kalusamobela@gmail.com)

Parish Administrator Elizabeth Ocampo

• Sisters of La Sainte Union, 51 Freegrove Road N7 9RG Tel: 020 7609 7160
• Pentonville Prison Chaplains Valentine Ambe, Mary Ebbasi (See HM Prison Service)

HOMERTON + IMMACULATE HEART OF MARY AND ST DOMINIC

Sunday Mass (Sat 6.30pm), 9, 11; **Holy Day Mass** 9.30, 7.30pm; **Weekday Mass** 9.30; **Exposition** for Priests / Vocations Tue 10-10.30; **Confession** Sat 5.30-6pm

Fr Patrick Allsop, Fr Christian de Lisle
Presbytery, Ballance Road E9 5SS Tel: 020 8985 1495
Email: homerton@rcdow.org.uk   Web: www.immaculatehearthomerton.org
Ballance Road
Hackney Deanery (1873; cons 30 June 1884)

HOUNSLOW + SS MICHAEL AND MARTIN

Sunday Mass (Sat 6.15pm), 9, 10.30, 12noon, 6pm; **Holy Day Mass** (Vigil 6pm), 7.30, 9, 6pm 7.30pm; **Weekday Mass** Mon–Sat 9, Mon–Thu 6pm, Fri 7pm.; **Exposition**, followed by **Benediction** Sat 4.30-5.30pm; **Confession** Fri 6-6.30pm, Sat 9.30-10.15, 4.30-5.15pm
Ethnic Chaplaincy Masses 3pm Syro-Malabar Mass *1st Sun only*, 4pm Sinhalese Mass *2nd Sun only*, 4pm Goan Mass *3rd Sun only*

Spiritans (CSSp) Fr Augustine Nwosu, Fr Gerald Bonaventure Peter, Fr Daniel Adayi (also Chaplain, Heathrow Airport Tel: 020 8570 1693 ext 6)
94 Bath Road, Hounslow TW3 3EH Tel: 020 8570 1693
Email: hounslow@rcdow.org.uk Web: parish.rcdow.org.uk/hounslow
Hounslow Deanery (1884; 1929; cons 12 October 1938)
Administrator Lavina Fernandes
Parish Catechists Colette Joyce, Lionel Pereira
Youth Worker Ivan Cižmárik

HOXTON + ST MONICA'S PRIORY A

Sunday Mass (Sat 6.30pm), 9, (followed by **Rosary Hour**) 11 (with Children's Liturgy, *First Sun only*), 7pm; **Holy Day Mass** (Vigil 7pm), 9.30, 7pm; **Weekday Mass** 9.30, preceded by **Morning Prayer** 9.10; **Mass** with **Healing Prayers** and **Benediction** 7pm *First Fri only*; **Bank Holiday Mass** 11; **Exposition** Sat 5-6pm, followed by **Vespers** 6pm; **Confession** Sat 5-6pm and on request

Augustinians (OSA) Fr Gabriel Hassan, Fr Jacob Choi, Fr Anthony Zabbey (Prior)
19 Hoxton Square N1 6NT Tel: 020 7739 5006
Email: hoxton@rcdow.org.uk Web: parish.rcdow.org.uk/hoxton
Off Old Street, at Shoreditch Town Hall
Hackney Deanery (1864)
Parish Secretary Ingrid Bowie

• Little Sisters of Jesus, 148 Fellows Court, Weymouth Terrace E2 8LW
Tel: 020 7729 3605 Email: lsj.hackney@virgin.net Web: www.jesuscaritas.info/lsj
• Shalom Catholic Community 150 Kingsland Road E2 8EB Tel: 07432 501250
Email: london@comshalom.org Web: http://www.comshalom.org/en
• Ashwell House, Shepherdess Walk N1 7NA Tel: 020 7490 3296
Hall of residence for women university students
Pastoral care entrusted to Prelature of Opus Dei

• Mildmay Mission Hospital

ISLE OF DOGS: *SEE MILLWALL*

ISLEWORTH + OUR LADY OF SORROWS AND ST BRIDGET OF SWEDEN

Sunday Mass (Sat 6pm), 8, 10, 12noon; **Holy Day Mass** 9, 7pm; **Bank Holiday Mass** 10; **Weekday Mass** Mon-Thu 9, Mon, Fri 7pm, Sat 10; **Exposition** Mon-Thu half hour before Mass, Fri, Sat half hour after Mass, with **Benediction** Fri; **Confession** Sat 10.30-11, 5-5.30pm

Divine Word Missionaries (SVD) Fr Nicodemus Lobo Ratu, Fr Kieran Fitzharris
Memorial Square, 112 Twickenham Road, Isleworth TW7 6DL Tel/Fax: 020 8560 1431
Email: isleworth@rcdow.org.uk Web: parish.rcdow.org.uk/isleworth /
www.stbridgets.org.uk
Corner of South Street (traffic lights); opposite Gumley House
Hounslow Deanery (1675; 1910; cons 6 October 1910)

• Faithful Companions of Jesus, Gumley House Convent, 251 Twickenham Road,
Isleworth TW7 6DN Tel: 020 8232 9570
Email: generalsecretary@fcjgeneralate.org Web: www.fcjsisters.org
The Generalate, central administration of the Community, is based here.

ISLINGTON + ST JOHN THE EVANGELIST

Sunday Mass (Sat 6pm), 9, 10.30 (Sung), 12noon (Sung), 6pm; **Holy Day Mass** 10, 7.30pm; **Weekday Mass** 10; **Exposition** Sat 10.30-11.30; **Confession** Sat 10.30-11, 5.15-5.45pm

Mgr Séamus O'Boyle, Fr Allan Alvarado Gil, Fr Lawrence Milby (in residence)
(clergy also serve Copenhagen Street)
39 Duncan Terrace N1 8AL Tel: 020 7226 3277 Fax: 020 7704 8988
Email: islington@rcdow.org.uk Web: www.st-johns-islington-org
2 mins from Angel TfL Stn, via Islington High Street, right into Duncan Street, left into Duncan
Terrace Islington Deanery (1839; 1843; cons 26 June 1873)

• Sisters of the Cross and Passion, 40 Duncan Terrace N1 8AL Tel: 020 7359 8719

ITALIAN CHURCH + ST PETER'S

Sunday Mass (Sat 7pm), 9.30, 11 (Sung), 12.30pm, 7pm; **Holy Day Mass** 10, 12.15pm, 7.30pm; **Weekday Mass** Mon-Fri 12.15pm; **Confession** (Italian, English, Sunday during Mass & on request)

Pallottine Fathers (SAC) Fr Andrea Fulco, Fr Giuseppe De Caro, Fr Ryszard Wrobel
St Peter's Italian Church, 136 Clerkenwell Road EC1R 5DL
(Correspondence etc. to 4 Back Hill EC1R 5EN)
Tel: 020 7837 1528 Fax: 020 7837 9071
Email: italianchurch@rcdow.org.uk Web: www.italianchurch.org.uk
Opposite the top end of Hatton Garden
Westminster Deanery (1863)

SECTION 3

KENSAL NEW TOWN + OUR LADY OF THE HOLY SOULS

Sunday Mass (Sat 6pm), 9, 11 (Family); **Holy Day Mass** 9.30, 7.30pm; **Weekday Mass** as announced; **Confession** Sat 5.15-5.45pm & on request

Fr Philip Baptiste
68 Hazlewood Crescent W10 5DJ Tel: 020 8969 2660
Email: kensalnewtown@rcdow.org.uk Web: parish.rcdow.org.uk/kensalnewtown
In Bosworth Road, off Kensal Road (near Halfpenny Bridge)
North Kensington Deanery (1862; 1882; cons 10 Nov 2012)
Parish Sister Sr Margarita RSM **Parish Administrator** Stephanie Mackay

• Missionaries of Charity, 177 Bravington Road W9 3AR Tel: 020 8960 2644
• Sisters of Mercy, 76 Fifth Avenue W10 4DP Tel: 020 8960 2505

KENSAL RISE + CHURCH OF THE TRANSFIGURATION A

Sunday Mass (Sat 6pm), 9, 11, 12.30pm (Italian); **Holy Day Mass** 10, 7pm; **Weekday Mass** Mon, Fri 7pm, Tues, Wed, Thurs, Sat 10 with **Exposition** one hour before each Mass; **Holy Hour** and **Benediction** Fri 6 pm; **Confession** Sat 10.30-11.15, 5-5.45pm

Fr Sean Thornton
Presbytery, 1 Wrentham Avenue NW10 3HT Tel: 020 8964 4040
Email: kensalrise@rcdow.org.uk Web: www.transfigparishkensalrise.org.uk
Corner of Wrentham Avenue and Chamberlayne Road, near Kensal Rise BR Stn
Brent Deanery (1977)
Parish Administrator Chelsea Bottomley (9:30-2:30pm, Mon-Wed, Fri)

• Sisters of Jesus and Mary, 200 Chamberlayne Road NW10 3JX
Tel: 020 8451 1957
• Stigmatine Fathers (CSS), 2 Leigh Gardens NW10 5HP
Tel/Fax: 020 8969 1414 Email: donnatalino@btinternet.com Fr Natalino Mignolli
• St Mary's Cemetery, 679-681 Harrow Road NW10 5NU Tel: 020 8969 1145

KENSINGTON 1 + OUR LADY OF VICTORIES

Sunday Mass (Sat 6.30pm), 9, 10.30, 12noon, 6.30pm; **Holy Day Mass** 7.30, 10, 7pm; **Weekday Mass** Mon-10, Sat 10; **Exposition** Wed 10.30-12noon, *First Sat only* 10.30-12noon; **Confession** Sat 10.35-11.30, 5.30-6.25pm & on request

Mgr Jim Curry, Fr Daniel Herrero Peña, Fr Frederick Jackson (in residence)
The Clergy House, 16 Abingdon Road W8 6AF Tel: 020 7937 4778 Fax: 020 7937 4221
Email: kensington1@rcdow.org.uk Web: parish.rcdow.org.uk/kensington1
235a High Street; south side of High Street, between Abingdon Road & Earls Court Road; not far from Kensington High Street Stn (TfL)
Kensington & Chelsea Deanery (1794; 1812; 1869; 1958)
Co-ordinator for Sacramental Programmes Sr Maureen McNamara RSM

• Daughters of St Paul, Pauline Books & Media, 199 Kensington High Street W8 6BA
Tel: 020 7937 4890 (Community), 020 7937 9591 (Book Centre)
Email: london@pauline-uk.org   Web: www.paulineuk.org
• Augustinian Recollects (OAR), 18 Cheniston Gardens W8 6TQ Tel: 020 7937 7681
Fr Robert Riezu

KENSINGTON 2 + OUR LADY OF MOUNT CARMEL & ST SIMON STOCK

Sunday Mass (Sat 6pm), 8.30, 10 (Family), 11 (Choir), 12.15pm, 6pm (Folk); **Holy Day Mass** (Vigil 6pm), 8, 12.15pm, 6pm; **Weekday Mass** 8, 12.15pm, 6pm; **Confession** Mon-Fri 5.40-6pm, Sat 10.30-11.30, 5-6pm

Discalced Carmelites (OCD) Fr Christopher Clarke
Carmelite Priory, 41 Kensington Church Street W8 4BB
Tel: 020 7937 9866 Fax 020 7938 1470
Email: kensington2@rcdow.org.uk   Web: www.carmelitechurch.org
500 yards north of Kensington High Street
Kensington & Chelsea Deanery (1862; 1959)
Community: Frs Christopher Clarke (Prior & Parish Priest), Alexander Ezechukwu, John McGowan, Tijo Xavier

• Adoratrices, Handmaids of the Blessed Sacrament and of Charity, 38/39 Kensington Square W8 5HP Tel: 020 7937 5237   Email: adorlonuk@hotmail.com
Web: www.adoratrices.com Hostel for Working Women & Students Tel: 020 7937 5237
• Religious of the Assumption, Convent of the Assumption, 20 Kensington Square W8 5HH Tel: 020 7361 4720 Email: enquiries@assumptionreligious.org
Web: www.assumptionreligious.org
Lay Volunteer Co-ordinator Helen Granger
Email: vc@assumptionvolunteers.org.uk Web: www.assumptionvolunteers.org.uk
Milleret House Retreat centre
Administrator Amy Holland Tel: 020 7361 4756
Email: enquiries@assumptionreligious.org
Web: www.assumptionreligious.org/Milleret-House
• Religious of Mary Immaculate, 15-16 Southwell Gardens SW7 4RN
Tel: 020 7373 2738 Email: rmilondon@btconnect.com
Hostel for working girls and students of all nationalities
Email: book@rmilondonhostel.org Web: www.rmilondonhostel.org
Social services for *au pairs*
Tel: 020 7373 3869 Email: socialservices@rmilondonhostel.org
Spanish Social Centre Tel: 020 7373 3869
• Cromwell Hospital

KENTISH TOWN + OUR LADY HELP OF CHRISTIANS

Sunday Mass (Sat 6pm), 9 (Sung), 11 (Family), 6pm; **Holy Day Mass** 10, 7pm; **Weekday Mass** 10; **Divine Office** 9.35, 12noon, 6pm; **Rosary** 10.35; **Confession** Sat 10.30-11

SECTION 3

Fr John Deehan
4 Lady Margaret Road NW5 2XT Tel: 020 7485 4023
Email: kentishtown@rcdow.org.uk Web: parish.rcdow.org.uk/kentishtown
Corner of Falkland Road; 3 mins from Kentish Town Stn (TfL)
Camden Deanery (1859; cons 2 June 1925; new church 1970; cons 20 September 1979)
Parish Welfare Project Co-ordinator Richard Mallon Tel: 07951 600451

• Sisters of La Sainte Union, Croft Lodge, Highgate Road NW5 1RP
LSU Provincialate, 53 Croftdown Road NW5 1EL Tel: 020 7482 7225

KENTON + ALL SAINTS
Sunday Mass (Sat 6.30pm), 9, 11; **Holy Day Mass** as announced; **Weekday Mass** 9.15;
Confession Sat 5.30-6pm

Fr Hector Rouco Gutierrez
The Presbytery, 2a Salehurst Close, Harrow HA3 0UG Tel: 020 8204 3550
Email: kenton@rcdow.org.uk Web: parish.rcdow.org.uk/kenton
*Church at 531 Kenton Road HA3 0UL, corner of Claremont Avenue; 600 yards west of
Kingsbury Circus/Kingsbury Stn (TfL); bus 183*
Harrow Deanery (1932; 1963)
Parish Administrator Elizabeth Galea
Catechetical Co-ordinator Pat Edwards Email: patedwards@rcdow.org.uk

KILBURN + SACRED HEART OF JESUS
Sunday Mass (Sat 6pm), 10, 12.30pm, 7pm; **Holy Day Mass** 10, 12.15pm, 7pm; **Weekday
Mass** Mon-Fri 10, 12.15pm, Sat 12noon; **Filipino Mass** *3rd Sun* 3pm; **Adoration** Fri 1-
4pm; **Confession** Sat 10.30-12noon, 5-6pm

Oblates of Mary Immaculate (OMI) Fr Terence Murray, Fr Thomas Devereux, Fr Johnson
Susai Raj
New Priory, Sacred Heart Church, Quex Road NW6 4PS
Tel: 020 7624 1701 Fax 020 7328 8176
Email: kilburn@rcdow.org.uk Web: www.oblateskilburn.com
Camden Deanery (1864; 1879; cons 18 June 1909)
Community: Frs Paschal Dillon, Michael Phelan, Terence Murray, Thomas Devereux, Brian
Maher (Superior), Johnson Susai Raj

• The Missionary Association of Mary Immaculate (MAMI), 237 Goldhurst Terrace NW6
3EP Fr Paschal Dillon OMI Tel: 020 7328 8610
Catechetical Co-ordinator Awaiting appointment
Mazenod Centre Manager Anna Redmond Tel: 020 7624 5517
• Oblate Partners in Mission Office, Denis Hurley House, 14 Quex Road NW6 4PL
Tel: 020 7624 7296 Fr Brian Maher
• Oblate Vocations Director Fr John McFadden **New Priory, Sacred Heart Church, Quex
Road NW6 4PS** Tel: 020 7624 1701 Email: j.mcfadden@oblates.co.uk

- Oblate Youth Service, Denis Hurley House, 14 Quex Road NW6 4PL
Tel: 020 7624 7296
- Sisters of the Holy Family of Bordeaux, 2 Aberdare Gardens NW6 3PX
Tel: 020 7624 7573
- Jesuits (SJ) Copleston House, 221 Goldhurst Terrace NW6 3EP Tel: 020 7604 5860
Community: Frs Michael Holman (Superior), Michael Barnes, Peter Gallagher, Pedro
McDade, Joseph Munitiz, Patrick Vance Nogoy, Richard Salmi, Chester Yacub

KILBURN WEST + IMMACULATE HEART OF MARY

Sunday Mass 9, 11.30; Holy Day Mass 9; Weekday Mass Tue, Fri 9; Exposition Sat 9.30-
10.30; Confession Sat 9.45 & before & after each Mass

Oblates of Mary Immaculate (OMI) Fr Terence Murray, Fr Thomas Devereux, Fr Johnson
Susai Raj (all in residence at New Priory, Sacred Heart Church, Quex Road NW6 4PS)
Immaculate Heart of Mary Presbytery, 1 Stafford Road NW6 5RS Tel: 020 7624 2188
Email: kilburnwest@rcdow.org.uk Web: parish.rcdow.org.uk/kilburnwest
Off Kilburn Park Road
Camden Deanery (1948)
Community: Fr John McFadden, Br Michael Moore
Marian Parish Centre Caretaker Francis Philip Bangura Tel: 020 3665 9697 / 07737
470350

KINGSBURY GREEN + ST SEBASTIAN AND ST PANCRAS A

Sunday Mass (Sat 6pm), 8, 9.30 (Family), 11 (Parish), 12.30 (Romanian, with Confession
available 11-12 noon); Holy Day Mass 9.15, 7.30pm; Weekday Mass Mon-Wed 9.15, Tue
7.30pm (Romanian), Thu 7.30pm, Fri-Sat 9.15; Confession Sat 12-1pm

Fr Stewart Keeley, Fr Marcelin Blaj (in residence, Romanian Chaplain, contact details below)
The Presbytery, 22 Hay Lane NW9 0NG Tel: 020 8204 2834 / 2117
Email: kingsburygreen@rcdow.org.uk Web: parish.rcdow.org.uk/kingsburygreen
Off Edgware Road, Colindale
Brent Deanery (1926; 2001)
(Fr Blaj Tel: 020 8204 4392 Email: romanianchaplaincy@gmail.com)

KING'S CROSS, EAST: *SEE COPENHAGEN STREET;*   WEST: *SEE SOMERS TOWN*

KINGSLAND + OUR LADY AND ST JOSEPH A

Sunday Mass (Sat 6.30pm), 8, 9.30 (Family), 11 (Sung), 12.30pm, 6.30pm; Holy Day Mass
(Vigil 7pm), 9, 12noon, 7pm; Weekday Mass Mon-Fri 9, 6pm, Sat 12noon followed by
Novena & Benediction; Exposition Sat 5.30-6.15pm, Sun 5.15-6.15pm with Benediction;
Confession Sat 11-11.45, 5.30-6.15pm

Fr Derek Hyett, Fr Saimon Gudime, Fr Dermot Power (in residence)
Presbytery, 100a Balls Pond Road N1 4AG Tel: 020 7254 4378
Email: kingsland@rcdow.org.uk Web: www.olsj.org
Off Kingsland High Street; at top end of Essex Road
Hackney Deanery (1854; 1964)

SECTION 3

Parish Administrator Mrs Ann-Marie Burnett-Charles
Email: amburnettcharles@rcdow.org.uk
Parish Sister Sr Winifred Quinlan UJ
• Ursulines of Jesus (UJ), Pax, 6 King Henry's Walk N1 4PB Tel: 020 7254 3319
• Nigerian National Chaplaincy, 8 King Henry's Walk N1 4PB Tel: 07710 512244
Chaplains Fr Matthew 'Gbenga Madewa, Fr Peter Tochukwu Egboo, Fr Alexander Izang Atu
• St Martin of Tours House, 162 New North Road N1 7BH
Rehabilitation Centre Tel: 020 7226 7516
• St Vincent's (SVP shop and counselling centre) 484/486 Kingsland Road E8 4AE
Tel: 020 7272 1263

KNEBWORTH + ST THOMAS MORE A

Sunday Mass (Sat 6pm), 8, 10 (Sung); **Holy Day Mass** 9.30, 8pm; **Weekday Mass** Mon 7.15 pm, Tue-Fri 9.30, Sat 10; **Exposition** Fri after Mass-12noon; **Confession** Sat 5.15-5.45pm

Canon Daniel Cronin
72 London Road, Knebworth SG3 6HB Tel: 01438 813303
Email: knebworth@rcdow.org.uk Web: www.knebworthcatholicchurch.org
Stevenage Deanery (1929; 1936)
Office Manager / PA to Parish Priest Theresa Taylor-Brookes

LEBANESE MARONITE CHURCH + OUR LADY OF LEBANON

Sunday Mass (Maronite Rite) (Sat 7pm), 12.30pm, 7pm; **Weekday Mass** Wed, Fri 7pm. All Masses celebrated at Our Lady of Sorrows, Paddington

Lebanese Maronite Order (LMO) Fr Fadi Kmeid, Fr Antoine Achkar, Fr Aziz Azzi
6 Dobson Close NW6 4RS Tel: 020 7586 1801
Email: lebanesechurch@rcdow.org.uk Web: www.maronitechurch.org.uk

LEICESTER SQUARE, WC2: *SEE FRENCH CHURCH*

LETCHWORTH GARDEN CITY+ ST HUGH OF LINCOLN

Sunday Mass (Sat 7pm), 8, 9.30, 11.30, 1pm (Polish); **Holy Day Mass** 9.30, 7.30pm; **Weekday Mass** Mon-Thu 9.30, **Liturgy of the Word** with **Holy Communion** Fri 9.30; **Morning Prayer** Mon-Fri 9.10; **Exposition** with **Confession** Thu, Sat 10, **Benediction** 10.30; **Confession** also Sat 6.15-6.45pm and on request

Fr James Garvey
84 Pixmore Way, Letchworth Garden City SG6 3TP Tel: 01462 510015
Email: letchworth@rcdow.org.uk Web: parish.rcdow.org.uk/letchworth
Stevenage Deanery (1907; 1963; cons 2007)
Parish Administrator Aimee Barnes Mon-Thu 9-12noon

• Sisters of Charity of Jesus and Mary, Provincial House, 108 Spring Road, Letchworth Garden City SG6 3SL Tel: 01462 682153 Email: elizabeth@scjm.org
Web: www. scjmangloirishprovince.co.uk
• Garden House Hospice

LIMEHOUSE + OUR LADY IMMACULATE AND ST FREDERICK A   S

Sunday Mass 12 noon; Mass in Word and Sign *2nd Sun only* 6pm *(not August)*; Holy Day Mass 7.15; Confession on request

Fr Keith Stoakes (also serves Poplar and is resident at Clergy House, 9 Pekin Street E14 6EZ Tel: 020 7987 4523)
Island Row, 636 Commercial Road E14 7HS
Email: limehouse@rcdow.org.uk Web: parish.rcdow.org.uk/limehouse
(A13), between Limehouse DLR Stn and Burdett Road
Tower Hamlets Deanery (1881; 1934; cons 17 October 1945)

LINCOLN'S INN FIELDS + ST ANSELM AND ST CECILIA

Sunday Mass (Sat 6pm), 10 (Family), 12noon (Sung Latin), 4pm (Filipino, *2nd Sun only*), 6pm; Holy Day Mass (Vigil 6pm), 12.30pm, 6pm (Sung); Weekday Mass Mon, Wed, Fri 12.30pm, 6pm, Tue, Thu 6pm; Exposition Mon-Sat 4-6pm; Confession Mon, Wed, Fri 12-12.20pm, Mon-Fri 5.30-5.50pm, Sat 5-5.40pm

Fr David Barnes, Mgr John Conneely (in residence)
70 Lincoln's Inn Fields WC2A 3JA Tel: 020 7405 0376
Email: lincolnsinnfields@rcdow.org.uk Web: parish.rcdow.org.uk/lincolnsinnfields
On east side of Kingsway, a few steps south of Holborn Stn (TfL)
Westminster Deanery (1687; 1909; cons November 1959)
Parish Administrator / Bookkeeper Mrs Mandy O'Sullivan-Whiting

• Hospital for Sick Children, Great Ormond Street
Chaplain Anne Marie O'Riordan Tel: 020 7813 8232
• National Hospital for Neurology & Neurosurgery
Chaplains Fr Peter Harries OP, Fr Serge Stasievich Tel: 020 3447 3007

LITHUANIAN CHURCH + ST CASIMIR A

Sunday Mass 10 (Lithuanian/English), 12noon (Lithuanian), 6pm (Lithuanian); Holy Day Mass 7pm; Weekday Mass 7pm; Confession (Lithuanian, Russian) daily before Mass & on request
Fr Petras Tverijonas, Fr Petras Gucevicius
21 The Oval, Hackney Road E2 9DT Tel: 020 7739 8735
Email: lithuanianchurch@rcdow.org.uk Web: www.londonas.co.uk
Tower Hamlets Deanery (1901; 1912)

LONDON COLNEY + OUR LADY, ST MARY OF WALSINGHAM A

Sunday Mass 11.30; Holy Day Mass as announced; Weekday Mass Mon 10, *Monthly* Wed 7pm as announced (in Radlett, see newsletter), Thu 10 ; Prayer Group Fri 8-9pm; Filipino Adorers *4th Fri only* 9pm-midnight; Confession Sun 11.10-11.25
Radlett: Sunday Mass 10; Holy Day Mass as announced; Weekday Mass Tue 10, *Monthly* Wed 7pm as announced; Confession Sun 9.30-9.50
Shenley: Sunday Mass (Sat 5pm); Holy Day Mass as announced; Weekday Mass Wed 9.30, *Monthly* 7pm as announced (in Radlett, see newsletter); Exposition Sat 4.15pm, with Benediction 4.50pm; Confession Sat 4.15-4.45pm

Fr Kevin Moule, Rev Tony Barter (Deacon), Rev Anthony Curran (Deacon) (clergy also serve Radlett and Shenley, Parish Priest is resident at 22 The Crosspath, Radlett WD7 8HN Tel: 01923 635541)
Haseldine Road, London Colney AL2 1RP
Email: radlett@rcdow.org.uk Web: parish.rcdow.org.uk/londoncolney
At junction of Haseldine Road and High Street,
St Albans Deanery (1959)
Parish Administrator Mrs Catherine King Tel: 01923 635541

MAIDEN LANE: *SEE COVENT GARDEN*

MANOR HOUSE + ST THOMAS MORE

Sunday Mass (Sat 6pm), 10 (Sung), 12noon (Sung), 5pm (Portuguese); Holy Day Mass 12.30pm; Weekday Mass Mon 9, Thu 12.30pm, Fri 9; Confession On request

Fr Clive Lee, Rev Kassa Tsegaye (Deacon, contact details below)
9 Henry Road N4 2LH Tel: 020 8802 9910
Email: manorhouse@rcdow.org.uk Web: parish.rcdow.org.uk/manorhouse
Off Portland Rise, south of Finsbury Park (near Manor House TfL Stn)
Hackney Deanery (1969; 1975)
(Rev Kassa Tsegaye Tel: 07930 416927)
Parish Administrator Ingrid Bowie

• Ursulines of Jesus Administration Flat 14 Kimpton Court, 2 Murrain Road N4 2BN
Tel: 020 8442 8800 Web: www.ursulinesjesus.org Sisters Flat 15 Kimpton Court, 2 Murrain Road N4 2BN Tel: 020 8800 4486

MARYLEBONE + OUR LADY OF THE ROSARY A

Sunday Mass (Sat 6pm), 8.30, 11 (Family), 6pm (Folk); Holy Day Mass 12.30pm, 6pm; Weekday Mass Mon-Sat 12.30pm; Exposition and Benediction Sat 5-5.30pm; Confession Sat 11-11.30, 5-5.30pm

Fr Michael Johnston
211 Old Marylebone Road NW1 5QT Tel: 020 7723 5101
Email: marylebone@rcdow.org.uk Web: parish.rcdow.org.uk/marylebone
South side of Old Marylebone Road, by junction with Marylebone Road
Marylebone Deanery (1855; 1963; cons 18 February 2006)
Parish Administrator Mrs Marion Egan

• Tyburn Convent (Adorers of the Sacred Heart OSB), 8 Hyde Park Place W2 2LJ
Tel: 020 7723 7262 Email: admin@tyburnconvent.org.uk
Web: www.tyburnconvent.org.uk
Perpetual Exposition of the Blessed Sacrament; chapel open daily 6.15(am)-8.30 pm
Sunday Mass 10, Weekday Mass Mon-Fri 7.30, Sat 10, Bank Holidays 10; Vespers 4.30pm
Chaplain Fr Brendan Carmody SJ
• St Mary's (Praed Street), Western Eye Hospital

Sunday Mass 11; Weekday Mass Thu 12.30pm
Chaplains Fr Giles Pinnock, Fr Blaise Amadi CM Tel 020 3312 1508
• Charter Nightingale Hospital

MILE END + THE GUARDIAN ANGELS

Sunday Mass (Sat 7.30pm), 9, 11, 6pm; Holy Day Mass (Vigil as announced), as on
weekdays; Weekday Mass Mon, Wed 9.30, Tue, Thu 9, Fri 7pm, Sat 12.30pm; Confession
Sat 11.30-12.15pm & on request

Fr John D A Elliott, Fr Bryan Jones (in residence), Rev Jeremy Yates (Deacon)
377 Mile End Road E3 4QS Tel: 020 8980 1845
Email: mileend@rcdow.org.uk Web: parish.rcdow.org.uk/mileend
Near Grove Road/Burdett Road junction; 2 mins from Mile End Stn (TfL)
Tower Hamlets Deanery (1868; 1901; cons 20 October 1927)

• Neo-Catechumenate Communities Paul Dennis Tel: 07855 826086
• Mile End Hospital & The Bancroft Unit, Pat Shaw House

MILL END (& MAPLE CROSS) + ST JOHN THE EVANGELIST

Sunday Mass (Sat 6pm), 10.30; Holy Day Mass as announced; Weekday Mass Mon, Wed
9.30; Exposition Sat 5.30-5.55pm; Confession on request & by appointment
Chorleywood: Sunday Mass (Sat 6pm), 9; Holy Day Mass as announced; Weekday Mass Tue,
Fri 9.30; Confession on request & by appointment
Rickmansworth: Sunday Mass 8.30, 11, 6pm; Holy Day Mass 9.30, 8pm; Weekday Mass Mon,
Tue, Thu, Fri 9.30, Sat 10; Exposition and Confession Sat 10.30-11.30

Fr Shaun Church, Fr Damian Ryan (clergy also serve Chorleywood and Rickmansworth
and are resident at 5 Park Road, Rickmansworth WD3 1HU Tel: 01923 773387)
Berry Lane, Rickmansworth WD3 7HG
Email: rickmansworth@rcdow.org.uk Web: parish.rcdow.org.uk/millend
Watford Deanery (1969; cons 30 April 2016))

MILL HILL + SACRED HEART AND MARY IMMACULATE

Sunday Mass (Sat 6pm), 8.30, 10 (Family), 11.30, 6pm; Holy Day Mass 10, 12.15pm,
7.30pm; Weekday Mass daily 10, also Mon 7.30pm; Exposition Mon 8-9pm, Wed, Thu
10.30-12noon, Sat 10.30-11.30; Confession Sat 10.30-11.30

Vincentians (CM) Fr Eugene Curran
2 Flower Lane NW7 2JB Tel: 020 8959 1021
Email: millhill@rcdow.org.uk   Web: www.shmi.info
The Broadway, just off Watford Way (A4) at Mill Hill Circus
Barnet Deanery (1889; 1922; cons 6 December 1923; 1995; cons 25 September 1996)
Community: Frs Eugene Curran (Superior), Akobundu Anywanwu, Raymond Armstrong,
Chinedu Enuh, Noel Travers
Parish Administrator Melanie Gibbons

• Daughters of Charity, Provincial House, The Ridgeway NW7 1RE Tel: 020 8906 3777
Email: secretariat@dcmillhill.org Web: www.daughtersofcharity.org.uk

• Franciscan Sisters of Mill Hill, St Mary's Convent, 118 Chalet Estate, Hammers Lane NW7 4DN Tel: 020 8959 1364 Email: osfsistersmillhill@gmail.com

MILLWALL + ST EDMUND

Sunday Mass (Sat 6pm), 9, 11; **Holy Day Mass** 9.15, 8pm; **Weekday Mass** Mon-Wed, Fri 9.15; **Holy Hour** with **Exposition** Sat 5pm; **Confession** Sat 5-5.45pm.

Priest in Charge Fr Christopher Silva
297 Westferry Road E14 3RS Tel: 020 7987 4114
Email: millwall@rcdow.org.uk Web: parish.rcdow.org.uk/millwall
Westferry Road
Tower Hamlets Deanery (1846; 1874; 2000; cons 22 September 2000)
Parish Secretary Katherine Woznicka
• Canary Wharf Catholic Chaplaincy, The Prayer Room, Unit 11, 2 Churchill Place E14 5RB Correspondence to 1 St Catherine's Apartments, 179a Bow Road E3 2SH
Web: www. cwcc.org.uk
Chaplain Mgr Vladimir Felzmann **Tel: 020 7477 1073 / 07810 116508**
Mass Tue 12.30pm

MOORFIELDS + ST MARY MOORFIELDS

Sunday Mass 9.30; **Holy Day Mass** (Vigil 7pm) 8.05, 12noon, 12.30 pm, 1.05pm, 5.30pm; **Weekday Mass** Mon-Fri 8.05, 1.05pm; **Exposition** as announced; **Confession** Mon-Fri 12.30-12.50pm, 1.30-1.50pm

Fr Christopher Vipers (also serves Bunhill Row)
4/5 Eldon Street EC2M 7LS Tel: 020 7247 8390
Email: moorfields@rcdow.org.uk Web: www.stmarymoorfields.net /
parish.rcdow.org.uk/moorfields
100 yards west of Liverpool Street Stn (BR/TfL); just before the Red Lion
Westminster Deanery (1710; 1903)

• St Bartholomew's Hospital Tel: 020 3416 5000
Chaplains Fr Rory Murphy IVD, Fr James McMahon OSB **Tel: 020 3465 7220**
Emails: Rory.Murphy3@nhs.net, James.McMahon2@nhs.net
Hospital Church of St Bartholomew the Less
Weekday Mass Thu 12.30pm

MUCH HADHAM: *SEE BISHOP'S STORTFORD*

MUSWELL HILL + OUR LADY OF MUSWELL A

Sunday Mass (Sat 6.30pm), 10, 11.45; **Holy Day Mass** 10, 7.30pm; **Weekday Mass** Mon-Thu, Sat 10, Fri 7.30pm; **Exposition** Sat 10.45-11.45; **Confession** Sat 10.45-11.45

Fr Mark Anwyll
1 Colney Hatch Lane N10 1PN Tel: 020 8883 5607 Fax: 020 8444 3464
Email: muswellhill@rcdow.org.uk Web: parish.rcdow.org.uk/muswellhill
Haringey Deanery (1917; 1938; cons 23 September 1959)

- Sisters of Marie Auxiliatrice, 20 Elgin Road N22 7UE Tel: 020 8881 8547
and Flats 8 and 15 The Paddock, Meadow Drive N10 1PL
- St Luke's Woodside Hospital

NEASDEN + ST PATRICK A

Sunday Mass (Sat 6.30pm), 9.30, 11.30; Holy Day Mass 9.30, 7.30pm; Weekday Mass 9.30 or as announced; Confession Sat 5.45-6.15pm

Fr Patrick McLoughlin
The Presbytery, Hardie Close NW10 0UH Tel: 020 8451 0367
Email: neasden@rcdow.org.uk Web: parish.rcdow.org.uk/neasden
Just off North Circular Road (A406), west side, adjacent to IKEA main entrance off Drury Way
Brent Deanery (1981)

- Little Aisha Nursery Tel: 020 8423 6353

NEW BARNET + MARY IMMACULATE AND ST PETER

Sunday Mass (Sat 6pm), 9.30, 11, 6pm; Holy Day Mass as announced; Weekday Mass Mon-Sat 9.30, preceded by Morning Prayer 9.10 & followed by Rosary; Exposition Fri 7-7.30pm; Confession Sat 10-10.30 & on request

Spiritans (CSSp) Fr James Ademola Fasakin, Fr Terkura Igbe (in residence, School Chaplain), Fr Dominic Alih
63 Somerset Road, New Barnet EN5 1RF Tel: 020 8449 1961
Email: newbarnet@rcdow.org.uk Web: www.stpetersnewbarnet.org.uk
Barnet Deanery (1912; 1938)
Parish Secretary Paula Lefevre
Parish Catechetical Co-ordinator Carol Ward

NEW SOUTHGATE + OUR LADY OF LOURDES A

Sunday Mass (Sat 6.30pm), 8.30, 9.45 (Choir), 11.15 (Family), 12.30pm, 6.30pm; Holy Day Mass 8, 10, 7.30pm; Weekday Mass Mon-Fri 8, 10, Sat 10; Exposition Fri 10.30-11, 7-8pm; Confession Sat 10.30-11, 5.30-6pm

Fr David Reilly, Fr Andrew Bowden, Fr Johnson Alexander (in residence, Keralan Chaplaincy), Rev Ian Coleman (Deacon)
373 Bowes Road N11 1AA Tel: 020 8368 1638
Email: newsouthgate@rcdow.org.uk Web: www.ourladynewsouthgate.org.uk
200 yards right from Arnos Grove Stn (TfL)
Enfield Deanery (1923; 1935; 1990)

- Congregation of Our Lady of the Missions, 2 Brookdale N11 1BL Tel: 020 8361 6848
- Sisters of St Louis, 16 Chaucer Close N11 1AU
Tel: 020 8617 0529 Email: philomenamorris@talktalk.net

SECTION 3

NORTHFIELDS (WEST EALING) + SS PETER AND PAUL A

Sunday Mass (Sat 6.30pm), 8.30, 10 (Family/Children's Liturgy), 11.30 (Sung), 6.30pm;
Sunday Mass (Sat 6.30pm), 8.30, 10 (Family/Children's Liturgy), 11.30 (Sung), 6.30pm;
Holy Day Mass 9.30, 8pm; **Weekday Mass** Mon-Wed, Fri, Sat 9.30, with **Rosary**;
Weekday Morning Prayer *(Advent & Lent only)* 9.15; **Holy Hour** Tue 10-11; **Confession**
Sat 10-10.30, 6-6.30pm

Fr Jim Duffy, Rev Andrew Goodall (Deacon)
38 Camborne Avenue W13 9QZ Tel: 020 8567 5421
Email: northfields@rcdow.org.uk   Web: parish.rcdow.org.uk/northfields
Off Northfield Avenue, 1/4 mile north of Northfields Stn
Ealing Deanery (1926; 1931; cons 29 October 1959)
Parish Administrator Rosa Bambury
Pastoral Assistant Anna Dupelycz **Email:** northfieldscat@rcdow.org.uk

• Medical Mission Sisters, 109 Clitherow Avenue W7 2BL Tel: 020 8567 1504
Email: unit.uk.office@gmail.com Web: www.medicalmissionsisters-uk.org
• Religious of the Sacred Heart of Mary, Provincial House, 54 Grange Road W5 5BX
Tel: 020 8567 7228 Web: www.rshm-nep.org
also **44 The Park** W5 5NP Tel: 020 8567 4722

NORTHOLT: *SEE HARROW SOUTH*

NORTHWOOD + ST MATTHEW

Sunday Mass (Sat 6pm), 9, 11.15, 6pm; **Holy Day Mass** Weekday Mass time and 7.30pm
as announced; **Weekday Mass** Mon, Tue 10, Thu 7.30, Fri 10, (10 Masses preceded by
Morning Prayer 9.45); **Exposition** Tue, Sat 10.30, with **Benediction** 11.15; **Confession**
Sat 10.30-11.15, 5-5.45pm & by appointment

Fr Brian O'Mahony
32 Hallowell Road, Northwood HA6 1DW Tel: 01923 840736
Email: northwood@rcdow.org.uk Web: parish.rcdow.org.uk/northwood
Off Green Lane (shopping centre); near Northwood Stn
Hillingdon Deanery (1924; cons 12 October 1954)
Administration Assistant Cheryl Myring
RE Co-ordinator Eileen O'Sullivan
Safeguarding Co-ordinator Peggy Lovett

• Society of African Missions (SMA) White House, Watford Road, Northwood HA6 3PW
Tel: 01923 828015
Frs Thyagu Arputham, Anthony Cussen
• Joint Support Unit, Northwood HQ, Mount Vernon Hospital, Bishops Wood Hospital,
Michael Sobell House

NOTTING HILL + ST FRANCIS OF ASSISI

Sunday Mass (Sat 6pm), 10, 11.30, 6pm; **Holy Day Mass** 9.30, 7pm; **Weekday Mass** Mon, Tue, Thu-Sat 9.30; **Rosary** Tue, Sat after Mass; **Exposition** Mon, Thu, Fri 10-11; **Confession** Sat 10-10.30

Fr Gerard Skinner
St Francis of Assisi Church, The Presbytery, Pottery Lane W11 4NQ Tel: 020 7727 7968
Email: nottinghill@rcdow.org.uk Web: www.stfrancisnottinghill.org.uk
North Kensington Deanery (1860)
Parish Administrator Paula Lopes McDermid Tel: 020 7727 7968

• Sisters of Jesus in the Temple, 28 Penzance Street W11 4QX Tel: 020 7603 3329

OGLE STREET + ST CHARLES BORROMEO

Sunday Mass (Sat 6pm, 8.15pm with Neo-Catechumenate), 9, 11; **Holy Day Mass** as weekday Mass; **Weekday Mass** Mon-Wed 12.30pm, Thu, Fri 6pm, for Bank Holidays see newsletter; **Confession** Daily after Mass & on request

Fr David Barrow, Fr Gary Walsh (in residence, Albanian Chaplaincy)
8 Ogle Street W1W 6HS Tel: 020 7636 2883
Email: oglestreet@rcdow.org.uk Web: oglestreetblog.wordpress.com
Off New Cavendish Street, near BT Tower
Marylebone Deanery (1862; cons 4 October 1921)
Parish Assistant Sr Pauline Forde DC
Neo-Catechumenate Communities Michael Anderson Tel: 020 7584 2579

• University Chaplaincy: see *University & Institutes of Higher Education* entry in this section
• Portland Hospital for Women & Children Tel: 020 7580 4400
Chaplains Fr Giles Pinnock, Fr Blaise Amadi CM Tel 020 3312 1508
• University College Hospital, including **Elizabeth Garrett Anderson Wing**
Sunday Mass 9.45; **Holy Day Mass** 1.30pm; **Weekday Mass** Mon-Thu 1.30pm, Fri 12.15pm
Chaplains Fr Peter Harries OP, Fr Serge Stasievich, Sr Pauline Forde DC
Tel: 020 3447 3007

OLD HALL GREEN & PUCKERIDGE + ST EDMUND OF CANTERBURY & ENGLISH MARTYRS

Sunday Mass (Sat 6pm, Puckeridge); 11.30 (Old Hall Green); **Holy Day Mass** 10.30 (Puckeridge); **Weekday Mass** Wed 10.30 (Puckeridge); **Confession** Sat 5.15-5.45pm (Puckeridge)
Buntingford: **Sunday Mass** 9.15 (with term time Children's Liturgy, *2nd & 4th Sun only*) ; **Holy Day Mass** 7pm; **Weekday Mass** Tue, Thu 9.30, Fri 10.30, with **Exposition** and **Benediction** 11-11.30, Sat 9.30; **Confession** Sat 10-11

Fr Cyril Chiaha (also serves Buntingford and is resident at **3 Station Road, Buntingford SG9 9HT** Tel: 01763 271471)
Email: oldhallgreen@rcdow.org.uk Web: parish.rcdow.org.uk/oldhallgreen

Old Hall Green + St Edmund and the English Martyrs

SECTION 3

To rear of St Edmund's College (off A10 as signposted)
Lea Valley Deanery (1769; 1818; new church cons 2 December 1911)

Puckeridge + St Thomas of Canterbury
Off the A10, at end of Puckeridge High Street (opposite school)
Lea Valley Deanery (1926)

• St Edmund's College, Old Hall Green, Ware SG11 1DS (1793; 1853) Tel: 01920 821504
Priest-in-Residence Fr Peter Lyness Tel: 01920 821504
Lay Chaplain Paula Pierce Tel: 01920 821334

ORATORY + IMMACULATE HEART OF MARY

Sunday Mass (Sat 6pm), 8, 9 (Low Mass), 10 (Sung English), 11 (Solemn Latin), 12.30pm, 4.30pm, 7pm; **Holy Day Mass** (Vigil 6.30pm), 7, 8 (Low Mass), 10, 12.30pm, 5.30pm, 6.30pm (Solemn Latin); **Weekday Mass** Mon-Fri 7, 8 (Low Mass, St Philip's Altar), 12.30pm, 6pm (Latin), Sat 7, 8 (Low Mass, St Philip's Altar), 10; **Sunday Vespers** and **Benediction** 3.30pm; **Holy Day Vespers** and **Benediction** (Vigil 5.30pm); **Benediction** Tue 6.30pm; **Holy Hour** Thu 6.30pm; **Confession** (French, German, Italian, Spanish) Sat 10-12.55pm, 3-6pm, Sun after each morning Mass, 6-6.50pm, Mon-Fri at all times except 12.30-3pm & 6-7.45pm

Fathers of the Oratory of St Philip Neri (Oratorians) Fr Michael Lang
The Oratory SW7 2RP Tel: 020 7808 0900 Fax 020 7584 1095
Email: oratory@rcdow.org.uk Web: www.bromptonoratory.co.uk
Beside V&A Museum at convergence of Brompton Road and Thurloe Place; near South Kensington Stn (TfL)
Kensington & Chelsea Deanery (1854; 1884; cons 16 April 1884)
Community: Frs Julian Large (Provost), Edward van den Bergh, George Bowen, Ronald Creighton-Jobe, Charles Dilke, Patrick Doyle, John Fordham, Michael Lang, Rupert McHardy
The Little Oratory: Exercises of the Brotherhood Sun 4.30pm

• Congregation of Our Lady (Canonesses of St Augustine), 51 Clareville Street SW7 5AX
Tel: 020 7370 6217 / 07365 270599 Email: mgabrielrobin@outlook.com
• More House, 53 Cromwell Road SW7 2EH Tel: 020 7584 2040 (Hostel); see also
University & Institutes of Higher Education entry in this section
• Brompton Hospital

OSTERLEY + ST VINCENT DE PAUL

Sunday Mass 9.30 (with term time Children's Liturgy), 11.30, 6pm; **Holy Day Mass** 9.30, 7.30pm; **Weekday Mass** Mon, Wed-Sat 9.30, Tue 7.30pm; **Morning Prayer** Mon, Wed-Sat 9.10; **Rosary** Mon, Wed, Thu, Fri after Mass, Tue 7pm before Mass; **Exposition** Sat 10-11 followed by **Benediction** at 11; **Confession** Sat 10-10.30 & on request

Fr Mark Leenane
2 Witham Road, Osterley, Isleworth TW7 4AJ Tel: 020 8560 4737
Email: osterley@rcdow.org.uk Web: parish.rcdow.org.uk/osterley
Between Eversley Crescent & Spring Grove Road
Hounslow Deanery (1934; cons 1936; 2004; cons 24 September 2005)

PADDINGTON + OUR LADY OF SORROWS A

Sunday Mass 9.30 **Holy Day Mass** as Weekday Mass (Mon, Fri at Harrow Road); **Weekday Mass** Tue, Thu, Sat 10; **Exposition** and **Benediction** Tue, Thu, Sat 9-10; **Confession** Sat 9-10 or on request

Fr Michael Jarmulowicz (also serves Harrow Road, resident at **Presbytery, 337 Harrow Road** W9 3RB Tel: 020 7286 2170)
17 Cirencester Street W2 5SR Tel: 020 7286 2672
Email: paddington@rcdow.org.uk Web: parish.rcdow.org.uk/paddington
Off Harrow Road, near Royal Oak Stn (TfL)
North Kensington Deanery (1912; cons 1998)
Parish Administrator Mrs Mandy O'Sullivan-Whiting **Thu 10-2pm**
Maronite Rite: Sunday Mass (Sat 7pm), 12.30pm, 7pm; **Weekday Mass** Wed, Fri 7pm (see *Lebanese Church* entry in this section)

PALMERS GREEN + ST MONICA

Sunday Mass (Sat 6pm), 7.45, 9, 10.30 (with Children's Liturgy), 12noon, 3.30pm (Polish), 5.30pm; **Holy Day Mass** 7, 9.30, 7.30pm; **Weekday Mass** 9.30 daily, preceded by **Morning Prayer** Mon-Fri 9.10, see weekly newsletter for other times; **Exposition** Sat 10-10.50, Mon, Wed 4-5pm, *First Fri only* 10-6.30pm; **Rosary Hour** Thu 7pm; **Saturday Rosary** Sat 9.10; **Confession** Sat 10-10.50, 5.15-5.45pm

Fr Mehall Lowry, Fr Stewart Hasker
(for Polish Chaplain, see details below)
The Presbytery, 1 Stonard Road N13 4DJ Tel: 020 8886 9568
Email: palmersgreen@rcdow.org.uk Web: www.stmonica.co.uk
Enfield Deanery (1910; 1914; cons 6 October 1985)
Parish Sister Sr Joyce Dionne, Daughters of Providence (St Brieuc) **c/o The Presbytery**
Youth Programme Co-ordinator Anna McMullan
Parish Centre, Cannon House, Cannon Hill N14 7HG

• **Polish Chaplain** Fr Maciej Michałek **c/o Holy Family Convent, 52 London Road, Enfield EN2 6EN** Email: jeszuam@interia.pl
• Grovelands Priory Psychiatric Hospital

PARSONS GREEN + HOLY CROSS

Sunday Mass (Sat 6.30pm), 9.30 (Family), 11.30 (**Sunday Mass in August** (Sat 6.30pm), 10.30); **Holy Day Mass** as announced; **Weekday Mass** 9.30 (except Wed), with **Morning Prayer** 9.15, *1st Sat only* 9.30, then **Exposition** and **Benediction**; **Confession** Sat 5.45-6.15pm & on request

Fr Michael Daley, Fr Tibor Borovsky (in residence, Slovak and Czech Chaplaincy)
22 Cortayne Road SW6 3QA Tel: 020 7736 1068
Email: parsonsgreen@rcdow.org.uk

SECTION 3

Web: http://www.holycrosschurchparsonsgreen.org.uk
Ashington Road off New Kings Road, opposite Munster Road; between Parsons Green & Putney Bridge Stns (TfL)
Hammersmith & Fulham Deanery (1843; 1884; 1924; cons 11 October 1928)
Parish Administrator Mrs Annie D'Souza, Office Hours 8.30–1.30pm Mon-Fri (except Wed)

Catechetical Co-ordinator / Pastoral Assistant Mrs Alexandra Fisher

PERIVALE + ST JOHN FISHER

Sunday Mass (Sat 6.30pm), 9.30 (Family), 11.30, 6.30pm; **Holy Day Mass** (Vigil 7.30pm), 10; **Weekday Mass** Mon, Tue, Thu, Fri 10; **Exposition** Mon 10.30, Sat 5-6pm; **Confession** Sat 5.15-5.45pm & on request

Fr Agustin Conesa
41/42 Langdale Gardens, Perivale, Greenford UB6 8DQ Tel/Fax: 020 8997 3164
Email: perivale@rcdow.org.uk   Web: parish.rcdow.org.uk/perivale
On north side of Western Avenue (A40), just past the Hoover building
Ealing Deanery (1936; 1970)
Parish Office Manager Mrs Ana Hains (Mon 9:30-2:30pm, Tue 10:30-3:30pm, Wed-Fri 9:30-2:30pm)

PIMLICO + HOLY APOSTLES A

Sunday Mass (Sat 6pm), 9, 10.30 (Family), 12.30pm (Spanish) **Albanian Sunday Mass** 3 pm, *every 2 weeks*; **Holy Day Mass** (Vigil 7pm), 10, 7pm; **Weekday Mass** 9.30 (10 if a funeral); **Exposition** Wed 10-11, Sat 5-5.45pm; **Confession** Sat 5-5.30pm & by appointment

Canon Pat Browne, Fr Charles Soyombo (in residence)
47 Cumberland Street SW1V 4LY Tel: 020 7834 6965 Fax: 020 7821 8609
Email: pimlico@rcdow.org.uk   Web: www.holyapostlespimlico.org
Winchester Street off Lupus Street, near Pimlico Stn (TfL)
Westminster Deanery (1917; 1957; cons 10 May 1974)
Parish Sister Sr Louise Callan DC

• Franciscan Sisters of the Heart of Jesus, 9-11 St George's Drive SW1V 4DJ
Tel: 020 7834 4020 (Convent) 020 7834 5356 (Hostel) Fax: 020 7976 6862
Email: fransisuk09@gmail.com
• Sisters of Notre Dame de Namur, Bella Best House, 5B Westmoreland Terrace SW1V 4AW Web: sndden.org
• Apostleship of the Sea, 39 Eccleston Square SW1V 1PX Tel: 020 7901 1931
Email: info@apostleshipofthesea.org.uk Web: www.apostleshipofthesea.org.uk
• Catholic Bishops' Conference of England and Wales, 39 Eccleston Square SW1V 1BX
Tel: 020 7630 8220 Fax: 020 7901 4820 Email: secretariat@cbcew.org.uk
• Missio (APF), 23 Eccleston Square SW1V 1NU Tel: 020 7821 9755
Fax: 020 7630 8466 Email: director@missio.org.uk

PINNER + ST LUKE

Sunday Mass (Sat 6pm), 9, 11; **Holy Day Mass** (Vigil 7.30pm), 10; **Weekday Mass** Mon-Fri 10; **Exposition** Tue 9.30-10; **Confession** Sat 11-11.30, 4.30-5pm

Canon Robert Plourde
28 Love Lane, Pinner HA5 3EX Tel: 020 8866 0098
Email: pinner@rcdow.org.uk Web: parish.rcdow.org.uk/pinner
In town centre, 3 mins from Pinner Stn (TfL), off Bridge Street
Harrow Deanery (1914; 1957)
Parish Secretary Mrs Pat Williams (Mon-Fri 8.30-1pm)
Pastoral Assistant (**Catechetics**) Norah O'Hare Tel: 020 8866 0098 ext. 3
Pastoral Outreach Worker Mariola Griffiths Tel: 020 8866 0098 ext. 4

• Daughters of Charity, 43 High Street, Pinner HA5 5PJ
Tel: 020 8866 4442 Email: pinnerdcs@hotmail.com
• Diocesan Centre for Youth Ministry, 125 Waxwell Lane, Pinner HA5 3EP
Tel: 020 3757 2516 Email: youth@rcdow.org.uk Web: http://dowym.com
(see under *Westminster Youth Ministry*, Section 2)
• SPEC, Waxwell House, 125 Waxwell Lane, Pinner HA5 3EP
Tel: 020 3757 2500 Email: spec@rcdow.org.uk
Diocesan Retreat Centre for Young People (see under *Westminster Youth Ministry*, Section 2)

POLISH CHURCH 1 + OUR LADY OF CZESTOCHOWA AND ST CASIMIR A

Sunday Mass (Sat 6pm), 9, 11, 12.30pm, 3.30pm, 7pm; **Holy Day Mass** 10.30, 7pm
Weekday Mass Mon-Fri 10.30, 7pm, Sat 7.30; **Confession** 30 min before Mass

Fr Bogdan Kołodziej, Fr Leszek Buba
2 Devonia Road N1 8JJ Tel: 020 7226 9944 Fax: 020 7359 8042
Email: polishchurch1@rcdow.org.uk Web: www.parafia-devonia.org.uk
Near Angel TfL Station
Islington Deanery (1905; 1930)
Parish Office Tue-Fri 5-6pm
• Polish Catholic Mission, 4 Devonia Road N1 8JJ
Tel: 020 7226 3439 Fax 020 7226 7677
Mgr Stefan Wylezek (Vicar Delegate), Canon Krzysztof Tyliszczak (Chancellor), Mgr Janusz Tworek (Financial Administrator)

POLISH CHURCH 2 + ST ANDREW BOBOLA

Sunday Mass (Sat 6pm), 8.30, 10, 12noon, 6pm; **Holy Day Mass** 10, 12noon, 7pm;
Weekday Mass 10, 7pm; **Confession** Mon-Fri 9.30-10, 6.30-7pm, Thu 7.30-9pm, Sat 5-6pm

Fr Marek Reczek
1 Leysfield Rd W12 9JF Tel: 020 8743 8848
Email: polishchurch2@rcdow.org.uk Web: www.bobola.church
Hammersmith & Fulham Deanery (1961)

POLISH CHURCH 3 + OUR LADY MOTHER OF THE CHURCH

Sunday Mass (Sat 7pm), 8.30, 10 (Family), 11.30, 1pm, 2.30pm (*Seasonal from Sep-Jun*) 5.15pm, 7pm (Youth), 8.30pm; **Weekday Mass** 8 (Latin), 10, 3.30pm *English on 1st Fri,* 7pm

Marian Fathers (MIC) Fr Michał Kozak, Fr Wiktor Gumienny, Fr Dariusz Mazewski, Fr Klaudiusz Rokicki, Fr Piotr Szyperski
2 Windsor Road W5 5PD Tel: 020 8567 1746
Email: polishchurch3@rcdow.org.uk Web: www.parafiaealing.co.uk
Ealing Deanery (1986)

• Sisters of the Holy Name of Jesus, 57 Mount Park Road W5 2PU Tel: 020 8997 2030
Sunday Mass (Sat 5pm, Polish)
• Sisters of the Resurrection, 84 Gordon Road W5 2AR Tel: 020 8998 8954
Weekday Mass Mon-Fri 7.30
• Divine Mercy Apostolate: see *Ealing* parish entry
• Kolbe House (Nursing Home) 18 Hanger Lane W5 3HH Tel: 020 8992 4978
Sunday Mass (Sat 4.30pm)

PONDERS END + CHURCH OF MARY, MOTHER OF GOD   A

Sunday Mass (Sat 6pm), 8, 9.30 (Family), 11 (Sung), 12.30pm (Italian), 6pm; **Holy Day Mass** 9.30, 12.30pm, 8pm; **Weekday Mass** Mon, Tue, Wed, Thu, Sat 9.30, Fri 7.30pm; **Confession** Sat 10-11

Fr John B. Shewring
192 Nags Head Road, Enfield EN3 7AR
Tel: 020 8804 2149 / 07973 539907 Fax: 020 8804 2749
Email: pondersend@rcdow.org.uk Web: www.marymotherofgod.church
Enfield Deanery (1912; 1921; cons 8 September 1985)
Parish Administrator Dorothy Eribankya Tel: 020 8804 2149

• Italian Catholic Centre
Fr Antonio Serra 197 Durants Road, Enfield EN3 7DE Tel: 020 8804 2307

POPLAR + SS MARY AND JOSEPH   S

Sunday Mass (Sat 6pm), 10; **Holy Day Mass** (Vigil 7pm), 10; **Weekday Mass** Mon-Thu 9.30, Fri 9.45 (may vary); **Confession** Sat 5.15pm

Fr Keith Stoakes (also serves Limehouse)
Clergy House, 9 Pekin Street E14 6EZ Tel: 020 7987 4523
Email: poplar@rcdow.org.uk Web: parish.rcdow.org.uk/poplar
Church at junction of Upper North Street and Canton Street
Tower Hamlets Deanery (1816; 1856; 1954; new church cons 12 October 1960)
• Faithful Companions of Jesus, The Lodge, Hale Street E14 0BS
Tel: 020 7517 9599 Email: nip65@msn.com Web: www.fcjsisters.org

POTTERS BAR + OUR LADY & ST VINCENT

Sunday Mass (Sat 6pm), 9, 11 (with Children's Liturgy) (**Sunday Mass August** (Sat 6pm), 10); **Holy Day Mass** (Vigil 7.30pm), 7, 10; **Weekday Mass** 10 as announced; **Confession** Sat 5.15– 5.45pm, Advent & Lent 10.30 – 11.30 (with **Exposition)**

Canon Shaun Lennard, Rev Donal Hopkins (Deacon, sabbatical), Rev Axcel Soriano (Transitional Deacon)
243 Mutton Lane, Potters Bar EN6 2AT Tel: 01707 654359
Email: pottersbar@rcdow.org.uk Web: www.olasv.org.uk
Enfield Deanery (2006; 2006)
Catechetical Co-ordinator Mrs Francesca Khaliq **Email:** pottersbarcat@rcdow.org.uk
Parish Safeguarding Representative Michael Sibley

• Sisters of Charity of St Jeanne Antide, 1a The Avenue, Potters Bar EN6 1EG
Tel: 01707 645901 Email: paxirene@live.co.uk
• Potters Bar District Hospital

QUEENSWAY + OUR LADY, QUEEN OF HEAVEN

Sunday Mass (Sat 5.30pm), 10, 11.30, 1pm (Ethiopian, Gheez rite); **Holy Day Mass** 9.30, 6pm; **Weekday Mass** Mon 6pm, Tue, Wed 9.30, Fri 6pm; **Holy Hour** Sat 4.15-5.15pm; **Confession** Sat 4.15-5.15pm & on request

Fr Saviour Grech
4a Inverness Place W2 3JF Tel: 020 7229 8153
Email: queensway@rcdow.org.uk Web: parish.rcdow.org.uk/queensway
Queensway, opposite Bayswater Stn (TfL); close to Queensway Stn (TfL)
North Kensington Deanery (1954; 1973; cons 21 April 2002)

• Prelature of Opus Dei, 4 Orme Court W2 4RL Tel: 020 7229 7574
Mgr Nicholas Morrish (Regional Vicar), Frs Peter Bristow, Paul Hayward, Gerard Sheehan, Andrew Soane

RADLETT + ST ANTHONY OF PADUA, AND SHENLEY + THE GOOD SHEPHERD

Radlett: Sunday Mass 10; **Holy Day Mass** as announced; **Weekday Mass** Tue 10; *Monthly* Wed 7pm as announced (see newsletter); **Confession** Sun 9.30-9.50

Shenley: Sunday Mass (Sat 5pm); **Holy Day Mass** as announced; **Weekday Mass** Wed 9.30; *Monthly* 7pm as announced (in Radlett, see newsletter); **Exposition** Sat 4.15pm, with **Benediction** 4.50pm; **Confession** Sat 4.15-4.45pm

London Colney: **Sunday Mass** 11.30; **Holy Day Mass** as announced; **Weekday Mass** Mon 10, *Monthly* Wed evening as announced (in Radlett, see newsletter), Thu 10; **Prayer Group** Fri 8-9pm; **Filipino Adorers** *4th Fri only* 9pm-midnight; **Confession** Sun 11.10-11.25

Fr Kevin Moule, Rev Tony Barter (Deacon), Rev Anthony Curran (Deacon) (clergy also serve London Colney)
22 The Crosspath, Radlett WD7 8HN Tel: 01923 635541

+ St Anthony of Padua
Email: radlett@rcdow.org.uk   Web: parish.rcdow.org.uk/radlett
St Albans Deanery (1905; new church 1910)
+ The Good Shepherd, Black Lion Hill, Shenley WD7 9DH
Email: radlett@rcdow.org.uk   Web: parish.rcdow.org.uk/shenley
St Albans Deanery (1969; 1976)
Parish Administrator Mrs Catherine King Tel: 01923 635541

REDBOURN (FLAMSTEAD AND MARKYATE) + ST JOHN FISHER

Sunday Mass (Sat 5.30pm), 9; **Holy Day Mass** as announced; **Weekday Mass** as announced; **Confession** Sat 9.45-10.15, 5.45-6.15pm

Fr Michael Mannion (also serves Wheathampstead)
1 Peppard Close, Redbourn, St Albans AL3 7EB Tel: 01582 792270
Email: redbourn@rcdow.org.uk Web: parish.rcdow.org.uk/redbourn
Dunstable Road, north of the village on the old A5
St Albans Deanery (1936; 1967; cons 22 June 2003)

RICKMANSWORTH + OUR LADY HELP OF CHRISTIANS

Sunday Mass 8.30, 11, 6pm; **Holy Day Mass** 9.30, 8pm; **Weekday Mass** Mon, Tue, Thu, Fri 9.30, Sat 10; **Exposition** and **Confession** Sat 10.30-11.30

Chorleywood: **Sunday Mass** (Sat 6pm), 9; **Holy Day Mass** as announced; **Weekday Mass** Tue, Fri 9.30; **Confession** on request & by appointment

Mill End: **Sunday Mass** (Sat 6pm), 10.30; **Holy Day Mass** as announced; **Weekday Mass** Mon, Wed 9.30; **Exposition** Sat 5.30-5.55pm; **Confession** on request & by appointment

Fr Shaun Church, Fr Damian Ryan (clergy also serve Chorleywood and Mill End)
5 Park Road, Rickmansworth WD3 1HU Tel: 01923 773387
Email: rickmansworth@rcdow.org.uk Web: parish.rcdow.org.uk/rickmansworth
On main road beside roundabout at bottom of Scots Hill (east end of High Street)
Watford Deanery (1886; 1909)

ROYSTON + ST THOMAS OF CANTERBURY AND THE ENGLISH MARTYRS A

Sunday Mass (Sat 6.30pm), 9, 10.30; **Holy Day Mass** 9.15, 7.30pm; **Weekday Mass** Tue 7.30pm Wed-Fri 9.15; **Confession** Sat 5.45pm & by appointment, with **Exposition** from 5.30pm

Fr Philip Knights
6 Melbourn Road, Royston SG8 7DB Tel: 01763 243117
Email: royston@rcdow.org.uk Web: www.roystoncatholicchurch.co.uk
Left side of A10 just beyond central roundabout, towards Cambridge
Stevenage Deanery (1911; 1917)

• Sisters of Providence (of the Immaculate Conception), Providence House, 4 Melbourn Road, Royston SG8 7DB Tel: 01763 250956 Email: providencemarian@yahoo.co.uk

RUISLIP + MOST SACRED HEART

Sunday Mass (Sat 6pm), 8.30, 10 (Family), 11.30 (Sung), 6pm; **Holy Day Mass** (Vigil 8pm), 8, 10, 8pm; **Weekday Mass** 10 and as announced; **Exposition** Mon-Fri 10.30-11, Sat 10.30-12noon; **Confession** Sat 10.30-11.30, 5.15-5.30pm

Fr Duncan Adamson, Fr Sebastian Joseph
73 Pembroke Road, Ruislip HA4 8NN Tel: 01895 632739
Email: ruislip@rcdow.org.uk Web: parish.rcdow.org.uk/ruislip
Ruislip Manor, near traffic lights; near Ruislip Manor Stn; 1/3 mile Ruislip Stn
Hillingdon Deanery (1921; new church cons 15 June 1939)
Administrator Mrs Anne O'Connor
Catechetical Co-ordinator Mrs Jo Marsh Tel: 01895 673983
Parish Youth Worker Siobhan Denny

RUISLIP SOUTH + ST GREGORY THE GREAT A

Sunday Mass (Sat 5.30pm), 10 (Sung), 6pm; **Holy Day Mass** 10, 8pm; **Weekday Mass** 10 (except Thu); **Exposition** Sat 10.30-11; **Confession** Sat 10.30-11, 6.30-7pm

Mgr Canon Paul McGinn *(to 31/12/2019);* awaiting appointment
447 Victoria Road, South Ruislip HA4 0EG Tel: 020 8845 2186
Email: ruislipsouth@rcdow.org.uk Web: www.st-gregory.org.uk
Corner of Angus Drive, near South Ruislip shops/Stn
Hillingdon Deanery (1958; 1967; cons 1 November 1975)
Pastoral Assistant Sr Joanna Whooley RSHM
Parish Administrator Gillian Harrington

ST ALBANS + SS ALBAN AND STEPHEN A

Sunday Mass (Sat 6pm), 8, 9.30, 11.30, 7pm; **Holy Day Mass** (Vigil 7pm) 10, 7pm; **Weekday Mass** Mon-Fri 10, Mon, Wed, Fri 7pm; **Confession** Sat 10.30-11.30, 6.45-7pm
Mass at St Albans Abbey, in the Lady Chapel Fri 12noon

Fr Michael O'Boy, Fr Julian Davies, Rev Steve Pickard (Deacon)
14 Beaconsfield Road, St Albans AL1 3RB Tel: 01727 853585
Email: stalbans@rcdow.org.uk Web: www.albanstephen.com
Close to St Albans City Stn
St Albans Deanery (1840; 1904; cons 1977)
Mass Centre, Marshalswick (St John Fisher School)
Sunday Mass 9

ST ALBANS SOUTH + ST BARTHOLOMEW

Sunday Mass (Sat 6pm), 8.30, 10.30; **Holy Day Mass** as announced; **Weekday Mass** Mon 12noon, Tue, Wed 9, Fri 9.30, Sat 9; **Exposition** Sat 9.30-10; **Confession** Sat 9.30-10, 5.15-5.45pm & by appointment
Mass at St Albans Abbey, in the Lady Chapel Fri 12noon

Fr Francis Antwi-Darkwah, Rev Justin Cross (Deacon)
47 Vesta Avenue, St Albans AL1 2PE Tel: 01727 850066
Email: stalbanssouth@rcdow.org.uk Web: parish.rcdow.org.uk/stalbanssouth
On Watling Street (A5183), just above the North Orbital Road/A414 roundabout
St Albans Deanery (1959; cons 9 November 1985)

• Brothers of the Sacred Heart, Watling House, 8 King Harry Lane, St Albans AL3 4AW
Tel: 01727 861969
Brs Nelson Dionne, Clement Pelletier, Daniel St Jacques, Paul Vaillancourt (Superior)

ST CHARLES SQUARE (NORTH KENSINGTON) + ST PIUS X

Sunday Mass (Sat 6pm), 9, 11; **Holy Day Mass** 8.20, 12.30pm; **Weekday Mass** Mon-Fri
8.20, preceded by **Morning Prayer** 8.05; **Confession** Sat 5.15-5.45pm

Fr Peter Wilson, Fr Brian Creak (in residence, University Chaplain, contact details below)
79 St Charles Square W10 6EB Tel: 020 8969 6844 Fax: 020 8960 6589
Email: stcharlessquare@rcdow.org.uk Web: parish.rcdow.org.uk/stcharlessquare
West of Ladbroke Grove, just north of Stn (TfL) & motorway bridge
North Kensington Deanery (1937; 1955)
(Fr Brian Creak Tel: 020 8968 3373)
Fr Gerard O'Brien in residence at 81 St Charles Square W10 6EB Tel: 020 8525 3032

• Carmelite Nuns, Monastery of the Most Holy Trinity, 87 St Charles Square W10 6EA
Tel: 020 8969 8702 Email: carmelnottinghill@talktalk.net
Web: carmelitesnottinghill.org.uk Chaplain Fr Marcus Winter Tel: 020 3673 9540
Daily Mass 8.15
• Little Sisters of Jesus, 41 Bonchurch Road W10 5NN Tel: 020 8960 0440
• Princess Louise Home
• St Charles Square Centre for Health and Wellbeing (Mental Health Units)
Tel: 020 8969 2488
• St Charles Square Palliative Care, Pembridge Hospice

ST JOHN'S WOOD + OUR LADY A

Sunday Mass (Sat 6pm), 9 (Sung), 10.30 (Solemn Sung Latin, Choir), 12noon (Sung,
Choir), 6pm; **Holy Day Mass** 6.30(am), 10, 7.30pm; **Weekday Mass** Mon-Wed 10, Thu
7pm, Fri-Sat 10; **Exposition** Mon-Sat 6(am)-Midnight; **Confession** Sat 10.30-11, 5.15-
5.45pm & by arrangement
Our Lady Queen of the World: see below

Fr Kevin Jordan, Fr Benjamin Woodley
54 Lodge Road NW8 8LA Tel: 020 7286 3214
Email: stjohnswood@rcdow.org.uk Web: www.rcsjw.org.uk
Top of Lisson Grove, close to junction with St John's Wood Road (by Lords Cricket Ground)
Marylebone Deanery (1833; 1836; cons 14 May 1925)
Catechetical Co-ordinator Margaret Wickware **Email:** margaretwickware@rcdow.org.uk
Parish Administrator Hantanirina Lessore **Email:** stjohnswood@rcdow.org.uk
Parish Sister Sr Brigid Collins RSM

• Handmaids of the Sacred Heart of Jesus, 25 St Edmund's Terrace NW8 7PY
Tel: 020 7722 2756 Email: provincialsec@aol.com Web: http://aciengland.org
Chapel of Our Lady, Queen of the World: Holy Day Mass as announced; Weekday Mass
Mon-Fri 8; Exposition daily 8.30-12noon

• Mercy Union Generalate, 11 Harewood Avenue NW1 6LD Tel: 020 7723 2527
9 Wimborne House, Harewood Avenue NW1 6NU Tel: 020 7723 4794
39 Alma Square NW8 9PY Tel: 020 7289 3657
91 Ashmill Street NW1 6RA

• Redemptoris Mater House of Formation, St Edward's Convent, 11 Harewood Avenue
NW1 6LD Tel: 020 7723 9364 Fax: 020 7258 3914 Email: rmhf.lnd@gmail.com
Fr Lorenzo Andreini

• Hospital of St John & St Elizabeth, 60 Grove End Road NW8 9NH Tel: 020 7806 4000
Chaplain Fr Hugh MacKenzie
Hospital chapel (Church of St John of Jerusalem)
Sunday Mass 11; Weekday Mass Tue 11

• Wellington Hospital Tel: 020 7586 5959
Chaplains Fr Giles Pinnock, Fr Blaise Amadi CM Tel 020 3312 1508

ST MARGARETS-ON-THAMES + ST MARGARET OF SCOTLAND

Sunday Mass (Sat 6.30pm), 8.30, 10.30, 6.30pm; Holy Day Mass 7.15, 10, 8pm; Weekday
Mass Mon-Wed, Fri, Sat 10; Confession Sat 10.30-11, Sun 10-10.20

Canon Peter Newby, Rev Joseph Estorninho (Deacon)
130 St Margarets Road, Twickenham TW1 1RL Tel: 020 8892 3902
Email: stmargaretsonthames@rcdow.org.uk Web: www. stmargarets-church.co.uk
Opposite St Margarets Stn (BR); close to Chertsey Road (A316) and Richmond Road (A305)
Upper Thames Deanery (1930; 1969)
Parish Administrator Jean McGinley

SAWBRIDGEWORTH: SEE BISHOP'S STORTFORD

SHENLEY + THE GOOD SHEPHERD: SEE RADLETT

SHEPHERDS BUSH + THE HOLY GHOST AND ST STEPHEN A

Sunday Mass (Sat 6pm), 9.15, 11 (Family), 12.30pm; Holy Day Mass 9.30, 8pm; Weekday
Mass Mon, Tue 9.30, Wed 7, Thu 7pm; Fri, Sat 9.30; Exposition Sat 10-10.45, with
Benediction; Confession Sat 10.15-10.45, 5.15-5.45pm

Fr Mark Vickers
44 Ashchurch Grove W12 9BU Tel: 020 8743 5196
Email: shepherdsbush@rcdow.org.uk Web: www.rcshepherdsbush.org
Off Askew Road, near junction with Goldhawk Road; nearest Stn Stamford Brook (TfL)
Hammersmith & Fulham Deanery (1889; 1904; cons 24 April 1936)

• Franciscan Missionaries of Mary (Provincialate), 5 Vaughan Avenue W6 0XS
Tel: 020 8748 4077 Email: provsecuk@aol.com Web: www.fmmii.org

SHEPPERTON + ST JOHN FISHER

Sunday Mass (Sat 6pm), 8.30, 10.30; **Holy Day Mass** 9.30, 7pm; **Weekday Mass** Tue-Fri 9.30, Sat 10; **Rosary** Wed after Mass; **Exposition** Fri after Mass; **Confession** Sat 5.30pm

Fr Shaun Richards

15 Wood Road, Shepperton TW17 0DH Tel: 01932 563116
Email: shepperton@rcdow.org.uk Web: www.sjfchurch.org.uk /
parish.rcdow.org.uk/shepperton
In Shepperton Green (sign on Shepperton-Staines road)
Upper Thames Deanery (1936; 1965)
Parish Administrator Nathalie Hasted **Email:** shepperton@rcdow.org.uk
Parish Bookkeeper Tracy Blundell **Email:** sheppertonbookkeeper@rcdow.org.uk

SOHO SQUARE + ST PATRICK

Sunday Mass (Sat 6pm), 11, 5pm, 6pm (Spanish); **Holy Day Mass** 8, 12.30pm, 1.05pm, 6pm; **Weekday Mass** Mon-Fri 12.45pm; **Exposition** Mon-Fri 1.30-6pm, Sat 7-9pm; **Confession** Mon-Fri 12.15-12.40pm, Sat 5.30-6pm

Canon Alexander Sherbrooke

21a Soho Square W1D 4NR Tel: 020 7437 2010
Email: sohosquare@rcdow.org.uk Web: www.stpatrickssoho.org
Near junction of Oxford Street and Charing Cross Road, south of Tottenham Court Road TfL Stn
Westminster Deanery (1792; 1893)
Parish Sister Sr Mary Kenefick SMG

• **Latin American Chaplaincy** Fr Carlos Abajos Eguileta Tel: 020 7820 1697
• **Shalom Catholic Community at St Patrick's**
Missionaries Emanuela Cardoso, Francisca de Fatima de Oliveira
Tel: 07432 501250 Email: london@comshalom.org Web: http://www.comshalom.org/en
• **SOS Prayer Line** Tel: 020 7434 9211
• **St Patrick's School of Evangelisation (SPES)** 21a Soho Square W1D 4NR
Tel: 020 7434 9965 Email: spes@stpatrickssoho.org Web: www.stpatrickssoho.org

SOMERS TOWN + ST ALOYSIUS A

Sunday Mass (Sat 6pm), 9.30, 11.30, 6pm; **Holy Day Mass** 7.30, 9.30, 12.30pm, 6pm; **Weekday Mass** Mon, Tue, Thu, Fri 9.30; **Confession** Sat 5pm & by appointment

Fr Jeremy Trood, Mgr James Overton (in residence), Fr Mark Walker (in residence, Diocesan Youth Chaplain)
20 Phoenix Road NW1 1TA Tel: 020 7387 1971
Email: somerstown@rcdow.org.uk Web: parish.rcdow.org.uk/somerstown
Off Eversholt Street, east of Euston Stn
Camden Deanery (1798; 1808; 1968; cons 24 May 1992)

• Faithful Companions of Jesus, 32 Phoenix Road NW1 1TA
Tel: 020 3435 8049 Email: fcjcommunity@fcjhouse-somerstown.co.uk

Web: www.fcjsisters.org
FCJ Spirituality Centre Email: enquiries.fcjcentre@fcjhouse-somerstown.co.uk
Web: www.fcjsisters.org/spirituality-centre-london
• Poor Servants of the Mother of God, St Philomena's Convent, 70-71 Euston Square
NW1 1DJ Tel: 020 7387 5855 Email: mary.kenefick@psmgs.org.uk /
frances.ennis@psmgs.org.uk Web: www.poorservants.org
• St Pancras Hospital (Evergreen, Rochester and Oakwood Wards)
Chaplains: Fr Peter Harries OP, Fr Serge Stasievich Tel: 020 3447 3007

SOUTHALL + ST ANSELM

Sunday Mass (Sat 6.30pm), 8, 9.45, 11.30, 6.30pm; Holy Day Mass 9.15, 12.15pm, 7.30pm;
Weekday Mass Mon-Fri 9.15; Holy Hour Sun 4.30pm; Novena Sun 5.30pm; Confession
Sat 11-12noon
Ethnic Chaplaincy Masses: Sri Lankan (Tamil) 1st Sun 2pm; Konkani (Goan) 3rd Sat
4pm; Malayalam 3rd Sun 3pm; Urdu last Sun 3pm

Jesuits (SJ) Fr Gerard Mitchell, Fr George Stephen Thayriam;
Rev Stephen Khokhar (Deacon)
St Anselm's Rectory, The Green, Southall UB2 4BE
Tel: 020 8574 3300 Fax: 020 8813 8784
Email: southall@rcdow.org.uk Web: stanselmchurchsouthall.com
To the south of Southall Stn (BR), opposite Osterley Park Road
Ealing Deanery (1906; 1930; 1968)
Parish Evanglisation Co-ordinator Susan Cawley Email susancawley@rcdow.org.uk

• Missionaries of Charity, 41 Villiers Road, Southall UB1 3BS Tel: 020 8574 1892

SPANISH PLACE + ST JAMES A

Sunday Mass (Sat 6pm), 8.30, 9.30 (Extraordinary Form), 10.30 (Sung Latin), 12noon,
4pm, 7pm; Holy Day Mass 7.15, 11 (Extraordinary Form), 12.30pm, 6pm, 7pm; Weekday
Mass Mon-Fri 7.15, 12.30pm, 6pm, Sat 10; Holy Hour Sat 4.45pm; Confession Mon-Fri
12-1pm; Sat 10.30-12noon, 5-5.45pm & on request

Fr Christopher Colven, Canon Stuart Wilson (contact details below), Fr Mark Elliott-Smith
(in residence, Ordinariate), Fr Hugh MacKenzie (in residence)
22 George Street W1U 3QY Tel: 020 7935 0943
Email: spanishplace@rcdow.org.uk Web: www.sjrcc.org.uk
Bottom of Marylebone High Street; Baker Street or Bond Street TfL Stns
Marylebone Deanery (1791; 1890; cons 28 April 1949)
(Canon Wilson, Vocations Promoter Tel: 07515 065696)

• University College on Westmoreland Street
Chaplains: Fr Peter Harries OP, Fr Serge Stasievich Tel: 020 3447 3007
• London Clinic, King Edward VII Hospital for Officers
• Harley Street Clinic
Chaplains Fr Giles Pinnock, Fr Blaise Amadi CM Tel 020 3312 1508

SECTION 3

• Princess Grace Hospital
Chaplains Fr Giles Pinnock, Fr Blaise Amadi CM **Tel** 020 3312 1508

SPITALFIELDS, E1: *SEE UNDERWOOD ROAD*

STAINES-UPON-THAMES + OUR LADY OF THE ROSARY

Sunday Mass (Sat 6.30pm) 9, 11; **Holy Day Mass** 7, mid-morning as announced, 7pm; **Weekday Mass** Tue-Thu 9.15, Fri as announced; **Exposition** Tue 9.35-9.50; **Confession** Sat 5.30-6pm

Fr Philip Dyer-Perry
The Presbytery, 59 Gresham Road, Staines TW18 2BD Tel: 01784 452381
Email: staines@rcdow.org.uk Web: parish.rcdow.org.uk/staines
Near Staines Stn (BR), opposite footbridge
Upper Thames Deanery (1890; 1932)

STAMFORD HILL + ST IGNATIUS   S

Sunday Mass (Sat 7pm), 8.30, 10 (Family), 11.30 (Sung), 1.30pm (Polish), 4.30pm (Latin American), 6pm, 7.30pm (Polish); **Holy Day Mass** 10, 6.30pm; **Weekday Mass** 10, 6.30pm; **Confession** Sat 10.30-11.15, 6-6.45pm

Jesuits (SJ) Fr Andrew Cameron-Mowat
27 High Road N15 6ND Tel: 020 8800 2121 Fax: 020 8802 8102
Email: stamfordhill@rcdow.org.uk Web: parish.rcdow.org.uk/stamfordhill
Corner of High Road (A10) & St Ann's Road near Seven Sisters Stn (TfL)
Haringey Deanery (1894;1903)
Community: Frs Edward Bermingham, Michael Bossy, Michał Karnawalski, Mateusz Konopinski, John Mahoney, Paul O'Reilly (Superior); David Stewart
Catechetical Co-ordinator Elwira Pniewski

• Servite Sisters, St Mary's Convent, 90 Suffolk Road N15 5RH Tel: 020 8800 2940
• Ursulines of Jesus, 149 Bethune Road N16 5DY Tel: 020 8800 4623
• Pope's Worldwide Prayer Network 27 High Road N15 6ND
National Promoter Fr David Stewart SJ Tel: 020 8442 5232
Email: prayernetwork@jesuit.org.uk Office hours Mon, Tue only

STANMORE + ST WILLIAM OF YORK

Sunday Mass (Sat 5.30pm), 8, 10 (Sung); **Holy Day Mass** 9.30, 7pm; **Weekday Mass** Mon-Wed, Sat 9.30, Fri 7pm; **Confession** Sat 10-10.30

Canon Michael Munnelly
1 Du Cros Drive, Stanmore HA7 4TJ Tel: 020 8954 1299
Email: stanmore@rcdow.org.uk Web: parish.rcdow.org.uk/stanmore
Off Marsh Lane, 1/4 mile south of The Broadway
Harrow Deanery (1938; 1960)
Parish Secretary Frances Bright

• Royal National Orthopaedic Hospital, Woodland Hall Home

STANWELL + ST DAVID

Sunday Mass (Sat 6pm), 10, 6pm; **Holy Day Mass** 9.30, 7.30pm; **Weekday Mass** Mon, Tue, Thu, Fri 9.30; **Rosary** Fri 6.45pm; **Exposition** Fri 7.15-8pm; **Confession** Sat 5.15-5.45pm

Sons of Divine Providence (FDP) Fr Sidon Sagar, Fr Carlo Mazzotta (clergy also serve Ashford and are resident at 112 Clarendon Road, Ashford TW15 2QD)
St David's, Everest Road, Stanwell, Staines TW19 7EE Tel/Fax: 01784 255973
Email: stanwellparish@rcdow.org.uk Web: parish.rcdow.org.uk/stanwell
Upper Thames Deanery (1964; 1967)

• Ashford Hospital

STEVENAGE PARISHES   A

Bedwell, St Joseph: **Sunday Mass** (Sat 6pm), 10.30, 12.15, 6pm; **Holy Day Mass** 9.15; **Weekday Mass** Wed 7pm, Thu, Fri 9.15; **Rosary** Wed, Thu after Mass; **Adoration**, then **Benediction** Wed 7.30-8.30pm; **Confession** Wed 7.30-8.30pm, Sat 5.15-5.45pm and on request
Old Town, Transfiguration: **Sunday** (Sat 5pm), 9; **Holy Day Mass** 9.30; **Weekday Mass** Mon, Fri 9.30; **Confession** Sat 4.30-4.45pm
Shephall, St Hilda: **Sunday Mass** (Sat 6.30pm), 9.30 (Sung), 11 (with Children's Liturgy); **Holy Day Mass** 9.30; **Weekday Mass** Mon, Tue, Sat 9.30; **Exposition** and **Benediction** Thu 8pm, Fri 10-11; **Confession** Sat 10, 6.15pm

Fr Michael Doherty SDS (resident at 9 Breakspear, Stevenage SG2 9SQ Tel: 01438 352182), Fr Nigel Woollen (resident at St Joseph's Presbytery, Bedwell Crescent, Stevenage SG1 1NJ Tel: 01438 351243)
Administrator for the three parishes Lynne Gasston

+ St Joseph (Stevenage Bedwell)
St Joseph's Presbytery, Bedwell Crescent, Stevenage SG1 1NJ
Email: stevenagebedwell@rcdow.org.uk Web: parish.rcdow.org.uk/stevenage
Off roundabout linking Bedwell Crescent and Fairlands Way
Stevenage Deanery

+ Transfiguration of Our Lord
Grove Road, Stevenage SG1 3PX (Stevenage Old Town)
Email: stevenageoldtown@rcdow.org.uk Web: www.stevenage-rc.org.uk
Off Church Lane, east of High Street
Stevenage Deanery (1912)

• Sisters of Charity of Jesus and Mary, 3 Hitchin Road, Stevenage SG1 3BJ
Tel: 01438 354247
• Lister Hospital Tel: 01438 314333

+ St Hilda (Stevenage Shephall)
9 Breakspear, Stevenage SG2 9SQ
Email: stevenageshephall@rcdow.org.uk Web: parish.rcdow.org.uk/stevenageshephall
Stevenage Deanery (1958; cons 1986)

STOKE NEWINGTON + OUR LADY OF GOOD COUNSEL

Sunday Mass (Sat 6.30pm), 9, 11; **Holy Day Mass** 10, 7pm; **Weekday Mass** Mon-Fri 10 (followed by Marian devotions); **Zimbabwean Mass** *First Sat only* 2pm; **Holy Hour** *First Sat only* 11; **Confession** Sat 11.30-12noon, 5.30-6pm & on request

Fr Martin Tate, Fr John Rufaro Mudereri (in residence, Zimbabwean Chaplaincy)
24 Bouverie Road N16 0AJ Tel: 020 8800 5250
Email: stokenewington@rcdow.org.uk Web: parish.rcdow.org.uk/stokenewington
Hackney Deanery (1882; 1936; 1976)

• Little Sisters of the Poor, St Anne's Home, 77 Manor Road N16 5BL
Tel: 020 8826 2500 Email: ms.stanne@lsplondon.co.uk Web: www.lsplondon.co.uk
Chaplain Fr Daniel Magnier

STONEBRIDGE + THE FIVE PRECIOUS WOUNDS A

Sunday Mass (Sat 6pm), 10 (Sung), 12noon (Family); **Holy Day Mass** 10, 7pm; **Weekday Mass** Mon-Fri 10; **Confession** Fri 10.30-11, Sat 5.15-5.45pm

Fr Antonio Ritaccio, Rev William Lo (Deacon)
The Presbytery, Brentfield Road NW10 8ER Tel: 020 8965 3313
Email: stonebridge@rcdow.org.uk Web: parish.rcdow.org.uk/stonebridge
Off Harrow Road (A404), 1/4 mile east of junction with North Circular Road
Brent Deanery (1926; 1957; cons 14 May 1967)

STROUD GREEN + ST PETER-IN-CHAINS A

Sunday Mass (Sat 6.30pm), 9.45 (Sung), 11.15 (Family), 7pm; **Holy Day Mass** 9, 7.30pm; **Weekday Mass** Mon-Sat 9; **Morning Prayer** 15 mins before weekday Mass; **Holy Hour** Fri 7.30-8.30pm; **Exposition** Sat 9.30-10; **Confession** Sat 9.30-10, 6-6.20pm

Fr Sean Carroll
12 Womersley Road N8 9AE Tel: 020 8340 3394
Email: stroudgreen@rcdow.org.uk   Web: www.stpeterinchains.com
Haringey Deanery (1894; 1896)

• Sisters of Christian Instruction (St Gildas), 36 Dickenson Road N8 9ET
Tel: 020 8340 7203 Web: sistersofstgildas.org.uk
• Sisters of Providence, 78 Oakfield Road N4 4LB Tel: 020 8340 1088
also 78a Oakfield Road N4 4LB Tel: 020 8341 1788
Email: prov.london@yahoo.com Web: www.providenceruillesurloir.com

SUDBURY + ST GEORGE

Sunday Mass (Sat 6.15pm), 8.30, 9.45 (Family), 11.15 (Solemn), 5.30pm (Sung); **Holy Day Mass** 9.30, 8pm; **Weekday Mass** 9.30; **Exposition** with **Benediction** Sat 5.15-6pm; **Confession** Sat 5.15-6pm

Mgr Jeremy Fairhead, Fr John Warnaby
970 Harrow Road, Sudbury, Wembley HA0 2QE
Tel: 020 8904 2552 Fax: 020 8904 0744
Email: sudbury@rcdow.org.uk Web: parish.rcdow.org.uk/sudbury
On corner of St Andrew's Avenue, east of Greenford Road / Sudbury Court Drive junction
Harrow Deanery (1924; 1926; cons 18 April 1928)
Parish Team Mgr Jeremy Fairhead, Fr John Warnaby, Mr Peter Kingsley (**Pastoral Assistant** and **Catechetical Co-ordinator**), Mrs Toni Miles (**Parish Secretary**)

• Northwick Park Hospital
• Wembley Hospital, Clementine Churchill Hospital

SUNBURY-ON-THAMES + ST IGNATIUS OF LOYOLA

Sunday Mass (Sat 6pm), 9.30, 11.30; **Holy Day Mass** 9, 11.30, 7pm; **Weekday Mass** 9.30; **Confession** Sat 9.30

Fr Michael Tuck
The Rectory, Green Street, Sunbury-on-Thames TW16 6QB Tel: 01932 783507
Email: sunburyonthames@rcdow.org.uk Web: parish.rcdow.org.uk/sunburyonthames
Main road, South Sunbury Stn (BR) / M3 interchange
Upper Thames Deanery (1862; 1869; cons 22 May 1884)
Parish Sister Sr Liza Randall
The Loyola Centre (opposite church, *Hall available for hire*) Tel: 07725 023811

• Sunbury Nursing Home, Ashton Lodge, Beechwood Court

SWISS COTTAGE + ST THOMAS MORE A

Sunday Mass 10, 12noon (Sung), 6.30pm; **Holy Day Mass** 7,10, 7pm; **Weekday Mass** Mon-Fri 7,10, Sat 10; **Exposition** Sun 5.15-6.15pm, Fri 10.30-4pm; **Confession** daily, before & after Mass

Fr Stefan Hnylycia, Fr Paul Diaper
Presbytery, Maresfield Gardens NW3 5SU Tel: 020 7435 1388
Email: swisscottage@rcdow.org.uk Web: parish.rcdow.org.uk/swisscottage
Off Fitzjohn's Avenue, near Finchley Road and Swiss Cottage TfL Stns
Camden Deanery (1938; 1968; cons 8 May 1977)

• Lakefield, Maresfield Gardens NW3 5RY Tel: 020 7794 5669
Web: www.lakefield.org.uk Catering and education centre
Pastoral Care entrusted to the Prelature of Opus Dei

SECTION 3

• Netherhall House, Nutley Terrace NW3 5SA Tel: 020 7435 8888
Web: www.nh.netherhall.org.uk   Hall of Residence for male University students
Pastoral Care entrusted to the Prelature of Opus Dei
Fr Dancho Azagra, Mgr Richard Stork
• Eden Hall (Marie Curie) Hospice

TEDDINGTON (& HAMPTON WICK) + THE SACRED HEART

Sunday Mass (Sat 6.30pm), 9.30 (Family), 11.15 (Sung); **Holy Day Mass** 9.30, 7.30pm;
Weekday Mass Mon-Thu 9.30; **Confession** Sat 6-6.30pm & by appointment

Fr Reg Dunkling
262 Kingston Road, Teddington TW11 9JQ Tel: 020 8977 2986
Email: teddington@rcdow.org.uk Web: www.loguk.com/sacredheart
Upper Thames Deanery (1882; 1893; cons 14 June 1944)

• Sons of Divine Providence (FDP), 25 Lower Teddington Road, Hampton Wick KT1 4HB
Tel: 020 8977 5130 Email: info@orionecare.org Web: orionecare.org
Sunday Mass 9.30 (English), 11 (Polish); **Weekday Mass** Mon-Fri 6.45pm
Community: Frs John C Perrotta (Superior), Henryk Halman
Orione Care Main Office 13 Lower Teddington Road, Hampton Wick KT1 4EU
Email: info@orionecare.org Web: orionecare.org
Colombo House, 1 Ferry Road, Teddington TW11 9NN Supported living flats for people
with learning disabilities
St John's, 1 Ferry Road, Teddington TW11 9NN Tel: 020 8977 7574 Residential Care for
people with learning disabilities

TOLLINGTON PARK + ST MELLITUS

Sunday Mass (Sat 6.30pm), 10.30, 6.30pm; **Holy Day Mass** as announced in newsletter;
Weekday Mass Mon-Wed 9, Fri 10; **Confession** Sat 10.30-11 and as announced in
newsletter

Fr Paul McDermott
The Presbytery, St Mellitus Church, Tollington Park N4 3AG Tel: 020 7272 3415
Email: tollingtonpark@rcdow.org.uk Web: parish.rcdow.org.uk/tollingtonpark
Off Stroud Green Road; north end of Fonthill Road, 5 mins from Finsbury Park Stn (BR/TfL)
Islington Deanery (1925; 1959)

TOTTENHAM + ST FRANCIS DE SALES

Sunday Mass (Sat 7pm), 8.30, 10.30, 12.15pm; **Holy Day Mass** 9.30, 7pm; **Weekday Mass**
Mon-Thu 9.30, Fri 7pm, Sat 10 with **Rosary** and **Exposition**; **Confession** Sat 10.30-
11.15, 6-6.45pm

Fr David Lucuy Claros
729 High Road N17 8AG Tel: 020 8808 3554
Email: tottenham@rcdow.org.uk Web: parish.rcdow.org.uk/tottenham
Main road, opposite Tottenham Hotspur FC Ground
Haringey Deanery (1793; 1895)

TOTTENHAM (SOUTH): *SEE STAMFORD HILL*

TOTTENHAM (WEST): *SEE WEST GREEN*

TOWER HILL + THE ENGLISH MARTYRS ♿ ♪

Sunday Mass (Sat 6.30pm), 9, 11; **Holy Day Mass** 9.30, 1pm; **Weekday Mass** Tue-Fri 1pm; **Exposition** Sat 12noon-1pm; **Confession** before and after Mass

Oblates of Mary Immaculate (OMI) Fr Angodage Don Joseph Alex, Fr Raymond Warren (Superior)
30 Prescot Street E1 8BB Tel: 020 7488 4654 Fax: 020 7488 1418
Email: towerhill@rcdow.org.uk Web: parish.rcdow.org.uk/towerhill
Close to junction with Mansell Street
Tower Hamlets Deanery (1865;1876)

• DeMazenod House, Spirituality Centre, 62 Chamber Street E1 8BL
Tel: 020 7702 0270 Email: demazenodhouse@oblates.co.uk

TRING + CORPUS CHRISTI ♿ ♪

Sunday Mass (Sat 6pm), 12.15pm; **Holy Day Mass** as announced; **Weekday Mass** Mon, Thu 10; **Confession** Sat 5.15-5.45pm

Fr David Burke (also serves Berkhamsted, and is resident at **Sacred Heart Church, Park Street, Berkhamsted HP4 1HX** Tel: 01442 863845)
Corpus Christi Church, Langdon Street, Tring HP23 6BA Tel: 01442 823161
Email: tring@rcdow.org.uk Web: parish.rcdow.org.uk/tring
St Albans Deanery (1910; 1913; cons 16 February 2001)

TWICKENHAM + ST JAMES A ♪

Sunday Mass (Sat 6pm) 8, 10.30,12.15pm; **Holy Day Mass** 9, 7.30pm; **Weekday Mass** Mon, Tue, Thu-Sat 9, **Eucharistic Service** Wed 9; **Confession** Sat 9.45-10.45

Fr Ulick Loring
61 Pope's Grove, Twickenham TW1 4JZ Tel: 020 8892 4578
Email: twickenham@rcdow.org.uk   Web: www. stjamestwickenham.org.uk
Upper Thames Deanery (1883; 1885; cons 23 July 1887)

• Religious of the Assumption, 259 Waldegrave Road, Twickenham TW1 4SY
Tel: 020 8744 1642 Email: christinercharlwood@gmail.com
Web: www.assumptionreligious.org
• Sisters of Mercy, 88 Pope's Grove, Twickenham TW1 4JX Tel: 020 8744 2812
• St Mary's University, Waldegrave Road, Strawberry Hill, Twickenham TW1 4SX
See entry below for *Universities and Institutes of Higher Education*

TWICKENHAM (EAST): *SEE ST MARGARETS-ON-THAMES*

UKRAINIAN CATHEDRAL: *SEE EASTERN CATHOLIC CHURCHES*

UNDERWOOD ROAD + ST ANNE

Sunday Mass 10.30 **Holy Day Mass** as announced; **Confession** by appointment.
See entry for *Brazilian Chaplaincy* under Ethnic Chaplaincies

Fr Paulo Bagini
St Anne's Church, Underwood Road E1 5AW Tel: 020 7247 7833
Email: braziliancp@rcdow.org.uk Web: parish.rcdow.org.uk/underwoodroad *and*
www.ccblondres.com
Off Vallance Road
Tower Hamlets Deanery (1850; 1855; cons 27 September 1905)
Parish and Chaplaincy Administrator Telma Melo
• **Brazilian Chaplaincy** Fr Paulo Bagini (Principal Chaplain)

UNIVERSITIES AND INSTITUTES OF HIGHER EDUCATION CHAPLAINCY A

Sunday Mass 10.30 (all year). *All other services termtime only:* Sunday 7.30pm; **Holy Day
Mass** as announced; **Weekday Mass** Mon-Fri 5.30pm; **Exposition** Sun 6.15-7.15pm, Tue
6-9pm, then **Benediction**; **Confession** Sun 6.15-7.15pm, Mon 6-7pm & on request

Newman House, 111 Gower Street WC1E 6AR Tel: 020 7387 6370
Email: enquiries@universitycatholic.net Web: www.universitycatholic.net

Particular Pastoral Responsibility Bishop John Sherrington

Senior Chaplain and Chaplain to LSE Fr Stephen Wang
Email: swang@universitycatholic.net
Finance and Operations Manager Alison Reilly
Email: alison@universitycatholic.net
Receptionist Team Elizabeth Elive, Ann Molloy, Louise Nicholson
Email: reception@universitycatholic.net
Pastoral Associate Chris Castell
Email: chris@universitycatholic.net

Chaplains
Fr David Barrow **(Pastoral Care of Students from the University of Westminster)**
Email: davidbarrow@rcdow.org.uk **(Ogle Street)**
Fr Andrew Connick **(Queen Mary University of London)**
Email: a.connick@qmul.ac.uk **(Wapping)**
Fr Brian Creak **(Goodenough College)**
Email: bcreak@mac.com **(St Charles Square)**
Sr Anabel Gonzalez FMVD **(City University)**
anabel.gonzalez@city.ac.uk
Fr Oliver Keenan OP **(Imperial College)**
Email: oliver.keenan@english.op.org

Sr Mary Kenefick SMG **(Brunel University, University College London)**
Email: mary.kenefick@brunel.ac.uk, m.kenefick@ucl.ac.uk
Fr Ivano Millico **(Newman House Chaplaincy Team)**
Sr Carolyn Morrison RA **(Social Outreach Chaplain, based in Newman House)**
Email: carolyn@universitycatholic.net
Olivia Raw **(SOAS)**
Email: or5@soas.ac.uk
Fr Thomas Skeats **(King's College, London)**
Email: thomas.skeats@english.op.org

• Goodenough College, Mecklenburgh Square WC1 2AB

 Sunday Mass 10

Fr Brian Creak (contact details above)

• **More House, 53 Cromwell Road SW7 2EH Tel: 020 7584 2040**

(Imperial College, Royal College of Art, Royal College of Music)

 Sunday Mass 6pm

• **St Mary's University, Waldegrave Road, Strawberry Hill, Twickenham TW1 4SX**
Email: chaplaincy@stmarys.ac.uk Web: stmarys.ac.uk/chaplaincy

 Sunday Mass 11 (all year), 6pm (*term only*); **Holy Day Mass** 1.05pm; **Weekday Mass** Mon-Fri 1.05pm (chapel); **Confession** Mon-Fri 12.30-1pm

Chaplain Canon Peter Newby **Tel: 020 8240 4006**
Email: peter.newby@stmarys.ac.uk
Deputy Chaplain (Pastoral) Caroline Stanton **Tel: 020 8240 4002**
Email: caroline.stanton@stmarys.ac.uk
Deputy Chaplain (Events) Louise Gordon **Tel: 020 8240 4331**
Email: louise.gordon@stmarys.ac.uk
Chaplaincy Administrator Grazia Hazell **Tel: 020 8240 2327**
Email: grazia.hazell@stmarys.ac.uk
Choral Director Martin Foster **Tel: 020 8240 2327**
Email: martin.foster@stmarys.ac.uk
Benedict XVI House (for students) 7 Waldegrave Road, Twickenham TW1 4JZ

• **University of Hertfordshire**

 Student Mass Sun 6pm at St Peter's, Hatfield South (see *Hatfield South* parish entry for other times)

Fr Julius Otoaye MSP **(Hatfield South)** St Peter's Presbytery, Bishop's Rise, Hatfield AL10 9HN Tel: 01707 262121 Email: juliusotoaye@rcdow.org.uk

UPPER HOLLOWAY: *SEE ARCHWAY*

SECTION 3

UXBRIDGE + OUR LADY OF LOURDES AND ST MICHAEL

Sunday Mass (Sat 6.30pm) 8.30, 10.30 (Solemn), 5pm; **Holy Day Mass** 9.30, 7pm; **Weekday Mass** Mon-Wed, Fri 9.30, Sat 10; **Holy Hour** Sun 3.45-4.45pm; **Confession** Sat 10.30-11

Fr Nicholas Schofield

Presbytery, Osborn Road, Uxbridge UB8 1UE Tel: 01895 233193
Email: uxbridge@rcdow.org.uk Web: www.catholicchurchuxbridge.org.uk
Beside Oxford Road, at junction with Harefield Road
Hillingdon Deanery (1891; 1931; cons 14 May 1936)
Pastoral Assistant Angela Atkins

• Sisters of the Sacred Hearts of Jesus and Mary, Pield Heath House, Pield Heath Road, Hillingdon UB8 3NW Tel: 01895 233092 Email: convent@pieldheathschool.org.uk
Special School Tel: 01895 258507
also Marian House Care Home, 100 Kingston Lane, Uxbridge UB8 3PW
Tel: 01895 253299
• Clare House Nursing Home

WALTHAM CROSS + OUR LADY OF THE IMMACULATE CONCEPTION AND ST JOSEPH

Sunday Mass (Sat 6.30pm, 8pm Polish), 8.30, 10 (Polish),11.30, 5pm (Italian), 6.30pm; **Holy Day Mass** 10, 8pm; **Weekday Mass** 10; **Ukrainian Rite Liturgy** as announced; **Exposition** Fri 9.15-9.45; **Confession** Sat 10.30-11, 5.45-6.15pm

Fr John Cunningham

204 High Street, Waltham Cross EN8 7DP Tel: 01992 623156
Email: walthamcross@rcdow.org.uk Web: parish.rcdow.org.uk/walthamcross
Lea Valley Deanery (1859; 1931; cons 3 July 1971)
Parish Secretary Jacqueline Farley

WAPPING + ST PATRICK

Sunday Mass (Sat 6.30pm), 10, 6.30pm; **Holy Day Mass** 10, 7.30pm; **Weekday Mass** Mon-Wed 10, Thu, Fri 6.30pm, Sat 10; **Exposition** Sun 5.30-6.15pm; **Confession** Sat, Sun 6pm

Fr Andrew Connick

The Presbytery, Dundee Street E1W 2PH Tel: 020 7481 2202
(St Patrick's Church is on Green Bank)
Email: wapping@rcdow.org.uk Web: parish.rcdow.org.uk/wapping
Off Wapping Lane; close to Wapping Stn (Overground)
Tower Hamlets Deanery (1871; 1892; cons 22 May 1902)
Parish Secretary Lucy Knights Email: lucyknights@rcdow.org.uk
Events Co-ordinator Joann Condon Email: joanncondon@rcdow.org.uk

• Hurtado Jesuit Centre, 2 Chandler Street E1W 2QT Tel: 020 7488 7325
Director Br Stephen Power SJ **Administrator** Rebecca Gormally Tel: 020 7488 7325

• Jesuit Refugee Service [JRS-UK] Director Sarah Teather **Tel: 020 7488 7310**
• **Jesuit Community (SJ):** Frs Michael Smith (Superior), Harry Elias, Keith McMillan, John Moffatt, David Smolira; Br Stephen Power **Tel: 020 3217 6922**

WARE + SACRED HEART OF JESUS AND ST JOSEPH A

Sunday Mass (Sat 6.30pm), 8.30, 10.30 (Sung & Family); **Holy Day Mass** 10, 7.30pm; **Weekday Mass** Mon 7pm, Tue-Thu 10; **Confession** Sat 11-11.30, 5.30-6pm *on first Sat of month* & on request

Fr Charles Cahill, Rev Adrian Cullen (Deacon)
1 King Edward's Road, Ware SG12 7EJ Tel: 01920 462140
Email: ware@rcdow.org.uk   Web: www.sacredheartware.com
Junction of New Road (off High Street)
Lea Valley Deanery (1870; 1921; 1939)

• Carmelite Monastery, Ware Park SG12 0DT   Tel: 01920 462154
Email: prioress@warecarmel.com Web: www.warecarmel.com
Chaplain Fr Anthony Baxter **The Lodge, Ware Park, Ware SG12 0DS Tel: 01920 487287**
Sunday Mass 11; Weekday Mass Mon-Sat 8
• Ashview, Ashwood, Highfield, Hillview, Nightingale, Riverside Place, Snowdrop House, Westgate, Willowthorpe Care Homes

WARWICK STREET + OUR LADY OF THE ASSUMPTION AND ST GREGORY

Sunday Mass (Sat 6pm), 10.30 (Solemn), 5pm; **Holy Day Mass** 8, 12.45pm; **Weekday Mass** Tue-Fri 8, Mon-Fri 12.45pm, Sat 12 noon (Extraordinary Form); **Exposition** Sat 5.15-5.45pm; **Confession** Mon-Fri 12.15-12.35pm & after Mass, Sat 5.15-5.45pm

in care of the Personal Ordinariate of Our Lady of Walsingham
Priest in Charge Fr Mark Elliott Smith **(Tel: 020 7935 0943 / 07815 320761),** Mgr Keith Newton (in residence, contact details below)
Presbytery address: 24 Golden Square W1F 9JR
(Church & Communication address: Warwick Street W1B 5LZ Tel: 020 7734 9313)
Email: warwickstreet@rcdow.org.uk Web: parish.rcdow.org.uk/warwickstreet
Between Beak Street/Glasshouse Street; off Regent Street, close to Piccadilly Circus
Westminster Deanery (1730; 1790; cons 24 July 1928)
(Mgr Newton **Tel: 020 7440 5750**)

WATFORD + HOLY ROOD

Sunday Mass (Sat 6pm), 8, 9.30 (Sung), 11 (Folk), 2.15pm (Polish), 5pm; **Holy Day Mass** (Vigil 7pm), 8.30, 12noon; **Weekday Mass** 8.30, 12noon followed by **Rosary,** Sat 11; **Malayalam Mass** *4th Sat* 3pm; **Exposition** Fri 7-8pm, Sat 4.30-5.30pm; **Confession** Sat 11.30, 5pm

Fr Derek McGuire, Fr Joseph Okoro, Rev Neville Dyckhoff (Deacon)
Holy Rood Rectory, Exchange Road, Watford WD18 0PJ Tel: 01923 224085
Email: watford@rcdow.org.uk Web: parish.rcdow.org.uk/watford

In town centre, corner of Market Street
Watford Deanery (1883; 1890; cons 5 July 1900)
Parish Secretary Martha Stuart-Berrisford Tel: 01923 224085 Tue-Fri 10-1pm
• Watford General Hospital Tel: 01923 244366
Chaplain Colette Lennon Tel: 01923 217994

WATFORD NORTH + ST HELEN A

Sunday Mass 9, 11, 6pm; **Holy Day Mass** 10, 7.30pm; **Weekday Mass** Tue-Thu 10, Fri 6pm, Sat 10; **Exposition** Sat 9-9.50 **Confession** Sat 9-9.50

Fr Peter Shekelton, Rev Liam Lynch (Deacon)
Church of St Helen, The Harebreaks, Watford WD24 6NJ Tel: 01923 223175
Email: watfordnorth@rcdow.org.uk Web: parish.rcdow.org.uk/watfordnorth
Watford Deanery (1925; 1935)
Parish Secretary Annette Nugent Tue-Thu 9.3pm
Tel: 01923 223175

WEALDSTONE (& HARROW WEALD) + ST JOSEPH

Sunday Mass (Sat 6pm), 8.15, 9.30 (Family), 11 (Sung), 12.30pm, 6pm; **Holy Day Mass** 7.30, 10, 7.15pm; **Weekday Mass** 7.30 (not Sat), 10; *First Fri only* Exposition and **Confessions** 6.15-6.45pm, **Mass** 7pm; **Baptism** Sun 3pm; **Confession** Sat 10.30-11, 7-7.30pm

Salvatorians (SDS) Fr Thomas Malal Muchail, Fr Fortunatus Banzi, Fr Mario Lainez, Fr Frank Waters
St Joseph's Presbytery, 191 High Road, Harrow Weald HA3 5EE
Tel: 020 8427 1955
Email: wealdstone@rcdow.org.uk Web: www.catholicwealdstone.org
On main road, half mile north of Harrow & Wealdstone Stn (BR)
Harrow Deanery (1898; 1901; 1931)
Parish Secretaries Terri Cousins Mon/Tue 9-5pm, Julie Conneely Wed/Thu/Fri 9-4pm
Salvatorians (SDS) Fr Noel Keane, Fr Peter Preston
Community House, 189 High Street, Wealdstone, Harrow HA3 5DY Tel: 020 8427 2808

• Congregation of Our Lady of the Missions, 108 Spencer Road, Wealdstone, Harrow HA3 7AR Tel: 020 8861 2656 Email: ukireprovsec@gmail.com
Web: www.rndm.org and www.rndm-ukireland.org

WELWYN GARDEN CITY PARISHES A

St Bonaventure: **Sunday Mass** 8, 10.30; **Holy Day Mass** as announced; **Weekday Mass** Tue, Fri 9.30, Sat 10; **Confession** Sat 10.30-11

Digswell, Holy Family: **Sunday Mass** 9.30, 6pm; **Holy Day Mass** as announced; **Weekday Mass** Wed, Thu 9.30; **Confession** Thu 10-10.30

East, Our Lady Queen of Apostles: **Sunday Mass** (Sat 6pm), 11.30; **Holy Day Mass** as announced; **Weekday Mass** Mon 9.30, Tue, Fri 7 pm; **Confession** Sat 5-5.30pm

Fr Norbert Fernandes (resident at Our Lady, Queen of Apostles Tel: 01707 323234), Fr
Tony Thomas (resident at Holy Family Church Tel: 01707 327434)
Parish Secretary Kathryn Hubbard Tel: 01707 322579

+ St Bonaventure (Welwyn Garden City)
(in residence, Bishop Paul McAleenan)
81 Parkway, Welwyn Garden City AL8 6JF
Email: welwyngdncity@rcdow.org.uk Web: www.wgc-catholics.org.uk
Stevenage Deanery (1925; 1926; cons 14 September 1974)

+ Holy Family (Welwyn Garden City Digswell)
194 Knightsfield, Shoplands, Welwyn Garden City AL8 7RQ
Email: welwyngdncitydigs@rcdow.org.uk
Web: www.wgc-catholics.org.uk
Stevenage Deanery (1967; cons 13 May 2007)

+ Our Lady Queen of Apostles (Welwyn Garden City East)
141 Woodhall Lane, Welwyn Garden City AL7 3TP
Email: welwyngdncityeast@rcdow.org.uk Web: www.wgc-catholics.org.uk
Stevenage Deanery (1961; cons 18 December 1973)

• Focolare Movement (Residential Conference Centre) 69 Parkway, Welwyn Garden City
AL8 6HH Tel: 01707 323620 Fr Francis Johnson (in residence)
• Queen Elizabeth II Hospital Tel: 01438 314333
• Queen Victoria Memorial Hospital, Danesbury Hospital, Isabel Hospice

WEMBLEY 1 + ST JOSEPH A

Sunday Mass (Sat 6.30pm), 9, 12noon, 7.30pm; Holy Day Mass (Vigil 7.30pm) 9.30,
12noon; Weekday Mass Mon-Thu 7, 9.30, Fri 7, 12noon, Sat 9.30; Confession (also
Exposition) Sat 10-10.45

Carmelites of Mary Immaculate (CMI) Fr John Menonkari, Fr Joseph Kaduthanam, Fr Tebin
Puthenpurackal
St Joseph's Presbytery, 339 High Road, Wembley HA9 6AG Tel: 020 8902 0081
Email: wembley1@rcdow.org.uk   Web: parish.rcdow.org.uk/wembley
At 'The Triangle' (junction of High Road, Harrow Road & Wembley Hill Road)
Brent Deanery (1901; 1957)

WEMBLEY 2 + ENGLISH MARTYRS

Sunday Mass (Sat 6pm), 9, 11 (Family/with Children's Liturgy), 6pm; Holy Day Mass 9.30,
7pm; Weekday Mass Mon, Tue, Thu-Sat 9.30, preceded by Morning Prayer 9.15, also
Wed 7pm; Filipino Mass *2nd Sun only* 2pm; Exposition Thu after Mass until 11, Sun 5-
5.45pm; Novena to Our Lady of Perpetual Help Sat after morning Mass; First Friday
Devotion 7-8pm; Confession Sat 10-10.30, 5.15-5.45pm & on request

Fr Albert Ofere

The Presbytery, Chalkhill Road, Wembley Park HA9 9EW Tel: 020 8904 2306
Email: wembley2@rcdow.org.uk Web: parish.rcdow.org.uk/wembleypark
Blackbird Hill, corner of Chalkhill Road, below Blackbird Cross
Brent Deanery (1930; 1970)

WEMBLEY 3 + ST ERCONWALD (PRESTON ROAD)

Sunday Mass (Sat 5.30pm), 9, 11.30; **Holy Day Mass** (Vigil 7pm) 9.30, 7pm; **Weekday Mass** Mon-Wed, Fri 9.30; **Confession** Sat 4.30-5pm

Fr Anthony Psaila

112 Carlton Avenue East, Wembley HA9 8NB Tel: 020 8904 6031
Email: wembley3@rcdow.org.uk   Web: www.erconwald.org.uk
Off Preston Road, 400 yds east
Brent Deanery (1932; 1970)
Parish Hall Manager Elizabeth Patten **Email:** wembley3@rcdow.org.uk

• Sisters of La Sainte Union, 128 Elmstead Avenue, Wembley HA9 8NZ
Tel: 020 8908 3715
• Kenbrook, Birchwood Grange, Brook House, Preston Lodge

WEST DRAYTON AND YIEWSLEY + ST CATHERINE OF ALEXANDRIA

Sunday Mass (Sat 7pm), 9, 11 (Sung/with Children's Liturgy), 6pm (not Easter Day, Sunday before New Year),; **Holy Day Mass** 9, 11, 7.30pm, (*School holidays* 9.30, 7.30pm); **Weekday Mass** Mon-Fri 9.30 as announced, Sat 10; **Confession** Sat 10.30, 6.30pm

Fr Brian Smith, Rev Nick Agule (Deacon)

20 The Green, West Drayton UB7 7PJ Tel: 01895 442777
Email: westdrayton@rcdow.org.uk Web: parish.rcdow.org.uk/westdrayton
Hillingdon Deanery (1867; 1869; cons 29 September 1893)

WEST GREEN + ST JOHN VIANNEY A

Sunday Mass (Sat 6pm), 9, 11; **Holy Day Mass** 9.15, 10 (*when school attending*), 7.30pm; **Weekday Mass** 9.15; **Confession** Sat 9.45-10.15

Fr Joe Ryan (Tel: 020 8888 9036)

4 Vincent Road N15 3QH Tel: 020 8888 5518 (Parish Office)
Email: westgreen@rcdow.org.uk Web: stjohnvianneywestgreen.co.uk
Haringey Deanery (1927; 1959; cons 20 June 1964)
Parish Sister Sr Devy Pranadjaja Tel: 07455 544065

• Sisters of St John of God, 103 Black Boy Lane N15 3AS Tel: 020 8374 1693
• Sisters of Verbum Dei Missionary Fraternity, 4a Vincent Road N15 3QH
Tel: 020 8351 4986 Email: verbumdei.lon@gmail.com Web: uk.verbumdei.org
• Justice and Peace Commission Office, 4 Vincent Road N15 3QH
Tel: 020 8888 4222 Email: justice@rcdow.org.uk

• London Catholic Worker, Giuseppe Conlon House, 49 Mattison Road N4 1BG
Tel: 020 8348 8212
• Haringey Migrant Support Centre, 386 West Green Road N15 3QL Tel: 07544 078332
Email: info@haringeymsc.org Web: www.haringeymsc.org
Assessment sessions on Mondays (not Bank Holidays), registration 11-1pm.

WHEATHAMPSTEAD + ST THOMAS MORE

Sunday Mass 11 (with Children's Liturgy), 5pm; **Holy Day Mass** as announced; **Weekday Mass** as announced; **Confession** as announced

Redbourn: **Sunday Mass** (Sat 5.30pm), 9; **Holy Day Mass** as announced; **Weekday Mass** as announced; **Confession** Sat 9.45-10.15, 5.45-6.15pm

Fr Michael Mannion (also serves Redbourn, resident at 1 Peppard Close, Redbourn,
St Albans AL3 7EB Tel: 01582 792270)
7 Marford Road, Wheathampstead AL4 8AY Tel: 01582 832114
Email: wheathampstead@rcdow.org.uk Web: parish.rcdow.org.uk/wheathampstead
St Albans Deanery (1936; 1938; 1978)

WHETSTONE + ST MARY MAGDALEN

Sunday Mass (Sat 6pm), 9 (with Children's Liturgy), 11 (Solemn and with Children's Liturgy), 4pm (Polish); **Holy Day Mass** 9.30, 7pm; **Weekday Mass** 9.30, preceded by **Morning Prayer**; **Exposition** Sat 4.45-5.45pm, except in August (replaced in Lent by Stations of the Cross at 5pm); **Confession** Sat 10-10.30, 4.45-5.45pm

Fr Gladstone Liddle
6 Athenaeum Road N20 9AE Tel: 020 8445 0838
Email: whetstone@rcdow.org.uk Web: www.stmarymagdalens.com
Off High Road (A1000), Totteridge Lane/Oakleigh Road intersection
Barnet Deanery (1926; 1958; cons 1979)
Catechist Co-ordinator Winnie Brady Tel: 07702 094650

• Sisters of the Sacred Heart of Jesus (St Jacut), 6 Oakleigh Park South N20 9JU
Tel: 020 8445 4655 Email: dbissonnette1942@gmail.com
Web: www.soeursdusacrecoeurdeJesus.com

WHITECHAPEL, E1: *SEE COMMERCIAL ROAD, GERMAN CHURCH AND UNDERWOOD ROAD*

WHITE CITY + OUR LADY OF FATIMA   S

Sunday Mass (Sat 6pm), 9, 11, 6pm; **Holy Day Mass** 9.15, 7pm; **Weekday Mass** 9.15, preceded by **Morning Prayer** 9; **Exposition** *First Fri only* all day, Wed 5-6pm, Sat 5-5.40pm; **Confession** Sat 10-10.30, 5-5.30pm

Fr Richard Nesbitt, Fr Ephrem Andom (in residence, Eritrean Chaplaincy)
The Catholic Presbytery, Commonwealth Avenue, White City W12 7QR
Tel: 020 8743 8334 (Fr Ephrem Andom Tel: 020 8743 8315)
Email: whitecity@rcdow.org.uk Web: www.ourladyoffatima.biz

Off Bloemfontein Road, between Western Avenue / Uxbridge Road
Hammersmith & Fulham Deanery (1951; 1965; cons 17 May 1980)
Parish Office Mon, Wed, Fri, 10-4pm

WHITTON + ST EDMUND OF CANTERBURY A   S

Sunday Mass (Sat 6.30pm), 9.30 (Family), 11.15 (Sung), 6pm; **Holy Day Mass** 9.30,
7.30pm; **Weekday Mass** Mon-Fri 9.15, Sat 10.30; **Exposition** *First Fri* 24 hours from 10;
Confession Sat 11-11.30

Fr Nigel Griffin
Presbytery, St Edmund's Lane, 213 Nelson Road, Whitton TW2 7BB Tel: 020 8894 9923
Email: whitton@rcdow.org.uk Web: parish.rcdow.org.uk/whitton
Right at Whitton BR Stn, left at Nelson Pub; presbytery behind the church
Upper Thames Deanery (1934; 1935; cons 1972)
Administrator Paul Hampartsoumian
Co-ordinator of Lay Ministry Chiara Aletti

WILLESDEN + OUR LADY OF WILLESDEN

Sunday Mass (Sat 6pm), 9, 11 (Sung), 5.30pm (Extraordinary Form); **Holy Day Mass**
(Vigil 7pm), 7, 10, 7.30pm (Sung); **Weekday Mass** 10, 7pm; **Exposition** Tue 10.30-
6.50pm, Sat 10.30-5.50pm; **Shrine Prayers** Tue 7.30pm (*see* Catholic Societies and
Organisation, Section 6, *Guild of Our Lady of Willesden*); **Confession** Tue 6.30-7pm, Sat
10.30-11.30, 5-5.45pm

Fr Stephen Willis, Fr Andrew Jaxa-Chamiec
The Presbytery, 1 Nicoll Road NW10 9AX Tel: 020 8965 4935
Email: willesden@rcdow.org.uk Web: parish.rcdow.org.uk/willesden
At junction of Acton Lane, near Jubilee Clock, Harlesden
Brent Deanery (1886; 1931)
Shrine of Our Lady of Willesden
Catechetical Co-ordinator AnneMarie Sylvester-Charles

• **Brazilian Sunday Mass** (Sat 7.30pm), 2pm; **Weekday Mass** Wed, Fri 7.30pm

WILLESDEN GREEN + ST MARY MAGDALEN A

Sunday Mass (Sat 6.30pm), 9, 10.30 (Sung), 12noon (Sung), 6.30pm; **Holy Day Mass** 9.30,
7pm; **Weekday Mass** Mon-Sat 9.30, Fri 6.30pm; **Holy Hour** *(first Fri only)* 7-8pm;
Exposition Mon-Sat 8.30-9.30, Sat 5.30-6.15pm; **Confession** Sat 10-10.30, 5.30-6.15pm
Mgr Roger Reader, Fr Sudham Maharage Perera (in residence, Sri-Lankan (Sinhalese)
Chaplaincy)
Clergy House, Peter Avenue NW10 2DD Tel: 020 8451 4677
Email: willesdengreen@rcdow.org.uk Web: parish.rcdow.org.uk/willesdengreen
Harlesden Road, south side of High Road, via St Andrew's Road; not far from Willesden Green
Stn (TfL)
Brent Deanery (1901; 1939; cons 1958)

Parish Administrator Kathleen Reddington
Safeguarding Claudia Tugbobo **Email:** willesdengreensg3@rcdow.org.uk

• Congregation of Jesus (CJ), 244 Willesden Lane NW2 5RE
Tel: 020 8459 5378 Web: www.cjengland.org, www.congregatiojesu.org,
https://www.facebook.com/cjenglishprovince
• Daughters of Wisdom (La Sagesse), 9 The Oaks, 25 Brondesbury Park NW6 7BY
Tel: 020 8830 2530
• Missionary Sisters of Christ the King (MChR) 180 Walm Lane NW2 3AX
Tel: 020 3638 4753 Email: michalik.mchr@op.pl Web: www.mchr.pl
• Sisters of the Holy Family of Bordeaux, 83 St Gabriel's Road NW2 4DU
Tel: 020 8452 3844 Email: stgabriels@holyfamilybordeaux.org
Web: www.holyfamilybordeaux.org
• St Boniface Secular Institute (English Region), 44 Exeter Road NW2 4SB
Tel: 020 8438 9628 Email: hostel@institut-st-bonifatius.de
Web: www.hostel-lioba-house.de (see also *German Church* entry)
• Divine Word Missionaries (SVD), 8 Teignmouth Road NW2 4HN
Tel: 020 8452 8430 Email: svdlondon@gmail.com
Frs Albert Escoto (Praeses), Eamonn Donnelly, Krzysztof Krzyskow, John McCarthy, Martin McPake, Kevin O'Toole
• Hospitaller Order of St John of God (OH), 52 Kenneth Crescent NW2 4PN
Tel: 020 8452 8879 Email: johnoneill@sjog.org.uk Web: www.hospitaller.org.uk
Brs Malachy Brannigan (Prior), Bonaventure Gerrard, John O'Neill, Andrzej Zach
• Jesuits (SJ), Our Lady of Mercy, 182 Walm Lane NW2 3AX Tel: 020 8452 4304
Email: londyn@jezuici.pl Web: polishjesuits.co.uk
Frs Adam Baczewski, Leszek Szuta, Adam Tomaszewski (Superior)
Sunday Mass (Polish) 10.30, Noon; Mon-Sat 7.30 (English), Wed 7.30pm (Polish)
St Francis of Assisi, Fleetwood Road NW10 1NQ
Sunday Mass (Polish) 9, 10.30, Noon, 7 pm; Weekday Mass (Polish) Mon, Tue, Thu, Fri 7pm;
Exposition, with Confession Thu 7.30-8pm;
Lectio Divina: lectio.divinaOLM@gmail.com; Men of St Joseph: london.msj@gmail.com
• Montfort Missionaries, 27 St Gabriel's Road NW2 4DS Tel: 020 8450 4291 / 07525 220255
Frs Nelson Cabanero, Kieran Flynn
• De Paul Trust, 247 Willesden Lane NW2 5RY Tel: 020 8830 1093
• Willesden General Hospital Tel: 020 8438 7000

WOOD GREEN + ST PAUL THE APOSTLE
Sunday Mass (Sat 6.30pm), 8, 10 (Family), 12noon (Sung); **Holy Day Mass** 9.30, 7.30pm; **Weekday Mass** Mon-Fri 9.30, Sat 10.30; **Holy Hour** Sat 11-12noon; **Confession** Sat 11-12noon, 5.30-6pm

Fr Perry Sykes, Fr Jonathan Stogdon
Presbytery & Communication Address: 22 Bradley Road N22 7SZ Tel: 020 8888 2390
(Church address: Station Road N22 7SY)
Email: woodgreen@rcdow.org.uk Web: parish.rcdow.org.uk/woodgreen

---

Wood Green TfL Stn (Piccadilly line), near junction with Mayes Road
Haringey Deanery (1882; 1904; 1970)
Parish Administrator Rose Mary Correia

• Daughters of Divine Love, **82/84 Sylvan Avenue N22 5HY** Tel: **020 8888 1898**
Email: divinelovedaughters@yahoo.co.uk Web: www.ddlenglishregion.org

YEADING + ST RAPHAEL

Sunday Mass (Sat 7pm), 9, 10.30 (Sung), 12noon; **Holy Day Mass** 9.30, 7.30pm;
Weekday Mass (incorporates **Morning Prayer**) Mon-Thu 9.30, Fri, Sat 12noon; **Rosary**
30 mins before Weekday Mass; **Exposition** *First Fri only* 7pm; **Confession** Sat 11.30,
6.30pm

Fr John Welsh
St Raphael's House, Morrison Road, Yeading UB4 9JP Tel: 020 8845 1919
Email: yeading@rcdow.org.uk Web: parish.rcdow.org.uk/yeading
In Ayles Road, off Kingshill Avenue (west of Yeading Lane)
Hillingdon Deanery (1957; 1961; cons 4 May 1975)
Catechetical Co-ordinator Jane Foskett
Parish Administrator Paulina Louison

MASS IN THE EXTRAORDINARY FORM

Masses regularly celebrated in the Extraordinary Form of the Roman Rite are as follows:

Westminster Cathedral, Most Precious Blood	2nd Saturday 4pm, (but 1st Saturday 4pm from January 2020) Low Mass (Lady Chapel)
Baldock, Holy Trinity	1st Sunday 3pm Low Mass
Covent Garden, Corpus Christi	Monday 6.30pm Sung Mass
	2nd Friday 6.30pm Low Mass
Ely Place, St Etheldreda	1st Friday 6pm Low Mass
Hackney, St John the Baptist	1st & 3rd Fridays 6pm Low Mass
Moorfields, St Mary Moorfields	Dates as publicised Sung Mass
Old Hall Green, St Edmund of Canterbury & English Martyrs	3rd Sunday 3pm Low Mass
Oratory, Immaculate Heart of Mary	Sunday 9 Low Mass
	Monday - Friday 8 Low Mass (St Joseph's Altar)
	Saturday 8 Low Mass (St Wilfrid's Chapel)
	Holy Days 8 Low Mass
Spanish Place, St James	Sunday 9.30 Low Mass
	Holy Days 11 Low Mass
Uxbridge, Our Lady of Lourdes and St Michael	1st Friday 7pm Sung Mass
Warwick Street, Our Lady of the Assumption and St Gregory	Wednesday 7pm Sung Mass
	Saturday Noon Low Mass
Willesden, Our Lady of Willesden	Sunday 5.30pm Low Mass

By decision of the Bishops' Conference, ratified by the Holy See, the Solemnity of the Ascension of the Lord will henceforth by celebrated on its traditional day. The Solemnity of Corpus Christi may be celebrated in the Extraordinary Form on the traditional day (in 2020 this will be Thursday 11 June), but the obligation to attend Mass is transferred to the following Sunday. The Solemnity of the Epiphany is kept on its proper date, unless it falls on a Saturday or Monday, in which case it is observed on the Sunday (in 2020 on Sunday 5 January)

Anyone wishing to attend any of the Masses listed above is advised to check that it is taking place; for further details, see the Latin Mass Society entry in Section 6, Catholic Societies and Organisations

For listings of Ordinary Form Masses in Latin in the diocese visit the website of the Association for Latin Liturgy, also in Section 6, Catholic Societies and Organisations.

SECTION 3

CHAPLAINCIES

Information about Chaplaincies can be found at **www.rcdow.org.uk/chaplaincies**

AIRPORT CHAPELS

GATWICK AIRPORT (Diocese of Arundel & Brighton) Chapels in North and South
Terminals (Diocese of Arundel & Brighton); for times of services **Tel: 01293 505540**
Web: www.gatwickairportchapel.org
HEATHROW AIRPORT St George's Chapel
See page 87 in Parish Directory.

ARMED FORCES, PRINCIPAL CHAPLAINCIES

ARMY Fr Michael Fava CBE QHC, **Deputy Chaplain General, Army Headquarters, MOD
Chaplains (A), Blenheim Building, Marlborough Lines, Monxton Road, Andover SP11 8HT**
Tel: 01264 887170 E-mail: michael.fava553@mod.gov.uk

ROYAL AIR FORCE Rev (Sqn Ldr) David E. Skillen RAF, **Station Chaplain, The Chaplaincy
Centre, RAF Odiham, Hook RG29 1QT**
Tel: 01256 367497 E-mail: David.Skillen100@mod.gov.uk

ROYAL NAVY Fr David Conroy QHC MA MMS IMS(Dip) QCVS RN **Catholic Chaplain
and Chaplaincy Team Leader, HMS SULTAN, Military Road, GOSPORT PO12 3BY**
Tel: 02392 542686 E-mail: david.conroy977@mod.gov.uk

EASTERN CATHOLIC CHURCHES

Episcopal Vicar for Eastern Catholic Churches Mgr John Conneely

BELARUSIAN CATHOLIC CHURCH

Chaplain:	Fr Serge Stasievich
Address:	Church of St Cyril of Turau and All the Patron Saints of the Belarusian People, adjacent to Marian House, Holden Avenue N12 8HY
Tel:	020 8446 3378
Email:	belarusmission@gmail.com
Mass times:	Sunday 10 (Slovak), 11.30 (Belarusian)

CHALDEAN CATHOLIC CHURCH

Chaplain:	Fr Andrawis Toma
Address:	38-40 Cavendish Avenue W13 0JQ
Tel:	020 8997 6370
Web:	www.chaldeans.uk
Mass times:	*Acton West*, Sunday 12.45pm

GHEEZ RITE (Eritrea)

Chaplain:	Fr Ephrem Andom
Address:	The Catholic Presbytery, Commonwealth Avenue W12 7QR (*White City*)
Tel:	020 8743 8315

Email: abbaephrem@yahoo.co.uk
Mass times: *Acton East,* Sunday 1pm

GHEEZ RITE (Ethiopia)

Chaplain: Fr Ufayissa Dea Madalcho CM
Address: 1 Waller Road SE14 5LE
Tel: 07498 328188
Email: ufiyeedm@gmail.com
Mass times: *Queensway,* Sunday 1pm

KNANAYA

Chaplain: Fr Joshy Philip
Address: The Presbytery, Esdaile Lane Hoddesdon EN11 8DS *(Hoddesdon)*
Tel: 01992 440986 / 07491 623832
Email: joshymsp@gmail.com
Mass times: *St Alban, Hornchurch RM12 5JX (Brentwood),* 1st and 3rd Sunday 2.30pm
Our Lady of Gillingham, Gillingham ME7 1YL (Southwark) 2nd Sunday 3pm

MARONITE CATHOLIC CHURCH

Chaplains: Fr Antoine Achkar, Fr Aziz Azzi, Fr Fadi Kmeid
Address: 6 Dobson Close NW6 4RS
Tel: 020 7586 1801 (10.30-1.30pm)
Email: admin@maronitechurch.org.uk
Web: www.maronitechurch.org.uk
Mass times: (for Lebanese) *Paddington,* Saturday 7pm; Sunday 12.30, 7pm; Wednesday, Friday 7pm
(for Cypriots) *Holy Family Convent, 52 London Road, Enfield EN2 6EN* Sunday 10.30

MELKITE CATHOLIC CHURCH

Chaplain: Archimandrite Shafiq Abouzayd
Address: 46 Sunderland Avenue, Oxford OX2 8DU
Tel: 01865 514041 / 07977 495150
Email: melkitelondon@gmail.com
Web: www.melkite.uk
Mass times: *St Barnabas C of E Church, Pimlico Road SW1W 8PF* Sunday 12noon

SYRIAC CATHOLIC CHURCH

Chaplain: Awaiting appointment

SYRO-MALABAR CHURCH (see *Other Jurisdictions*, page 150)

Chaplain: Fr Joseph Anthiamkulam MCBS **(in charge of 9 Centres in Brentwood Diocese)**
Address: 132 Shernhall Street E17 9HU
Tel: 020 8520 5877
Email: joseajmcbs@gmail.com

SECTION 3

Chaplain: Fr Sebastian Chamakala John
Address: 165 Arlington Road NW1 7EX *(Our Lady of Hal)*
Tel: 07429 307307
Email: sebchamakala@yahoo.com
Mass times: *Edmonton,* 4th Sunday 4 pm (2.30-3.30pm Catechism; 3.30-4pm Rosary & Confessions, BVM Novena)
Harefield, 2nd Sunday 5 pm (4pm-5pm Catechism & Confessions, Rosary, BVM Novena)
Hayes, 2nd Sunday 2.30pm-3pm Confessions & Rosary, BVM Novena; 4th Friday 5pm
Hounslow, 1st Sunday 3 pm (2pm-3pm Catechism, Rosary & Confessions)
Stevenage Bedwell 3rd Saturday 10 (11.30-12.30pm Adoration, Catechism & Confessions)
Ware, 3rd Wednesday 5pm
Watford, 2nd Friday 4.30pm
4th Saturday 4 pm (followed by BVM Novena)
Wembley 1, 4th Sunday 4pm

SYRO-MALANKARA CHURCH

Chaplain: Fr John Alex
Address: St John the Baptist, 349 Wanstead Park Road, Cranbrook, Ilford IG1 3TS
St John the Baptist, Ilford (Brentwood)
Tel: 020 8554 3763

UKRAINIAN CATHOLIC CHURCH (see *Other Jurisdictions,* page 150)

Clergy: Very Rev David J Senyk, Fr Irineu Kraiczyi OSBM, Fr Carlos Mekekiuk, Fr Mark Woodruff (English Liturgy)
Address: Cathedral of the Holy Family, Duke Street W1K 5BQ (Correspondence etc. to 22 Binney Street W1K 5BQ)
Tel: 020 7629 / 07561 473888
Email: cathedral@ukrainianchurch.org.uk
Web: www.ucc-gb.com
Mass times: *Cathedral,* Sunday 8, 10, 12noon, 6.15pm; Holy Day as weekdays, also 10.30; Weekday 7, 6.15pm (Monday 6.15pm only); 2nd Saturday 4pm; Confession daily before Divine Liturgy
Feltham, 2nd Sunday 3pm
Waltham Cross, as announced

ETHNIC CHAPLAINCIES

Particular Pastoral Responsibility   Bishop Paul McAleenan

Episcopal Vicar for Ethnic Chaplaincies Fr David Irwin
Where a Chaplaincy is based at a parish, the name of the parish is given in italics after the address. Parish names are also in italics in the list of Mass times - please refer to the Parish Directory for the parish address.

AFRICAN CATHOLIC MISSION IN BRITAIN

Chaplain:	Rev Joseph Baffour-Awuah (Deacon)
Address:	St George's Presbytery, 132 Shernhall Street E17 9HU
Tel:	020 8521 2359 / 07786 501371
Email:	africath@clara.co.uk

ALBANIAN – KOSOVAN

Chaplain:	Fr Gary Walsh
Address:	8 Ogle Street W1W 6HS *(Ogle Street)*
Tel:	07791 054137
Email:	garywalsh2001@yahoo.com
Mass times:	*Pimlico,* 2nd and 4th Sunday 3pm
	Wood Green, 1st and 3rd Sunday 1.30pm

BRAZILIAN

Principal Chaplain:

	Fr Paulo Bagini
Chaplains:	Awaiting appointment
Address:	St Anne's Church, Underwood Road E1 5AW *(Underwood Road)*
Tel:	020 7247 7833
Email:	braziliancp@rcdow.org.uk
Web:	www.ccblondres.com
Mass times:	(Brazilian Masses)
	Brixton (Southwark), Sunday 7pm
	Crystal Palace (Southwark), Sunday 9
	Manor House, Sunday 5pm
	Underwood Road, Thursday 7.30pm, Saturday 7pm; Sunday 12.30pm
	Willesden, Wednesday 7.30pm, Saturday 7.30pm, Sunday 2pm

CARIBBEAN

Chaplain:	Rev Jon Dal Din (Deacon)
Address:	112 Kelmscott Road SW11 6PT
Tel:	07527 758729 / 07889 536957
Email:	jondaldin@rcdow.org.uk
President:	Lloyd Booker
Address:	17a Cambray Road SW12 0DX
Tel:	020 8675 0607

CHINESE

Chaplain:	Fr Joseph Liang
Address:	Assumption Priory, Victoria Park Square E2 9PB *(Bethnal Green)*
Tel:	020 8709 5281 / 07753 471611
Email:	josephliang1998@gmail.com
Web:	http://londonccc.wordpress.com
Mass times:	*Bethnal Green,* (Chinese) Sunday 2.15pm

SECTION 3

CONGOLESE

Chaplain:	Fr Julien Matondo Mboko
Address:	2 Lukin Street E1 0AA *(Commercial Road)*
Tel:	020 7790 2211/ 07452 772111
Email:	julienmboko@hotmail.fr / julienmboko@rcdow.org.uk
Mass times:	*Highbury*, (Lingala) Sunday 2pm

CROATIAN

Chaplain:	Fr Ljubomir Šimunović OFM
Address:	17 Boutflower Road SW11 1RE
Tel:	020 7223 3530
Email:	hkmlondon@gmail.com
Web:	www.hkmlondon.org
Mass times:	*Sacred Heart Church (Cathedral Chapel of Ease), Horseferry Road SW1P 2EF,* Sunday 4pm

CZECH

Please contact the Slovak Chaplaincy

FILIPINO

Chaplain:	Fr Cirino Potrido CM **(Co-ordinator)**
Address:	1 Waller Road SE14 5LE
Tel:	07857 709545
Email:	cgpotrido@yahoo.com
Chaplain:	Fr Luc Nguyen **(Southwark)**
Address:	20 Brixton Road SW9 6BU
Tel:	020 7735 8235
Mass times:	*Bethnal Green,* 4th Sunday 5pm
	Feltham, 4th Saturday 3pm
	Kilburn, 3rd Sunday 3pm
	Lincoln's Inn Fields, 2nd Sunday 4pm
	Mill Hill, 2nd Saturday 7pm
	Stonebridge, 1st Sunday 3pm

FRENCH

Chaplains:	Fr Pascal Boidin sm, Fr Hubert Bonnet-Eymard sm, Fr Damien Diouf sm, Fr Kevin Duffy sm, Br Ivan Vodopivec sm
Address:	Notre Dame de France, 5 Leicester Place WC2H 7BX *(French Church)*
Tel:	020 7437 9363
Mass times:	See *French Church* in Parish Directory

GERMAN

Chaplain:	Fr Andreas Blum
Address:	St Boniface, 47 Adler Street E1 1EE *(German Church)*
Tel:	020 7247 9529
Email:	pfarrer@dkg-london.org

Mass times: See *German Church* in Parish Directory

GHANAIAN

Chaplain: Fr Dominic Yaw Assuahene
Address: St Mary Magdalen Church, 71 Comerford Road SE4 2BA
Tel: 020 8305 8004 / 07393 613906
Email: dyassuahene@gmail.com

GOAN

Chaplain: Fr Patrick D'Souza SFX
Address: (Office) St Thomas of Canterbury School, Commonside East, Mitcham, CR4 1YG
Tel: 020 8665 2176
Email: goanchaplaincy@gmail.com
Address: (Home) Ss Peter and Paul Church, 1 Cranmer Road, Mitcham CR4 4LD
Mass times: *Cranford,* (Konkani) 4th Sunday 5pm
Hounslow, (Konkani) 3rd Sunday 4pm
Mitcham (Southwark), (Konkani) 2nd Sunday 3pm
Heathrow Airport, (Konkani) 2nd Saturday 5pm
Southall, (Konkani) 3rd Saturday 4pm
Wembley 1, (Konkani) 1st Sunday 4 pm

HUNGARIAN

Chaplain: Fr János Csicsó
Address: 62 Little Ealing Lane W5 4EA
Tel: 020 8566 0271
Email: hungarian.chaplaincy@btinternet.com
Web: www.magyarkatolikusok.co.uk
Mass times: *62 Little Ealing Lane,* 1st & 3rd Sunday 11.30

IRISH

CEO: Eddie Gilmore
Address: 52 Camden Square NW1 9XB
Tel: 020 7482 5528
Email: info@irishchaplaincy.org.uk
Web: www.irishchaplaincy.org.uk
Mass times: 12noon *(First Friday only)*

ITALIAN CHURCH

Chaplains: Fr Andrea Fulco SAC, Fr Giuseppe De Caro SAC
Fr Ryszard Wrobel SAC
Address: St Peter's Italian Church, 4 Back Hill EC1R 5EN *(Italian Church)*
Tel: 020 7837 1528
Email: italianchurchlondon@gmail.com
Mass times: See *Italian Church* in Parish Directory

SECTION 3

ITALIAN MISSION

Chaplain: Fr Antonio Serra
Address: 197 Durants Road, Enfield EN3 7DE *(Ponders End)*
Tel: 020 8804 2307
Email: mci.london@hotmail.com
Web: www.mcilondon.org
Mass times: *Italian Centre* Sunday 9.30, Tue, Fri 7.30pm; Adoration Fri 6.30pm
Hoddesdon, Saturday 4pm
Ponders End, Sunday 12.30pm
Waltham Cross, Sunday 5pm
Confessions: 30 min before each Mass.

JAPANESE

There is no Japanese Chaplaincy at present.

KERALAN / MALAYALAM (Latin Rite)

Chaplains: Fr Johnson Alexander, Fr Sebastian Joseph *(resident at Ruislip)*
Address: 373 Bowes Road N11 1AA *(New Southgate)*
Tel: 07438 182888 / 07958376955
Email: fr.johnsonalexander@gmail.com
Mass times: *East Ham (Brentwood),* 2nd & 4th Sunday 4pm, preceded by Catechism 3pm and Rosary 3.30pm, 1st Saturday 7pm Rosary & Charismatic Prayer
Forest Gate (Brentwood), 2nd Tuesday 7.10pm & Novena to St Anthony 7pm
New Southgate, 2nd Sunday 3.30pm & Perpetual Help Novena 3pm
Pollards Hill (Southwark), 1st Sunday 3.30pm & Perpetual Help Novena 3pm
Ruislip, 1st Sunday 4pm
Southall, 3rd Sunday 3pm, preceded by Adoration and Confession 2pm

KOREAN

Chaplain: Fr Joong Hee Kwon
Address: Korean Catholic Community, 104-106 Benhill Wood Road, Sutton SM1 3SR
Tel: 020 8644 1223
Email: londoncatholic@gmail.com
Web: www.londoncatholic.net
Mass times: (Saturday 7pm), Sunday 11

LATIN AMERICAN

Chaplains: Fr Carlos Abajos OAR, Fr Gerardo Cortes OAR
Address: 363 Kennington Lane SE11 5QY
Tel: 020 7820 1697
Email: capellanialatinoamericana@gmail.com
Mass times: *St George's Cathedral (Southwark),* Sunday 1pm
St Anthony, Forest Gate (Brentwood), Sunday 3pm

St Anne, Vauxhall (Southwark), Sunday 1.30pm
Stamford Hill, Sunday 4.30pm
Soho Square, Sunday 6pm

LITHUANIAN

Chaplains:	Fr Petras Tverijonas, Fr Petras Gucevicius
Address:	21 The Oval, Hackney Road E2 9DT *(Lithuanian Church)*
Tel:	020 7739 8735
Email:	parish@londonas.co.uk
Mass times:	See *Lithuanian Church* in Parish Directory

MALTESE

Chaplain:	Fr Victor Camilleri OFM
Address:	47 Adler Street E1 1EE *(German Church)*
Tel:	07930 198251
Email:	victor-camilleri@hotmail.com

NIGERIAN

Chaplains:	Fr Matthew 'Gbenga Madewa, Fr Peter Tochukwu Egboo, Fr Alexander Izang Atu
Address:	8 King Henry's Walk N1 4PB *(Kingsland)*
Tel:	07399 434762 (Fr Matthew); 07440 653821 (Fr Peter); 07432 048440 (Fr Alexander);
Email:	ncchaplaincy@ncchapeng.org / admin@ncchapeng.org
Web:	ncchapeng.org
Mass times:	*Dagenham (Brentwood),* 1st Sunday 2pm
	Feltham, 4th Sunday 2.30pm
	Kingsland, 3rd Sunday 2pm
	Mill Hill, 4th Sunday 2pm
	Peckham (Southwark), 1st Sunday 2pm
	Tottenham, 1st Sunday in third month of the quarter 2pm
	Language Masses 2nd Sundays 2pm
	Night Vigil 3rd Fridays *Walworth (Southwark)*

POLISH

Vicar Delegate:	Mgr Stefan Wylezek
Address:	2-4 Devonia Road N1 8JJ
Tel:	020 7226 3439
Email:	biuro@pcmew.org
Mass times:	See *Polish Church 1, 2 & 3* in the Parish Directory

PORTUGUESE

Chaplain:	Fr Carlos M F Gabriel
Address:	Portuguese Catholic Mission, 6 Minerva Close SW9 6NZ
Tel:	020 7587 0881 / 07443 885815
Email:	carlosgabriel@rcdow.org.uk, ukportuguesechaplain@gmail.com

SECTION 3

Mass times: *Bayswater,* Sunday 11
                Camden Town, Sunday 5pm
                Clapham Common (Southwark), Sunday 5pm
                Fulham 1, Sunday 3pm
                Northwood, dates as announced 7.30pm

ROMANIAN

Chaplain:	Fr Marcelin Blaj,
Address:	Presbytery, 22 Hay Lane NW9 0NG *(Kingsbury Green)*
Tel:	020 8204 4392 / 07424 372813
Chaplain:	Fr Gabriel Ciobanu
Address:	The Presbytery, 98 Manford Way, Hainault IG7 4DF
Tel:	07986 988969
Email:	romanianchaplaincy@gmail.com
Mass times:	*Kingsbury Green,* Sunday 12.30pm, Tuesday 7.30pm
	Canning Town (Brentwood) Sunday 4pm
	South Croydon (Southwark) Sunday 11.30

SLOVAK (see also CZECH)

Chaplain:	Fr Tibor Borovsky
Address:	14 Melior Street SE1 3QP *(Bermondsey-Melior Street, Southwark)*
Tel:	07597 637411
Email:	info@scmlondon.org, secretary@scmlondon.org
Mass times:	Sunday 1pm, *1* Oct-30 Jun 7.30pm
	Wednesday, Friday 7.30pm
Confession	Sunday 12.30-12.50pm, 2.45-3.30pm, 7-7.20pm
	Wednesday, Friday 6.45-7.20pm
Exposition	*1st Friday* 8-8.30pm
	3rd Wednesday 6.30-7.20pm
Rosary	30 minutes before each Mass

SLOVENE

Chaplain:	Fr Stanislav Cikanek
Address:	62 Offley Road SW9 0LS *(Kennington Park, Southwark)*
Tel:	020 7735 6655
Email:	cikanek@msn.com
Mass times:	*62 Offley Road,* Sunday 11, 2nd Sunday 4pm

SPANISH

                Please contact the Latin American Chaplaincy

SRI-LANKAN (SINHALESE-SPEAKING)

Chaplain:	Fr Sudham Maharage Perera
Address:	Clergy House, Peter Avenue NW10 2DD *(Willesden Green)*
Tel:	020 8451 4677

Email: sudhamperera@rcdow.org.uk
Mass times: *Hounslow,* 2nd Sunday 4pm
Willesden Green, Last Sunday of the month 4.30pm
Woolwich (Southwark), 3rd Sunday 3pm

SRI-LANKAN (TAMIL-SPEAKING)

Chaplain: Fr Elmo Arulnesan Jeyarasa
Address: 304 Garratt Lane SW18 4EH
Tel: 020 8870 6257
Email: elmojeyarasa@rcdow.org.uk
Web: www.tamil-rcchaplaincy.org.uk
Mass times: *Earlsfield (Southwark),* 4th Sunday 4.30pm
Forest Gate (Brentwood), 4th Sunday 4.30pm
Kenton, 1st Sunday 4pm
Lewisham (Southwark), 2nd Sunday 3.45pm
Southall, 1st Sunday 1.30pm
Wembley 1, 3rd Sunday 3.30pm

TRAVELLER, GYPSY AND ROMA COMMUNITIES

National
Chaplain: Fr Dan Mason
Address: 21 Laindon Road, Billericay CM12 9LL *(Brentwood)*
Tel: 01277 624891
Email: frdanmason@gmail.com

Pastoral
Co-ordinator: Sr Petronia Williams
Address: 12 Clevelys Road E5 9JN
Tel: 020 8880 0257
Email: petroniawilliams@rcdow.org.uk / petroniaosm@yahoo.co.uk

UGANDAN   There is no Ugandan Chaplaincy, but communities meet for Mass

Mass times: Blessed Jildo Irwa & Daudi Okello Uganda Catholic Community
Kingsland, 2nd Sunday 3pm
Uganda Martyrs Catholic Community
Archway, Last Sunday of the month 3pm
Ugandan Croydon Catholic Community
South Norwood (Southwark), 2nd Sunday 2pm

VIETNAMESE

Chaplains: Fr Simon Thang Duc Nguyen, Fr Tam Huu Nguyen, Fr Van Dien Nguyen
Rev Paul Song Trong Ly (Deacon)
Address: 117 Bow Common Lane E3 4AU *(Bow Common)*
Tel: 020 7987 3477 / 07920 044275
Email: Simon_hue@yahoo.co.uk

Mass times: *130 Poplar High Street E14 0AG,* Catechesis School for Vietnamese
Catholic Children Tel: 020 7536 2844
Sunday Mass 1pm (except school holidays)
Bow Common, Sunday 12noon, Monday, Tuesday 10, Thursday, Friday
8pm, Saturday 10

ZAMBIAN

Chaplain: Fr Henry Mobela
Address: 62 Eden Grove N7 8EN *(Holloway)*
Tel: 020 7607 3594 / 07495 866069
Email: kalusamobela@gmail.com
Mass times: *Clerkenwell,* 4th Saturday 3pm

ZIMBABWEAN

Chaplain: Fr John Rufaro Mudereri
Address: 24 Bouverie Road N16 0AJ
Tel: 020 3802 2911 / 07943 875189 (Tue-Fri)
Email: zimbabweanchaplaincy@rcdow.org.uk
Mass times: *Stoke Newington,* 1st Saturday 2pm

HM PRISON SERVICE

Particular Pastoral Responsibility Bishop Paul McAleenan, assisted by Mgr Martin Hayes

PRISON CHAPLAINCIES
National Catholic Chaplain for Prisons Fr Paul Douthwaite
CBCEW, 39 Eccleston Square SW1V 1BX
Tel: 020 7901 4857 Email: Prisons.Chaplain@cbcew.org.uk
Her Majesty's Prison and Probation Service
Roman Catholic Internal HQ Advisor Rev Paul Hargreaves
Tel: 07562 433656 Email: paul.hargreaves@justice.gov.uk

Adviser and Co-ordinator for the Diocese Awaiting appointment

Bovingdon: HM Prison The Mount, Molyneaux Avenue, Hemel Hempstead HP3 0NE
Chaplain Kim Davey Tel: 01442 836300 Email: kim.davey@hmps.gsi.gov.uk
Bronzefield: HM Prison, Woodthorpe Road, Ashford TW15 3JZ
Chaplain Karen Connaughton Tel: 01784 425690
Email: Karen.Connaughton@hmps.gsi.gov.uk
Feltham: HM Young Offenders Institution and Remand Centre, Bedfont Road, Feltham
TW13 4ND
Chaplains Barry Phillips-Devaney, Bridget Brinkley Tel: 020 8844 5326
Email: barry.devaney@hmps.gsi.gov.uk, bridget.brinkley@hmps.gsi.gov.uk
Pentonville: HM Prison, Caledonian Road N7 8TT
Chaplains Valentine Ambe, Mary Ebbasi Tel: 020 7023 7217
Email: Valentine.Ambe@hmps.gsi.gov.uk, Mary.Ebbasi@hmps.gsi.gov.uk

Wormwood Scrubs: HM Prison, PO Box 757, London W12 0AE
Chaplain Fr Chima Ibekwe **Tel: 020 8588 3200 Email: chima.ibekwe@hmps.gsi.gov.uk**

HOSPITAL AND HOSPICE CHAPLAINS

Particular Pastoral Responsibility Bishop Paul McAleenan, assisted by Mgr Martin Hayes

Cardinal's Advisor for Healthcare Chaplaincy and Programme Consultant at St Mary's University Fr Peter-Michael Scott **279 High Road N2 8HG**
Tel: 020 8834 4234 Email: peterscott@rcdow.org.uk
Assistant Co-ordinators of Healthcare Chaplains Fr Giles Pinnock, Rev Anthony Clark (Deacon)

For further information please see **www.rcdow.org.uk/healthcare**
In light of the Data Protection Act 1998, please indicate on entering hospital that your details may be passed to the RC Chaplain. Also state that you would like the RC Chaplain to visit you.

Hospital telephone numbers are listed after the name of the hospital, followed by the name and telephone number of the specially appointed Hospital Chaplain, where there is one, or the name in italics of the parish from which the hospital is served and the parish's telephone number.
Ashford Hospital **Tel: 01784 884488** Chaplain: Frances Castledine Tel: 01784 884488

Barnet Hospital **Tel: 0845 111 4000** Chaplain: Awaiting appointment
Bishops Wood **Tel: 01923 835814** *Northwood* Tel: 01923 825639
Bushey BUPA **Tel: 020 8950 9090** *Bushey* Tel: 020 8950 2077

Capio Nightingale **Tel: 020 7535 7700** *Marylebone* Tel: 020 7723 5101
Central Middlesex **Tel: 020 8965 5733** Chaplain: Fr Agustin Paunon Tel: 020 8869 2113 (Sun-Thu 9-5pm) Email: LNWH-tr.Chaplaincy@nhs.net
Charing Cross **Tel: 020 3311 1056** Chaplains: Fr Giles Pinnock, Fr Blaise Amadi CM Tel: 020 3312 1508
Chase Farm **Tel: 0845 111 4000** Chaplain: Awaiting appointment
Chelsea & Westminster **Tel: 020 8746 8000** Chaplain: Awaiting appointment
Clayponds **Tel: 020 8560 4011** *Brentford* Tel: 020 8560 1671
Clementine Churchill **Tel: 020 8872 3872** *Sudbury* Tel: 020 8904 2552
Colindale **Tel: 020 8952 2381** *Kingsbury Green* Tel: 020 8204 2834 / 2117
Cromwell **Tel: 020 7460 2000** *Kensington 2* Tel: 020 7937 9866

Ealing **Tel: 020 8967 5000** Chaplain: via Tel: 020 8967 5130
Email: LNWH-tr.Chaplaincy@nhs.net
East London & The City Mental Health NHS Trust **Tel: 0845 155 5000** Chaplain: Awaiting appointment
Edenhall Marie Curie Centre **Tel: 020 7794 0066** *Swiss Cottage* Tel: 020 7435 1388
Edgware Community **Tel: 020 8952 2381** Chaplain: Awaiting appointment
Elizabeth Garrett Anderson Wing Chaplains: Fr Peter Harries OP, Fr Serge Stasievich Tel: 020 3447 3007

Finchley Memorial **Tel: 020 8349 3121** *Finchley Church End* Tel: 020 8346 2459
Fitzroy Nuffield **Tel: 020 7723 1288** *Spanish Place* Tel: 020 7935 0943

Garden House Tel: **01462 679540** *Letchworth* Tel: 01462 683504
Gordon (The) Tel: **020 8746 8733** Chaplain: Fr Giles Pinnock
Tel: 020 3312 1508
Great Ormond Street Tel: **020 7405 9200** Chaplain: Anne-Marie O'Riordan

Hammersmith, Queen Charlotte's & Chelsea Tel: **020 3313 4574** Chaplains: Fr Giles Pinnock,
Fr Blaise Amadi CM Tel: 020 3312 1508
Harefield Tel: **01895 823737** *Harefield* Tel: 01895 822365
Harley Street Clinic Tel: **020 7935 7700** Chaplains: Fr Giles Pinnock, Fr Blaise Amadi CM Tel:
020 3312 1508
Harpenden BUPA Tel: **01582 763191** *Harpenden* Tel: 01582 712245
Hendon Tel: **020 8457 4500** *Hendon* Tel: 020 8202 0560
Hertfordshire Partnership Foundation Trust Tel: **01727 804814**
Hillingdon Tel: **01895 238282** Lead Chaplain: Fr Jack Creagh Tel: 01895 279433
Homerton Tel: **020 8510 5555** Chaplain: Awaiting appointment

King Edward VII Tel: **020 7486 4411** *Spanish Place* Tel: 020 7935 0943

Lister (The) Tel: **020 7730 3417** *Chelsea 1* Tel: 020 7589 5487
Lister Stevenage (The) Tel: **01438 314333** Chaplain: John O'Neil Tel: 01438 314333
London Clinic Tel: **020 7935 4444** *Spanish Place* Tel: 020 7935 0943

Meadow House Hospice Tel: **020 8746 8000**
Mildmay Mission Hospital Tel: **020 7613 6300** Lead Chaplain: Sr Bernie Devine SP
Tel: 020 7613 6307
Mile End Tel: **020 7377 7000** *Mile End* Tel: 020 8980 1845
Moorfields Eye Tel: **020 7253 3411** *Moorfields* Tel: 020 7247 8390
Mount Vernon Tel: **01923 826111** Chaplain: Tel: 01438 314333

National Hospital for Neurology & Neurosurgery Chaplains: Fr Peter Harries OP, Fr Serge
Stasievich Tel: 020 3447 3007
North London Hospice Tel: **020 8343 8841** *Finchley North* Tel: 020 8446 0224
North London Nuffield Tel: **020 8366 2122** *Enfield* Tel: 020 8363 2569
North Middlesex Tel: **020 8887 2000** *Edmonton* Tel: 020 8803 6631
Northwick Park Tel: **020 8864 3232** Chaplain: Fr Agustin Paunon Tel: 020 8869 2113 (Sun-
Thu 9-5pm) Email: LNWH-tr.Chaplaincy@nhs.net

Peace Hospice (The) Tel: **01923 330330** *Watford* Tel: 01923 224085
Portland Hospital for Women & Children Tel: **020 7580 4400** Chaplains: Fr Giles Pinnock, Fr
Blaise Amadi CM Tel: 020 3312 1508
Potters Bar Tel: **01707 653286** *Potters Bar* Tel: 01707 654359
Princess Grace Tel: **020 7486 1234** Chaplains: Fr Giles Pinnock, Fr Blaise Amadi CM
Tel: 020 3312 1508

Queen Elizabeth II Tel: **01438 314333** Chaplain: John O'Neil Tel: 01438 314333
Queen Victoria Memorial Tel: **01707 365291** *Welwyn Garden City (Digswell)* Tel: 01707 327
434

Royal Brompton Tel: **020 7352 8121** Chaplain: Fr Edward van den Bergh Tel: 020 7808 0900

Royal Free Tel: **020 7794 0500** Chaplain: Fr John McCarthy Tel: 020 7830 2742
Royal London (Whitechapel) Tel: **020 3416 5000** Chaplains: Fr Rory Murphy IVD, Fr James McMahon OSB Tel: 020 3594 2070, Sr Andrena Mulligan SM, Sr Frances Rowe RSM
Royal Marsden Tel: **020 7352 8171** Chaplain: Fr Joseph McCullough Tel: 07881 464236
Royal National Orthopaedic Tel: **020 8954 2300** *Stanmore* Tel: 020 8954 1299
Royal National ENT and Eastman Dental Hospitals Chaplains: Fr Peter Harries OP, Fr Serge Stasievich Tel: 020 3447 3007

St Alban's City Tel: **01727 866122** Chaplain: Colette Lennon Tel: 01923 217994
St Andrew's at Harrow Bowden House Clinic Tel: **020 8966 7000** *Harrow-on-the-Hill* Tel: 020 8422 2513
St Bartholomew's Tel: **020 3416 5000** Chaplains: Fr Rory Murphy IVD, Fr James McMahon OSB Tel: 020 3465 7220
St Bernard's Tel: **020 8967 5000** Chaplain: Awaiting appointment
St Charles Square Centre for Health and Wellbeing (Mental Health Units) Tel: **020 8969 2488**
St Charles Square Palliative Care, Pembridge Hospice *St Charles Square* Tel: 020 8969 6844
St John and St Elizabeth & St John's Hospice Tel: **020 7806 4000**
Chaplain: Fr Hugh MacKenzie Tel: 020 7806 4040
St Joseph's Hospice Tel: **020 8525 6000** Chaplain: Fr Gerard O'Brien Tel: 020 8525 3032
St Luke's Kenton Grange Hospice Tel: **020 8382 8000** *Kenton* Tel: 020 8204 3550
St Luke's Woodside Tel: **020 8219 1800** *Muswell Hill* Tel: 020 8883 5607
St Mark's (Northwick Park) Tel: **020 8864 3232** Chaplain: Fr Augustin Paunon
Tel: 020 8869 2113 (Sun-Thu 9-5pm) E-mail: LNWH-tr.Chaplaincy@nhs.net
St Mary's Tel: **020 3312 1508** Chaplains: Fr Giles Pinnock, Fr Blaise Amadi CM
St Pancras Hospital Tel: **020 7530 3500** Chaplain: Awaiting appointment
St Pancras Hospital (Evergreen, Rochester & Oakwood Wards) Chaplains: Fr Peter Harries OP, Fr Serge Stasievich Tel: 020 3447 3007

University College (UCLH) Chaplains: Fr Peter Harries OP, Fr Serge Stasievich, Sr Pauline Forde DC Tel: 020 3447 3007
University College on Westmoreland Street Chaplains: Fr Peter Harries OP, Fr Serge Stasievich Tel: 020 3447 3007

Watford General Tel: **01923 244 366** Chaplain: Colette Lennon Tel: 01923 217994
Wellington (The) Tel: **020 7586 5959** Chaplains: Fr Giles Pinnock, Fr Blaise Amadi CM
Tel: 020 3312 1508
West Middlesex Tel: **020 8321 5447** Chaplain: Sr Clementina Nasimiyu
Western Eye Tel: **020 3312 1508** Chaplains: Fr Giles Pinnock, Fr Blaise Amadi CM
Whittington Tel: **020 7272 3070** Chaplain: Fr Oliver Ugwu Tel: 020 7288 5337
Willesden Community Tel: **020 8459 1292** *Willesden Green* Tel: 020 8451 4677

SPORT

Chaplain Mgr Vladimir Felzmann **Vaughan House, 46 Francis Street SW1P 1QN**
Tel: **07810 116508** Email: Info@jp2f4s.org

UNIVERSITIES AND INSTITUTES OF HIGHER EDUCATION

See pages 124/5 in Parish Directory

OTHER JURISDICTIONS

BISHOPRIC OF THE FORCES

Wellington House, St Omer Barracks, Thornhill Road, Aldershot GU11 2BG
Tel: 01252 348234

Bishop of the Forces Paul Mason (2016; 2018) Email: Paul.mason111@mod.gov.uk
Wellington House, St Omer Barracks, Thornhill Road, Aldershot, Hants GU11 2BG
Vicar General Fr Nicholas Gosnell Email: stmichael.stgeorge@live.co.uk
Chancellor Fr Stephen Sharkey RAChD Email: Stephen.sharkey941@mod.gov.uk
Secretary Diane Restall Email: Diane.restall654@mod.gov.uk

EPARCHY OF THE HOLY FAMILY OF LONDON

The Eparchy serves Ukrainian and Belarusian Catholics, and also Slovakian Greek Catholics
Chancery, 22 Binney Street W1K 5BQ Tel: 020 7629 1073
Eparch Awaiting appointment
Apostolic Administrator Rt Rev Mykola Matwijiwskyj **Chancellor** Very Rev David J Senyk
See *Ukrainian Cathedral* and *Belarusian Catholic Church* under Eastern Catholic Churches
in the listing above.

ORDINARIATE OF OUR LADY OF WALSINGHAM

On 15 January 2011 the Congregation for the Doctrine of the Faith published a Decree
which formally established a 'Personal Ordinariate' in England and Wales for groups of
Anglican faithful and their clergy who wish to enter into full communion with the Catholic
Church.

The Ordinariate of Our Lady of Walsingham, 24 Golden Square W1F 9JR
Tel: 020 7440 5750
Email: enquiries@ordinariate.org.uk Web: www.ordinariate.org.uk
Ordinariate Clergy in the Diocese: Mgr Keith Newton (Ordinary), Frs Simon Chinery,
Mark Elliott-Smith, Alan Griffin, Antony Homer (see Other Priests in the Diocese, Section 4,
for contact details)
Warwick Street Parish is in the care of the Ordinariate; and a Sunday Mass is also
celebrated in **Hemel Hempstead West Parish.**

PERSONAL PRELATURE OF THE HOLY CROSS AND OPUS DEI

Prelate (resident in Rome) Mgr Fernando Ocáriz
Regional Vicar for Great Britain Mgr Nicholas Morrish MA STD
(1) 4 Orme Court W2 4RL Tel: 020 7229 7574 (Queensway)
Other centres in the diocese:
(2) Pembridge House, 29 Pembridge Square W2 4DS Tel: 020 7221 0588 (Bayswater)

(3) Dawliffe Hall, 2 Chelsea Embankment SW3 4LG Tel: 020 7351 0719 (Chelsea 1)

(4) Lakefield, 41a Maresfield Gardens NW3 5RY Tel: 020 7794 5669 (Swiss Cottage)

(5) Netherhall House, Nutley Terrace NW3 5SA Tel: 020 7435 8888 (Swiss Cottage)

(6) Westpark, 1 Leopold Road W5 3PB Tel: 020 8992 3954 (Chiswick)

(7) Woodlands, 12 Gunnersbury Avenue W5 3NJ Tel: 020 8992 4025 (Chiswick)

(8) Ashwell House, Shepherdess Walk N1 7NA Tel: 020 7490 3296 (Hoxton)

(9) Elmore, 8 Orme Court W2 4RL Tel: 020 7243 9411 (Queensway)

Priests: Azagra, Dancho (5), Bristow, Peter (9), Diaper, Paul (5), Hayward, Paul (1), Hnylycia, Stefan (5), Marsh, Bernard (6), Morrish, Mgr Nicholas (1), Sheehan, Gerard (9), Soane, Andrew (1), Stork, Mgr Richard (5)

Opus Dei Information Office, 6 Orme Court W2 4RL Tel: 020 7221 9176

Fax: 020 7243 9400   Email: info.uk@opusdei.org   Web: www.opusdei.org.uk

SYRO-MALABAR EPARCHY OF GREAT BRITAIN

Pope Francis established the Syro-Malabar Eparchy of Great Britain on 28 July 2016 for members of the Syro-Malabar community in England, Scotland and Wales.

Eparch Bishop Joseph Srampickal (2016)

Eparchial Curia, St Alphonsa Cathedral, St Ignatius Square, Preston PR1 1TT

Tel: 01722 396065   Email: smcuria@gmail.com   Web: www.eparchyofgreatbritain.org

SECTION 3

LISTED BUILDINGS

in order of Parish, Building, Address, Local Authority and Grade

Cathedral, Most Precious Blood Victoria Street SW1P 1QW City of Westminster I

Allen Hall Seminary Chapel Beaufort Street SW3 5AA Kensington & Chelsea II

Ashford, St Michael Clarendon Road TW15 2QD Spelthorne II

Bayswater, St Mary of the Angels Church and Presbytery Moorhouse Road W2 5DJ, City of Westminster II*,

Bethnal Green, Our Lady of the Assumption Victoria Park Square E2 9PB Tower Hamlets II

Bishops Stortford, St Joseph & the English Martyrs Windhill CM23 2ND East Herts II

Bow, Our Lady Refuge of Sinners and St Catherine of Siena 177 Bow Road E3 2SG Tower Hamlets II

Brentford, St John the Evangelist Boston Park Road TW8 9JF Hounslow II

Brook Green, Holy Trinity Brook Green W6 7BL Hammersmith & Fulham II*

Buntingford, St Richard of Chichester Station Road SG9 9HT East Herts II

Chelsea, St Mary Cadogan Street SW3 2QR Kensington & Chelsea II*

Chelsea, Most Holy Redeemer & St Thomas More Cheyne Row SW3 5HS Kensington & Chelsea II

Chiswick, Our Lady of Grace & St Edward High Road W4 4PU Hounslow II

Chorleywood, St John Fisher Shire Lane WD3 5NH Three Rivers II

Clerkenwell, Ss Peter & Paul Amwell Street EC1R 1UL Islington II

Commercial Road, St Mary & St Michael Lukin Street E1 0AA Tower Hamlets II

Covent Garden, Corpus Christi Maiden Lane WC2E 7NB City of Westminster II

Ealing, Abbey Church of St Benedict Charlbury Grove W5 2DY Ealing II
Ely Place, St Etheldreda Holborn Circus EC1N 6RY Camden I

Farm Street, The Immaculate Conception Farm Street W1K 3AH City of Westminster II*
French Church, Notre Dame de France Leicester Place WC2H 7BX City of Westminster II*
Fulham, St Thomas of Canterbury Rylston Road SW6 7HW Hammersmith & Fulham **Church** II*, **Presbytery** II, **War Memorial & Adjacent Tomb** II
Fulham Road, Our Lady of Dolours Fulham Road SW10 9EL Kensington & Chelsea II

Golders Green, St Edward the Confessor Finchley Road NW11 7NE Barnet II

Hammersmith, Sacred Heart School Hammersmith Road W6 7DG Hammersmith & Fulham II*
Hampstead, St Mary Holly Place NW3 6QU Camden II*
Harpenden, Our Lady of Lourdes Kirkwick Avenue, Harpenden AL5 2QH St Albans II
Harrow on the Hill, Our Lady & St Thomas of Canterbury Roxborough Park HA1 3BE Harrow II
Hatfield, Marychurch, Salisbury Square, Old Hatfield AL9 5JD Welwyn Hatfield II
Haverstock Hill, St Dominic Southampton Road NW5 4LB Camden II*
Hertford, Immaculate Conception & St Joseph St John's Street SG14 1RX East Herts II
Highgate, St Joseph Highgate Hill N19 5NE Islington II*
Holloway, Sacred Heart of Jesus Eden Grove N7 8EN Islington II
Hoxton, St Monica Hoxton Square N1 6NT Hackney II

Islington, St John the Evangelist Duncan Terrace N1 8AL Islington II
Italian Church, St Peter Clerkenwell Road EC1R 5DL Camden II*

Kensal New Town, Our Lady of the Holy Souls Bosworth Road W10 5DJ Kensington & Chelsea II
Kensington 1, Our Lady of Victories Kensington High Street W8 6AF Kensington & Chelsea II
Kensington 2, Our Lady of Mt. Carmel & St Simon Stock Kensington Church Street W8 4BB Kensington & Chelsea II
Kensington 2, Assumption Convent Kensington Square W8 5HH Kensington & Chelsea II
Kentish Town, Our Lady Help of Christians Lady Margaret Road NW5 2XT Camden II

Lincoln's Inn Fields, Ss Anselm & Cecilia Kingsway WC2A 3JA Camden II

Marylebone, Our Lady of the Rosary Old Marylebone Road NW1 5QT City of Westminster II
Mile End, Guardian Angels Mile End Road E3 4QS Tower Hamlets II
Moorfields, St Mary Eldon Street EC2M 7LS City of London II

Notting Hill, St Francis of Assisi Pottery Lane W11 4NQ Kensington & Chelsea II*

Ogle Street, St Charles Borromeo Ogle Street W1W 6HS City of Westminster II
Oratory, Immaculate Heart of Mary Brompton Road SW7 2RP Kensington & Chelsea II*

Pinner, St Luke Love Lane HA5 3EX Harrow II
Polish Church, Our Lady of Czestochowa Devonia Road N1 8JJ Islington II
Poplar, St Mary & St Joseph Pekin Street E14 6EZ Tower Hamlets II

Queensway, Our Lady Queen of Heaven Inverness Place W2 3JF City of Westminster II

Ruislip South, St Gregory the Great (Church and Hall) Victoria Road HA4 0EG Hillingdon II

St John's Wood, Chapel of the Hospital of St John and St Elizabeth
Grove End Road NW8 9NH City of Westminster II
St John's Wood, Our Lady Lisson Grove NW8 8LA City of Westminster II
St John's Wood, St Edward's Convent Harewood Avenue NW1 6LD City of Westminster II*
St Margarets-on-Thames, St Margaret St Margaret's Road TW1 1RL Richmond II
Shepherds Bush, The Holy Ghost and St Stephen (Church and Presbytery)
Ashchurch Grove W12 9BU Hammersmith & Fulham II
Soho Square, St Patrick Soho Square W1D 4NR City of Westminster II *
Spanish Place, St James George Street W1U 3QY City of Westminster
(Church II*, Presbytery II)
Stamford Hill, St Ignatius High Road N15 6ND Haringey II
Stanmore, St William of York Du Cros Drive HA7 4TJ Harrow II
Sudbury, St George Harrow Road HA0 2QE Brent II
Swiss Cottage, St Thomas More Maresfield Gardens NW3 5SU Camden II

Tollington Park, St Mellitus Tollington Park N4 3AG Islington II
Tower Hill, English Martyrs Prescot Street E1 8BB Tower Hamlets II
Twickenham, St Mary's University Waldegrave Road TW1 4ST Richmond I
Ukrainian Cathedral, Holy Family Duke Street W1K 5BQ City of Westminster II
Underwood Road, St Anne Underwood Road E1 5AW Tower Hamlets II*
University Chaplaincy 111 Gower Street WC1E 6AR Camden II

Wapping, St Patrick Dundee Street E1W 2PH Tower Hamlets II
Ware, Chapel of St Edmund's College Old Hall Green SG11 1DS East Herts I
Warwick Street, Our Lady of the Assumption & St Gregory Golden Square W1F 9JR
City of Westminster II*
Watford, Holy Rood Market Street WD18 0PJ Watford I
Wealdstone, St Joseph Wealdstone High Road HA3 5EE Harrow II
Wembley I, St Joseph High Road, Wembley HA9 6AG Brent II
West Drayton, St Catherine's The Green, West Drayton UB7 7PJ Hillingdon II
Willesden, Our Lady of Willesden Acton Lane NW10 9AX Brent II

SECTION 3

CENTRAL LONDON CHURCHES

CHURCHES NEAR RAILWAY TERMINALS

CANNON STREET; FENCHURCH STREET; LONDON BRIDGE:
The English Martyrs, 26 Prescot Street E1 8BB *(Tower Hill)*
CHARING CROSS: Corpus Christi, 1 Maiden Lane WC2E 7NB *(Covent Garden)*
EUSTON; KING'S CROSS (West side); ST PANCRAS & EUROSTAR TERMINAL: St
Aloysius, Phoenix Road NW1 1TA *off Eversholt Street (Somers Town)*
KING'S CROSS (East side): The Blessed Sacrament, 165 Copenhagen Street N1 0SR
off York Way (Copenhagen Street)
LIVERPOOL STREET: St Mary Moorfields, 4-5 Eldon Street EC2M 7LS *(Moorfields)*
LONDON BRIDGE: Our Lady of La Salette & St Joseph, 14 Melior Street SE1 3QP
Tel: 020 7407 1948 *(Southwark)*
MARYLEBONE; PADDINGTON: Our Lady of the Rosary, 211 Old Marylebone Road
NW1 5QT *(Marylebone)*
VICTORIA: Westminster Cathedral, Victoria Street SW1P 1QW *(Cathedral)*
WATERLOO: St Patrick's, 26 Cornwall Road SE1 8TW Tel: 020 7928 4818 *(Southwark)*

CENTRAL LOCATIONS

Services in the Churches listed will be found in the Parish Directory section, under the entry indicated here in bold and italic.

CITY (I) St Mary Moorfields, Eldon Street EC2M 7LS *north of Finsbury Circus, near Liverpool Street Stn & Moorgate TfL Stn* Tel: 020 7247 8390 *(Moorfields)*

CITY (II) The English Martyrs, 26 Prescot Street E1 8BB *off Mansell Street, near Tower of London* Tel: 020 7488 4654 *(Tower Hill)*

CITY (III) St Joseph, Lamb's Buildings EC1Y 8LE *off Bunhill Row, near Barbican Centre* Tel: 020 7628 0326 *(Bunhill Row)*

HOLBORN CIRCUS St Etheldreda, Ely Place EC1N 6RY *off Charterhouse Street, beside Holborn Circus* Tel: 020 7405 1061 *(Ely Place)*

HOLBORN KINGSWAY St Anselm and St Cecilia, Kingsway WC2A 3JA *east side just south of Holborn TfL Stn* Tel: 020 7405 0376 *(Lincoln's Inn Fields)*

LEICESTER SQUARE Notre Dame de France, Leicester Place WC2H 7BX *north side of Leicester Square* Tel: 020 7437 9363 *(French Church)*

MAYFAIR Immaculate Conception, Farm Street W1K 3AH *entrance also in Mount Street, between South Audley Street and Berkeley Square* Tel: 020 7493 7811 *(Farm Street)*

PICCADILLY CIRCUS The Assumption, Warwick Street W1R 3PA *close to Piccadilly Circus* Tel: 020 7437 1525 *(Warwick Street)*

SOHO St Patrick, Soho Square W1D 4NR *in angle between Oxford Street and Charing Cross Road; near Tottenham Court Road TfL Stn* Tel: 020 7437 2010 *(Soho Square)*

STRAND Corpus Christi, 1 Maiden Lane WC2E 7NB *off Southampton Street on north side of the Strand; near Covent Garden* Tel: 020 7836 4700 *(Covent Garden)*

VICTORIA Westminster Cathedral, Ashley Place SW1P 1QW *south side of Victoria Street, close to Victoria Stn* Tel: 020 7798 9097 *(Cathedral)*

WEST END (I) St Charles Borromeo, Ogle Street W1W 6HS *off eastern end of New Cavendish Street* Tel: 020 7636 2883 *(Ogle Street)*

WEST END (II) St James, George Street W1U 3QY *eastern end, near junction with Marylebone High Street* Tel: 020 7935 0943 *(Spanish Place)*

WEST END (III) Our Lady of the Rosary, Old Marylebone Road NW1 5QT *south side of Old Marylebone Road, by junction with Marylebone Road* Tel: 020 7723 5101 *(Marylebone)*

WEST END (IV) Tyburn Convent, 8 Hyde Park Place W2 2LJ *in Bayswater Road, close to Marble Arch* Perpetual Exposition of the Blessed Sacrament Tel: 020 7723 7262 *(Marylebone)*

SECTION 3

PARISHES AND LONDON POSTAL DISTRICTS

Parishes are listed according to the postal address of the church or presbytery; postal district numbers following the name of a parish indicate that parts of those districts are also within the parish. Districts south of the Thames (Southwark Diocese) or east of the Lea (Brentwood) are not included.

E1	Commercial Road		N10	Muswell Hill N2
E1	German Church		N11	New Southgate N13, N14, N20, N22
E1	Tower Hill EC3		N12	Finchley (North) N3, N20
E1	Underwood Road E2		N13	Palmers Green N14, N21
E1	Wapping		N14	Cockfosters N21
E2	Bethnal Green E1		N15	Stamford Hill N16, E5
E2	Lithuanian Church		N15	West Green N8, N17, N22
E3	Bow		N16	Stoke Newington N4
E3	Bow Common E14		N17	Tottenham
E3	Mile End E1		N19	Highgate N6, N8, NW5
E5	Clapton E8, N16		N19	Archway
E5	Clapton Park E9		N20	Whetstone N12
E9	Hackney E8		N22	Wood Green N8, N11, N17
E9	Homerton E5			
E14	Limehouse		NW1	Somers Town WC1
E14	Millwall		NW1	Marylebone W1, W2
E14	Poplar		NW1	Camden Town N1, N7
			NW2	Cricklewood NW3, NW11, NW6
EC1	Bunhill Row		NW2	Dollis Hill NW10
EC1	Clerkenwell WC1, N1		NW3	Hampstead
EC1	Ely Place EC4		NW3	Swiss Cottage NW6, NW8
EC1	Italian Church		NW4	Hendon NW7, NW9
EC2	Moorfields EC1, EC3, EC4, E1		NW5	Haverstock Hill NW3, NW1
			NW5	Kentish Town NW1, N7, N19
N1	Copenhagen Street		NW6	Kilburn NW2, NW8
N1	Hoxton E2, EC2, EC1		NW6	Kilburn West
N1	Islington EC1		NW7	Mill Hill
N1	Kingsland N5, N16, E8		NW8	St John's Wood NW1, W2, W9
N1	Polish Church 1		NW9	Grahame Park
N2	Finchley (East) N3, N6, N12, NW11		NW9	Hendon (West) NW4
N3	Finchley (Church End) N12, NW11, NW7		NW9	Kingsbury Green
N4	Manor House		NW10	Kensal Rise NW6
N4	Tollington Park N7, N19		NW10	Neasden
N5	Highbury N4		NW10	Stonebridge
N7	Holloway N5, N19		NW10	Willesden
N8	Stroud Green N4, N19		NW10	Willesden Green NW2, NW6
N9	Edmonton N13, N18, N21		NW11	Golders Green NW3, N2

SECTION 3

SW1	Westminster Cathedral
SW1	Pimlico
SW3	Chelsea 1 SW1
SW3	Chelsea 2 SW10
SW6	Fulham
SW6	Parsons Green
SW6	Stephendale Road
SW7	Oratory SW1, SW3, W2, W8
SW10	Fulham Road SW3, SW5, SW7
W1	Farm Street SW1
W1	Ogle Street WC1
W1	Soho Square EC1, WC2
W1	Spanish Place
W1	Warwick Street SW1
W2	Bayswater W11
W2	Paddington
W2	Queensway
W3	Acton
W3	East Acton NW10, W10, W12
W3	West Acton W5

W4	Chiswick W3, W5
W4	Grove Park
W5	Ealing W13
W5	Polish Church 3
W6	Brook Green W12, W14
W6	Hammersmith SW6
W7	Hanwell W13
W8	Kensington 1 SW5, W11, W14
W8	Kensington 2 SW5, SW7, W11
W9	Harrow Road
W10	Kensal New Town W9
W10	St Charles Square
W11	Notting Hill W10
W12	Polish Church 2
W12	Shepherd's Bush W3, W6
W12	White City
W13	Northfields W5, W7
WC2	French Church
WC2	Lincoln's Inn Fields EC4, WC1
WC2	Covent Garden SW1

DIOCESAN STATISTICS

Priests of the Diocese

Working in the Diocese	184
Chaplains / Teaching	20
Further Studies	2
Others working outside the Diocese	23
Sabbatical	1
Retired / Supply	92
Total (includes 5 Bishops)	**326**

Priests of other Dioceses

From England & Wales	5
From other countries (includes Poland)	26
Eastern Catholic (14, not resident in diocese 4,	
Diocesan Priest 1; Religious 6)	10
Ethnic Chaplains (excludes Deacons, Religious)	27
Ethnic Chaplains resident in diocese	19
(also excludes those otherwise counted, e.g. Religious)	
Ordinariate OLW	5
Prelature of Opus Dei	10
Total working in the diocese	**87**
Total resident in the diocese	**68**

Priests of Religious Congregations & Societies of Apostolic Life, including Chaplains

African Missions Society 2; Assumptionists: 5; Augustinians: 7; Augustinian Recollects: 1; Benedictines (Annunciation): 1; Benedictines (English): 12; Benedictines (Olivetan): 1; Carmelites (Discalced): 4; Carmelites of Mary Immaculate: 3; Chemin Neuf Community: 2; Claretians: 5; Columban Fathers: 4; Comboni Missionaries 4; Congregation of the Sacred Hearts: 5; Consolata Fathers: 2; Divine Providence, Sons of: 4; Divine Word Missionaries: 8; Dominicans: 8; Franciscans: 2; Institute of Charity: 2; Jesuits: 34; Lebanese Maronite: 3; Marian Fathers: 6; Marist Fathers: 4; Mill Hill Missionaries: 2; Missionaries of Africa: 15; Missionaries of St Paul: 4; Missionary Society of St Thomas the Apostle: 1; Monaci Studiti Ucraini: 1; Montfort Missionaries: 2 Oblates of Mary Immaculate: 10; Oratorians: 9; Pallottine Fathers: 7; Passionists: 5; Salvatorians: 9; Scalabrini Fathers: 1; Servites: 4; Society of Christ: 1; Society of Divine Vocations: 2; Spiritans 8; Stigmatines: 1; Vincentians 5

Total (includes 3 Bishops)	**219**
Total for Other & Religious Priests	**305**
Other & Religious Priests resident in the diocese	**286**

Permanent Deacons	31
Parishes	210

PARISH STATISTICS 2018

In the Parish Directory each parish has its deanery noted thus: *Westminster Deanery*.
The following tables are compiled from the parish returns; where no figures are given,
returns have not been received..

Mass attendance for 2019 has been counted over the last two Sundays in September and
the first two Sundays of October, following a decision of the Bishops' Conference.

Parish	Sunday Mass	Baptisms	Receptions	Marriages
Barnet Deanery				
Barnet	778	27	1	7
Burnt Oak	638	42	2	3
Cricklewood	873	50	0	16
Edgware	794	33	2	2
Finchley Church End	636	9	0	1
Finchley East	522	21	0	2
Finchley North	670	20	0	3
Golders Green	670	10	0	5
Grahame Park	300	10	0	0
Hendon	497	14	0	3
Hendon West	272	3	0	4
Mill Hill	778	32	1	10
New Barnet	457	24	3	3
Whetstone	671	35	1	6
Brent Deanery				
Dollis Hill	695	27	0	4
Kensal Rise	451	21	1	2
Kingsbury Green	774	163	0	16
Neasden	202	15	0	0
Romanian Chaplaincy	583	123	5	10
Stonebridge	370	18	0	0
Wembley 1	2161	69	0	60
Wembley 2	937	33	0	10
Wembley 3	483	12	1	1
Willesden	901	27	2	5
Willesden Green	1007	85	0	7

Parish	Sunday Mass	Baptisms	Receptions	Marriages
Camden Deanery				
Camden Town	400	8	0	7
Hampstead	673	29	8	2
Haverstock Hill	529	45	3	11
Kentish Town	550	14	0	4
Kilburn	1458	123	3	10
Kilburn West	174	8	0	0
Somers Town	401	28	1	2
Swiss Cottage	365	9	1	0
Ealing Deanery				
Acton	885	74	0	3
Acton East	411	68	3	5
Acton West	283	11	0	1
Ealing	1350	81	2	16
Greenford	2003	105	1	3
Hanwell	988	8	0	1
Northfields	830	38	0	8
Perivale	562	9	2	0
Polish Church 3	4280	151	0	6
Southall	2006	94	1	12
Enfield Deanery				
Cockfosters	414	8	0	1
Cuffley	128	15	0	0
Edmonton	1020	46	0	8
Enfield	2110	98	4	13
New Southgate	1450	42	1	2
Palmers Green	1456	80	1	1
Ponders End	1150	40	6	7
Potters Bar	555	36	0	4
Hackney Deanery				
Clapton	415	18	0	4
Clapton Park	163	13	2	0
Hackney	626	7	0	0
Homerton	349	16	0	0
Hoxton	412	26	0	12
Kingsland	932	54	2	0
Manor House	202	17	0	2
Stoke Newington	221	19	0	1

SECTION 3

Parish	Sunday Mass	Baptisms	Receptions	Marriages
Hammersmith & Fulham Deanery				
Brook Green	970	64	5	9
Fulham 1	730	25	1	13
Fulham 2 (Stephendale Road)	243	26	2	2
Hammersmith	901	53	8	12
Parsons Green	520	72	1	0
Polish Church 2	1361	0	30	28
Shepherds Bush	654	36	2	9
White City	509	23	0	4
Haringey Deanery				
Muswell Hill	861	34	2	2
Stamford Hill	1570	124	2	105
Stroud Green	539	31	1	3
Tottenham	788	4	11	5
West Green	640	1	4	10
Wood Green	970	38	2	5
Harrow Deanery				
Harrow-on-the-Hill	1009	50	1	11
Harrow North	798	22	1	7
Harrow South and Northolt	864	9	0	1
Headstone Lane	450	36	2	3
Kenton	762	28	1	4
Pinner	696	22	0	0
Stanmore	417	14	0	0
Sudbury	1575	48	5	8
Wealdstone & Harrow Weald	1381	53	1	3
Hillingdon Deanery				
Eastcote	335	12	2	0
Harefield	301	9	0	2
Hayes	1817	80	0	7
Heathrow Airport	143	5	0	0
Hillingdon	670	28	0	1
Northwood	451	9	0	2
Ruislip	1134	56	1	15
Ruislip South	678	22	0	0
Uxbridge	773	35	1	2
West Drayton	666	16	4	4
Yeading	786	34	4	2

Parish	Sunday Mass	Baptisms	Receptions	Marriages
Hounslow Deanery				
Brentford	475	19	0	1
Chiswick	1586	42	2	1
Cranford	595	32	0	3
Feltham	2020	112	8	4
Grove Park	96	5	0	0
[Gunnersbury	58	0	0	0]
Heston	615	31	5	5
Hounslow	3863	99	1	1
Isleworth	789	50	1	9
Osterley	522	18	0	4
Islington Deanery				
Archway	348	8	1	1
Bunhill Row	81	3	1	0
Clerkenwell	194	9	0	0
Copenhagen Street	162	16	1	0
Highbury	615	47	2	5
Highgate	629	75	1	7
Holloway	458	11	3	2
Islington	495	65	3	4
Polish Church 1	1338	42	0	4
Tollington Park	297	35	1	4
Kensington and Chelsea Deanery				
Chelsea 1	617	27	2	5
Chelsea 2	1151	31	2	7
Fulham Road	568	38	2	5
Kensington 1	1686	54	5	9
Kensington 2	826	31	1	1
Oratory	2248	163	11	30
Lea Valley Deanery				
Bishop's Stortford	918	68	2	16
Buntingford	83	7	1	1
Cheshunt	263	19	0	3
Hertford	444	46	1	9
Hoddesdon	490	42	1	2
Old Hall Green and Puckeridge	64	0	0	2
Waltham Cross	1323	61	2	12
Ware	319	38	1	5

Parish	Sunday Mass	Baptisms	Receptions	Marriages
Marylebone Deanery				
Farm Street	552	76	7	28
Marylebone	507	8	2	1
Ogle Street	370	10	1	3
St John's Wood	965	31	1	1
Spanish Place	1308	77	4	20
University	361	11	3	1
North Kensington Deanery				
Bayswater	734	51	2	4
Harrow Road	198	10	0	0
Kensal New Town	381	22	2	4
Lebanese Church (at Paddington)	225	9	0	5
Notting Hill	619	46	0	3
Paddington	70	3	0	0
Queensway	312	9	1	0
St Charles Square	394	7	1	0
St Albans Deanery				
Berkhamsted	374	21	0	1
Borehamwood	479	51	1	2
Borehamwood North	245	2	0	0
Harpenden	775	49	3	6
Hemel Hempstead East Parishes	650	38	2	3
Hemel Hempstead West Parishes	532	65	0	6
London Colney	374	9	0	2
Radlett	178	5	0	0
Redbourn	141	13	0	4
St Albans	1114	103	4	15
St Albans South	510	18	1	3
Shenley	78	4	0	0
Tring	175	6	1	2
Wheathampstead	153	8	0	2

Parish	Sunday Mass	Baptisms	Receptions	Marriages
Stevenage Deanery				
Baldock	317	23	2	5
Hatfield	185	11	2	0
Hatfield South	485	28	0	1
Hitchin	380	26	1	3
Knebworth	302	6	0	2
Letchworth	509	35	0	4
Royston	337	15	0	4
Stevenage Bedwell	730	46	4	3
Stevenage Old Town	276	0	0	0
Stevenage Shephall	618	51	3	3
Welwyn Garden City	192	24	0	2
Welwyn Garden City Digswell	329	13	0	0
Welwyn Garden City East	413	57	9	8
Tower Hamlets Deanery				
Bethnal Green	250	19	1	3
Bow	480	21	1	3
Bow Common	621	82	2	3
Commercial Road	348	59	1	3
German Church	70	4	0	1
Limehouse	156	8	0	3
Lithuanian Church	395	201	1	6
Mile End	343	18	1	0
Millwall	370	19	1	1
Poplar	300	37	1	4
Tower Hill	144	7	0	2
Underwood Road	121	9	0	0
Wapping	361	20	0	2
Upper Thames Deanery				
Ashford	501	62	3	5
Hampton Hill	463	32	0	0
Hampton-on-Thames	261	18	1	0
St Margarets-on-Thames	394	24	1	0
Shepperton	160	8	0	0
Staines-upon-Thames	647	36	3	5
Stanwell	281	14	0	1
Sunbury-on-Thames	362	26	2	4
Teddington	397	17	3	9
Twickenham	478	54	7	5
Whitton	878	50	0	0

SECTION 3

Parish Statistics

Parish	Sunday Mass	Baptisms	Receptions	Marriages
Watford Deanery				
Abbots Langley	398	41	9	3
Bushey & Oxhey	879	55	7	6
Carpenders Park	185	33	5	0
Chipperfield	141	19	0	0
Chorleywood	96	1	0	0
Croxley Green	194	6	0	0
Garston	545	57	5	6
Mill End and Maple Cross	228	5	0	0
Rickmansworth	312	31	0	8
Watford	1443	45	2	6
Watford North	519	70	4	3
Westminster Deanery				
Cathedral	3641	91	21	13
Covent Garden	268	2	0	0
Ely Place	144	39	0	42
French Church	660	73	2	3
Italian Church	600	113	6	19
Lincoln's Inn Fields	425	19	0	0
Moorfields	71	13	2	8
Pimlico	608	37	0	3
Soho Square	572	15	2	4
Warwick Street	115	0	0	1
TOTAL FOR DIOCESE	**139,650**	**7,607**	**367**	**1,113**

Note to the Statistics: These figures do not include those which are reported separately to Rome, e.g. those for the Eastern Catholic Churches and chaplaincies. Baptisms, Marriages and Receptions undertaken by Ethnic Chaplaincies and recorded in parish registers are included in the above statistics. However, Sunday Mass attendances for the majority of the Ethnic Chaplaincies are not included.

JUSTICE AND PEACE CONTACTS

Here are listed the Justice and Peace contacts for each parish. If the parish is not noted below, then please contact the Parish Priest with regard to Justice and Peace matters. Please contact justiceandpeace@rcdow.org.uk if the details below need updating.

Cathedral Mary Wogar

Archway Rachel McGonigal

Berkhamsted David & Lesley Brinsden
Bishop's Stortford Astrid Davies
Bunhill Row Martin Pendergast
Burnt Oak Joey Flores
Bushey Sue Schmitt

Chelsea 1 John Wilson
Chiswick Hugh Caldin
Cockfosters Frances Halliday
Copenhagen Street Sr Miriam Bruder

Ealing Abbey Martha Rumian
Edmonton Lauri Clarke
Enfield Tony Sheen

Finchley Church End Anne Godwin
Finchley East Daniel Servini
Fulham 1 Kevin Lawler
Fulham Road Henry Stovell

Garston Deacon Paul Quinn
Greenford Teresa Byrne

Hackney Tigger Cullinan
Hammersmith Social Justice Forum Manager
Hampstead Santana Luis
Hampton Hill Bernie McKay
Hanwell Angie Harris
Harpenden Graham & Liz Ryan
Harrow North Elspeth Everitt
Harrow Road Patricia McAllister
Harrow-on-the-Hill Angela Gannon
Hatfield Angela Madden
Haverstock Hill Keiran Proffer
Hayes Ann Mullaney
Headstone Lane Dominic Rodriguez
Hemel Hempstead Boxmoor Richard Dodd

Hemel Hempstead East David Toorawa
Hemel Hempstead West Camille Fidgett
Heston Martin Birdseye
Highgate Edmund Tierney
Hillingdon Jill Rhodes
Hitchin One World Group
Hoddesdon Tony Barrell
Hounslow Corrine Lynch

Kensal Rise Oonagh O'Toole
Kentish Town Margaret Harvey
Kenton Colette Lennon
Kilburn Fr Lylie Fernando
Kilburn West Benedict Ogbolu
Kingsbury Green Ann Wade
Kingsland Henrietta Cullinan

Letchworth Garden City Mary Ryan

Manor House Barbara Kentish
Mill End Sue Schmitt

New Barnet Sheila Gallagher & Fausta Valentine
New Southgate John Donnelly
Northfields Anna Maria Dupelycz

Osterley Nicolette Robson

Pimlico Judyann Masters
Pinner Ian & Belinda Brandon
Potters Bar Rosaleen Pinto

Queensway Evelyn Lopez

Radlett Deacon Tony Barter
Redbourn Mark Yate
Rickmansworth Judy Gordon
Ruislip Robert Nunn

St Albans Anne Romain
St Charles Square Vanessa Davies
St John's Wood Priscilla Sharp
St Margarets-on-Thames Judith Burman

SECTION 3

Sawbridgeworth Eugene Keddy
Shepperton Daphne Argent
Stamford Hill Fr David Ardagh-Walter
Stevenage Bedwell Sr Geraldine
Stevenage Transfiguration Hannah Wright
Stroud Green Sr Anne Hogan
Sudbury Anne Nemeth
Sunbury-on-Thames Colin Bennet

Tollington Park Jo Bownas
Tottenham Innocent Uworibhor
Tring Michael Demidecki

University Chaplaincy Sr Carolyn Morrison
Uxbridge Ken Lobo

Ware Deacon Adrian Cullen
Wealdstone Ellen Teague
Welwyn Garden City East John Fogarty
Welwyn Garden City Kathryn Hubbard
Welwyn Garden City Digswell CAFOD
Group
Wembley I Rebecca Chatelier
West Green Mariantha Fomenky
Wheathampstead Marie Rose Law
White City Hilda McCafferty
Willesden Bernadette Ogombu
Willesden Green Brigid Hegarty

Section 4

ARCHBISHOPS OF WESTMINSTER SINCE THE RESTORATION OF THE HIERARCHY

Cardinal Nicholas Patrick Stephen Wiseman
Born Seville, Spain, 3 August 1802; ordained Priest 11 March 1825;
ordained as Vicar Apostolic Coadjutor for the Midland District 8 June 1840;
translated to the newly-erected Diocese of Westminster 29 September 1850;
created Cardinal 30 September 1850; died 1 February 1865.

Cardinal Henry Edward Manning
Born Totteridge House, London 15 July 1808; ordained Priest 16 June 1851;
ordained as Archbishop of Westminster 8 June 1865; created Cardinal 15 March 1875; died 14 January 1892.

Cardinal Herbert Vaughan
Born Gloucester 15 April 1832; ordained Priest 28 October 1854;
ordained as Bishop of Salford 28 October 1872; translated to Westminster 8 April 1892;
created Cardinal 16 January 1893; died 19 June 1903.

Cardinal Francis Alphonsus Bourne
Born Clapham, London 23 March 1861; ordained Priest 11 June 1884;
ordained as Bishop Coadjutor of Southwark 1 May 1896; succeeded as Bishop 9 April 1897;
translated to Westminster 11 September 1903; created Cardinal 27 November 1911; died 1 January 1935.

Cardinal Arthur Hinsley
Born Selby, Yorkshire 25 August 1865; ordained Priest 23 December 1893;
ordained Bishop of the titular see of Sebastopolis in Armenia 30 November 1926;
translated to the titular see of Sardis 9 January 1930; translated to Westminster 25 March 1935; created Cardinal 13 December 1937; died 17 March 1943.

Cardinal Bernard William Griffin
Born Birmingham 21 February 1899; ordained Priest 1 November 1924;
ordained as Auxiliary Bishop of Birmingham 30 June 1938; translated to Westminster 18 December 1943; created Cardinal 18 February 1946; died 20 August 1956.

Cardinal William Godfrey
Born Liverpool 25 September 1889; ordained Priest 1916; ordained Bishop as Apostolic Delegate 21 December 1938; translated to Liverpool 14 November 1953; translated to Westminster 3 December 1956; created Cardinal 15 December 1958; died 22 January 1963.

Cardinal John Carmel Heenan
Born Ilford, Essex 26 January 1905; ordained Priest 6 July 1930; ordained as Bishop of Leeds 12 March 1951; translated to Liverpool 17 May 1957; translated to Westminster 2 September 1963; created Cardinal 22 February 1965; died 7 November 1975.

Cardinal George Basil Hume OSB OM
Born Newcastle-upon-Tyne 2 March 1923; ordained Priest 23 July 1950; ordained as Archbishop of Westminster 25 March 1976; created Cardinal 24 May 1976; died 17 June 1999.

Cardinal Cormac Murphy-O'Connor
Born Reading 24 August 1932; ordained Priest 28 October 1956; ordained as Bishop of Arundel and Brighton 21 December 1977; translated to Westminster 22 March 2000; created Cardinal 21 February 2001; retired 3 April 2009; died 1 September 2017.

Cardinal Vincent Nichols
Born Crosby, Liverpool 8 November 1945; ordained Priest 21 December 1969; ordained as Auxiliary Bishop of Westminster 24 January 1992; translated to Birmingham 29 March 2000; translated to Westminster 21 May 2009; created Cardinal 22 February 2014.

SECTION 4

PRIESTS OF THE DIOCESE

Seniority by year of ordination; **r** indicates a priest who is retired.

1950
r Miles, Mgr Canon Frederick
1951
r Garvey, Charles A
1953
r Miller, John M
1955
r Crowe, Bernard
1956
r Stark, Mgr Anthony
1957
r Dwyer, Peter
r O'Halloran, John
r Young, Henry

1960
r Scholes, Canon Bernard
r Stanley, Cedric
1961
r Coghlan, Mgr John
r Fullam, Seamus
r Ward, Brian
1962
r Berry, Canon Vincent
r Helm, John
r Matthews, Canon Edward
r Reynolds, Brian
r Seeldrayers, Anthony
1963
r Crewe, Hilary
Tuck, Michael
1964
r Brunning, Antony
r Wilby, William
1965

Delany, Stephen
Garnett, Michael
r Sharratt, Aidan
r Wahle, Francis
1966
r Egan, Patrick
r Turner, Mgr Canon Henry
1967
r Boylan, Bernard
r Brockie, Canon Michael
r Duffy, James
r Egan, Mgr Canon Thomas
1968
r Murphy, Seamus
1969
r Baker, Desmond
r Crewe, Vincent
Felzmann, Mgr Vladimir
r McDevitt, Kevin
r McGeoghan, Seamus
Nichols, Cardinal Vincent
r Whatling, Colin

1970
r Ardagh-Walter, David
r Maher, Peter
r Sharp, Peter
r Wilson, David
1971
Convery, Antony
r Foley, Patrick
Leonard, Francis
r McCumiskey,

Bernard
Ryan, Joseph
1972
McGinn, Mgr Canon Paul
r O'Brien, Eamonn
1973
r Doyle, Anthony
Munnelly, Canon Michael
r O'Connor, Timothy
r Overton, Mgr James
1974
Browne, Canon Patrick
Carroll, Patrick
r Cross, Canon Philip
Davies, Jeremy
Ponsonby Meredyth
McNicholas, James
Magnier, Daniel
Sawyer, Guy
1975
r Carroll, Edward
Connor, Christopher
Deehan, John
Lebasi, Kidane
r Mallon, James
Plourde, Canon Robert
Rowland, Mgr Phelim
Wiley, John
r Williamson, David
Zsidi, Gabriel
1976
Barltrop, Mgr Keith
Barnes, David
Byrne, John
Seabrook, John

Shewring, John
1977
Azzopardi, Frans
Buckley, John
Cronin, Canon Daniel
Cunningham, John
r Forde, Thomas
Kelly, David
Law, Philip
Psaila, Anthony
1978
Baxter, Anthony
r Kirinich, Roger
Price, Richard
Winter, Marcus
1979
Conlon, Antony
Doyle, Michael
Power, Dermot

1980
Brady, Mgr Vincent
Creak, Brian
r Gullan-Steel, Stuart
Kennedy, Jim
Liddle, Gladstone
McGuckin, Terence
Ryan, Canon Paschal
1981
Doe, Anthony
Donaghy, Michael
Johnston, Michael
r McLean, Colin
O'Boyle, Mgr Seamus
Press, Francis
Scurlock, Anthony
1982
O'Neill, Dermot
r Stewart, Michael

r Whooley, John

1983

Anwyll, Mark

Duffy, James

Paris, Anthony

Phipps, Canon Terence

Stoakes, Keith

Stokes, John

Webb, Christopher

1984

Dwyer, Canon Anthony

r Gray, John

Hayes, Mgr Martin

King, Canon Gerard

McPartlan, Mgr Paul

Quinn, Gerard

Smith, Brian

r White, John

1985

Healy, Bruno

Leathem, Michael

Letellier, Robert

McAleenan, Bishop Paul

Skehan, William

Sykes, Perry

1986

r Boland, John

Cahill, Charles

r Carter, Joseph

Curry, Mgr James

Dunkling, Reginald

Hudson, Bishop Nicholas

McLoughlin, Patrick

Mannion, Michael

1987

Davies, Canon Colin

Loring, Ulick

Sherrington, Bishop John

1988

Carroll, Sean

Conneely, Mgr John

Fernandes, Norbert

Hannigan, Neil

r Harrington, Thomas

r Hutton, Timothy

Poole, Robert

Sherbrooke, Canon Alexander

r Stevens, Michael

1989

Adamson, Duncan

Booth, Michael

Middleton, Shaun

r Stevens, Peter

Thornton, Sean

1990

Andom, Ephrem

Grech, Saviour

Langham, Mgr Mark

Newby, Canon Peter

Piccolomini, Charis

Seasman, Terence

Wadsworth, Mgr Andrew

1991

Byrne, Dominic

Garvey, James

James, Howard

Lowry, Mehall

Morris, Allen

Przyjalkowski, Voytek

Scott, Peter-Michael

1992

r Dean, Timothy

Dermody, John

O'Doherty, Michael

O'Leary, Canon John

Salvans, Albert

1993

O'Connell, Andrew

Tastard, Terry

Wagay, Gideon

Whitmore, Mgr Philip

1994

Antwi-Darkwah, Francis

Campbell, David

r de Lord, Richard

Harris, Peter

Lennard, Canon Shaun

McKenna, Dominic

Welsh, John

1995

Andrew, Richard

Cullinan, Michael

Evans, David

Fairhead, Mgr Jeremy

r Graham, Donald

Irwin, David

Lyness, Peter

MacKenzie, Hugh

McGuire, Derek

r Marriott, Canon Richard

Reader, Mgr Roger

Reynolds, Neil

Touw Tempelmans-Plat, Dennis F P

Tuckwell, Canon Christopher

Woodruff, Mark

1996

r Burgess, Robin

Coker, Stephen

Colven, Christopher

Edgar, Timothy

Hasker, Stewart

r Klyberg, Mgr John

r Palmer, David

Willis, Stephen

Wilson, Canon Stuart

1997

Griffin, Nigel

Griffiths, Brian

r Jackson, Frederick

Robinson, Alan

Silva, Christopher

Vipers, Christopher

Wilson, Peter

1998

Arnold, Paul

Baptiste, Philip

Gosnell, Nicholas

Lee, Clive,

Leenane, Mark

Parsons, Richard

r Rimini, Kenneth

Wang, Stephen

1999

Heslin, Matthew

Jordan, Kevin

Miller, Philip

Nguyen, Simon

Ritaccio, Antonio

r Sammarco, Anthony

2000

r Ablewhite, John

Everson, Simon

McDermott, Paul

O'Boy, Michael

Pham, John Hai

Taylor, Canon Roger

r Usher, Thomas

2001

Barrow, David

r Burton, Edward

Church, Shaun

r Horan, Danny

Shekelton, Peter

Trood, Jeremy

2002

Eastell, Kevin

Knights, Philip

Sarsfield, Denis

SECTION 4

Skinner, Gerard
2003
Pachuta, Robert
Schofield, Nicholas
Vickers, Mark
2004
Braz, Cristiano
Dunne, Michael
Dyer-Perry, Philip
Master, Alexander
r Pellegrini, Anthony
Ruiz-Ortiz, F Javier
2005
Daley, Michael
Mulligan, Jim
Rouco Gutierrez, Hector
Witoń Sławomir
2006
Conesa, Agustin
McKenna, John
2007
Elliott, John D A
Nesbitt, Richard
2008
Arulananthem, Thevakingsley
Moule, Kevin
Neal, James
Reilly, David
2009
Nicol, William

2010

O'Brien, Gerard
Seaton, Stuart
2011
Bagini, Paulo
Connick, Andrew
Gallagher, Andrew
Richardson, Paul
Stokes, Graham

2012
Addison, Kim
Andreini, Lorenzo
Millico, Ivano
2013
Ardila, Oscar
Downie, Jeffrey
Pantisano, Fortunato
Pinnock, Giles
Plunkett, Martin
Steel, Jeffrey
Tate, Martin
Walker, Mark
2014
Hyett, Derek
Jaxa-Chamiec, Andrew
O'Mahony, Brian
Richards, Shaun
2015
Bowder, Bill
Burke, David
Chiaha, Cyril
Humphreys, Daniel
Lucuy Claros, David
2016
de Lisle, Christian
Montgomery, Tom
Ryan, Damian
Scott, John
Thomas, Tony
Udo, Chinedu
2017
Albornoz Bolivar, Julio
Bowden, Andrew J
Jarmulowicz, Michael
McMahon, Brian
Maguire, Michael
Okoro, Joseph
Quito, Carlos
Warnaby, John
2018

Allsop, Patrick
Alvarado Gil, Allan
Dunglinson, Mark
Herrero Peña, Daniel
Michael, Rajiv
Pineda, Antonio
Stogdon, Jonathan
Tabor, John
2019
Julian Davies
Benjamin Woodley

CLERGY OF THE DIOCESE

In alphabetical order, figures following each surname indicate year of birth and of ordination to the priesthood, a place name in brackets refers to an entry in the Parish Directory section. Unless stated otherwise, all email addresses are formed: **first name+surname@rcdow.org.uk**

ARCHBISHOP

Nichols (1945; 1969) PhL, MA, MEd, STL, His Eminence Cardinal Vincent; **Archbishop's House, Ambrosden Avenue SW1P 1QJ**

AUXILIARY BISHOPS

Hudson (1959; 1986) MA, PhB, STB, STL, Right Rev Nicholas; **Archbishop's House, Ambrosden Avenue SW1P 1QJ Tel: 020 7931 6061**

McAleenan (1951; 1985) Right Rev Paul; **Archbishop's House, Ambrosden Avenue SW1P 1QJ Tel: 020 7931 6062**

Sherrington (1958; 1987) MA, STL, Right Rev John; **Archbishop's House, Ambrosden Avenue SW1P 1QJ Tel: 020 7798 9060**

PRIESTS

Ablewhite (1943; 2000) John; **46 Tower Court, Ely CB7 4XS Tel: 01353 968056**

Adamson (1948; 1989) Duncan; **73 Pembroke Road, Ruislip HA4 8NN Tel: 01895 632739 (Ruislip)**

Addison (1975; 2012) Kim; **The Presbytery, Rant Meadow, Hemel Hempstead HP3 8PG Tel: 01442 210610 (Hemel Hempstead East)**

Albornoz Bolivar (1981; 2017) Julio; **Cathedral Clergy House, 42 Francis Street SW1P 1QW Tel: 020 7931 6097 (Cathedral)**

Allsop, Patrick (1952; 2018); **The Presbytery, Ballance Road E9 5SS Tel: 020 8985 1495 (Homerton)**

Alvarado Gil (1982; 2018) Allan; **39 Duncan Terrace N1 8AL Tel: 020 7226 3277 (Islington, Copenhagen Street)**

Andom (1960; 1990) STB, STL, MTh Ephrem; **The Catholic Presbytery, Commonwealth Avenue W12 7QR Tel: 020 8743 8315 (White City, Eritrean Chaplaincy)**

Andreini (1977; 2012) Lorenzo; **11 Harewood Avenue NW1 6LD (Superior, Redemptoris Mater House of Formation)**

Andrew (1953; 1995) MA, Richard; **41 Brook Green W6 7BL Tel: 020 7603 3832 (Brook Green)**

Antwi-Darkwah (1957; 1994) STB, DIP. COUNS, Francis A; **47 Vesta Avenue, St Albans AL1 2PE Tel: 01727 850066 (St Albans South)**

Anwyll (1957; 1983) DIP. S.Comm, STL, MA, Mark; **1 Colney Hatch Lane N10 1PN Tel: 020 8883 5607 (Muswell Hill)**

Ardagh-Walter (1941; 1970) BA, David; **17 St Ann's Road N15 6NG Tel: 020 8800 8374 / 07399 881072**

Ardila (1976; 2013) Oscar; **(on loan, Diocese of Plymouth)**

Arnold (1953; 1998) MA, Paul; St Elizabeth's Centre, South End, Much Hadham SG10 6EW
Tel: 01279 842145 (Bishop's Stortford)

Arulananthem (1973; 2008) BA, STB, MA, Thevakingsley; 17 Kenninghall Road E5 8BS
Tel 020 8985 2178 (Clapton)

Azzopardi (1951; 1977) Frans; Flat 3 Copper Beeches, 6 Witham Road, Isleworth TW7 4AW
Tel: 020 8568 6581

Bagini (1980; 2011) Paulo; St Anne's Church, Underwood Road E1 5AW
Tel: 020 7247 7833 (Underwood Road, Brazilian Chaplaincy)

Baker (1940; 1969) Desmond; 75 Fern Road, St Leonards-on-Sea TN38 0UP
Tel: 01424 423769 / 07986 785429

Baptiste (1971; 1998) Eugene Philip; 68 Hazlewood Crescent W10 5DJ (Kensal New Town)

Barltrop (1947; 1976) MA, STL, Mgr Keith; The Presbytery, Moorhouse Road W2 5DJ
Tel: 020 7229 0487 (Bayswater)

Barnes (1944; 1976) BA, LicPsych, David; 70 Lincoln's Inn Fields WC2A 3JA
Tel: 020 7405 0376 (Lincoln's Inn Fields)

Barrow (1963; 2001) BSc, MSc, STB, David; 8 Ogle Street W1W 6HS
Tel: 020 7636 2883 (Ogle Street)

Baxter (1944; 1978) MA, BD, MPhil, PhD, Anthony; The Lodge, Ware Park, Ware SG12 0DS
Tel: 01920 487287 (Chaplain, Ware Carmel)

Berry (1937; 1962) Canon Vincent; 14 The Hyde, Weston Turville, Bucks HP22 5RP
Tel: 01296 615976

Boland (1947; 1986) John; Nazareth House, 162 East End Road N2 0RU (Chaplain)

Booth (1954; 1989) STL, MFT, KHS, Michael; 5970 Rancho Mission Road #248, San Diego,
CA 92108, USA Tel: 619 990 1288 Email: boothmichael1954@icloud.com

Bowder (1946; 2015) Bill; Parish House, 2 Tynemouth Street SW6 2QT
Tel: 020 7736 4864 (Fulham 2 Stephendale Road)

Bowden (1971; 2017) BD, PgDL, STB, Andrew; 373 Bowes Road N11 1AA
Tel: 020 8368 1638 (New Southgate)

Boylan (1942; 1967) Bernard; St Vincent's Nursing Home, Wiltshire Lane, Eastcote HA5 2NB
(Chaplain)

Brady (1956; 1980) Mgr Vincent G; 54 Parkside SW19 5NE Tel: 020 8944 7189 (Nunciature)

Braz (1974; 2004) STB, Cristiano; 52 Uxbridge Road W7 3SU (Hanwell)

Brockie (1942; 1967) JCL, Canon Michael; 7 St Joseph's Cottages, 38 Cadogan Street
SW3 2QU Tel: 020 7581 0868

Browne (1948; 1974) Canon Patrick; 47 Cumberland Street SW1V 4LY
Tel: 020 7834 6965 (Pimlico)

Brunning (1940; 1964) Antony; Flat 19, St Joseph's House, 42 Brook Green W6 7BL

Buckley (1950; 1977) John; 35 Cricklewood Lane NW2 1HR
Tel: 020 8452 2475 (Cricklewood)

Burgess (1949; 1996) MA, Robin; 20 Willowmead Close W5 1PT Tel: 020 8998 4710

Burke (1975; 2015) MA, STB, David; Sacred Heart Church, Park Street, Berkhamsted HP4
1HX Tel: 01442 863845 (Berkhamsted, Tring)

Burton (1940; 2001) AKC, Edward; 20 Wilbury Grange, Wilbury Road, Hove BN3 3GN
Tel: 01273 774271
Byrne (1955; 1991) MA, JCD, STL, Dominic; 110 Station Road, Hampton-on-Thames TW12
2AS Tel: 020 8979 3596 (Hampton-on-Thames)
Byrne (1951; 1976) John; St Lawrence's Presbytery, The Green, Feltham TW13 4AF
Tel: 020 8890 2367 / 07879 058732 (Feltham)

Cahill (1955; 1986) Charles; 1 King Edward's Road, Ware SG12 7EJ
Tel: 01920 462140 (Ware)
Campbell (1955; 1994) David; c/o Archbishop's House SW1P 1QJ
Carroll (1933; 1975) Edward; 2 Delmer Court, Aycliffe Road, Borehamwood WD6 4HS
Tel: 020 8236 9565
Carroll (1947;1974) Patrick; 4 Church Close, Cuffley, Herts EN6 4LS
Tel: 01707 873308 (Cuffley)
Carroll (1956; 1988) Sean; 12 Womersley Road N8 9AE Tel: 020 8340 3394 (Stroud Green)
Carter (1936; 1986) Joseph; 10 Stevenson Park, Lurgan, Craigavon, Co. Armagh BT67 9DR
Chiaha (1981; 2015) BA, BPhil, MBA, BD, STB, Cyril; 3 Station Road, Buntingford SG9 9HT
Tel: 01763 271471 (Buntingford, Old Hall Green and Puckeridge)
Church (1964; 2001) STB, BA, Shaun; 5 Park Road, Rickmansworth WD3 1HU
Tel: 01923 773387 (Rickmansworth. Chorleywood and Mill End)
Coghlan (1934;1961) Mgr John; c/o Archbishop's House SW1P 1QJ
Coker (1953; 1996) Stephen P; 3 Wissen Drive, Letchworth Garden City SG6 1FT
Tel: 07976 400954
Colven (1945; 1996) BA, Christopher G; 22 George Street W1U 3QY
Tel: 020 7935 0943 (Spanish Place)
Conesa (1973; 2006) STB Agustin; 42 Langdale Gardens, Perivale, Greenford UB6 8DQ
Tel: 020 8997 3164 (Perivale)
Conlon (1949; 1979) HEL, PhD, Antony; R.C. Rectory, Ferry Lane, Goring-on-Thames
RG8 9DX Tel: 01491 872181 (On loan, Archdiocese of Birmingham)
Conneely (1956; 1988) JCL, Mgr John; 70 Lincoln's Inn Fields WC2A 3JA
Tel: 020 7405 0376 (Lincoln's Inn Fields, Judicial Vicar, Episcopal Vicar for Eastern Catholic
Churches)
Connick (1982; 2011) Andrew; The Presbytery, Dundee Street E1W 2PH
Tel: 020 7481 2202 (Wapping, University Chaplaincy)
Connor (1947; 1975) MA, Christopher; 165 Arlington Road NW1 7EX
Tel: 07947 561414 (Camden Town, School Chaplain)
Convery (1947; 1971) Antony; 700 Finchley Road NW11 7NE
Tel: 020 8455 1300 (Golders Green)
Creak (1940; 1980) MA, PhD, Brian; 79 St Charles Square W10 6EB
Tel: 020 8968 3373 (St Charles Square, University Chaplaincy)
Crewe (1933; 1963) Hilary; Bramley House, Half Acre, Brentford TW8 8BH
Tel: 020 8847 4550 (Chaplain)
Crewe (1930; 1969) Vincent; c/o Archbishop's House SW1P 1QJ

SECTION 4

177

Cronin (1952; 1977) LLM, KCHS, Canon Daniel; **72 London Road, Knebworth SG3 6HB**
Tel: 01438 813303 (Knebworth)

Cross (1936; 1974) Canon Philip; **St Anne's Home, 77 Manor Road N16 5BL**
Tel: 020 8826 2500

Crowe (1930; 1955) Bernard; **Nazareth House, 162 East End Road N2 0RU**
Tel: 020 8803 1104

Cullinan (1957; 1995) MA, MASt, PhD, STD, Michael; **36 Chiswick Court, Moss Lane, Pinner
HA5 3AP Tel: 020 8429 3349 (Director of Maryvale Higher Institute of Religious Sciences,
Director of BDiv Programme, and Reader in Moral Theology, Maryvale Institute,
Birmingham)**

Cunningham (1952; 1977) John; **204 High Street, Waltham Cross EN8 7DP**
Tel: 01992 623156 (Waltham Cross)

Curry (1960; 1986) KCHS, STB, Mgr James; **The Clergy House, 16 Abingdon Road W8 6AF**
Tel: 020 7937 4778 (Kensington 1)

de Lisle (1988; 2016) MA, STB, Christian; **The Presbytery, Ballance Road E9 5SS**
Tel: 020 8985 1495 (Homerton)

de Lord (1946; 1994) STB, Richard; **18 Rannoch Court, Adelaide Road, Surbiton, Surrey
KT6 4TE Tel: 020 8251 2036**

Daley (1959; 2005) BA, BSc, (Hons) STB, MA, RGN, Cert.Ed, Michael; **22 Cortayne Road
SW6 3QA Tel: 020 7736 1068 (Parsons Green)**

Davies (1948; 1987) Canon Colin; **4 Thirleby Road, Burnt Oak, Edgware HA8 0HQ**
Tel: 020 8959 1971 (Burnt Oak)

Davies (1935; 1974) Jeremy Ponsonby Meredyth ; **52 Castle Street, Luton LU1 3AG**

Davies (1960; 2019) Julian; **14 Beaconsfield Road, St Albans AL1 3RB (St Albans)**

Dean (1942;1992) Timothy; **7 Hutchings Lodge, High Street, Rickmansworth WD3 1EY**
Tel 07812 248234

Deehan (1949; 1975) MA, STB, LSS, John; **4 Lady Margaret Road NW5 2XT**
Tel: 020 7485 4023 (Kentish Town)

Delany (1940; 1965) Stephen; **c/o Archbishop's House SW1P 1QJ**

Dermody (1955; 1992) BA, John P; **Priests House, Gravel Hill N3 3RJ**
Tel: 020 8346 2459 (Finchley Church End)

Doe (1950; 1981) BA, MA, STL, PhD, Anthony; **Via di Monserrato 45, 00186 Rome, Italy**
Tel: 00390 6686 8546 (Venerable English College)

Donaghy (1956; 1981) BD, PGCE, Michael; **Cathedral Clergy House, 42 Francis Street SW1P
1QW Tel: 020 7798 9048 (Cathedral)**

Downie 1970; 2013) Jeffrey; **St Luke's, 14 Sellers Grange, Orton Goldhay, Peterborough
PE2 5XX Tel: 01733 370877 Email: saintlukesparish@yahoo.co.uk (on loan, Diocese of
East Anglia)**

Doyle (1948; 1973) Anthony; **Paraíso de la Bahia, Bloque 10-2J, 29690, Casares Costa,
Provincia de Málaga, Spain**

Doyle (1948; 1979) Michael; **Allen Hall, 28 Beaufort Street SW3 5AA Tel: 020 7349 5610**
(Seminary)

Duffy (1938; 1967) MEd, James A; 4 Merry Hill Road, Bushey WD23 1DY
Tel: 020 8950 8985 / 07885 670483 Email: jimduffy@rcdow.org.uk
Duffy (1956; 1983) James; 38 Camborne Avenue W13 9QZ
Tel: 020 8567 5421 (Northfields)
Dunglinson (1959; 2018) Mark; 41 Brook Green W6 7BL
Tel: 020 7603 3832 (Brook Green)
Dunkling (1962; 1986) Reginald; 262 Kingston Road, Teddington TW11 9JQ
Tel: 020 8977 2986 (Teddington)
Dunne (1964; 2004) BA, Michael; 247 High Road W4 4PU
Tel: 020 8994 2877 (Chiswick)
Dwyer (1952; 1984) Canon Anthony; 1 Kirkwick Avenue, Harpenden AL5 2QH
Tel: 01582 712245 (Harpenden)
Dwyer (1933; 1957) BA, MA, Peter; 31 Monks Horton Way, St Albans AL1 4HA
Tel: 01727 761183
Dyer-Perry (1976; 2004) STB, Philip; The Presbytery, 59 Gresham Road, Staines TW18 2BD
Tel: 01784 452381 (Staines)

Eastell (1942; 2002) BA, STh, MEd, PhD, Kevin; 7 rue de la Breche, Les Verchers sur Layon,
49700 France Tel: 0033 241 599750 (Chaplain to English-speaking community in Diocese of
Angers)
Edgar (1956; 1996) MA, BD, AKC, Timothy; 4 Egerton Gardens NW4 4BA
Tel: 020 8202 0560 (Hendon & Hendon West)
Egan (1937; 1966) MA, MSc, Patrick; Domino's Chapel, 24 Frank Lloyd Wright Drive,
PO Box 466, Ann Arbor, Michigan 48106-0466 USA Email: fatheregan@gmail.com
Egan (1942; 1967) BEd, Mgr Canon Thomas; Flat 2, 90 Station Road N22 7SY
Tel: 07803 891545
Elliott (1962; 2007) John D A; 377 Mile End Road E3 4QS Tel: 020 8980 1845
Email: jdaelliott@rcdow.org.uk (Mile End)
Evans (1959; 1995) BSc, BTh, David; 3 King Edward's Road E9 7SF
Tel: 020 8985 2496 (Hackney)
Everson (1958; 2000) BA, Simon; Farleigh School, Red Rice, Andover SP11 7PW
Tel: 01264 710747 (Headmaster/Chaplain)

Fairhead (1960; 1995) MA, BTh, Mgr Jeremy; 970 Harrow Road, Sudbury, Wembley HA0
2QE Tel: 020 8904 2552 (Sudbury)
Felzmann (1939; 1969) KCHS, DD, MSc(Eng), Mgr Vladimir; 1 St Catherine's Apartments,
179a Bow Road E3 2SH Tel: 07810 116508 (Canary Wharf Chaplaincy, Catholic Chaplain
for Sport)
Fernandes (1964; 1988) BD, Norbert; 141 Woodhall Lane, Welwyn Garden City AL7 3TP
Tel: 01707 323234 (Welwyn Garden City Parishes)
Foley (1944; 1971) Patrick; c/o Archbishop's House SW1P 1QJ
Email: pjtwomeyfoley@gmail.com
Forde (1943, 1977) Thomas; Garden Flat, 6 Leighton Crescent NW5 2QY
Fullam (1932; 1961) Seamus; c/o Archbishop's House SW1P 1QJ

Gallagher (1981; 2011) Andrew; **Cathedral Clergy House, 42 Francis Street SW1P 1QW**
Tel: 020 7798 9098 (Cathedral)

Garnett (1935; 1965) MA, PhL, Michael; **Santa Apolonia 146, Apartado 319, Cajamarca, Peru**
Tel: 0051 7636 3517 Email: miguelgarnett@yahoo.es (On loan)

Garvey (1926; 1951) MA, Charles Austin; **Nazareth House, 162 East End Road N2 0RU**
Tel: 020 8883 1104

Garvey (1962; 1991) James P; **84 Pixmore Way, Letchworth Garden City SG6 3TP**
Tel: 01462 683504 (Letchworth)

Gosnell (1958; 1998) VG, SRN, BTh, MA(Ed), MA, Nicholas; **Dean, St Michael and St George, The Cathedral Church of the Bishopric of the Forces, Queens Avenue, Aldershot GU11 2BY**
Tel: 01252 315042 (Vicar General of HM Forces)

Graham (1952; 1995) STB, Donald; **Flat 4 Francis Court, Caddington Road NW2 1RP**
Tel: 020 3609 6711

Gray (1944; 1984) John; **11 St Mary's Close, Longridge, Preston. PR3 3NW**
Tel: 07739 904456

Grech (1965; 1990) MTh, MA, Saviour; **4a Inverness Place W2 3JF**
Tel: 020 7229 8153 (Queensway)

Griffin (1948; 1997) MA, BSc, Dip Th, FRSA, Nigel; **The Presbytery, St Edmund's Lane, 213 Nelson Road, Whitton TW2 7BB Tel: 020 8894 9923 (Whitton)**

Griffiths (1960; 1997) Brian; **The Presbytery, Everglade Strand NW9 5PX**
Tel: 020 8205 6830 (Grahame Park)

Gullan-Steel (1943; 1980) BD, Stuart; **26a Salisbury Square, Hatfield AL9 5JD**

Hannigan (1947; 1988) Neil; **131 Glenarm Road E5 0NB Tel: 020 8525 1929 (Clapton Park)**

Harrington (1935; 1988) Thomas; **St Joseph's, Carrowmore Meadows 32, Knock, Co Mayo, Ireland**

Harris (1951; 1994) BEd, MTh, Peter; **St Joseph's, 3 Windhill, Bishop's Stortford CM23 2ND**
Tel: 01279 654063 (Bishop's Stortford)

Hasker (1961; 1996) BA, CQSW, Stewart P; **1 Stonard Road N13 4DJ Tel: 020 8886 9568 (Palmers Green)**

Hayes (1956; 1984) VG, BA, BD, KCHS, Mgr Martin; **St Mary's Rectory, Draycott Terrace SW3 2BG Tel: 020 7931 6076 (Vicar General)**

Healy (1952; 1985) Bruno J; **Tan Y Cefn, Garnfadryn, Pwllheli, Gwynedd LL53 8TG** (Eremitical Life)

Helm (1936; 1962) John; **41 Parkside, Welwyn AL6 9DQ Tel: 01438 718524**

Herrero Peña (1989; 2018) Daniel; **The Clergy House, 16 Abingdon Road W8 6AF**
Tel: 020 7937 4778 (Kensington 1)

Heslin (1960; 1999) BA, HDipEd, STB, Matthew; **160 Long Lane, Hillingdon UB10 0EH**
Tel: 01895 234577 (Hillingdon)

Horan (1934; 2001) Danny; **1 Nettleden Avenue, Wembley HA9 6DP**
Tel: 07973 913989

Humphreys (1974; 2015) Daniel; **Cathedral Clergy House, 42 Francis Street SW1P 1QW**
Tel: 020 7798 9180 (Cathedral)

Hutton (1944; 1988) TD, FCII, Timothy; **56 Pinner Court, Pinner Road, Pinner HA5 5RN**
Tel: **020 3417 2193**
Hyett (1979; 2014) BA (Hons), STB, Derek; **The Presbytery, 100a Balls Pond Road N1 4AG**
Tel: **020 7254 4378** (Kingsland)

Irwin (1944; 1995) AKC, David; **32 Beech Road, Findon Village, West Sussex BN14 0UR**
Tel: **07786 769392** (Episcopal Vicar for Ethnic Chaplaincies)

Jackson (1943; 1997) BA, Frederick; **The Clergy House, 16 Abingdon Road W8 6AF**
Tel: **020 7937 4778** (Kensington 1)
James (1959;1991) MA, BSc, STB, Howard; **(On loan, West Indies)**
Jarmulowicz (1950; 2017) BSc, MB.BS, BDiv, FRCPath, KSG Michael; **Presbytery, 337 Harrow Road W9 3RB** Tel: **020 7286 2170** (Harrow Road, Paddington)
Jaxa-Chamiec (1976; 2014) Andrew; **The Presbytery, 1 Nicoll Road NW10 9AX**
Tel: **020 8965 4935** (Willesden)
Johnston (1946; 1981) MTh, MA, BD, Dip Ed, Michael; **211 Old Marylebone Road NW1 5QT**
(Marylebone)
Jordan (1968;1999) BVetMed, STB, Kevin; **54 Lodge Road NW8 8LA** Tel: **020 7286 3214**
(St John's Wood)

Kelly (1953; 1977) David; **c/o Archbishop's House SW1P 1QJ**
Kennedy (1943; 1980) Jim; **c/o Archbishop's House SW1P 1QJ** (On loan)
King (1960; 1984) Canon Gerard; **60 Highbury Park N5 2XH**
Tel: **020 7226 0257** (Highbury)
Kirinich (1953; 1978) MA, STL, Roger; **c/o Archbishop's House SW1P 1QJ**
Klyberg (1931; 1996), Mgr Charles John; **Balgowan Care Home, 46 Bartholomew Lane,**
Hythe CT21 4BX Tel: **01303 266782**
Knights (1960; 2002) MA, BA, PhD, Philip; **6 Melbourn Road, Royston SG8 7DB** (Royston)

Langham (1960; 1990) MA, STL, STD, Mgr Mark; **Fisher House, Guildhall Street, Cambridge**
CB2 3NH Tel: **01223 742192** (Cambridge University Catholic Chaplaincy)
Law (1950; 1977) Philip; **19 Deanscroft, Knebworth SG3 6BD** Tel: **01438 816444**
Leathem (1960; 1985) Michael; **c/o Archbishop's House SW1P 1QJ**
Lebasi (1946; 1975) STL, Kidane; **St Joseph's House, 42 Brook Green W6 7BW**
Lee (1959; 1998) Clive; **9 Henry Road N4 2LH** Tel: **020 8802 9910** (Manor House)
Leenane (1964; 1998) BSc (Surv), BA, Mark; **2 Witham Road, Osterley, Isleworth TW7 4AJ**
Tel: **020 8560 4737** (Osterley)
Lennard (1957; 1994) Canon Shaun; **243 Mutton Lane, Potters Bar EN6 2AT** Tel: **01707**
654359 (Potters Bar)
Leonard (1936; 1971) Francis; **4 Basils Road, Stevenage SG1 3PX** Tel: **01438 364165**
Letellier (1953; 1985) MA, MLitt, PhD, SSL, STD, Robert Ignatius; **7 Parker Street, Cambridge**
CB1 1JL (Further Studies)
Liddle (1948; 1980) BA, Gladstone; **6 Athenaeum Road N20 9AE**
Tel: **020 8445 0838** (Whetstone)

SECTION 4

Loring (1946; 1987) MA, BD, BACP, Ulick; 61 Pope's Grove, Twickenham TW1 4JZ
Tel: 020 8892 4578 (Twickenham)

Lowry (1961; 1991) Mehall; 1 Stonard Road N13 4DJ Tel: 020 8886 9568 (Palmers Green)

Lucuy Claros (1975; 2015) David; 729 High Road N17 8AG
Tel: 020 8808 3554 (Tottenham)

Lyness (1948; 1995) MA, Peter; St Edmund's College, Old Hall Green, Ware SG11 1DS
Tel: 01920 821504 (Priest-in-Residence)

MacKenzie (1962; 1995) MSc, PhL, Hugh; 22 George Street W1U 3QY Tel: 020 7935 0943
Email: hughm1@aol.com (Spanish Place, Further Studies, Hospital Chaplain)

McCumiskey (1938; 1971) MA, BSc(Psy), STL, JCL, Bernard; 53 Village Court, Whitley Bay, Tyne
and Wear NE26 3QA Tel: 0191 670 4858 / 07712 328218

McDermott (1970; 2000) Paul; The Presbytery, St Mellitus Church, Tollington Park N4 3AG
Tel: 020 7272 3415 (Tollington Park)

McDevitt (1943; 1969) Kevin; Blackwater, Enniscorthy, Co. Wexford, Ireland Y21 W283
Tel: 00353 851 886834 Email: kevinmcdevitt43@gmail.com

McGeoghan (1945; 1969) Seamus; St Vincent's Nursing Home, Wiltshire Lane, Eastcote,
Pinner HA5 2NB

McGinn (1947; 1972) Mgr Canon Paul; 80 Pembroke Road, Ruislip HA4 8NE
Tel: 07900 887088

McGuckin (1950; 1980) BA, STL, MA, MLitt, BD, DD, Terence; c/o Archbishop's House SW1P
1QJ

McGuire (1967; 1995) Derek; Holy Rood House, Exchange Road, Watford WD18 0PJ
Tel: 01923 224085 (Watford)

McKenna (1950;1994) Dominic; 291 Shenley Road, Borehamwood WD6 1TG
Tel: 020 8953 1294 (Borehamwood & Borehamwood North)

McKenna (1966; 2006) BA, STB, MTh, John; 82 Union Street, Barnet EN5 4HZ
Tel: 020 8449 3338 (Barnet)

McLean (1934; 1981) Colin; Flat 2, 165 Arlington Road NW1 7EX
Tel: 020 7267 0214

McLoughlin (1947; 1986) BD, CertSp, MBTI, MA(Sp), Patrick; The Presbytery, Hardie Close
NW10 0UH Tel: 020 8451 0367 (Neasden)

McMahon (1958; 2017) MSc, BA, FdA, Brian; 186 St John's Road, Boxmoor HP1 1NR
Tel: 01442 391759 (Hemel Hempstead West)

McNicholas (1944; 1974) BD, MTh, James; Sacred Heart Presbytery, London Road, Bushey
WD23 1BA Tel: 020 8950 2077 (Bushey and Oxhey)

McPartlan (1955; 1984) MA, STL, DPhil, Mgr Paul; Carl J Peter Professor of Systematic
Theology and Ecumenism, School of Theology and Religious Studies, The Catholic University
of America, Washington DC 20064 USA Tel: 001 202 319 6515 Email: mcpartlan@cua.edu

Magnier (1949; 1974) Daniel J; St Anne's Home, 77 Manor Road N16 5BL
Tel: 020 8802 0362 (Chaplain)

Maguire (1978; 2017) BSc, BD, STB, PGDip, Michael; 247 High Road W4 4PU
Tel: 020 8994 2877 (Chiswick)

Maher (1944; 1970) Peter; **St Peter's, 7a Station Road, Biggleswade SG18 8AL**
Tel: 01767 312013 / 07957 626829
Mallon (1940; 1975) James; **Flat 2, 8 Morpeth Terrace, SW1P 1QE**
Tel: 07850 640179
Mannion (1952; 1986) Michael; **7 Marford Road, Wheathampstead AL4 8AY** (Redbourn
and Wheathampstead)
Marriott (1938; 1995) MA, Richard; **c/o Archbishop's House SW1P 1QJ**
Master (1976; 2004) Alexander; **Archbishop's House, Ambrosden Avenue SW1P 1QJ**
Tel: 020 7798 9041 (Private Secretary to the Cardinal Archbishop)
Matthews (1937; 1962) LTL, Canon Edward; **16 Halls Drive, Faygate, Horsham, West Sussex
RH12 4QN Tel: 01293 851503**
Michael (1978; 2018) Rajiv; **Cathedral Clergy House, 42 Francis Street SW1P 1QW**
Tel: 020 7798 9055 (Cathedral)
Middleton (1962; 1989) STB, MA, Shaun; **St Mary's Rectory, Draycott Terrace SW3 2BG**
Tel: 020 7589 5487 (Chelsea I)
Miles (1925; 1950) ProtAp, MA, Mgr Canon Frederick A; **2a Meadow Road SW8 1QH**
Tel: 020 7793 1338
Miller (1923; 1953) John M; **13 Highlands, 131 Oakleigh Road North N20 9HA**
Tel: 020 8445 8896
Miller (1966; 1999) MA, PhD, STL, Philip; **The Presbytery, Esdaile Lane, Hoddesdon
EN11 8DS Tel: 01992 440986** (Hoddesdon)
Millico (1972; 2012) MA, MSc, BD (Hons), STB, Ivano; **5 Amwell Street EC1R 1UL**
(Clerkenwell)
Montgomery (1973; 2016) BTh, Tom; **390b Northolt Road, South Harrow HA2 8EX**
Tel: 020 8864 5455 (Harrow South and Northolt)
Morris (1956;1991) MA, BA, BD, Allen; **243 Jockey Road, Sutton Coldfield B73 5US**
Tel: 0121 354 1763 (on loan, Archdiocese of Birmingham)
Moule (1954; 2008) Kevin; **22 The Crosspath, Radlett WD7 8HN**
Tel: 01923 635541 (Radlett and Shenley, London Colney)
Mulligan (1946; 2005) MA, BTh, James; **St Paul's House, 2 Merle Avenue, Harefield
UB9 6DG Tel: 01895 822365** (Harefield)
Munnelly (1949; 1973) BD, MA, Canon Michael; **1 Du Cros Drive, Stanmore HA7 4TJ**
Tel: 020 8954 1299 (Stanmore)
Murphy (1937; 1968) Seamus; **3 Lut Na Greine, opp. St Michael's Church, Creeslough, Co.
Donegal, Ireland**

Neal (1962; 2008) MA, STL, James; **The Presbytery, 17 Mandeville Road, Northolt UB5 5HE**
Tel: 020 8864 5455 (Harrow South and Northolt)
Nesbitt (1966; 2007) Richard; **The Catholic Presbytery, Commonwealth Avenue, White City
W12 7QR Tel 020 8743 8334** (White City)
Newby (1958; 1990) MA, PhL, Canon Peter; **130 St Margarets Road, Twickenham TW1 1RL**
Tel: 020 8892 3902 (St Margarets-on-Thames, Chaplain, St Mary's University)

SECTION 4

Nguyen (1958; 1999) MA, STB, Simon Thang Duc; 117 Bow Common Lane E3 4AU
Tel: 020 7987 3477 / 07920 044275 Email: Simon_hue@yahoo.co.uk (Bow Common, Vietnamese Chaplaincy)

Nicol (1952; 2009) William; Allen Hall, 28 Beaufort Street SW3 5AA (Seminary)

O'Boy (1968; 2000) BA, PhD, STB, MTh, STL, Michael; 14 Beaconsfield Road, St Albans AL1 3RB (St Albans)

O'Boyle (1957; 1981) STL, Mgr Séamus; 39 Duncan Terrace N1 8AL
Tel: 020 7226 3277 (Islington, Copenhagen Street, Episcopal Vicar for Safeguarding)

O'Brien (1948; 1972) Dip RE, Eamonn; c/o Archbishop's House SW1P 1QJ

O'Brien (1963; 2010) Gerard; 81 St Charles Square W10 6EB Tel: 020 8525 3032
(St Charles Square, St Joseph's Hospice Chaplain)

O'Connell (1963; 1993) Andrew; 45B Pemberton Gardens N19 5RR
Email: andrewoconnell@rcdow.org.uk

O'Connor (1949; 1973) BA, Dip Rel Ed, Timothy; c/o Archbishop's House SW1P 1QJ

O'Doherty (1964; 1992) Michael; 216 Dollis Hill Lane NW2 6HE
Tel: 020 8452 6158 (Dollis Hill)

O'Halloran (1924; 1957) MA, John; Nazareth House, 162 East End Road N2 0RU

O'Leary (1967; 1992) STB, PhL, PhD, Canon John; Allen Hall, 28 Beaufort Street SW3 5AA
Tel: 020 7349 5600 (Seminary, Vocations Director)

O'Mahony (1978; 2014) BA (Hons), BD, STB, STL, Brian; 32 Hallowell Road, Northwood HA6 1DW Tel: 01923 840736 (Northwood)

O'Neill (1959; 1982) Dermot; 51 Nether Street N12 7NN Tel: 020 8446 0224
(Finchley North)

Okoro (1977; 2017) Joseph; Holy Rood House, Exchange Road, Watford WD18 0PJ
Tel: 01923 224085 (Watford)

Overton (1941; 1973) MA, STL, BD, Mgr James; 20 Phoenix Road NW1 1TA
Tel: 07930 908264

Pachuta (1977; 2003) Robert; 5 Garratt Road, Edgware HA8 9AN
Tel: 020 8952 0663 (Edgware)

Palmer (1933; 1996) BA, David; 29 Manor House Way, Isleworth TW7 6BJ
Tel: 020 8847 4632

Pantisano (1979; 2013) Fortunato; Our Lady and St Michael Catholic Church, Crown Rise, Garston WD25 0NE Tel: 01923 673239 (Garston)

Paris (1956; 1983) Anthony B; The Presbytery, 4 Lord's Croft, Amesbury, Wiltshire SP4 7EP
Tel: 01980 622177 (on loan, Diocese of Clifton)

Parsons (1946; 1998) BD, MTh, MPhil, STL, DProf, AKC, Richard; 22 Boniface Walk, Harrow HA3 6PU Tel: 020 8428 3260 / 020 8864 8021 (Headstone Lane)

Pellegrini (1940; 2004) KSG, KMCO, BA, BTh, ARCO, Anthony; 16 Elm Close, North Harrow HA2 7BT Email: asjp@btopenworld.com

Pham (1966; 2000) STB, John Hai; 165 Arlington Road NW1 7EX
Tel: 020 7485 2727 (Camden Town)

Phipps (1950; 1983) MA, STL, Canon Terence; **23 St John's Street, Hertford SG14 1RX**
Tel: 01992 582109 (Hertford)
Piccolomini (1955; 1990) Charis; **c/o Archbishop's House SW1P 1QJ**
Pineda (1970; 2018) STL, STB, MA, BSc, Antonio; **291 Shenley Road, Borehamwood
WD6 1TG** Tel: 020 8931 4124 (Borehamwood & Borehamwood North)
Pinnock (1967; 2013) Giles; **c/o Archbishop's House SW1P 1QJ** (Imperial College Trust
Hospitals Chaplaincy)
Plourde (1944; 1975) Canon Robert; **28 Love Lane, Pinner HA5 3EX**
Tel: 020 8866 0098 (Pinner)
Plunkett (1968; 2013) Martin; **32 Field End Road, Eastcote, Pinner HA5 2QT**
Tel: 020 8866 6581(Eastcote)
Poole (1955; 1988) Robert; **c/o Archbishop's House SW1P 1QJ**
Power (1952; 1979) BA, BD, STL,STD, Dermot; **The Presbytery, 100a Balls Pond Road N1
4AG** Tel: 020 7254 4378
Press (1955; 1981) Francis; **St Anne's Home, 77 Manor Road N16 5BL**
Price (1947; 1978) Richard; **The Presbytery, Moorhouse Road W2 5DJ** Tel: 020 7229 0487
(Bayswater)
Przyjalkowski (1955; 1991) BD MTh,Voytek; **c/o Archbishop's House SW1P 1QJ** (Sabbatical)
Psaila (1952; 1977) Anthony; **112 Carlton Avenue East, Wembley HA9 8NB**
Tel: 020 8904 6031 (Wembley 3)

Quinn (1955; 1984) BA, STL, Gerard; **44 Boston Park Road, Brentford TW8 9JF**
Tel: 020 8560 1671 (Brentford)
Quito (1990; 2017) Carlos; **St Joseph's, 3 Windhill, Bishop's Stortford CM23 2ND**
Tel: 01279 654063 (Bishop's Stortford)

Reader (1958; 1995) KHS, BA, Mgr Roger; **Clergy House, Peter Avenue NW10 2DD**
Tel: 020 8451 4677 (Willesden Green)
Reilly (1978; 2008) MA, David; **373 Bowes Road N11 1AA**
Tel: 020 8368 1638 (New Southgate)
Reynolds (1938; 1962) Brian; **186a St John's Road, Boxmoor HP1 1NR**
Tel: 01442 382118
Reynolds (1959; 1995) BEd Hons, Neil Francis; **The Presbytery, Vale Lane W3 0DY**
Tel: 020 8992 1308 (Acton West)
Richards (1962; 2014) BTh, Shaun; **15 Wood Road, Shepperton TW17 0DH** (Shepperton)
Richardson (1947; 2011) Paul; **86 Fitzalan Street SE11 6QU** Tel: 020 7091 4299
Rimini (1942; 1998) MISM, AIM, Kenneth; **c/o Archbishop's House SW1P 1QJ**
Ritaccio (1970;1999) STB, Antonio; **The Presbytery, Brentfield Road NW10 8ER**
Tel: 020 8965 3313 (Stonebridge)
Robinson (1953; 1997) KHS, MA, Alan Ian P; **Corpus Christi Presbytery, Maiden Lane
WC2E 7NB** Tel: 020 7836 4700 (Covent Garden)
Rouco Gutierrez (1972; 2005) BA, BATS, Hector; **The Presbytery, 2a Salehurst Close,
Kenton HA3 0UG** Tel 020 8204 3550 (Kenton)

Rowland (1949; 1975) Mgr Phelim; **4 Holly Place NW3 6QU**
Tel: 020 7435 6678 (Hampstead)
Ruiz-Ortiz (1976; 2004) STB, SSL, STD, F Javier; **177 Bow Road E3 2SG**
Tel: 020 8980 3961 (Bow)
Ryan (1981; 2016) Damian; **5 Park Road, Rickmansworth WD3 1HU**
Tel: 01923 773387 (Rickmansworth, Chorleywood and Mill End)
Ryan (1946; 1971) Joseph; **4 Vincent Road N15 3QH** Tel: 020 8888 5518 (West Green)
Ryan (1955; 1980) Canon Paschal; **7 Cheyne Row SW3 5HS**
Tel: 020 7352 0777 (Chelsea 2)

Salvans (1959; 1992) MTh, Albert; **c/o Archbishop's House SW1P 1QJ** (Missions)
Sammarco (1940: 1999) Anthony; **Flat 1, Croft Court, Brickwall Lane, Ruislip HA4 8JT**
Tel: 01895 638771
Sarsfield (1962; 2002) STB, Denis; **Holy Trinity Church, London Road, Baldock SG7 6LQ**
Tel: 01462 893127 (Baldock)
Sawyer (1946; 1974) Guy; **22 Roxborough Park, Harrow-on-the-Hill HA1 3BE**
Tel: 020 8422 2513 (Harrow-on-the-Hill)
Schofield (1975; 2003) MA, STB, FSA, FRHistS, Nicholas; **The Presbytery, Osborn Road,**
Uxbridge UB8 1UE Tel: 01895 233193 (Uxbridge, Archivist Tel: 020 7938 3580)
Scholes (1936; 1960) MA, Canon Bernard; **186b St John's Road, Boxmoor HP1 1NR**
Tel: 01442 385118
Scott (1952; 2016) John; **Cathedral Clergy House, 42 Francis Street SW1P 1QW**
Tel: 020 7931 6041 (Cathedral)
Scott (1970; 1991) STB, Peter-Michael; **279 High Road N2 8HG** Tel: 020 8883 4234
(Finchley East, Cardinal's Advisor for Healthcare Chaplaincy)
Scurlock (1951;1981) Anthony John; **c/o Archbishop's House SW1P 1QJ**
Seabrook (1947; 1976) BD, MA, John; **1 Bolton Road W4 3TE**
Tel: 020 8994 6861 (Grove Park)
Seasman (1990) MA, BACP, Terence; **c/o Archbishop's House SW1P 1QJ**
Seaton (1975; 2010) BA, MA, Stuart; **9 Meadow View, Harrow-on-the-Hill HA1 3DN**
Tel: 020 8422 1862 (Harrow-on-the-Hill, Catholic Chaplain, Harrow School)
Seeldrayers (1937; 1962) Anthony; **8 Burroughs Gardens NW4 4AU**
Tel: 07811 221787
Sharp (1938; 1970) Peter; **23 The Homestead, Henry Street, Lytham, Lancs FY8 5LJ**
Tel: 01253 730803
Sharratt (1940; 1965) BA, STL, Aidan; **2 Lukin Street E1 0AA**
Tel: 020 7790 5911
Shekelton (1970; 2001) Peter; **Church of St Helen, The Harebreaks, Watford WD24 6NJ**
Tel: 01923 223175 (Watford North)
Sherbrooke (1957; 1988) Canon Alexander; **21a Soho Square W1D 4NR**
Tel: 020 7437 2010 (Soho Square)
Shewring (1941; 1976) John; **192 Nags Head Road, Enfield EN3 7AR**
Tel: 020 8804 2149 (Ponders End)

Silva (1949; 1997) BSc, Christopher; **297 Westferry Road E14 3RS**
Tel: **020 7987 5187** (Millwall)
Skehan (1960;1985) William; **2 Lukin Street E1 0AA**
Tel: **020 7790 5911** (Commercial Road)
Skinner (1970; 2002) GRSM, LRAM, PhB, STL, Gerard; **St Francis of Assisi Church, The Presbytery, Pottery Lane W11 4NQ** Tel: **020 7727 7968** (Notting Hill)
Smith (1958; 1984) SLitDip, Brian; **20 The Green, West Drayton UB7 7PJ**
Tel: **01895 442777** (West Drayton)
Stanley (1935; 1960) MBE, Cedric; **1 Dunster Close, Harefield UB9 6BS**
Tel: **01895 824229**
Stark (1932; 1956) Prot. Ap. KCHS, Mgr Anthony G; **Nazareth House, 162 East End Road N2 0RU**
Steel (1969; 2013) BA, MDiv, Lit Cert, STB, PhD Jeffrey; **c/o Archbishop's House SW1P 1QJ**
Stevens (1935; 1988) Michael; **5 Layfield Road, Newcastle-upon-Tyne NE3 5AA**
Tel: **01912 368101** Email: micste68@msn.com
Stevens (1931; 1989) Peter Francis; **St Anne's Home, Manor Road N16 5BL**
Tel: **07979 822520** Email: peter@stevens75.orangehome.co.uk
Stewart (1935; 1982) Michael; **50 Bull Stag Green, Hatfield AL9 5DE**
Tel: **01707 264213**
Stoakes (1958; 1983) Keith; **Clergy House, 9 Pekin Street E14 6EZ**
Tel: **020 7987 4523** (Poplar, Limehouse)
Stogdon (1988; 2018) Jonathan; **22 Bradley Road N22 7SZ**
Tel: **020 8888 2390** (Wood Green)
Stokes (1972; 2011) Graham; **80 Imperial Close, Harrow HA2 7LW**
Tel: **020 8868 7531** (Harrow North)
Stokes (1945; 1983) John; **c/o Archbishop's House SW1P 1QJ** (Chaplain, HMP Isle of Wight)
Sykes (1959; 1985) Perry; **22 Bradley Road N22 7SZ** Tel: **020 8888 2390** (Wood Green)

Tabor (1973; 2018) BD, John; **St Lawrence's Presbytery, The Green, Feltham TW13 4AF**
Tel: **020 8890 2367** (Feltham)
Tastard (1947; 1993) MA, PhD, Terry; **38 Mulberry Court, Bedford Road N2 9DZ**
Tel: **020 3224 3039**
Tate (1954; 2013) Martin; **24 Bouverie Road N16 0AJ**
Tel: **020 8800 5250** (Stoke Newington)
Taylor (1951; 2000) MA, STB, MA, Canon Roger; **Allen Hall, 28 Beaufort Street SW3 5AA**
Tel: **020 7349 5600** (Seminary)
Thomas (1972; 2016) Tony; **194 Knightfield, Shoplands, Welwyn Garden City AL8 7RQ**
Tel: **01707 327434** (Welwyn Garden City Parishes)
Thornton (1964; 1989) Sean; **Presbytery, 1 Wrentham Avenue NW10 3HT**
Tel: **020 8964 4040** (Kensal Rise)
Touw Tempelmans-Plat (1949; 1995) MA, Dennis F P; **60 Rylston Road SW6 7HW**
Tel: **020 7385 4040** (Fulham 1)
Trood (1961; 2001) MA, STB, MCL, JCL, ACA Jeremy; **20 Phoenix Road NW1 1TA**
Tel: **020 7387 1971** (Somers Town, Chancellor)

SECTION 4

Tuck (1939; 1963) Michael; The Rectory, Green Street, Sunbury-on-Thames TW16 6QB
Tel: 01932 783507 (Sunbury-on-Thames)
Tuckwell (1945; 1995) Canon Christopher; Cathedral Clergy House, 42 Francis Street
SW1P 1QW Tel: 020 7798 9374 (Cathedral)
Turner (1941; 1966) Mgr Canon Henry; 8 Rothamsted Court, Harpenden AL5 2BZ
Tel: 01582 965207 (Ecumenical Chaplaincy at St Albans Abbey)

Udo (1982; 2016) BD, STB, Chinedu; 45 London Road, Enfield EN2 6DS
Tel: 020 8363 2569 (Enfield)
Usher (1942; 2000) BA, Thomas; c/o Archbishop's House SW1P 1QJ

Vickers (1966; 2003) BA, STB, Mark; 44 Ashchurch Grove W12 9BU
Tel: 020 8743 5196 (Shepherds Bush)
Vipers (1963; 1997) BA, Christopher J; 4/5 Eldon St EC2M 7LS Tel: 020 7247 8390 (Bunhill
Row, Moorfields, Director of Agency for Evangelisation)

Wadsworth (1961; 1990) MA, GTCL, LTCL, LRAM, Mgr Andrew; ICEL Secretariat, 1100
Connecticut Avenue, NW, Suite 710, Washington DC 20036-4101, USA
(Executive Director, ICEL)
Wagay (1953; 1993) BA, MA, STB, Gideon; 62 Eden Grove N7 8EN
Tel: 020 7607 3594 (Holloway)
Wahle (1929; 1965) STL, BSc, Francis; 17 Chiltern Court, Baker Street NW1 5TD
Tel: 020 7487 5956 Email: franciswahle@yahoo.com
Walker (1985; 2013) Mark; 20 Phoenix Road NW1 1TA
Tel: 020 7387 1971 (Somers Town, Diocesan Youth Chaplain)
Wang (1966; 1998) MA, PhL, STL, PhD, Stephen; Newman House, 111 Gower Street
WC1E 6AR Tel: 020 7387 6370 (University Chaplaincy)
Ward (1937; 1961) Brian; 2 Evergreen Park, Tanderagee, Binion, Clonmany,
Co Donegal, Ireland Tel: 0035 37493 78887
Warnaby (1960; 2017) MA, BD, John; 970 Harrow Road, Sudbury, Wembley HA0 2QE
Tel: 020 8904 2552 (Sudbury)
Webb (1953; 1983) Christopher; c/o Archbishop's House SW1P 1QJ (On loan)
Welsh (1946; 1994) John; St Raphael's House, Morrison Road, Yeading UB4 9JP
Tel: 020 8845 1919 (Yeading)
Whatling (1929; 1969) Colin; 2B Eton Avenue, Heston TW5 0HB
Tel: 020 8606 9544
White (1952; 1984) John; 32 Old Brewery Close, Aylesbury HP21 7SH
Tel: 01296 481776
Whitmore (1959; 1993) MA, DPhil, STL, Mgr Philip; Via di Monserrato 45, 00186 Rome, Italy
Tel: 00390 6686 8546 Email: philipjwhitmore@gmail.com (Venerable English College)
Whooley (1942; 1982) John; 24 The Crosspath, Radlett WD7 8HN
Wilby (1939; 1964) William; St Wilfred's Convent, 29 Tite Street SW3 4JX
Tel: 020 7351 5339 (Chaplain)

Wiley (1947; 1975) KJSJ, MA, BD, John; **185 Baldwins Lane, Croxley Green, Rickmansworth WD3 3LL Tel: 01923 231969 (Croxley Green)**

Williamson (1945; 1975) STD, David; **Nazareth House, 162 East End Road N2 0RU**

Willis (1965; 1996) BA, Stephen A; **The Presbytery, 1 Nicoll Road NW10 9AX**
Tel: **020 8965 4935 (Willesden)**

Wilson (1938; 1970) David; **c/o Archbishop's House SW1P 1QJ**

Wilson (1965; 1997) BA, HDipEd, Peter J; **79 St Charles Square W10 6EB**
Tel: **020 8969 6844 (St Charles Square)**

Wilson (1947; 1996) MA, BSc, Canon Stuart M P; **22 George Street W1U 3QY**
Tel: **020 7935 0943 (Spanish Place), 07515 065696 (Vocations Promoter)**

Winter (1948; 1978) Marcus; **The Lodge, 87 St Charles Square W10 6EA**
Tel: **020 3673 9540 (Notting Hill Carmel Chaplain)**

Witoń (1975; 2005) STB, Sławomir; **45 London Road, Enfield EN2 6DS**
Tel: **020 8363 2569 (Enfield)**

Woodley (1973: 2019) BMus, ARCM, STL, Benjamin; **54 Lodge Road NW8 8LA**
Tel: **020 7286 3214 (St John's Wood)**

Woodruff (1959; 1995) BA, Mark; **c/o Sainsbury Family Charitable Trusts, The Peak, 5 Wilton Road SW1V 1AP Tel: 020 7410 0330 (English Liturgy Chaplain and Co-ordinator, Ukrainian Cathedral)**

Young (1932; 1957) MA, Henry; **63 Heathfield Court, Heathfield Terrace W4 4LS**

Zsidi (1951; 1975) Gabriel; **c/o Archbishop's House SW1P 1QJ**

PERMANENT DEACONS

Abrahams (1960; 2017) Reginald; **160 Long Lane, Hillingdon UB10 0EH**
Tel: **01885 234577 Email: reginaldabrahams@rcdow.org.uk (Hillingdon)**

Agule (1966; 2012) BSc (Acct), BA (Theol), MBA, FCA, Nick; **20 The Green, West Drayton UB7 7PJ Tel: 01895 442777 Email: nickagule@rcdow.org.uk**
(West Drayton and Yiewsley)

Barter (1956; 2017) Tony; **22 The Crosspath, Radlett WD7 8HN Tel: 01923 635541**
Email: tonybarter@rcdow.org.uk (Radlett, Shenley and London Colney)

Burke (1953; 2018) MTh, BD (Hons), PGCE, NPQH, FdA, QTS, Alex; **Ealing Abbey Parish Office, 2 Marchwood Crescent W5 2DX Tel: 020 8862 2162**
Email: alexburke@rcdow.org.uk (Ealing)

Clark (1945; 2008) BA, BD, LicPhil, Anthony; **700 Finchley Road NW11 7NE**
Tel: **020 8455 1300 Email:anthonyclark@rcdow.org.uk (Golders Green)**

Coleman (1965; 2019) MA, LGSM, FRCO Ian; **373 Bowes Road N11 1AA**
Tel: **020 8368 1638 Email: iancoleman@rcdow.org.uk (New Southgate)**

Cross (1975; 2014) FdA, BSc(Econ), MA, ACIS, Justin; **47 Vesta Avenue, St Albans AL1 2PE**
Tel: **01727 850066 Email: justincross@rcdow.org.uk (St Albans South)**

Cullen (1957; 2009) MBA, BSc (Hons), Adrian; **1 King Edward's Road, Ware SG12 7EJ**
Tel: **01920 462140 Email: adriancullen@rcdow.org.uk (Ware)**

SECTION 4

Curran (1971; 2012) MA, BA (Hons), PhB, Dip Coun, Anthony; 22 The Crosspath, Radlett WD7 8HN Tel: 01923 635541 Email: anthonycurran@rcdow.org.uk (Radlett and Shenley, London Colney)

Dyckhoff (1941; 2006) OBE, FIH, FRSPH, Neville; Holy Rood House, Exchange Road, Watford WD18 0PJ Tel: 01923 224085 Email: nevilledyckhoff@rcdow.org.uk (Watford)

Edwards (1965; 2014) FdA, BEng, PgDip, CEng, MIET, Ian; Ealing Abbey Parish Office, 2 Marchwood Crescent, Ealing, London W5 2DX Tel: 020 8862 2162 Email: ianedwards@rcdow.org.uk (Ealing)

Estorninho (1960; 2019) BEd, FdA, Joseph; 130 St Margarets Road, Twickenham TW1 1RL Tel: 020 8892 3902 Email: josephestorninho@rcdow.org.uk (St Margarets-on-Thames)

Goodall (1957; 2019) FdA, Andrew; 38 Camborne Avenue W13 9QZ Tel: 020 8567 5421 Email: andrewgoodall@rcdow.org.uk (Northfields)

Hemming (1962; 1997) BA, MA, MPhil, PhD, Laurence; 5 Westmoreland Place SW1V 4AB Tel: 020 7828 2737 Email: laurencehemming@rcdow.org.uk

Hopkins (1950; 2011) FD, BA (Hons), Donal; 243 Mutton Lane, Potters Bar EN6 2AT Tel: 01707 654359 Email: donalhopkins@rcdow.org.uk (Potters Bar, Sabbatical)

Izundu (1952; 2018) BA, BSc (Hons), MSC, PhD, MRTPI, Kingsley; 17 Kenninghall Road E5 8BS Tel: 020 8985 2178 Email: kingsleyizundu@rcdow.org.uk (Clapton)

Joiris de Caussin (1971; 2017) Stéphane; Email: stephanejoirisdecaussin@rcdow.org.uk (Kensington and Chelsea Deanery)

Khokhar (1968; 2014) FD (Telecom Engineer) Stephen; St Anselm's Rectory, The Green, Southall UB2 4BE Email: stephenkhokar@rcdow.org.uk (Southall)

Levett (; 2005) Robert; St George's Chapel, Heathrow Airport, Hounslow TW6 1BP Tel: 020 8745 4261 Email: robertlevett@rcdow.org.uk (Heathrow Airport)

Lo (1966; 2019) HDFCT, FdA, LLB, LLM, William; The Presbytery, Brentfield Road NW10 8ER Tel: 020 8965 3313 Email: williamlo@rcdow.org.uk (Stonebridge)

Lynch (1980; 2017) BSc (Hons), MA, PGdip, PGcert (Edu), QTS, Liam; Church of St Helen, The Harebreaks, Watford WD24 6NJ Tel: 01923 223175 Email: liamlynch@rcdow.org.uk (Watford North)

MacPherson (1940; 1992) MA, DMin, KHS, Duncan; 16 Ormond Drive, Hampton TW12 2TN Tel: 020 8274 0210 Email: duncanmacpherson@rcdow.org.uk

Macken (1962; 2018) FdA, Colin; St Lawrence's, 9 The Green, Feltham TW13 4AF Tel: 020 8890 2367 Email: colinmacken@rcdow.org.uk (Feltham)

Nunn (1956; 2008) Gordon; Ealing Abbey Parish Office, 2 Marchwood Crescent W5 2DX Tel: 020 8862 2162 Email: gordonnunn@rcdow.org.uk (Ealing)

O'Reilly (1970; 2019) FdA, Wayne; 60 Rylston Road SW6 7HW Tel: 020 7385 4040 Email: waynoreilly@rcdow.org.uk (Fulham I)

Pereira (1963; 2007) BA (Hons) QTS, FCoT, Tito; Our Lady of Lourdes, 5 Berrymead Gardens W3 8AA Tel: 020 8992 2014 Email: titopereira@rcdow.org.uk (Acton)

Pickard (1945; 2009) Steve; 14 Beaconsfield Road, St Albans AL1 3RB Tel: 01727 853585 Email: stevepickard@rcdow.org.uk (St Albans)

Quinn (1972; 2017) FdA, Paul; Our Lady & St Michael, Crown Rise, Garston, Watford WD25 0NE Tel: 01923 673239 Email: paulquinn@rcdow.org.uk (Garston)

Tsegaye (1943; 2007) BA, MSc, MCILIP, Kassa; **St Thomas More, 9 Henry Road N4 2LH**
Tel: **020 8802 9910** Email: kassatsegaye@rcdow.org.uk (Manor House)
Wright (1953; 2008) BSc, PhD, Simon; **186 St John's Road, Boxmoor HP1 1NR**
Tel: **01442 391759** Email: simonwright@rcdow.org.uk
(Hemel Hempstead West Parishes)
Yates (1967; 2017), FdA, MA, MSC, PhD, Jeremy; **377 Mile End Road E3 4QS**
Tel: **020 8980 1845** Email: jeremyyates@rcdow.org.uk (Mile End)

DEACONS IN FORMATION FOR PRIESTHOOD IN WESTMINSTER

Amari (1980; 2015) Guido
Balzanella (1990; 2019) Alexander **(Venerable English College, Rome)**
Dora (1992; 2019) Adam
Knight (1974; 2019) David **(Allen Hall / New Southgate)**
Seery (1960; 2017) Ronald
Soriano (1991; 2019) Axcel **(Potters Bar)**

SEMINARIANS IN FORMATION FOR PRIESTHOOD IN WESTMINSTER

Allen Hall Seminary
Redemptoris Mater **House of Formation**
John Casey
Daniel Daley
Matteo Di Giuseppe
Paolo Gambardella
Michael Guthrie
Jakub Joszko
Kiril Kovatchev
Martin Krizmanić
Marco Lazzaron
Tim Mangatal
Domagoj Matokovic
Marco Salvagnini
Robert Smialek
Juan Sola Garcia
Piotr Staniszewski

Extended Pastoral Placement & Itinerancy:
Thomas Blackburn
William Johnstone
Marcin Nadolski
Michał Pastuszka
Dominic Quirke
Francis Thomas

Beda College, Rome
Patrick van der Vorst

OBITUARIES

Fr Robert Barry RIP

Robert Joseph Barry will be remembered by relatives, friends and colleagues in the priesthood as a truly holy man. His holiness was evident because of his closeness to, and unfailing trust in, God. He believed in God and he heard and followed God's call to priesthood and to the Religious Life. His vocation was lived out with simplicity, humility and courage, especially in the face of illness and the restrictions that living with Multiple Sclerosis imposed.

Bob was born, educated and grew up in Ballybunion, County Kerry in Ireland. He was the fourth of six children born to Joseph and Margaret (née Keane) Barry, on 26 January 1945 and baptised two days later at St John's Church, Ballybunion, the church in which he was confirmed on 26 April 1957. His father was an honest and hard-working farmer, and Bob brought experience and knowledge of farming to his employment on local farms. When he was 17 Bob left Ireland in search of work in England and joined his siblings who were living in Kingsbury, North West London. He worked in construction as a labourer, along with so many others who had emigrated to England to earn their living and provide for their families in Ireland. At this time his spiritual life was developing, and by 1963 he had become aware that God was calling him to the priesthood. He attended daily evening Mass and Benediction twice weekly at Ss Sebastian and Pancras church in Kingsbury Green while continuing in employment. The parish clergy, Frs John O'Callaghan and Paul Dewe Mathews, were supportive of Bob's desire to be a priest of the diocese of Westminster. However, Bob was very aware that he would struggle with studies and so was put in contact with the Dominican Sr Catherine of St James' School in Burnt Oak. She saw his potential, and gave him weekly lessons in English and also Latin for a year, and employed him at the convent. She described him as having 'fine qualities of soul', a man ready to respond to God's call. With the encouragement of those who knew him, he applied and was accepted as a student for the diocese and sent to Campion House, Osterley for studies in preparation for seminary formation.

After two years at Campion House Bob was sent to Allen Hall Seminary in Ware. He was a hard-working and conscientious student, but struggled academically. The Superior at Campion House endorsed Bob's vocation. He reported: 'There is no mistaking the sincerity and good will of this man. He is never going to be brilliant academically, but has compensating qualities of good sense and perseverance'. Sr Catherine OP wrote: 'If there is patience over his initial difficulties, I believe he will make a holy priest'. The Rector of Allen Hall, Mgr (later Bishop) James O'Brien, described Bob as a student who: 'is conscientious, tries hard … works well and is a good member of the community'. Bob was ordained to the priesthood on 10 July 1976 at Eden Grove, Holloway by Bishop Victor Guazzelli, following ministry in the parish as a Deacon in formation.

Fr Bob's first appointment was to the parish of Our Lady of Lourdes, Acton where he served from 1976-78. He was then appointed as Assistant Priest at Hertford until 1980. Fr

Bob had spoken with Cardinal Heenan, Archbishop of Westminster, about a sense of calling to the monastic life. He had a deeply contemplative spirit, and spoke to the new Archbishop, the Benedictine Basil Hume, to ask permission to try his vocation with the Carthusians at St Hugh's Charterhouse, Parkminster in West Sussex. In April 1980 Cardinal Hume wrote to Fr Bob, having given permission for him to go to Parkminster: 'I do wish you all that is best. I only ask that if you discover that this Carthusian life is not for you … you will be received back into the diocese with open arms. But there is a side of me that prays and hopes that this is truly God's will for you'. Himself a monk, Cardinal Hume recognised and supported this monastic vocation. And so, in 1980, Fr Bob became Dom Joseph and lived in a cell at Parkminster living a radical life of prayer and contemplation, sharing in the silence and work of the community.

Dom Joseph embraced the monastic life in response to God's call. He found happiness and peace in the monastery, and enjoyed every day of the seven years he remained there. In 1985, at the time of renewal of temporary profession, the Novice Master wrote of him: 'All who meet him quickly notice his sincerity, his real faith, his dedication to the life of prayer. He has never had any doubt about his vocation. He tends to play himself down to identify with the underdog … it is interesting to note how he regularly impresses the more intellectual among our aspirants … all speak highly of him'. Dom Joseph is remembered by a contemporary at Parkminster for his humour and humility. His strong Kerry accent seems to have fascinated, amused, and at times confused his brother-monks! However, he was diagnosed with serious illness, Multiple Sclerosis, necessitating his departure from the monastic life as lived as a member of the Order of St Bruno in October 1987. This was a great disappointment and challenge for him. He had met the philanthropist Group Captain Leonard Cheshire, who had established homes for people with serious disabilities, and he went to the Cheshire Home in Cavendish, Suffolk as resident Chaplain. The Prior of Parkminster, Fr Bernard, had visited the home and described Fr Bob's accommodation as: 'a little cell of two rooms, quiet and remote, where he can continue to live a life of prayer and solitude, very like our own'. The Prior wrote to Cardinal Hume, saying: 'Fr Barry was very well liked and respected in this community, and we were sorry to lose him. He accepts his infirmity and disappointment in great peace and acceptance of God's will … he is very close to God, and will bring down many graces in your diocese by his life of prayer, and the suffering that is inevitable in his condition'. Fr Bob was happy and content at Cavendish, but declining health meant another change in 1990 – this time to the Diocesan Pastoral Centre at London Colney for four years.

His next move was to the parish of Southall, with the presbytery adapted for his needs. He was pleased to give assistance to the parish priest in the sacramental and pastoral life of the parish. He had a particular gift as a confessor and counsellor, able to listen to people's concerns and burdens, and showing them understanding, kindness and mercy. But deteriorating health meant another move, in 2000, to Nazareth House. After a few years Fr Bob moved to the new St Vincent's Nursing Home in Eastcote, where he remained a resident until his death at Northwick Park Hospital on 15 December 2018 with members of his family at his bedside.

Since his departure from the monastery, Fr Bob continued to live a monastic life in other places and circumstances. He was respected by all with whom he came into contact. His faithfulness to prayer and to God's will, with its challenges, inspired members of his family and his friends. He modelled courage and dedication to his vocations, living a life of quiet simplicity and evident joy without complaint about his personal cross of illness and suffering. He seems to have made his own the motto of the Carthusian Order: *Stat crux dum volvitur orbis*, the Cross is steady while the world is changing. He readily saw the good in others, and was unfailingly complimentary about people that others may have found difficult. He was always grateful for the understanding, support and friendship given by his family, friends and brother priests, and by the diocese. He, in turn, gave to all an example of faithful service to God and to the Church.

May he rest in peace.

Fr Gerard Thomas Burke RIP

Because of his love for, and commitment to, the priesthood and the diocese, Fr Gerry will be fondly remembered and sorely missed by the bishops, priests, deacons, Religious and lay people who knew him. And because of his love for, and commitment to, his family and friends, they too will miss him greatly and treasure their memories of him as a brother, uncle and companion. Gerard Thomas Burke (known as Gerry by almost everybody except his family) was born on 18 April 1935 in Willesden, the first of four sons born to Thomas and Ethel, parishioners at the church of Our Lady of Willesden. Thomas Burke had come from a large family with roots in Ireland, and moved from Wallsend in the North East of England to London in search of work. Here he met and married Ethel, who came from Holloway. Gerry knew himself to be 'half-Geordie', and remained proud of his heritage and kept in touch with family members.

Educated at Sacred Heart Primary School close to the family home in Ruislip, he became an altar server at the parish church and a member of the scout troop, always keen to learn new skills. His education continued at Gunnersbury Grammar School where, along with academic study, Gerry developed practical skills. He was high-spirited and enjoyed life at school, with occasional brushes with authority. He enjoyed comedy, notably the weekly 'Goon Show' broadcast by the BBC, and he developed a strong, and at times zany, sense of humour. He remained a lifelong fan and imitator of the Goons. In his mid-teens Gerry's sense of vocation to the priesthood led to his acceptance as an ecclesiastical student by Archbishop Myers, with the support of his parents and parish priest. In 1951 he was sent to St Edmund's College, Ware as a boarder to complete his secondary education and prepare him for seminary life. Gerry was a conscientious student, intelligent and grounded in reality. He joined the College's cadet corps, putting his musical skills to use as a member of the corps' band, playing the large bass drum and taking part in parades.

In 1953 he moved to the Venerable English College in Rome as a seminarian and studied at the Gregorian University. He remained in Rome for seven years, with one visit home for the summer three years into his priestly formation. While in Rome Gerry became proficient in Italian, and he developed a love of cooking, Italian style. He enjoyed travel to other parts of Italy during breaks from study, travelling with, and enjoying the company of, friends from the College and other seminaries in Rome. Because he had practical skills and ingenuity, he was called upon to attend to various repairs and odd jobs, with varying degrees of success, hence the nickname 'bodger' that friends continued to use, as he did of himself, long after life at the English College. On 12 March 1960 Gerry was ordained to the priesthood by Cardinal Traglia at the Basilica of St John Lateran. Fr Gerry's first appointment was to the parish of Holy Cross, Parsons Green as Assistant Priest for one year before moving to St James', Spanish Place where he served as Assistant Priest from 1961-64. He then moved to Archbishop's House, having been appointed Private Secretary. In 1967 he was appointed Assistant Priest at Barnet, until 1973. Fr Gerry's next appointment was to Isleworth, as Assistant Priest and Chaplain to Gumley House School until 1980 when he was appointed Parish Priest at Poplar, where he remained until 1983. In Poplar he found parishioners as robust in their understanding of the faith as he was robust in challenging them to a renewed understanding, and what follows from it. They were well matched!

Fr Gerry took part in preparations for the National Pastoral Congress held in Liverpool in 1980, with 2,000 delegates from England and Wales. He was involved with a 'theological road show', travelling around the diocese to address packed meetings in the Pastoral Areas, explaining ecclesial models and theological concepts. It was a time of great hope, and he was an optimist. He helped many 'ordinary' Catholics to grasp the difference between the BOC and the POG – the Body of Christ and the People of God, drawing inspiration from the teachings of the Second Vatican Council. From 1983 to 1986 he served as Pastoral Director at Allen Hall Seminary. At this time the 'Ministry to Priests' programme was being introduce to the diocese, and he was appointed Diocesan Director from 1986 to 1995. In that role, and running the Centre for Human Development based in Kensington Square, he worked tirelessly to support and promote the growth of priests in every aspect of their lives – spiritual, pastoral, intellectual and in their humanity and personhood. The programme was a response to the question 'Who ministers to the minsters, and how?' The need for such support was recognized in other countries, and Fr Gerry was invited by the Bishops' Conference of South Africa to set up and run the Ministry to Priests programme based in Pretoria. With the blessing of Cardinal Hume, he went to South Africa in 1995 and remained there for three years. During his years working with the Centre for Human Development, Fr Gerry travelled to many other English-speaking counties to share his knowledge of, and passion for, the life and ministry of priests and the need for organised support and means for personal growth for them.

In March 1998 he returned to the diocese and was appointed Parish Priest of St Lawrence's parish, Feltham. He enjoyed life and ministry there, perhaps more so than he had in Poplar, and he remarked to a colleague, speaking of the parishioners: 'I have never seen people as generous and loving as these', and to another: 'these have been the happiest years of my life'. The response of the parishioners to Fr Gerry's commitment to shared responsibility for the ministry and mission of the Church brought him much satisfaction. As a Parish Priest Fr Gerry had his own thoughts about matters such as the age of First Reconciliation and the manner of the celebration of Reconciliation with adults, and he articulated these verbally and in writing. But above his personal preferences, based on his knowledge and experience, he respected the authority of the Bishop and the unity of practice in the diocese. From 2001 to 2006 Fr Gerry served as a member of the Cathedral Chapter of Canons.

Throughout his life as a priest Fr Gerry remained close to his family and to his friends. Many visited him in his various parishes and while he was in South Africa, and have stories to tell of his zest for life, fun and adventure, and of the animated conversations around the table while enjoying the results of his cooking. He was an intelligent and articulate priest, and a good listener to the ideas, and to the joys and sorrows, of others. He brought humour to many situations, helping people not to take themselves too seriously, while supporting people with kindness and compassion as they faced serious situations. Many colleagues and parishioners appreciated his prophetic teaching and preaching, inspired by Vatican II, but others found him challenging, while maintaining respect for him, perhaps in recognition of his evident integrity.

In 2010, at the customary retirement age for priests, he retired to what he described as 'a bijou little bungalow' in Feltham, where he was able to indulge his twin passions of cooking and gardening (his passion for sailing had featured in earlier years), while remaining among his adopted parish family of St Lawrence's. In his letter to the Vicar General he wrote: 'This parish, more than any other, has become my family, and if I could retire locally I would be near many friends and, no less importantly, close to the various hospitals and medical facilities of which I have had to avail myself…'. He remained active in ministry, giving assistance in the parish and giving his successors support while never interfering. Fr Gerry died peacefully on 20 March after a short illness, having recently moved from his bungalow to the nearby Derwent Lodge Care Home where his needs were met, and where he continued to receive the support of family, friends and colleagues. He knew he was close to death, and he was without fear. He was ready to be embraced by the Lord whom he knew, loved and served. This much-loved man and priest died at the age of 83 years, having served as a priest for 59 years.

May he rest in peace.

Fr Barry Ffrench RIP

Barry Ffrench came from Rosslare, County Wexford in Ireland. He was born on 23 October 1936 and ordained to the priesthood by Cardinal Godfrey in Westminster Cathedral on 24 May 1962. He returned to his home county to live in retirement, and later moved to a nursing home where he died peacefully on 1 October 2019. His Funeral Mass took place at St Brigid's Church, Askamore on 4 October with the Bishop of Ferns, the Rt Rev Denis Brennan presiding and preaching, and with representation from the diocese of Westminster.

Fr Barry died on the annual day dedicated to the memory of St Thérèse of the Child Jesus, and was buried on the day dedicated to St Francis of Assisi. His formation for priesthood, and the early years of his ministry, were with the Oblates of St Charles. The Oblates were founded as an English institute of diocesan priests in 1857, with a rule of life based on that kept by the Oblates of Milan, founded by St Charles Borromeo. The Oblates lived as communities of priests dedicated to the ministry and mission of the local Church, including

SECTION 4

pastoral work and the education of children and young people.

Following his ordination to the priesthood, Fr Barry was appointed Assistant Priest at St Mary of the Angels, Bayswater from 1962-64. His next appointment as Assistant Priest was to St Francis of Assisi, Notting Hill where he remained until 1966 before returning to Bayswater. In 1967 he was appointed Priest in Charge at Our Lady of Sorrows, Paddington where he remained until 1969. Our Lady of Lourdes, New Southgate was his next appointment, as Assistant Priest until his appointment as Diocesan Youth Chaplain, based at London Colney, from 1973-76. He was then appointed Parish Priest at St John the Baptist, Hackney where he remained until 1983. He then moved west to Yeading, as Parish Priest at St Raphael's. In 2003 Fr Barry went on sabbatical leave, but health issues necessitated retirement from full-time parish ministry the following year, and he returned to Ireland where he gave much valued assistance in the local parish, and was close to members of his family. On 25 May 2012 Fr Barry celebrated his Golden Jubilee of Ordination with a Mass and party at St Brigid's, Askamore at which he was delighted to be joined by the retired Archbishop of Westminster, the late Cardinal Cormac Murphy-O'Connor. His 80th birthday was then marked with Mass and a party on 23 October 2016. He always loved a party! In Askamore he gave pastoral support for 12 years until failing health prevented further public ministry, although he continued to celebrate Mass privately in his home. However, with the advance of years and deteriorating health, his needs required additional care and he took up residence at The Moyne Nursing Home, Enniscorthy. There Fr Barry was well cared for and secure, with many regular visitors.

Many people will treasure their memories of him, 'a people's priest'. During his years of active ministry he was known for the warmth of welcome and hospitality extended to family, friends, brother priests and parishioners. He was a friend to everyone, especially the young and less fortunate. At his Funeral Mass children from three local schools formed a guard of honour. People of all ages expressed their sadness at the loss of a much-loved priest, and shared their stories of his engagement with them. He was attentive and responsive to people's needs, and was seldom unavailable to callers. In his prime Fr Barry attracted people to the Church, and he had a winning way with children and young people. There were many altar servers and members of uniformed groups in his parishes and youth clubs flourished. The pilgrimages he organized, to Lourdes and to Rome, attracted young adults and he inspired them in their faith and commitment to the Church. As diocesan Youth Chaplain his commitment to young people had a lasting influence on many. He was known to be a sympathetic confessor. For many years he had a dog, favouring spaniels as a breed. While in Yeading he named his dog Pod, the name by which a popular Auxiliary Bishop of Westminster, Pat O'Donoghue, was known. This brought amusement to the late Cardinal Basil Hume who enjoyed Fr Barry's sense of humour, as did so many people over the years.

Fr Barry will be fondly remembered by parishioners and friends alike, and missed by all who knew him. At the Funeral Mass a message from Cardinal Vincent Nichols was read to the congregation: '… We pray that our Blessed Lord will bring this faithful servant of his to his Heavenly Father, so that he might enfold him in his mercy and ensure eternal rest in his loving presence.'

May he rest in peace.

Fr Christopher Gawecki RIP

Born in Poland on 1 March 1939 and ordained to the priesthood as a Carmelite Friar on 22 February 1968 by Bishop Julian Groblicki, Auxiliary Bishop of Kraków, Fr Christopher Gawecki was the second of seven children born to Anthony and Francesca Gawecki. His first appointment as a priest was to a parish in Gdansk. In 1972 he was appointed to serve in Tadcaster as Assistant Priest, then in 1975 to Sittingbourne, followed by his appointment to Aylesford Priory in 1977, where he was Master of Ceremonies.

In 1979 he was appointed Assistant Priest at St Charles Square in the diocese of Westminster. Two years later he moved to serve as Assistant Priest at Ruislip, followed by appointment the following year to Berkhamsted. His next assignment was to Spanish Place, in 1988. In 1994 he was appointed to Hillingdon, where he remained until 2002. He was then appointed Assistant Priest at St Margarets-on-Thames, until his premature retirement from full-time parish ministry early in 2008. While at Hillingdon and St Margarets-on-Thames he served as a Chaplain at Hillingdon Hospital, but retired from this ministry in 2006.

Fr Christopher's request for early retirement, five years before the customary age, was supported by the diocese. He went to live with his elderly and disabled brother Stan in Putney. After the death of his brother, he felt the pain of loss deeply, and this seems to have remained with him. He generously offered to help locally, both in the Archdiocese of Southwark and in Westminster, as a supply priest. In recent months he had become unwell, and after a relatively short illness he died peacefully at home on 4 August 2019. His sister was with him at the time of his death, as was the local parish priest.

At his Funeral Mass on 13 August at the parish of Our Lady and St Simon Stock in Putney, the homilist, who had come to know Fr Christopher well, spoke of his endearing sense of humour and lightheartedness, his devotion to the Mass and the Sacraments of the Church, and his care for people who were unwell. He lived frugally, perhaps as a legacy of wartime experience as he grew up in Poland and his experience of life in the Polish navy. When sent to England for ministry in a Carmelite parish, he had to learn English quickly, adopting English customs and turns of phrase. Because English was not his first language, his sense of humour and expressions could on occasion seem odd and subject to possible misinterpretation. He will be remembered for letting people know that: 'I am British and have sworn allegiance to the Queen!'

In February 2018 Fr Christopher celebrated the Golden Jubilee of his ordination to the priesthood. He responded to Cardinal Vincent's letter of congratulations by including mention of his admiration for his fellow-countryman Pope St John Paul II. He wrote: 'While responding to my vocation in the seminary in Poland, I had the privilege of experiencing the guidance of Fr Karol Wojtyla, who was later elevated to the papacy and then canonised'. He celebrated his Jubilee, he continued, '… where it all started, in Poland.' It was his wish that his mortal remains return to Poland for burial following his Funeral Mass. After Masses, in the sacristy, Fr Christopher would often look at the Crucifix and say: 'Thank you, Jesus.' For all the good that he achieved as a priest, and for God's mercy in the reality

of his faults and failings, 'Thank you, Jesus.' And thank you, Fr Christopher, for your generous response to God's call to the priesthood and for your ministry to God's people.
May he rest in peace.

Fr Séamus Noctor RIP

Fr Séamus Noctor spent the final years of his life living back in Ireland, at the Glenashling Nursing Home in Celbridge, County Kildare where his sister Maura was in residence at the time of his arrival there. Maura died on 13 January and that of her brother followed on 16 January. Their Funeral Mass took place in the Chapel at Glenashling on 19 January, followed by burial in the family grave in Mount Jerome Cemetery. Fr Séamus was 90 years of age, and was a priest of the diocese of Westminster for 61 years.
Séamus was born in Dublin on 2 September 1928, the son of James and Sarah Noctor. The family home was in the Harold's Cross area of the city. He had five siblings. Educated at St Laurence O'Toole Secondary School, he went on to study book keeping, shorthand and typing. His skills led to employment in a local office with a company involved with imports and exports. For recreation he enjoyed dancing, and learnt waltz, quickstep and jive. He had a good voice and enjoyed singing – a gift he would bring to his priestly ministry.
Séamus was accepted as a student for the priesthood and ordained to the diaconate in the Chapel at St Mary's College, Oscott on 22 September 1956 by Bishop Humphrey Bright, Auxiliary Bishop of Birmingham; and then to the priesthood on 16 March 1957 at Holy Cross College, Clonliffe in Dublin by Archbishop John Charles McQuaid. A contemporary at Allen Hall, St Edmund's College, described the older Séamus as a student who was interested more in billiards and snooker than in table tennis, favoured by the younger seminarians. Following ordination, Fr Séamus was appointed Assistant Priest at the Church of the Blessed Sacrament, Copenhagen Street, from 1957 to 1972 when he was appointed to serve as Assistant Priest at St Joseph's, Wembley with the understanding that his ministry would commence at the beginning of October. However, there was a delay in him taking the appointment. He was given permission by the Cardinal to return to Dublin to attend to family matters, including the family business – a pub. Thirteen months later the Vicar General, Mgr David Norris, wrote to Fr Séamus, on behalf of Cardinal Heenan, to ask when he might return to the diocese to take up his appointment! It seems that there were some difficulties trying to sell the business on Lower Sherriff Street, described by Fr Séamus in correspondence with the diocese as being a 'no-go area', with a bad reputation. In January 1973 Fr Séamus wrote a lengthy letter to the Vicar General letting him know that there were still difficulties with selling the pub, and reassuring him that he was involved with Church life by celebrating two Sunday Masses in a local church and attending clergy gatherings at Clonliffe College. He concluded his letter: '…as requested, as soon as it is possible for me to return to my duties in the diocese I will let you know.' The Vicar General sent a two-sentence reply, expressing the hope that he would soon return. Three days later, on 11 January, the Cardinal wrote a very directive letter, expressing concern for him and making clear what was required. Fr Séamus replied by return of post, promising to return as soon as possible. The Vicar General had to write again to Fr Séamus, in March, which

elicited the reply that the pub would be sold the following month and then he would return and take up his appointment in Wembley.

Fr Séamus served as Assistant Priest at Wembley from mid-April 1973 until his next appointment, as Parish Priest at St Augustine's, Harringay in 1974 in succession to Fr Hugh Bishop. He remained there until his retirement from full-time parish ministry in April 2009. Symptoms of dementia had become evident. The parish of St Augustine was then merged with the parish of St John Vianney, West Green – it had been founded from West Green in 1964, but turned out to be non-viable. He was very happy at St Augustine's, and devoted all his time and energy to the parish. As well as for his kindness to parishioners and devotion to the Mass, he is remembered for sartorial elegance and his large vintage car. He never regretted becoming a priest, even when he was distracted by the family business; he had a good sense of humour, indeed of mischief, and an easy rapport with those with whom he came into contact.

In 2009 Fr Séamus retired from St Augustine's to live at St Anne's Nursing Home in Stoke Newington where his needs were met by the Sisters and staff. With increasing dementia, his needs had to be met elsewhere, and his family arranged for him to return to Ireland, to Glenashling Nursing Home. He took up residence there in the summer of 2015 and was well cared and provided for until his death. In 2017 he was invited by Cardinal Vincent to return to London to celebrate his Diamond Jubilee of Ordination – 60 years – with fellow Jubilarians, but he was unable to accept due to his circumstances. He was remembered then, as he is now and always will be, with affection for his dedication to the Church and the people of God.

May he rest in peace.

Fr Thomas Quinn RIP

Before a priest reaches his 75th birthday, he is required to write to his Bishop to offer resignation from ecclesiastical office, and to retire. Priests sometimes ask if they can remain in their current appointments, and this Fr Tom did when he wrote to Cardinal Vincent in February 2018, a month before turning 75. His request was granted, to his delight and that of the parishioners at Shepperton. However, seven months later he wrote again to let the Cardinal know that due to a rapid deterioration of his health he was asking to stand down. 'My health has deteriorated to the point where I can no longer shoulder the responsibility of a parish', he wrote in a letter accompanied by a medical report. The Cardinal accepted his request, thanking him for all he had done while in active ministry and acknowledging his wisdom in coming to this decision. In September 2018 Fr Tom went to live at Nazareth House, East Finchley, where he quickly felt at home and secure. He was popular among fellow residents and with Sisters and staff. Over the next few months his health continued to deteriorate, despite the medical attention he received at Nazareth House and at the Royal Free and Whittington Hospitals. He died peacefully in his sleep at the Whittington Hospital on 2 August 2019.

Born on 20 March 1943 in Ashton-under-Lyne, Manchester, Tom Quinn was educated at St Willibrord's Catholic School in Clayton. After some years of employment locally, as a wages clerk and also as a watchmaker and jeweller, he felt called to the priesthood and was accepted for formation by the Blessed Sacrament Fathers in 1968. Tom's novitiate was in Leicester, going on to study alongside diocesan seminarians at Allen Hall in Ware. He was ordained to the priesthood on 10 May 1975 in Liverpool. His ministry there was effective, as a sought-after confessor who ministered to a wide range of people in the city, including Travellers, becoming known as the 'Gypsy Priest'. He also ministered in Glasgow and Dublin. Within a few years he decided to take some time out from active ministry, being unsure of his true vocation. He set up home in Dublin, then went to live and work in Aberdeen. After nine years of personal vocational discernment he decided that he should resume priestly ministry. In 1988 the Provincial Superior of the Blessed Sacrament Fathers wrote to Cardinal Hume, then Archbishop of Westminster, to ask if Fr Tom could be given a placement in the diocese to live and work with a priest who would help with continuing discernment. In preparation for this Fr Tom undertook to do the Spiritual Exercises of St Ignatius in Wales while living in a presbytery. His continuing discernment included working as a driving instructor in Colwyn Bay, to the surprise of his Religious Superiors!

His desire to resume priestly life and ministry was recognized and supported by the diocese of Westminster. He went to live in parish accommodation at Cockfosters, then gave assistance in the parish of St Peter's, South Hatfield for 18 months. In September 1990 Cardinal Hume wrote to him to confirm his appointment as Assistant Priest at St Anselm's, Southall. Whilst there Fr Tom requested to be incardinated as a priest of the diocese, and this was widely welcomed. His gentle, open and sympathetic manner earned him an excellent reputation in his pastoral work. He had great empathy with people who had personal difficulties, on occasion becoming personally involved due to his generosity of spirit. Priests with whom he lived and worked saw in him a kind and thoughtful colleague with a deep spiritual life, who was easy to get on with. He was incardinated by Cardinal Hume in a simple ceremony at Archbishop's House on 29 September 1992, remaining at Southall until 1994, when he was appointed Parish Priest at Our Lady of the Rosary, Staines. In 1997 Fr Tom was appointed Parish Priest at Ss Peter and Paul, Northfields. His only sibling, John, died suddenly in December 2005 at the age of 60; this, being unexpected, caused much sadness. Fr Tom's next appointment was to St Mary and St Michael, Commercial Road in 2010, where he remained until 2013 when he was appointed Parish Priest at St John Fisher, Shepperton.

When he arrived to take up residence and begin his ministry there, he brought just three carrier bags of personal belongings. He was asked by a parishioner if he needed help to bring the rest of his possessions. Responding with a smile, he said: 'I have everything here.' Fr Tom was a man and priest who lived simply, without extravagance in any form. His clothes came from charity shops and jumble sales. He remained close to his sister-in-law and to his two nephews after the death of his beloved brother. Parishioners whom Fr Tom served will remember him for his warmth, kindness and approachability. He was patient and tolerant of others, giving people the gift of his time, generously. In his ministry he gave priority to the sick and suffering, and to the dying and bereaved. He had an easy rapport with young people, and served as their Chaplain on the diocesan pilgrimages to Lourdes. Visits to HMP Bronzefield were a feature of hiss weekly schedule, as was a game of golf before the decline of his health. He became an easily recognizable figure and well-known to parishioners and the wider community in Shepperton, perhaps in part due to his imposing height and unkempt shoulder-length hair. His wish was to return to Shepperton for his Funeral Mass and for his mortal remains to be taken back to Manchester for burial. As Fr Tom said with warmth and kindness at the conclusion of many conversations, we now say to him: 'Wish you well', as we pray in thanksgiving for his life and ministry and now for the repose of his soul.

May he rest in peace

Fr Adrian Walker RIP

Fr Adrian Walker will be fondly remembered by many who knew him over his 58 years of priestly life and ministry as an intelligent, gifted and self-effacing man. He was generous with his time and energy. Enduring, and endearing, characteristics of humility and generosity remain in evidence following his death. He made it known that the homily to be given at his funeral should have: 'few biographical references but concentrate on the manner in which I have lived my priesthood and on the influence the programme and spirituality of Alcoholics Anonymous has had in my life since November 1968'. He also wrote about his desire for his mortal remains to be given for the benefit of scientific research. Not everything that is requested can be granted. In May 1992 the diocesan newspaper, the Westminster Record, published a profile of Fr Adrian under the heading 'Enthusiasm at its best'. The article described some of Fr Adrian's qualities and achievements, 32 years into his ministry. He was: 'a doer… something of a whirlwind…'

Adrian Walker was born on 6 August 1931. Both parents were converts to Catholicism, and they sent their son to be educated by Jesuits at Stonyhurst College in Lancashire. His father's embrace of the Catholic faith was inspired by the example of a Catholic Chaplain in the Great War, and Adrian, in his turn, was inspired by his father. He served in the Navy. Despite his obvious intelligence, he eschewed any thought of a commission – he was never ambitious for status or preferment throughout his life. Accepted as a student for the priesthood by Cardinal Griffin, he was sent to Allen Hall at St Edmund's, Ware and ordained to the priesthood on 11 June 1960 by Cardinal Godfrey. He was then sent to Rome for further studies in philosophy at the Angelicum University, and lived at the Pontifical Beda College. On his return to the diocese, Fr Adrian's first appointment was to Edmonton, as Assistant Priest where he served from 1964-1971, when he was appointed to work as a Chaplain to London University, living at Newman House in Gower Street. After two years he was given a new appointment, as Assistant Priest at Bayswater. In 1976 he was appointed Parish Priest at Stevenage, Pin Green and in 1981 appointed further to have oversight of the four Stevenage parishes. His commitment to ecumenism was vitally expressed during his 11 years there, with the church building shared by Anglicans, Catholics and Methodists. After five years at Stevenage the team ministry was established. The new arrangements preserved the geographical identities of the four parishes, but with a shared church for all. Fr Adrian put all his energy into this project, supported by other priests and religious Sisters on the Parish Team, and by local Christian ministers. The local Catholic and wider community were broadly supportive of this innovative ecumenical plan; as anticipated, there were some detractors. The years at Stevenage allowed Fr Adrian's liturgical and theological creativity to flourish. This was coupled with zeal for the pastoral care of his parishioners and their formation in liturgy and theology. However, he knew that, after 11 years, it was time to ask for another appointment.

From 1987 to 1994 the parish of Staines was to benefit from Fr Adrian's intelligence, experience and commitment, and his unconventional way of facing and progressing challenging situations. He re-ordered the church, positioning the altar away from the sanctuary and into the north aisle, complete with the wooden baldacchino. The result made for more intimacy in the church, spreading into the parish. The parish hall expanded, occupying space in the adjacent presbytery which provided modest accommodation for the Parish Priest. In 1990 the parish celebrated its centenary, and Fr Adrian invited Cardinal Hume to lead the celebrations. With his care for detail and well in advance, he sent the Cardinal briefing notes on the history of the parish, the list of invited guests, and matters deserving of attention in the homily.

His appointment was next to Millwall, a parish without a church (the old church was closed in December 1994, having been declared structurally unsafe and then demolished in the summer of 1995), hall or presbytery, but in need of a priest with experience, vision and energy. The parish, in the developing Docklands area, was changing and Fr Adrian was well-suited to the emerging needs of the parish and neighbourhood. Cardinal Hume gave him much encouragement, including a large donation to the building fund, and went to Millwall to bless the foundation stone for the new church, writing a message of support for the ambitious fundraising efforts in 1999. Parishioners from Staines also gave great support. The newly-built church and complex was opened for use in 2000 with Cardinal Cormac celebrating Mass there in September. In 2004 Fr Adrian retired from full-time parish ministry, having requested this some two years before the usual age of 75. He knew that it was time to stand down and embrace a new rhythm of priestly living.

Fr Adrian will be remembered for his informality, and for being somewhat unconventional in his approach and practice. He will also be remembered, and admired, for 50 years of sobriety supported by, and giving support to, the fellowship of Alcoholics Anonymous, for which he made time to prepare and give retreats at annual AA gatherings in Aylesford He was devoted to his priesthood, and gave little time for his hobbies of cooking, reading and classical music.

On 24 January 2019 he died peacefully in hospital, having been admitted the previous evening. He had been retired from full-time parish ministry for 15 years, but kept himself busy with supply ministry in parishes close to his home in Maidenhead, remaining faithful to an hour of prayer every morning and the daily celebration of Mass. The onset of Alzheimer's in his 80s did not alter his disposition of kindness and respect for others, especially those who treated him and cared for him. A friend commented: 'Doesn't Adrian realise that everyone feels better when he comes into the room?' And now we pray that Fr Adrian will be welcomed by the God he knew, loved and served, to take his place in heaven.

May he rest in peace.

Fr Denis Patrick Watters RIP

Non nobis, Domine, sed nomine tuo da gloriam, Not to us, Lord, not to us, but to your name give the glory – this was Fr Denis' motto that featured on his personal stationery in correspondence from his home in Ballyheigue, Co. Kerry in Ireland. Taken from Psalm 113 in the Vulgate numbering of the Psalms, it was also the motto of the Knights Templar, the Order that cared for pilgrims travelling to sites in the Holy Land and seeking to journey closer to God. As a priest, Fr Denis cared for the parishioners he served, and they cared for him. He knew himself to be a fellow pilgrim, called to follow and called to serve, putting at the service of God and the Church his faith, his vocation and his humility.

Denis Patrick Watters was born in London on 29 March 1947, the son of Thomas and Josephine. He is survived by his younger sister Kate. He was baptised at St Joseph's, Wembley and educated at the parish primary school and St Gregory's High School, Kenton and at Breakspear College in Abbots Langley. Denis was good at sports, especially football. He played for his school teams, and for the Wembley Borough team, and had trials for West Ham United FC. He could have pursued a career as a footballer, but his sense of vocation led him to apply to the diocese and he was accepted and went to Allen Hall Seminary at St Edmund's College, Ware, as a seminarian, where he began studies in 1966. He was ordained to the Diaconate at St Edmund's College on 4 July 1971 and to the priesthood at St Joseph's, Wembley by Cardinal Heenan on 27 May 1972.

Fr Denis' first appointment as an Assistant Priest was to the parish of Ss Mary and Joseph, Poplar, from 1972 until 1978, the parish where he had served the previous year as a Deacon. While at Poplar Fr Denis played football for a local team in a Sunday morning league. With his skill, the team won the league and the local newspaper carried a photograph of the victorious team with the cup, including Fr Denis in team kit; the accompanying article mentioned that Fr Denis also fulfilled his priestly duties on Sundays! He was then appointed Assistant Priest at All Saints, Kenton and Chaplain at St Gregory's School until 1984. His next appointment was as Parish Priest at St Joseph's, Bunhill Row, serving as Chaplain to Moorfields Eye Hospital, where he remained until 1990 when he was appointed Parish Priest at St Gabriel's, Archway. In 1997 Fr Denis had sabbatical leave, including participation on a course at Palazzola, the Villa of the English College outside Rome. He was then appointed Parish Priest at Stevenage, living at St Joseph's, Bedwell from 1998 until his premature retirement from full-time parish ministry for reasons of poor health in June 2011.

Before being appointed to Stevenage, Fr Denis was asked if he would accept appointment as Vocations Director for the diocese, but he told Cardinal Hume that, after much prayer and thought, it would not be right for him to accept because of his introverted personality. He was grateful to Cardinal Hume for considering him for such a role, and for the Cardinal's confidence in his ability. He requested a return to parish ministry 'outside the capital' and this he was granted.

Writing to the diocese from his home in Ballyheigue in February 2012, Fr Denis commented on how much he missed active parish life as a priest: 'But I count myself fortunate in having a kind and considerate Parish Priest who tries to involve me in the activities that go on here', he wrote. Throughout his life he had a keen interest in all sports, including golf, fishing and basketball. In Co. Kerry he had more time for golf, living near the renowned Ballybunion course. Deteriorating health and the need for care then necessitated his return to England. In May 2016 he went to live at his sister's residential care home at Burnham Lodge, Slough where he enjoyed walking in the spacious grounds, with a subsequent move to Oaken Holt Nursing and Residential Home, Farmoor, near Oxford, where he died peacefully on Saturday 1 June.

Family members, friends and parishioners will have many stories to share as they recall the life of a faithful and well-loved priest. A humble man, he was dedicated to his ministry and faithful to his friends. A parishioner at Bunhill Row recalls him taking them down to the dark, unlit crypt of the church, populated with life size statutes of saints and martyrs, with graphic descriptions of how they died. Fr Denis explained that on his arrival the small church was full of them, 'leaving little room for the living'. He brought new life to the community.

An intelligent and insightful man, always respectful of the views of other people, he was able to analyse situations and face challenges, and win the respect and loyalty of parishioners. His abiding kindness and deep compassion for people who were troubled or suffering brought comfort to many. His self-effacing and dry sense of humour was never cynical or sarcastic, but able to bring a ray of light to a dark situation. He often told a humorous story at the end of each of his Masses, causing people to leave the church with a smile on their lips, as did the humorous photos and jokes that were characteristic of his parish newsletters.

  May he rest in peace.

DIOCESAN CLERGY ANNIVERSARIES

JANUARY

1	Cardinal Francis Bourne (1935)
	Fr Brendan Soane (2000)
2	Fr Sidney Dommersen (1970)
	Fr Alexander Wells (1970)
	Fr Cyril Wilson (1988)
3	Fr Donald Campbell (1985)
	Fr Denis Cantwell (1995)
4	Fr Bernard Canham (1990)
	Fr William Brown (2001)
6	Fr Thomas Anderson (1974)
	Fr Thomas McNamara (1976)
	Mgr Graham Leonard (2010)
	Mgr Ralph Brown (2014)
7	Fr John T Carberry (1988)
8	Fr John Kearsey (2004)
10	Mgr Ernest T Bassett (1990)
	Fr William Kahle (1993)
	Fr Patrick Nolan (2014)
11	Mgr Eustace Bernard (1972)
	Fr Mark Coningsby (2014)
12	Fr Arthur P Mintern (1993)
14	Cardinal Henry Manning (1892)
	Fr Peter Lyons (1998)
15	Canon James Hathway (1976)
	Fr Anthony Busuttil (2013)
16	Fr Edward Hinsley (1976)
	Canon Frederick Smyth (2007)
	Fr Seamus Noctor (2019)
17	Fr Edward Dering Leicester (1977)
	Fr George O'Connor (1989)
18	Fr Gerry Ennis (2000)
	Fr Robin Whitney (2012)
19	Fr Oldrich Trnka (2003)
20	Mgr George Leonard (1993)
	Fr Thomas Gardner (1995)
	Fr Stephen Bartlett (2012)
21	Preb Ronald Pilkington (1975)
22	Cardinal William Godfrey (1963)
23	Fr Derek Jennings (1995)
24	Fr Adrian Walker (2019)
25	Fr Bernard Fisher (1990)
26	Bishop Patrick Casey (1999)
29	Fr Frederick Vincent (1973)
30	Fr Joseph Fehrenbach (1985)

Fr Patrick Howard (2000)
Fr Philip Dayer (2005)

FEBRUARY

1	Fr Harold Gadsden (1972)
	Mgr Edward Dunderdale (2001)
2	Fr Charles Lowe (1978)
	Bishop Philip Harvey (2003)
	Fr James McCormick (2009)
3	Fr Hugh Bishop (1984)
6	Fr Patrick McEvoy (1974)
	Canon William Ward (1993)
	Canon Daniel Kay (2003)
	Fr Kenneth McCabe (2013)
7	Fr Bernard Ferry (1970)
	Fr George Haines (2000)
	Fr Michael John Groarke (2008)
9	Canon George Groves (1997)
11	Fr Alan Body (1988)
12	Fr Joseph Francis (1984)
	Canon Edward Armitage (1987)
	Mgr Canon Francis Bartlett (1992)
13	Fr Patrick O'Callaghan (1970)
	Mgr Canon Maurice Kelleher (1994)
15	Cardinal Nicholas Wiseman (1865)
	Fr Richard Wakeling (1988)
	Fr Leo Straub (2000)
	Mgr Canon Adrian Arrowsmith (2014)
16	Mgr Bernard Chapman (1999)
	Fr John Kirwin (2003)
	Canon Patrick Davies (2010)
19	Fr Ronald Aylward (2010)
20	Fr Joseph Scholles (1983)
21	Fr Michael Hollings (1997)
	Canon Peter Bourne (2001)
	Fr Cathal McGonagle (2010)
22	Deacon James Richards (2014)
23	Canon John O'Callaghan (1981)
24	Mgr Canon Arthur Rivers (1978)
25	Fr Charles McMenemy (1976)
	Fr Archibald Bardney (1985)
	Fr Andrew Clancy (1986)
26	Fr Brian Heaney (2013)
27	Fr Nicholas Lambert (1976)

SECTION 4

	Canon Michael Richards (1997)
	Canon Charles McGowan (2006)
	Canon Peter Moore (2006)
28	Fr Joseph Gilligan (1990)
	Fr John Taylor (2005)
29	Fr Frank Rochla (1992)
	Fr John McCoy (2012)

MARCH

6	Mgr Frederick Row (1974)
	Mgr Canon Clement Parsons (1980)
	Fr Geoffrey Webb (2014)
	Fr Timothy McCarthy (2018)
7	Fr Henry Dodd (1992)
	Fr Harold Riley (2003)
8	Fr Thomas Nobbs (1977)
9	Fr Paul Lenihan (1992)
13	Fr Patrick English (1971)
14	Bishop David Cashman (1971)
	Canon Jeremiah Galvin (1973)
	Fr Reginald Watt (1975)
15	Fr Walter Donovan (1981)
17	Cardinal Arthur Hinsley (1943)
	Fr Michael Buckley (1993)
	Fr Lionel Keane (1997)
	Fr Charles Connor (2005)
	Canon Digby Samuels (2018)
18	Fr John Nelson-Turner (2015)
20	Canon Desmond Swan (1995)
	Fr Edward Bushey (1996)
	Fr Nicholas Kavanagh (2018)
	Fr Gerard Burke (2019)
21	Fr James de Felice (1978)
22	Fr Edward Higgs (1988)
23	Fr Peter Day (2006)
24	Fr John Gill (1985)
	Fr Pat Heekin (2006)
25	Mgr Richard Kenefeck (1982)
27	Fr Cormac Rigby (2007)
	Fr James Brand (2013)
30	Fr William Hutchinson (1984)

APRIL

3	Fr Francis Kenney (1987)
4	Fr Peter Dunn (1974)
	Fr Robert Holmes-Walker (2010)
5	Fr Albert Parisotti (1970)
	Fr David Evans (1989)
7	Fr John Keep (2002)
9	Fr Ronald Cox (1994)
	Fr Thomas Hookham (1998)
	Fr James Wooloughan (2003)
	Fr Gerard Meaney (2010)
10	Mgr Canon John MT Barton (1977)
	Fr Brian Laycock (2004)
11	Fr John Bebb (1975)
	Bishop James O'Brien (2007)
12	Fr John Mills (1975)
	Fr Anton Cowan (2016)
13	Fr Albert Davey (1987)
14	Fr Michael Hendry (1994)
16	Fr Clement Tigar (1976)
	Mgr Canon Lancelot Long (1978)
	Fr Bernard McGuinness (1978)
17	Canon Lionel Dove (1971)
19	Fr Joseph McEntee (1978)
	Canon Harold Winstone (1987)
20	Fr Patrick Smyth (1978)
21	Canon Reginald Fuller (2011)
22	Fr Herbert Crees (1974)
	Fr Robert Tollemach (1998)
	Fr John Robson (2000)
23	Canon Frank Martin (2002)
24	Canon Clement Rochford (1978)
	Fr Derek McClughen (1991)
25	Canon Francis Hegarty (2004)
27	Fr Stanley Harrison (1973)
	Mgr John F McDonald (1992)
28	Canon John Longstaff (1986)
29	Fr Michael Moriarty (1996)

MAY

2	Fr John Farrelly (1990)
	Fr John Coughlan (1997)
	Fr Francis Finnegan (1999)
	Fr Edward Bilsborrow (2007)

4	Fr Peter Lowry (1972)
	Fr Raymond Tomalin (1996)
5	Canon Herbert Welchman (1982)
	Fr Denys Lucas (1995)
6	Fr John Hathway (1995)
	Fr Anthony Potter (2003)
7	Fr Alastair Russell (1997)
9	Fr Bernard Lagrue (1995)
10	Fr Patrick Keegan (1992)
	Mgr Canon Oliver Kelly (1995)
	Canon Denis Britt-Compton (2002)
	Fr Charles Mercer (2005)
	Fr Frederick de L'Orme (2016)
11	Fr Thomas Kean (1981)
13	Mgr Stephen Shaw (1998)
14	Fr Peter Boshell (1993)
15	Fr William O'Brien (2004)
	Fr Patrick Sammon (2018)
20	Fr Stanislaus Savage (1975)
	Fr Michael Markey (2014)
22	Fr Ronald Richardson (1999)
	Fr Charles MacMahon (2003)
23	Fr Bernard Bussy (1992)
	Fr Hugh McAleese (1994)
	Fr Matthew Burrows (2010)
24	Fr Denis Ward (1978)
	Fr Philip Rogers (1995)
	Fr Michael Garvey (2002)
	Fr Denis Nottingham (2002)
25	Mgr Canon John Bagshawe (1971)
	Mgr Denis McGuinness (1993)
	Fr John Oldland (1995)
26	Canon Patrick J Murphy (1974)
	Fr John Murray (1995)
30	Fr Albert Purdie (1976)
31	Canon Reginald Crook (1990)
	Fr John Luke (2003)
	Fr Kevin Greene (2004)

JUNE

1	Fr Philip Carpenter (1992)
	Bishop Victor Guazzelli (2004)
	Fr Denis Patrick Watters (2019)

2	Fr Stephen Finnegan (1993)
	Fr Damien McManus (1997)
4	Fr Joseph Rees (2007)
	Fr William McConalogue (2009)
7	Fr John O'Connell (1970)
8	Fr Harold Hamill (2016)
9	Mgr David Norris (2010)
10	Fr John Harrington (2007)
11	Fr Vincent McCarthy (1974)
	Fr Francis Davis (2003)
13	Canon Alfonso de Zulueta (1980)
14	Fr George Lee (1987)
16	Fr Michael Pinot de Moira (2013)
17	Cardinal Basil Hume OSB (1999)
18	Fr Michael Connor (2007)
19	Cardinal Herbert Vaughan (1903)
20	Fr Thomas Kiernan (2013)
21	Fr J Brian Campbell (1983)
22	Fr Anthony Turbett (2000)
26	Fr John Moran (1988)
	Mgr Canon Roderick More O'Ferrall (1991)
27	Fr Raleigh Addington, (1980)
28	Fr Cuthbert Boddy (1970)
	Canon Denis Crowley (1980)
29	Fr Richard Fitzgibbon (2006)
30	Fr Edmund R J Henry (1971)
	Fr William Anderson (1972)
	Fr Christopher Bedford (2008)

JULY

1	Mgr Anthony Howe (2011)
3	Fr William M Brown (1989)
	Fr George Ennis (2007)
4	Fr Joseph Anthony Carr (1999)
6	Fr Terence Wardle (2010)
7	Canon Alfred Cuming (1978)
	Fr Frank Morrall (1995)
	Fr John Power (2002)
8	Fr Joseph Gardner (1992)
9	Fr Christopher Pemberton (1983)
	Fr John Norton (1989)
10	Fr Peter Harris (1976)

SECTION 4

	Fr Thomas Kelly (1983)
12	Fr Daniel Higgins (1996)
14	Mgr Canon Joseph Williams (1991)
15	Fr Christopher McKenna (2003)
16	Fr Michael Giffney (1987)
	Canon John McKenzie (1988)
17	Fr Horatio Hosford (2014)
19	Fr Peter Pearson (1971)
	Canon Peter Gilburt (2017)
21	Canon Philip Moore (1976)
	Fr Anthony O'Sullivan (1997)
	Fr Norman Kersey (1999)
	Canon Herbert Veal (2005)
22	Fr Tom Allan (2007)
26	Fr George Fonseca (1998)
	Fr David Roderick (2005)
27	Fr Graham Feint (2000)
28	Fr Ralph Gardner (1976)
	Fr Patrick Whyte (1988)
	Deacon Sydney Adams (2005)
30	Fr Calum MacLean (1982)
	Fr Vincent Commerford (1997)
31	Fr Albert Vaughan (1995)

AUGUST

1	Fr Richard Johnson (1992)
	Fr Ignatius Tonna (1993)
2	Fr Thomas Stack (1984)
	Fr Michael Archer (2014)
	Fr Thomas Quinn (2019)
3	Mgr Canon John Mostyn (1981)
4	Fr Christopher Gawecki (2019)
5	Fr William Lynagh (1977)
	Fr Alan Fudge (2011)
6	Fr Anthony Sacré (2015)
9	Fr John Greene (1980)
11	Fr Laurence Allan (1981)
	Fr Guy Martin Heal (2009)
12	Fr Roderick Cuming (1981)
	Fr Wilfrid Soggee (1990)
	Fr John Milne (2001)
	Fr Joseph Finnegan (2002)
	Fr John D'Arcy Dutton (2013)

14	Fr Philip Dwerryhouse (1986)
15	Fr John Adam (1979)
	Fr Bernard Mortimore (1980)
16	Canon Denis O'Sullivan (1983)
	Fr Peter Latham (2005)
17	Mgr Walter Drumm (2015)
19	Canon George Davey (1986)
	Fr Leslie Cole (1997)
	Fr Michael Durand (2018)
20	Cardinal Bernard Griffin (1956)
	Fr Joseph McVeigh (1977)
	Fr Desmond Mullin (1988)
21	Fr Percival Fielden (1990)
	Fr Edward Houghton (2009)
24	Fr Patrick Cassidy (2007)
25	Fr James Gunston (1972)
	Mgr Canon Herbert Haines (2004)
	Fr Raymond Legge (2015)
	Fr Sean McWeeny (2016)
26	Fr Thomas Kilcoyne (1972)
	Fr Peter Keenan (1984)
27	Mgr John Coonan (1979)
	Fr Norman Wrigley (2015)
29	Fr Edward Fowler (1973)
	Fr Michael Lynam (1984)
31	Fr William Rees (1984)
	Canon Maurice O'Leary (1997)

SEPTEMBER

1	Cardinal Cormac Murphy-O'Connor (2017)
2	Fr Gerard Strain (1980)
3	Deacon Timothy Marsh (2013)
4	Fr John O'Neil (1971)
6	Canon Michael Roberts (2004)
7	Canon John F Marriott (1977)
10	Fr Thomas Burke (2018)
11	Fr William Erby (1974)
	Mgr Canon Cuthbert Collingwood (1980)
	Fr James Whitehead (1983)
12	Fr Leslie Wood (1984)
14	Fr William Ruhman (1978)

	Fr Leonard Collingwood (1985)
15	Fr Brian Connaughton (1979)
	Fr Robert Gates (2014)
16	Canon Nicholas Kelly (1988)
	Fr Patrick David O'Driscoll (2016)
17	Fr Frederick Thomas (1986)
	Fr John Pakenham (1987)
18	Canon John L Wright (1978)
19	Fr Alan Ashton (2014)
	Fr Patrick Lyons (2015)
20	Fr Des O'Neill (2008)
	Fr Austin Hart (2013)
21	Fr George Ingram (1992)
23	Fr Godfrey Wilson (1998)
24	Mgr Peter Anglim (2016)
26	Fr James Loughnane (1993)
	Fr Bernard Lang (2005)
	Fr Lance Joseph Boward (2011)
	Mgr Augustine Hoey (2017)
28	Fr Robert Newbery (1981)
	Fr Gerard Barry (1998)
30	Fr Michael O'Dwyer (1977)
	Fr Joseph Murray (1989)
	Fr John B Elliott (2017)

OCTOBER

1	Fr Barry Ffrench (2019)
2	Canon Des Sheehan (2004)
5	Fr John Fleming (1974)
	Fr Walter Meyjes (1987)
6	Fr Denis Murphy (1999)
	Fr George Dangerfield (2018)
7	Fr Thomas Daniel (1984)
	Canon Peter Phillips (2014)
8	Fr Thomas Allan (1982)
10	Fr Norman Fergusson (1986)
	Fr Arthur Moraes (2008)
11	Fr Joseph Davey (1970)
12	Fr James Finn (1977)
	Canon John P Murphy (1989)
13	Fr Norman Brown (2017)
14	Fr Henry Bryant (1972)
	Fr John Woods (2002)

	Fr Barry Carpenter (2012)
16	Mgr Canon Terence Keenan (1984)
18	Fr John Eveleigh Woodruff (1976)
	Fr John Murphy (2005)
19	Fr John Farrell (1983)
21	Fr Richard Berry (1989)
22	Fr David Cullen (1974)
	Fr Herbert Keldany (1988)
	Fr Ben Morgan (2005)
23	Fr Joseph O'Hear (1970)
	Fr Joe Gibbons (2002)
	Fr Dermot McGrath (2012)
24	Fr John Halvey (1990)
	Fr Ken Dain (2010)
25	Fr Andrew Moore (1994)
	Fr John Kearney (2007)
26	Fr John Clayton (1992)
	Fr George Talbot (2004)
27	Fr Colin Kilby (1985)
29	Canon Leo Ward (1970)
	Fr Joseph Eldridge (1993)
30	Canon William Gordon (1976)
31	Fr William Dempsey (2008)

NOVEMBER

1	Fr Horace Tennant (2000)
2	Mgr Canon George Tomlinson (1985)
	Fr Terence Brady (1989)
5	Fr Eric Chadwick (1993)
6	Fr Peter Geraerts (1980)
7	Cardinal John Carmel Heenan (1975)
	Canon Charles Carr (1985)
	Fr Raymond Geraerts (1995)
8	Fr Jeremiah Ryan (2001)
9	Fr George Barringer (1978)
	Fr James Ethrington (1981)
10	Fr Richard M Sutherland (1974)
	Fr John Spencer (1980)
11	Fr Gerald Freely (2013)
12	Fr James R Coughlan (1974)
	Fr Peter Johnson (2000)
14	Fr Maurice Ryan (1983)

SECTION 4

	Canon Louis Marteau (2002)
15	Fr James Stephenson (1970)
16	Fr Ian Dommerson (1996)
17	Fr Samuel Steer (1996)
20	Canon Louis Thomas (2017)
22	Mgr Reginald Butcher (1976)
	Fr Christopher Fullerton (1980)
24	Canon Edmund Hadfield (1982)
25	Fr Joseph Doyle (1978)
	Canon Joseph Geraerts (1979)
	Fr John Galvin (2010)
	Fr John Formby (2015)
26	Fr James Woodward (1976)
	Fr William Wood (1986)
	Fr Anthony John Cooke (2007)
27	Fr Joseph Scally (1995)
	Fr Peter O'Reilly (2005)
29	Fr Christopher Hamilton-Gray (2012)
	Fr Brian Nash (2014)
30	Canon Arthur Welland (1978)

	Canon John McDonald (2016)
21	Fr Clive Godwin (1974)
23	Fr Ian Dickie (2012)
24	Fr Manoel Gomes (1989)
25	Deacon Ron Saunders (2007)
	Canon Charles Acton (2016)
26	Fr Alan O'Connor (1992)
	Fr Bernard Lavin (1999)
27	Fr Andrew Morley (1993)
28	Mgr Canon Joseph Collings (1978)
	Fr Gerard Mulvaney (1996)
29	Fr Robert Bradley (1976)
30	Canon Alexander Stewart (1976)
31	Fr Wilfrid Trotman (1976)
	Fr Stephen Rigby (1978)
	Fr George Swanton (1979)
	Fr Dennis Skelly (1996)
	Fr Michael Ware (1998)

DECEMBER

3	Fr Harold Purney (1983)
4	Fr John Simcox (1972)
	Fr Peter Allen (1978)
	Mgr Wilfrid Purney (1987)
	Fr Benedict Westbrook (1989)
6	Fr John Harper-Hill (1998)
	Mgr Alexander Groves (1998)
11	Fr Dalton Haughey (1991)
12	Fr Laurence Kingseller (1975)
13	Fr Jeremiah Daly (1974)
14	Deacon Michael Bykar (2008)
15	Fr Francis Donovan (1983)
	Fr Robert Joseph Barry (2018)
16	Mgr George Tancred (2002)
	Fr John Donlan (2006)
18	Canon Bernard George (1980)
19	Canon John Shaw (1981)
	Fr Edward Gwilliams (1981)
	Fr Edward Scanlan (1992)
	Fr William Campling (1996)

OTHER PRIESTS IN THE DIOCESE

The entry in brackets following each surname indicates the diocese, order, congregation or society to which the priest belongs. A place name in brackets refers to a parish entry where further details may be found.

a.a.	Assumptionist	OCarm	Carmelite
CCN	Chemin Neuf Community	ODC	Carmelite (Discalced)
CM	Vincentian	OFM	Franciscan (Friar Minor)
CMF	Claretian Missionary	OFMCap	Capuchin Friar
CMI	Carmelite of Mary Immaculate	OMI	Oblate of Mary Immaculate
CP	Passionist	OP	Dominican
CS	Scalabrini Father	OSA	Augustinian
CSS	Stigmatine	OSB	Benedictine
CSSp	Spiritan	OSM	Servite
CSSR	Redemptorist	SAC	Pallottine
FDP	Sons of Divine Providence	SChr	Society of Christ
IC	Rosminian (Institute of Charity)	SCJ	Sacred Heart Father
IMC	Consolata Father	SDS	Salvatorian
LMO	Lebanese Maronite Order	SDV	Society of Divine Vocations
MAfr	Missionary of Africa (White Father)	SJ	Jesuit
MHM	Mill Hill Missionary	SM	Marist
Mccl	Comboni Missionary	SMA	Society of African Missions
MIC	Marian Father	SMM	Montfort Missionary
MSFS	Fransalian	SSC	Columban Father
MSP	Missionary Society of St Paul	SS.CC	Sacred Hearts Congregation
MSU	Monaci Studiti Ucraini	SSP	Society of St Paul
OAR	Augustinian Recollect	SVD	Divine Word Missionary

RETIRED BISHOPS

Campbell (OSA, Bishop Emeritus of Lancaster) Michael; **55 Fulham Palace Road W6 8AU (Hammersmith)**

Crowley (Bishop Emeritus of Middlesborough) John; **Flat 2, Francis Court, Caddington Road NW2 1RP Tel: 020 8452 6200 (Cricklewoood)**

Jabalé (OSB, Bishop Emeritus of Menevia) Mark; **Archbishop's House, Ambrosden Avenue SW1P 1QJ (Cathedral)**

PRIESTS

Achkar (LMO) Antoine; **6 Dobson Close NW6 4RS Tel: 020 7586 1801 (Lebanese Maronite Church)**

Adayi (CSSp) Daniel; **94 Bath Road, Hounslow TW3 3EH Tel: 020 8570 1693 (Hounslow, also Chaplaincy, Heathrow Airport)**

Addison (OSM) Paul; **264 Fulham Road SW10 9EL (Fulham Road)**

Akoeso (OSB) Bernard M; 32 High Street, Cranford, Hounslow TW5 9RG
Tel: 020 8759 9136 (Cranford)
Alex (OMI) Angodage Don Joseph; 30 Prescot Street E1 8BB (Tower Hill)
Alexander (Keralan Chaplaincy) Johnson; 373 Bowes Road N11 1AA
Tel 07438 182888 (New Southgate)
Alih (CSSp) Dominic 63 Somerset Road, New Barnet EN5 1RF (New Barnet)
Anywanwu (CM) Akobundu; 2 Flower Lane NW7 2JB Tel: 020 8959 1021 (Mill Hill)
Anzioli (MCCJ) Angelo; 16 Dawson Place W2 4TJ (Bayswater)
Armstrong (CM) Raymond; 2 Flower Lane NW7 2JB Tel: 020 8959 1021 (Mill Hill)
Arputham (SMA) Thyagu; White House, Watford Road, Northwood HA6 3PW
(Northwood)
Atu (Nigerian Chaplaincy) Alexander Izany; 8 King Henry's Walk N1 4PB
Tel: 07432 048440 (Kingsland)
Azagra (Opus Dei) PhD, MEng, Dancho; Netherhall House, Nutley Terrace NW3 5SA (Swiss
Cottage)
Azzi (LMO) Aziz; 6 Dobson Close NW6 4RS Tel: 020 7586 1801 (Lebanese Maronite
Church)

Baczewski (SJ) Adam; 182 Walm Lane NW2 3AX Tel: 020 8452 4304 (Willesden Green)
Bahati (a.a.) Antigon Claude; Assumption Priory, Victoria Park Square E2 9PB
(Bethnal Green)
Banayag (OSA) Thomas; 55 Fulham Palace Road W6 8AU (Hammersmith)
Banzi (SDS) Fortunatus; 191 High Road, Harrow Weald HA3 5EE (Wealdstone)
Barnes (SS.CC) Kenneth; 372 Uxbridge Road W5 3LH (Acton West)
Barnes (SJ) Michael; Copleston House, 221 Goldhurst Terrace NW6 3EP (Kilburn)
Beattie (SJ) Michael; 114 Mount Street W1K 3AH (Farm Street)
Bermingham (SJ) Edward; 27 High Road N15 6ND (Stamford Hill)
Bevan (OSB) Alexander; Ealing Abbey, Charlbury Grove W5 2DY (Ealing)
Blaj (Iasi, Romanian Chaplaincy) Marcelin; Presbytery, 22 Hay Lane NW9 0NG
(Kingsbury Green)
Blum (Cologne) Andreas; 47 Adler Street E1 1EE (German Church)
Boidin (SM) Pascal; 5 Leicester Place WC2H 7BX (French Church)
Bonelli (IMC) Carlo; 3 Salisbury Avenue N3 3AJ (Finchley Church End)
Bonnet-Eymard (SM) Hubert; 5 Leicester Place WC2H 7BX (French Church)
Borovsky (Slovak & Czech Chaplaincy) Tibor; 22 Cortayne Road SW6 3QA
(Parsons Green)
Bossy (SJ) Michael; 27 High Road N15 6ND (Stamford Hill)
Bowen (Oratorian) George; The Oratory, Brompton Road SW7 2RP (Oratory)
Bristow (Opus Dei) MA, STD, Peter; 8 Orme Court W2 4RL (Queensway)
Brunet (CCN) Christophe; 29 Bramley Road N14 4HE (Cockfosters)
Buba Leszek; 2 Devonia Road N1 8JJ Tel: 020 7226 9944 (Polish 1)
Burns (OSB) BA, STB, Peter; Ealing Abbey, Charlbury Grove W5 2DY (Ealing)
Byron (SJ) Timothy; Copleston House, 221 Goldhurst Terrace NW6 3EP (Kilburn)

Cabanero (SMM) Nelson; **27 St Gabriel's Road NW2 4DS (Willesden Green)**

Calcutt (MAfr) Richard; **64 Little Ealing Lane W5 4XF (Brentford)**

Cameron-Mowat (SJ) Andrew; **27 High Road N15 6ND (Stamford Hill)**

Camilleri (OFM, Maltese Chaplaincy) Victor; **47 Adler Street E1 1EE Tel: 07930 198251**
Email: camilleri_victor@hotmail.com (German Church)

Carmody (SJ) Brendan; **114 Mount Street W1K 3AH (Farm Street, Tyburn Convent)**

Chamakala John (Syro-Malabar Eparchy of Great Britain) Sebastian; **165 Arlington Road**
NW1 7EX (Camden Town)

Chantry (MHM) Anthony; **23 Eccleston Square SW1V 1NU (Pimlico)**

Chillman (OSB) BEd, Gregory; **Ealing Abbey, Charlbury Grove W5 2DY (Ealing)**

Chinery (Ordinariate) Simon; **19 Broadcroft, Hemel Hempstead HP2 5YX**
Tel: 01442 387195 Email: simon.chinery@ordinariate.org.uk (Hemel Hempstead North)

Choi (OSA) Jacob; **19 Hoxton Square N1 6NT (Hoxton)**

Ciebien Krzysztof; **2 Devonia Road N1 8JJ Tel: 020 7704 7662 (Polish 1)**

Clarke (OCD) Christopher; **41 Kensington Church Street W8 4BB (Kensington 2)**

Clifford (OSA) Barry; **55 Fulham Palace Road W6 8AU (Hammersmith)**

Creighton-Jobe (Oratorian) Ronald; **The Oratory, Brompton Road SW7 2RP (Oratory)**

Crotty (SS.CC) Fintan; **5 Berrymead Gardens W3 8AA (Acton)**

Csicsó (Pecs) János; **62 Little Ealing Lane W5 4EA (Brentford)**

Cummins (MAfr) Joseph; **64 Little Ealing Lane W5 4XF (Brentford)**

Cummins (MAfr) Thomas; **64 Little Ealing Lane W5 4XF (Brentford)**

Curci (MCCJ) Carmine; **16 Dawson Place W2 4TJ (Bayswater)**

Curran (CM) Eugene; **2 Flower Lane NW7 2JB (Mill Hill)**

Cussen (SMA) Anthony; **White House, Watford Road, Northwood HA6 3PW**
(Northwood)

Dabre (OSA) Gladson; **55 Fulham Palace Road W6 8AU (Hammersmith)**

Daly (SAC) Thomas; **358 Greenford Road, Greenford UB6 9AN (Greenford)**

Deidun (IC) Tom; **14 Ely Place EC1N 6RY (Ely Place)**

De Caro (SAC) Giuseppe; **4 Back Hill, Clerkenwell Road EC1R 5EN (Italian Church)**

De Marchi (MCCJ) Benito; **16 Dawson Place W2 4TJ (Bayswater)**

Devereux (OMI) Thomas; **New Priory, Quex Road NW6 4PS (Kilburn)**

Diaper (Opus Dei) MA, JCD, Paul; **The Presbytery, Maresfield Gardens NW3 5SU**
(Swiss Cottage)

Dilke (Oratorian) Charles; **The Oratory, Brompton Road SW7 2RP (Oratory)**

Dillon (OMI) Paschal; **237 Goldhurst Terrace NW6 3EP (Kilburn)**

Diouf (SM) Damien; **5 Leicester Place WC2H 7BX (French Church)**

Doherty (SDS) Michael; **9 Breakspear, Stevenage SG2 9SQ**
Tel: 01438 352182 (Stevenage Parishes)

Doherty (CP) Tiernan; **St Joseph's Retreat, Highgate Hill N19 5NE (Highgate)**

Donnelly (SVD) Eamonn; **8 Teignmouth Road NW2 4HN (Willesden Green)**

Doyle (Oratorian) Patrick; **The Oratory SW7 2RP (Oratory)**

Duffy (SM) Kevin; **5 Leicester Place WC2H 7BX (French Church)**

Dunn (OP) Michael; St Dominic's Priory, Southampton Road NW5 4LB (Haverstock Hill)

Edgar (OP) Leo; St Dominic's Priory, Southampton Road NW5 4LB (Haverstock Hill)
Egboo (Nigerian Chaplaincy) Peter Tochukwu; 8 King Henry's Walk N1 4PB
Tel: 07440 653821 (Kingsland)
Elias (SJ) Harold 2 Chandler Street E1W 2QT (Wapping)
Elliott-Smith (Ordinariate) MA, DipRAM, GRSM, LRAM, Mark; 22 George Street W1U 3QY
Tel: 020 7935 0943 / 07815 320761 Email: markelliottsmith@rcdow.org.uk
(Warwick Street)
Enuh (CM) Chinedu; 2 Flower Lane NW7 2JB (Mill Hill)
Escoto (SVD) Albert; 8 Teignmouth Road NW2 4HN (Willesden Green)
Ezechukwu (OCD) Alexander; 41 Kensington Church Street W8 4BB (Kensington 2)

Fasakin (CSSp) James Ademola; 63 Somerset Road, New Barnet EN5 1RF (New Barnet)
Fernandes (Goa and Daman) Linferd; 60 Rylston Road SW6 7HW
Tel: 020 7385 4040 (Fulham 1)
Fitzharris (SVD) Kieran; 8 Teignmouth Road NW2 4HN (Willesden Green)
Flynn (SMM) Kieran; 27 St Gabriel's Road NW2 4DS (Willesden Green)
Fordham (Oratorian) John; The Oratory, Brompton Road SW7 2RP (Oratory)
Frances (OAR) Jose; 18 Cheniston Gardens W8 6TQ (Kensington 1)
Fulco (SAC) Andrea; 4 Back Hill, Clerkenwell Road EC1R 5EN (Italian Church)

Gallagher (SJ) Peter; Copleston House, 221 Goldhurst Terrace NW6 3EP (Kilburn)
Gałuszka Marek; Priests House, Gravel Hill N3 3RJ Tel: 07523 545493 (Finchley Church
End)
Ganeri (OP) Martin St Dominic's Priory, Southampton Road NW5 4LB (Haverstock Hill)
Gerrard (MAfr) John; 15 Corfton Road W5 2HP (Ealing)
Gorham (OSB) STB, Timothy; Ealing Abbey, Charlbury Grove W5 2DY (Ealing)
Gowkielewicz (MIC) Andrzej; 1 Courtfield Gardens W13 0EY (Ealing)
Graham (OSA) Paul; 19 Hoxton Square N1 6NT (Hoxton)
Griffin (Ordinariate) Alan; 24 Cinnamon Street E1W 3NJ
Tel: 020 7265 1851   Email: a.h.f.griffin@gmail.com
Gucevicius (Vilnius) Petras; 21 The Oval, Hackney Road E2 9DT Tel: 020 7739 8735
(Lithuanian Church)
Gudime (Cuddapah) Saimon; The Presbytery, 100a Balls Pond Road N1 4AG
Tel: 020 7254 4378 (Kingsland)
Gumienny (MIC) Wiktor; 2 Windsor Road W5 5PD Tel: 020 8567 1746 (Polish 3)

Halman (FDP) Henryk; 25 Lower Teddington Road, Hampton Wick KT1 4HB
(Teddington)
Harries (OP) BSc, BD, Peter; St Dominic's Priory, Southampton Road NW5 4LB
(Haverstock Hill)
Hassan (OSA) Gabriel; 19 Hoxton Square N1 6NT (Hoxton)
Hayward (Opus Dei) LLB, JCD, Paul; 4 Orme Court W2 4RL (Queensway)

Heap (MAfr) Michael; 15 Corfton Road W5 2HP (Ealing)

Hemer (MHM) John; 28 Beaufort Street SW3 5AA Tel: 020 7349 5618 (Seminary)

Hewitt Stephen; St Joseph's, Oxhey Drive, South Oxhey, Watford WD19 7SW
Tel: 020 8428 2774 (Carpenders Park)

Hnylycia (Opus Dei) BSc, PGCE, Stefan; The Presbytery, Maresfield Gardens NW3 5SU
(Swiss Cottage)

Holman (SJ) Michael; Copleston House, 221 Goldhurst Terrace NW6 3EP (Kilburn)

Homer (Ordinariate, School Chaplain) Antony; Email: antonyhomer@rcdow.org.uk

Howard (SJ) Damian; 114 Mount Street W1K 3AH (Farm Street)

Hughes (OSB) Andrew; Ealing Abbey, Charlbury Grove W5 2DY (Ealing)

Hume (SJ) Patrick; 114 Mount Street W1K 3AH (Farm Street)

Igbe (CSSp) Terkura; 63 Somerset Road, New Barnet EN5 1RF (New Barnet, School
Chaplain)

Ikwuka (CSSp) Ugo; 15 St John's Villas N19 3EE Tel: 020 7272 8195 (Archway)

James (SDV) Vipin; 15 The Green, Heston Road, Heston TW5 0RL (Heston)

Januszkiewicz Canon Jerzy; c/o Polish Catholic Mission in England and Wales

Johnson (Focolare Movement) Francis Thomas; 138 Parkway, Welwyn Garden City
AL8 6HP Tel: 01707 339242 (Welwyn Garden City)

Jones Bryan; 377 Mile End Road E3 4QS Tel: 020 8980 1845 (Mile End)

Joseph (Quilon) Sebastian; 73 Pembroke Road, Ruislip HA4 8NN Tel: 01895 632739
(Ruislip)

Kaduthanam (CMI) Joseph; St Joseph's Presbytery, 339 High Road, Wembley HA9 6AG
(Wembley 1)

Karnawalski (SJ) Michał; St Ignatius Church, 27 High Road N15 6ND (Stamford Hill)

Kasereka (a.a.) Justin; Assumption Priory, Victoria Park Square E2 9PB (Bethnal Green)

Katsuva Kasine (a.a.) Euloge; 16 Nightingale Road, Hitchin SG5 1QS (Hitchin)

Katthula (CMF) Joseph; Botwell House, Botwell Lane, Hayes UB3 2AB (Hayes)

Keane (SDS) Noel; Salvatorian Community House, 189 High Street, Wealdstone, Harrow
HA3 5DY (Wealdstone)

Keeley (Lancaster) Stewart; Presbytery, 22 Hay Lane NW9 0NG
Tel: 020 8204 2834 (Kingsbury Green)

Keenan (OP) Oliver; St Dominic's Priory, Southampton Road NW5 4LB
(Haverstock Hill)

Kelly (CP) Christopher; Nazareth House, East End Road N2 0RU (East Finchley)

Kelly (MAfr) Peter; 64 Little Ealing Lane W5 4XF (Brentford)

Kmeid (LMO) Fadi; 6 Dobson Close NW6 4RS Tel: 020 7586 1801 (Lebanese Maronite
Church)

Kołodziej Bogdan; 2 Devonia Road N1 8JJ Tel: 020 7226 9944 (Polish 1)

Koloth (CP) George; St Joseph's Retreat, Highgate Hill N19 5NE (Highgate)

Konopinski (SJ) Mateusz; St Ignatius Church, 27 High Road N15 6ND (Stamford Hill)

Kozak (MIC) Michał; 2 Windsor Road W5 5PD Tel: 020 8567 1746 (Polish 3)

Kraiczyi (OSBM) Irineu; 22 Binney Street W1K 5BQ
Tel: 020 7629 1534 / 07772 111963 (Ukrainian Cathedral)
Krzyskow (SVD) Krzysztof; 8 Teignmouth Road NW2 4HN (Willesden Green)
Kukla Mgr Tadeusz; c/o Polish Catholic Mission in England and Wales

Lainez (SDS) Mario; 191 High Road, Harrow Weald HA3 5EE (Wealdstone)
Lang (Oratorian) Michael; The Oratory, Brompton Road SW7 2RP (Oratory)
Large (Oratorian) Julian; The Oratory, Brompton Road SW7 2RP (Oratory)
Leachman (OSB) James; Ealing Abbey, Charlbury Grove W5 2DY (Ealing)
Leggett (MAfr) Raymond; 15 Corfton Road W5 2HP (Ealing)
Lew (OP) Lawrence; St Dominic's Priory, Southampton Road NW5 4LB
(Haverstock Hill)
Liang (Jianxi, Chinese Chaplaincy) Joseph; Assumption Priory, Victoria Park Square E2 9PB
Tel: 07753 471611 (Bethnal Green)
Lobo Ratu (SVD) Nicodemus; 8 Teignmouth Road NW2 4HN (Willesden Green)
Loewenstein (OP) Rudolf; St Dominic's Priory, Southampton Road NW5 4LB (Haverstock
Hill)
Lodge (CP) Benedict; St Joseph's Retreat, Highgate Hill N19 5NE (Highgate)
Luoga (SDS) Christopher; The Presbytery, 96 The Crescent, Abbots Langley, Watford
WD5 0DS (Abbots Langley, Chipperfield)
Lynch (SAC) Eugene; 358 Greenford Road, Greenford UB6 9AN (Greenford)

McAneny (SS.CC) Christopher; 372 Uxbridge Road W5 3LH (Acton East)
McCambridge (OSB) Ambrose; Ealing Abbey, Charlbury Grove W5 2DY (Ealing)
McCarthy (SVD) John; 8 Teignmouth Road NW2 4HN (Willesden Green)
McDade (SJ) Pedro; Copleston House, 221 Goldhurst Terrace NW6 3EP (Kilburn)
McFadden (OMI) John; New Priory, Quex Road NW6 4PS (Kilburn, University Chaplaincy)
McFlynn (Irish Chaplaincy) Gerry; 52 Camden Square NW1 9XB Tel: 020 7482 5528
(Kentish Town)
McGowan (OCD) John; 41 Kensington Church Street W8 4BB (Kensington 2)
McHardy (Oratorian) Rupert; The Oratory, Brompton Road SW7 2RP (Oratory)
McLoughlin (SAC) Joseph; 358 Greenford Road, Greenford UB6 9AN (Greenford)
McMahon (OSB, St Bartholomew's / Royal London Chaplaincy) James; 2 Lukin Street E1
0AA (Commercial Road)
McMillan (SJ) Keith; 2 Chandler Street E1W 2QT (Wapping)
McPake (SVD) Martin; 8 Teignmouth Road NW2 4HN (Willesden Green)
MADEWA (Nigerian Chaplaincy) Matthew 'Gbenga; 8 King Henry's Walk N1 4PB
(Kingsland)
Maguire (SS.CC) Fergal; 85 Old Oak Common Lane W3 7DD (Acton East)
Maher (OMI) Brian; New Priory, Quex Road NW6 4PS (Kilburn)
Mahoney (SJ) John; 27 High Road N15 6ND (Stamford Hill)
Malal Muchail (SDS) Thomas; 191 High Road, Harrow Weald HA3 5EE (Wealdstone)
Markey (SSC) Gerard; 12 Blakesley Avenue W5 2DW (Ealing)
Marsh (Opus Dei) DIC, STD, Bernard; 1 Leopold Road W5 3PB (Chiswick)

Matwijiwskyj Rt Rev Mykola; 22 Binney Street W1K 5BQ Tel: 020 7629 1073 (Ukrainian Cathedral)

Mazewski (MIC) Dariusz; 1 Courtfield Gardens W13 0EY Tel: 07427 748605 (Ealing)

Mazzotta (FDP) Carlo; 112 Clarendon Road, Ashford TW15 2QD (Ashford, Stanwell)

Mboko (Congolese Chaplaincy) Julien Matondo; 2 Lukin Street E1 0AA (Commercial Road)

Mekekiuk Carlos; 22 Binney Street W1K 5BQ Tel: 020 7629 1073 (Ukrainian Cathedral)

Menonkari (CMI) John; 339 High Road, Wembley HA9 6AG (Wembley 1)

Michałek Maciej; c/o Holy Family Convent, 52 London Road, Enfield EN2 6EN
Email: jeszuam@interia.pl (Enfield)

Mignolli (CSS) Natalino; 2 Leigh Gardens NW10 5HP (Kensal Rise)

Milby (Buffalo, NY) Lawrence; 39 Duncan Terrace N1 8AL (Islington)

Minihane (OSA) Mark; 55 Fulham Palace Road W6 8AU (Hammersmith)

Mitchell (SJ) Gerard; St Anselm's Rectory, The Green, Southall UB2 4BE (Southall)

Mobela Henry; 62 Eden Grove N7 8EN Tel: 07495 866069 (Holloway)

Moffatt (SJ) John; 2 Chandler Street E1W 2QT (Wapping)

Morrish (Opus Dei) MA, STD, Mgr Nicholas; 4 Orme Court W2 4RL (Queensway)

Morrone (SDV) Luigi; 15 The Green, Heston Road, Heston TW5 0RL (Heston)

Mudereri (Zimbabwean Chaplaincy) John Rufaro; 24 Bouverie Road N16 0AJ (Stoke Newington)

Mullen (SS.CC) Pearse; 5 Berrymead Gardens W3 8AA (Acton)

Munitiz (SJ) Joseph; Copleston House, 221 Goldhurst Terrace NW6 3EP (Kilburn)

Murray (OMI) Terence; New Priory, Quex Road NW6 4PS (Kilburn)

Mway-Zeng (SDS) Richard; The Presbytery, 96 The Crescent, Abbots Langley, Watford WD5 0DS (Abbots Langley, Chipperfield)

Newman (CMF) Chris; Botwell House, Botwell Lane, Hayes UB3 2AB (Hayes)

Newton (Ordinariate) Mgr Keith; 24 Golden Square W1F 9JR
Tel: 020 7440 5750 (Warwick Street)

Nguyen (Vietnamese Chaplaincy) Tam Huu; 117 Bow Common Lane E3 4AU
Tel: 020 7987 3477 (Bow Common)

Nguyen (Vietnamese Chaplaincy) Van Dien; 117 Bow Common Lane E3 4AU
Tel: 020 7987 3477 (Bow Common)

Nicholson (SJ) Paul; 114 Mount Street W1K 3AH (Farm Street)

Nogoy (SJ) Patrick Vance; Copleston House, 221 Goldhurst Terrace NW6 3EP (Kilburn)

Nolan (MAfr) Francis; 64 Little Ealing Lane W5 4XF (Brentford)

Nunn (OSB) MMus, Alban; Ealing Abbey, Charlbury Grove W5 2DY (Ealing)

Nwosu (CSSp) Augustine; 94 Bath Road, Hounslow TW3 3EH Tel: 020 8570 1693 (Hounslow)

Nyarko Clement; 17 Churchfield Path, off Church Lane, Cheshunt EN8 9EG (Cheshunt)

O'Brien (OSM) Chris; 264 Fulham Road SW10 9EL (Fulham Road)

O'Brien (a.a.) Tom; 16 Nightingale Road, Hitchin SG5 1QS (Hitchin)

O'Byrne (CMF) John; Botwell House, Botwell Lane, Hayes UB3 2AB (Hayes)

O'Connell (OSM) Patrick; 264 Fulham Road SW10 9EL (Fulham Road)

O'Dell (a.a.) Andrew; 16 Nightingale Road, Hitchin SG5 1QS (Hitchin)

O'Donovan (SAC) Liam; 358 Greenford Road, Greenford UB6 9AN (Greenford)
O'Halpin (SSC) Aodh; 12 Blakesley Avenue W5 2DW (Ealing)
O'Malley (SSC) Daniel; 12 Blakesley Avenue W5 2DW (Ealing)
O'Reilly (OMI) Lorcan; 14 Quex Road NW6 4PL (Kilburn)
O'Reilly (SJ) Paul; 27 High Road N15 6ND (Stamford Hill)
O'Toole (SVD) Kevin; Nazareth House, 162 East End Road N2 0RU (Finchley East)
Ofere (Warri) Albert; The Presbytery, Chalkhill Road, Wembley Park HA9 9EW
Tel: 020 8904 2306 (Wembley 2)
Ogunnaike (MSP) Emmanuel; 115 Hertford Road N9 7EN (Edmonton)
Onyebuchi (MSP) Livinus; St Peter's Presbytery, Bishop's Rise, Hatfield, Herts AL10 9HN
(Hatfield Marychurch and Hatfield South, also University Chaplaincy)
Ostrynski (CCN) Sebastian; 29 Bramley Road N14 4HE (Cockfosters)
Otoaye (MSP) Julius; St Peter's Presbytery, Bishop's Rise, Hatfield, Herts AL10 9HN
(Hatfield South, also University Chaplaincy)

Paluku (AA) Jean-Marie Meso; 16 Nightingale Road, Hitchin SG5 1QS
Tel: 01462 459126 (Hitchin)
Panato (MCCJ) Pasquino; 16 Dawson Place W2 4TJ (Bayswater)
Paunon Agustin (Filipino/Hospital Chaplaincy, based at London North West Healthcare NHS
Trust HA1 3UJ); Room 235, Block 4, Hodgson Court, Nightingale Avenue, Harrow HA1
3GH Tel: 020 8869 2112 Mobile: 07880 558225 (Harrow-on-the-Hill)
Pedley (SJ) Christopher; 114 Mount Street W1K 3AH (Farm Street)
Perera (Colombo, Sri-Lankan (Sinhalese) Chaplaincy) Sudham; Clergy House, Peter Avenue
NW10 2DD Tel: 020 8451 4677 (Willesden Green)
Perrotta (FDP) John; 25 Lower Teddington Road, Hampton Wick KT1 4HB (Teddington)
Peter (CSSp) Gerald Bonaventure; 94 Bath Road, Hounslow TW3 3EH Tel: 020 8570 1693
(Hounslow)
Phelan (OMI) Michael; New Priory, Quex Road NW6 4PS (Kilburn)
Philip (Knanaya Chaplaincy) Joshy; The Presbytery, Esdaile Lane, Hoddesdon
EN11 8DS Tel: 01992 440986 (Hoddesdon)
Porter (SJ) Adrian; 114 Mount Street W1K 3AH (Farm Street)
Preston (SDS) Peter; Salvatorian Community House, 189 High Street, Wealdstone, Harrow
HA3 5DY (Wealdstone)
Puthenpurackal (CMI) Tebin; 339 High Road, Wembley HA9 6AG (Wembley 1)

Rajewski Bartosz; 167 West Hendon Broadway NW9 7EB Tel: 07449 801752
Email: chaplaincy@pcmew.org.uk Web: www.dalondon.org.uk (Hendon West)
Reczek, Marek; 1 Leysfield Road W12 9JF Tel: 07973 923026 (Polish 2)
Riezu (OAR) Robert; 18 Cheniston Gardens W8 6TQ (Kensington 1)
Robinson (SJ) Dominic; 114 Mount Street W1K 3AH (Farm Street)
Rockey (CP) Thomas; St Joseph's Retreat, Highgate Hill N19 5NE (Highgate)
Rokicki (MIC) Klaudiusz; 2 Windsor Road W5 5PD Tel: 020 8567 1746 (Polish 3)
Rossiter (OSB) JCL, DD, Abbot Francis; Ealing Abbey, Charlbury Grove W5 2DY (Ealing)

Rout (OFM) Paul; 15 The Green, Heston Road, Heston TW5 0RL Tel: 020 8570 1818 (Heston)

Ryall (OSM) Patrick; 264 Fulham Road SW10 9EL (Fulham Road)

Ryan (SSC) Thomas; 12 Blakesley Avenue W5 2DW (Ealing)

Sagar (FDP) Sidon; 112 Clarendon Road, Ashford TW15 2QD (Ashford, Stanwell)

Salmi (SJ) Richard; Copleston House, 221 Goldhurst Terrace NW6 3EP (Kilburn)

Salter (Eparchy of the Holy Family) John A T; 1 St James Close, Bishop Street N1 8PH Tel: 020 7359 0250 (Islington)

Sandambongo (CSSp) David; 15 St John's Villas N19 3EE (Archway) Tel: 020 7272 8195

Satur (OSM) Allan; 264 Fulham Road SW10 9EL (Fulham Road)

Sawadogo (MAfr) Augustin; 15 Corfton Road W5 2HP (Ealing)

Senyk Very Rev David; 22 Binney Street W1K 5BQ Tel: 020 7629 1073 (Ukrainian Cathedral)

Serra (Italian Mission) Antonio; 197 Durants Road, Enfield EN3 7DE Tel: 020 8804 2307 (Ponders End)

Sheehan (Opus Dei) MA, STD, Gerard; 8 Orme Court W2 4RL Tel: 020 7243 9411 (Queensway)

Shipperlee (OSB) BD, BA, Abbot Martin; Ealing Abbey, Charlbury Grove W5 2DY (Ealing)

Shorter (MAfr) Aylward; 64 Little Ealing Lane W5 4XF (Brentford)

Skeats (OP) Thomas; St Dominic's Priory, Southampton Road NW5 4LB (Haverstock Hill)

Smith (SJ) Michael; 2 Chandler Street E1W 2QT (Wapping)

Smith (MAfr) Peter; 64 Little Ealing Lane W5 4XF (Brentford)

Smolira (SJ) David; 2 Chandler Street E1W 2QT (Wapping)

Smyth (CMF) Paul; Botwell House, Botwell Lane, Hayes UB3 2AB (Hayes)

Soane (Opus Dei) BSc, STD, Andrew; 4 Orme Court W2 4RL (Queensway)

Soyombo Charles; 47 Cumberland Street SW1V 4LY (Pimlico)

Stachyra (SChr) Wojciech; 16 Wellington Road, Hampton Hill TW12 1JR (Hampton Hill)

Stapleford (OSB) BA, Thomas; Ealing Abbey, Charlbury Grove W5 2DY (Ealing)

Starkey (MAfr) Denis; 64 Little Ealing Lane W5 4XF (Brentford)

Stasievich (Belarusian) Serge; Marian House, Holden Avenue N12 8HY (Finchley North)

Stawicki (CMF) Krzysztof; Botwell House, Botwell Lane, Hayes UB3 2AB (Hayes)

Stewart (SJ) David; 27 High Road N15 6ND (Stamford Hill)

Stones (MAfr) Gerry; 64 Little Ealing Lane W5 4XF (Brentford)

Stork (Opus Dei) MSc, STD, Mgr Richard; 18 Netherhall Gardens NW3 5TH (Swiss Cottage)

Strange Mgr Roderick; St Mary's University, Waldegrave Road, Twickenham TW1 4SX Tel: 020 8240 8288 Email: roderick.strange@stmarys.ac.uk (Twickenham)

Susai Raj (OMI) Johnson; New Priory, Quex Road NW6 4PS (Kilburn)

Szuta (SJ) Leszek; 182 Walm Lane NW2 3AX Tel: 020 8452 4304 (Willesden Green)

Szyperski (MIC) Piotr; 2 Windsor Road W5 5PD Tel: 020 8567 1746 (Polish 3)

Taylor (OSB) Abbot Dominic; Ealing Abbey, Charlbury Grove W5 2DY (Ealing)

SECTION 4

Thayriam (SJ) George Stephen; St Anselm's Rectory, The Green, Southall UB2 4BE (Southall)
Thomas (Nottingham) Christopher; 39 Eccleston Square SW1V 1BX (CBCEW)
Thomas (IC) Tom; 14 Ely Place EC1N 6RY (Ely Place)
Toma Andrawis; 38 - 40 Cavendish Avenue W13)JQ
Tomas (IMC) Luis; 3 Salisbury Avenue N3 3AJ (Finchley Church End)
Tomaszewski (SJ) Adam; 182 Walm Lane NW2 3AX Tel: 020 8452 4304 (Willesden Green)
Travers (CM) Noel; 2 Flower Lane NW7 2JB (Mill Hill)
Tverijonas MA, Petras; 21 The Oval, Hackney Road E2 9DT (Lithuanian Church)
Tworek Mgr Janusz; 2 Devonia Road N1 8JJ Tel: 07970 150712 (Polish 1)
Tyliszczak Canon Krzysztof; 2 Devonia Road N1 8JJ Tel: 07710 198765 (Polish 1)

Ugwu (CSSp) Oliver; 15 St John's Villas N19 3EE Tel: 020 7272 8195 (Archway, Hospital Chaplaincy)
Umoren (MSP) Anthony; 115 Hertford Road N9 7EN (Edmonton)

van den Bergh (Oratorian) Edward; The Oratory, Brompton Road SW7 2RP (Oratory)
Velyanyk (Toulouse) Bogdan; 62 Eden Grove N7 8EN Tel: 020 7607 3594 (Holloway)
Vico (CS) Alberto; Villa Scalabrini, Green Street, Shenley WD7 9BB
Tel: 020 8207 5713 (Borehamwood North)

Wallbank (MAfr), Christopher; 64 Little Ealing Lane W5 4XF (Brentford)
Walsh (Albanian Chaplaincy) Gary; 8 Ogle Street W1W 6HS
Tel: 020 7636 2883 (Ogle Street)
Warren (OMI) Raymond; 30 Prescot Street E1 8BB (Tower Hill)
Waters (SDS) Francis; St Joseph's Presbytery, 191 High Road, Harrow Weald HA3 5EE (Wealdstone)
Wildsmith (MAfr) Edward; 15 Corfton Road W5 2HP (Ealing)
Woo (MAfr) Edward; 64 Little Ealing Lane W5 4XF (Brentford)
Woollen (Lyons) Nigel; St Joseph's Presbytery, Bedwell Crescent, Stevenage SG1 1NJ
Tel: 01438 351243 (Stevenage Parishes)
Wrobel (SAC) Ryszard; 4 Back Hill EC1R 5EN (Italian Church)
Wylezek Mgr Stefan; 2 Devonia Road N1 8JJ Tel: 020 7226 3439 (Polish 1)

Xavier (OCD) Tijo; 41 Kensington Church Street W8 4BB (Kensington 2)

Yacub (SJ) Chester; Copleston House, 221 Goldhurst Terrace NW6 3EP (Kilburn)

Zabbey (OSA) Anthony; 19 Hoxton Square N1 6NT (Hoxton)

SECTION 4

RELIGIOUS CONGREGATIONS AND SOCIETIES OF APOSTOLIC LIFE (MEN)

A place name in italics refers to a parish entry, where further details may be found.

African Missions, Society of (SMA)
White House, Watford Road, Northwood
HA6 3PW *(Northwood)*
Arputham, Thyagu **(Superior)**
Cussen, Anthony

Assumptionists (a.a.)
**(1) Assumptionist Priory, Victoria Park
Square E2 9PB** *(Bethnal Green)*
(2) 16 Nightingale Road, Hitchin SG5 1QS
(Hitchin)
Bahati, Antigon Claude (1)
Kasereka, Justin (1)
Katsuva Kasine, Euloge (2)
O'Brien, Tom (2)
O'Dell, Andrew (2)
Brother:
Tran, Joseph Quoc Cuong (1)

Augustinians (OSA)
(1) 55 Fulham Palace Road W6 8AU
(Hammersmith)
(2) 19 Hoxton Square N1 6NT *(Hoxton)*
Banayag, Thomas Jr (1)
Campbell, Bishop Michael (1)
Choi, Jacob (2)
Clifford, Barry (1) **(Parish Priest)**
Dabre, Gladson (1)
Hassan, Gabriel (2) **(Parish Priest)**
Minihane, Mark (1) **(Prior)**
Zabbey, Anthony (2) **(Prior)**
Brother:
David Tan

Augustinian Recollects (OAR)
18 Cheniston Gardens W8 6TQ
(Kensington 1)
Riezu, Robert **(Prior)**

Benedictines (OSB - English Congregation)
Charlbury Grove W5 2DY *(Ealing)*
Bevan, Alexander
Burns, Peter
Chillman, Gregory
Gorham, Timothy
Hughes, Andrew
Leachman, James
McCambridge, Ambrose **(Parish Priest)**
Nunn, Alban
Rossiter, Francis
Shipperlee, Martin
Stapleford, Thomas
Taylor, Dominic **(Abbot)**

Carmelites, Discalced (OCD)
41 Kensington Church Street W8 4BB
(Kensington 2)
Clarke, Christopher **(Prior & Parish Priest)**
Ezechukwu, Alexander
McGowan, John
Xavier, Tijo

Carmelites of Mary Immaculate (CMI)
**St Joseph's Presbytery 339 High Road,
Wembley HA9 6AG** *(Wembley 1)*
Kaduthanam, Joseph
Menonkari, John
Puthenpurackal, Tebin

Charity, Institute of (IC - Rosminians)
14 Ely Place EC1N 6RY *(Ely Place)*
Deidun, Tom
Thomas, Tom

Chemin Neuf Community (CCN)
29 Bramley Road N14 4HE
(Cockfosters)
Brunet, Christophe **(Parish Priest)**
Ostrynski, Sebastian **(Community Leader)**

Claretian Missionaries (CMF - Missionaries,
Sons of the Immaculate Heart of Mary)
**Botwell House, Botwell Lane, Hayes UB3
2AB** *(Hayes)*
Katthula, Joseph
Newman, Chris
O'Byrne, John
Smyth, Paul **(Major Superior)**
Stawicki, Krzysztof

Columban Fathers (SSC)
12 Blakesley Avenue W5 2DW *(Ealing)*
Markey, Gerard
O'Halpin, Aodh
O'Malley, Daniel **(Superior)**
Ryan, Thomas

Comboni Missionaries (MCCJ - Verona
Fathers)
Comboni House, 16 Dawson Place W2 4TJ
(Bayswater)
Anzioli, Angelo **(Superior)**
Curci, Carmine
De Marchi, Benito
Panato, Pasquino

Congregation of the Sacred Hearts (SS.CC)
(1) 372 Uxbridge Road W5 3LH *(Acton West)*
(2) 5 Berrymead Gardens W3 8AA *(Acton)*
(3) St Aidan of Lindisfarne W3 7DD *(Acton
East)*
Barnes, Kenneth (1)
Crotty, Fintan (2)
McAneny, Christopher (3), (1)
Maguire, Fergal (3), (2)
Mullen, Pearse (2)

Consolata Fathers (IMC)
3 Salisbury Avenue N3 3AJ
(Finchley Church End)
Bonelli, Carlo
Tomas, Luis **(Superior)**

Divine Providence, Sons of (FDP)
**(1) 25 Lower Teddington Road, Hampton
Wick KT1 4HB** *(Teddington)*
**(2) 112 Clarendon Road, Ashford
TW15 2QD** *(Ashford)*
Halman, Henryk (1)
Mazzotta, Carlo (2)
Perrotta, John C (1) **(Superior)**
Sagar, Sidon (2) **(Parish Priest)**

Divine Word Missionaries (SVD)
(1) 8 Teignmouth Road NW2 4HN
(Willesden Green)
**(2) 112 Twickenham Road, Isleworth TW7
6DL** *(Isleworth)*
Donnelly, Eamonn (1)
Escoto, Albert (1) **(Praeses)**
Fitzharris, Kieran (2)
Krzyskow, Krzysztof (1)
Lobo Ratu, Nicodemus (2)
McCarthy, John (1)
McPake, Martin (1)
O'Toole, Kevin *(Nazareth House, Finchley)*

Dominicans (OP - The Order of Preachers)
**St Dominic's Priory, Southampton Road
NW5 4LB** *(Haverstock Hill)*
Dunn, Michael
Edgar, Leo
Ganeri, Martin **(Provincial)**
Harries, Peter
Keenan, Oliver **(Parish Priest)**
Lew, Lawrence
Loewenstein, Rudolf
Skeats, Thomas

Franciscans (OFM)
Camilleri, Victor *(German Church)*
Rout, Paul *(Heston)*

Hospitaller Order of St John of God (OH)
52 Kenneth Crescent NW2 4PN
(Willesden Green)
Brothers:
Brannigan, Malachy **(Prior)**
Gerrard, Bonaventure
O'Neil, John
Zach, Andrzej

Jesuits (SJ - Society of Jesus)
**(1) Provincial Curia, 114 Mount Street
W1K 3AH** *(Farm Street)*
**(2) Farm Street Church, 114 Mount Street
W1K 3AH** *(Farm Street)*
**(3) St Ignatius Church, 27 High Road
N15 6ND** *(Stamford Hill)*
**(4) Polish Jesuits, 182 Walm Lane
NW2 3AX** *(Willesden Green)*
**(5) Copleston House, 221 Goldhurst
Terrace NW6 3EP** *(Kilburn)*
**(6) St Anselm's Rectory, The Green, Southall
UB2 4BE** *(Southall)*
**(7) Hurtado Jesuit Centre, 2 Chandler
Street E1W 2QT** *(Wapping)*
**(8) Tyburn Convent, 8 Hyde Park Place W2
2LJ** *(Marylebone)*
Baczewski, Adam (4)
Barnes, Michael (5)
Beattie, Michael (2)
Bermingham, Edward (3)
Bossy, Michael (3)
Cameron-Mowat, Andrew (3)
Carmody, Brendan (2,8)
Elias, Harold (7)
Gallagher, Peter (5)
Holman, Michael (5)
Howard, Damian (1,2) **(Provincial)**
Hume, Patrick (2)
Karnawalski, Michał (3)
Konopinski, Mateusz (3)

McDade, Pedro (5)
McMillan, Keith (7)
Mahoney, John (3)
Mitchell, Gerard (6)
Moffatt, John (7)
Munitiz, Joseph (5)
Nicholson, Paul (2)
Nogoy, Patrick Vance (5)
O'Reilly, Paul (3)
Pedley, Christopher (2)
Porter, Adrian (2)
Robinson, Dominic (2)
Salmi, Richard (5)
Smith, Michael (7)
Smolira, David (7)
Stewart, David (3)
Szuta, Leszek (4)
Thayriam, George Stephen (6)
Tomaszewski, Adam (4)
Yacub, Chester (5)
Power, Br Stephen (7)

Lebanese Maronite Order (LMO)
6 Dobson Close NW6 4RS
(Lebanese Church)
Achkar, Antoine
Azzi, Aziz
Kmeid, Fadi

Malta, Order of (SMOM)
13 Deodar Road SW15 2NP

Marian Fathers (MIC)
(1) 2 Windsor Road W5 5PD *(Polish Church 3)*
(2) 1 Courtfield Gardens W13 0EY *(Ealing)*
Gowkielewicz, Andrzej (2)
Gumienny, Wiktor (1)
Kozak, Michał (1) **(Parish Priest)**
Mazewski, Dariusz (1,2) **(Provincial
Delegate)**
Rokicki, Klaudiusz (1)
Szyperski, Piotr (1)

SECTION 4

Marist Fathers (SM)
5 Leicester Place WC2H 7BX
(French Church)
Boidin, Pascal **(Parish Priest)**
Bonnet-Eymard, Hubert **(Superior)**
Diouf, Damien
Duffy, Kevin
Vodopivec, Br Ivan

Mill Hill Missionaries
Chantry, Anthony *(Missio)*
Hemer, John *(Allen Hall Seminary)*

Missionaries of Africa (MAfr - White Fathers)
(1) 15 Corfton Road W5 2HP *(Ealing)*
(2) 64 Little Ealing Lane W5 4XF *(Brentford)*
Calcutt, Richard (2)
Cummins, Joseph (2)
Cummins, Thomas (2)
Gerrard, John (1) **(Superior)**
Heap, Michael (1)
Kelly, Peter (2)
Nolan, Francis (2)
Sawadogo, Augustin (1)
Shorter, Aylward (2)
Smith, Peter (2)
Starkey, Denis (2)
Stones, Gerry (2)
Wallbank, Christopher (2) **(Superior)**
Wildsmith, Edward (1)
Woo, Edward (2)
Brothers:
Murphy, Nicholas (1)
O'Reilly, Patrick (2)

Missionary Society of St Paul (MSP)
(1) 115 Hertford Road N9 7EN
(Edmonton)
(2) St Peter's Presbytery, Bishop's Rise, Hatfield AL10 9HN *(Hatfield Marychurch & Hatfield South)*
Ogunnaike, Emmanuel (1)
Onyebuchi, Livinus (2)
Otoaye, Julius (2)

Umoren, Anthony (1)

Montfort Missionaries (SMM)
27 St Gabriel's Road NW2 4DS
(Willesden Green)
Cabanero, Nelson
Flynn, Kieran

Oblates of Mary Immaculate (OMI)
(1) New Priory, Quex Road NW6 4PS
(Kilburn)
(2) 237 Goldhurst Terrace NW6 3EP
(Kilburn)
(3) 1 Stafford Road NW6 5RS *(Kilburn West)*
(4) 30 Prescot Street E1 8BB *(Tower Hill)*
(5) Denis Hurley House, 14 Quex Road NW6 4PL *(Kilburn)*
Alex, Angodage Don Joseph (4) **(Parish Priest)**
Devereux, Thomas (1)
Dillon, Paschal (2)
McFadden, John (3)
Maher, Brian (1)
Murray, Terence (1) **(Parish Priest)**
O'Reilly, Lorcan (5)
Phelan, Michael (1)
Susai Raj, Johnson (1)
Warren, Raymond (4)
Moore, Br Michael (3)

Oratorians
The Oratory, Brompton Road SW7 2RP
(Oratory)
van den Bergh, Edward
Bowen, George
Creighton-Jobe, Ronald
Dilke, Charles
Doyle, Patrick
Fordham, John
Lang, Michael **(Parish Priest)**
Large, Julian **(Provost)**
McHardy, Rupert

Pallottine Fathers (SAC)
(1) 358 Greenford Road, Greenford UB6 9AN *(Greenford)*
(2) 4 Back Hill EC1R 5EN *(St Peter's Italian Church)*
Daly, Thomas (1)
De Caro, Giuseppe (2)
Fulco, Andrea (2)
Lynch, Eugene (1)
McLoughlin, Joseph (1)
O'Donovan, Liam (1)
Wrobel, Ryszard (2)

Passionists (CP)
St Joseph's Retreat, Highgate Hill, N19 5NE *(Highgate)*
Doherty, Tiernan **(Rector)**
Kelly, Christopher *(Nazareth House, Finchley)*
Koloth, George **(Parish Priest)**
Lodge, Benedict
Rockey, Thomas

Sacred Heart, Brothers of the (SC)
8 King Harry Lane, St Albans AL3 4AW
(St Albans South)
Brothers:
Dionne, Nelson
Pelletier, Clement
St Jacques, Daniel
Vaillancourt, Paul **(Superior)**

Salvatorians (SDS - Society of the Divine Saviour)
(1) 96 The Crescent, Abbots Langley WD5 0DS *(Abbots Langley, Chipperfield)*
(2) Salvatorian Community House, 189 High Street, Wealdstone, Harrow HA3 5DY and **The Presbytery, 191 High Street, Wealdstone HA3 5EA** *(Wealdstone)*
(3) 9 Breakspear, Stevenage SG2 9SQ
(Stevenage Shephall)
Banzi, Fortunatus (2)
Doherty, Michael (3) **(Superior)**
Keane, Noel (2)

Lainez, Mario (2)
Luoga, Christopher (1)
Malal Muchail, Thomas (2)
Mway-Zeng, Richard (1) **(Provincial)**
Preston, Peter (2)
Waters, Frank (2)
Scalabrini Fathers (CS)
Green Street, Shenley WD7 9BB
(Borehamwood North)
Vico, Alberto

Servites (OSM - Friar Servants of Mary)
264 Fulham Road SW10 9EL *(Fulham Road)*
Addison, Paul **(Prior Provincial)**
O'Brien, Chris
O'Connell, Patrick
Ryall, Patrick **(Prior)**
Satur, Allan

Society of Christ (SChr)
16 Wellington Road, Hampton Hill TW12 1JR *(Hampton Hill)*
Stachyra, Wojciech

Society of Divine Vocations (SDV)
15 The Green, Heston Road, Heston TW5 0RL *(Heston)*
James, Vipin
Morrone, Luigi

Spiritans (CSSp - Congregation of the Holy Spirit)
(1) 63 Somerset Road, New Barnet EN5 1RF *(New Barnet)*
(2) 15 St John's Villas N19 3EE *(Archway)*
(3) 94 Bath Road, Hounslow TW3 3EH
(Hounslow)
Adayi, Daniel (3)
Alih, Dominic (1)
Fasakin, James Ademola (1)
Igbe, Terkura (1)
Ikwuka, Ugo (2)
Nwosu, Augustine (3)
Peter, Gerald Bonaventure (3)

SECTION 4

Sandambongo, David (2)

Stigmatine Fathers (CSS)
2 Leigh Gardens NW10 5HP *(Kensal Rise)*
Mignolli, Natalino

Vincentians (CM - Congregation of the
Mission)
2 Flower Lane NW7 2JB *(Mill Hill)*
Anywanwu, Akobundu
Armstrong, Raymond
Curran, Eugene **(Superior)**
Enuh, Chinedu
Travers, Noel

RELIGIOUS CONGREGATIONS AND SOCIETIES OF APOSTOLIC LIFE (WOMEN)

Place-names refer to a parish entry, where further details may be found.

Adoratrices, Handmaids of the Blessed Sacrament and of Charity (AASC): Kensington 2

Adorers of the Sacred Heart (OSB) - Tyburn Nuns: Marylebone

Capitanio Sisters (CS): Ealing

Carmelites (ODC): St Charles Square, Ware

Columban Sisters (MSSC): Bow

Comboni Missionary Sisters (CMS): Chiswick

Congregation of Jesus (CJ): Willesden Green

Congregation of Our Lady (Canonesses of St Augustine) (CSA): Oratory

Congregation of Our Lady of the Missions (RNDM): New Southgate, Wealdstone

Congregation of La Sainte Union des Sacrés Coeurs (LSU): Bethnal Green, Holloway, Kentish Town, Wembley 3

Congregation of the Sisters of Nazareth (CSN): Brook Green, Finchley East

Daughters of Charity of St Vincent de Paul (DC): Cathedral, Mill Hill, Pinner

Daughters of the Cross (Liege) (FC): Bishop's Stortford, Chelsea 1

Daughters of Divine Love (DDL): Borehamwood North, Wood Green

Daughters of Mary, Mother of Mercy DMMM): Edgware

Daughters of Providence (St Brieuc) : Palmers Green

Daughters of St Paul (FSP): Kensington 1

Dominican Sisters (Congr. of Newcastle, Natal) (OP): Bushey, Cricklewood, Edgware, Harpenden

Faithful Companions of Jesus (FCJ): Isleworth, Poplar, Somers Town

Franciscan Sisters of the Heart of Jesus (FCJ): Pimlico

Franciscan Missionaries of Mary (FMM): Shepherds Bush

Franciscan Sisters of Mill Hill (OSF): Mill Hill

Franciscan Sisters of Our Lady of Victories: Cathedral

Handmaids of the Holy Child Jesus (HHCJ): Edmonton

Handmaids of the Sacred Heart of Jesus (ACI): St John's Wood

Institute of the Blessed Virgin Mary (Loreto Sisters) (IBVM): Acton West

Institute of Our Lady of Mercy: Highbury

Little Company of Mary (LCM): Ealing, Gunnersbury

Little Sisters of Jesus: Hoxton, St Charles Square

Little Sisters of the Poor (LSP): Stoke Newington

Marist Sisters (SM): Archway

Medical Missionaries of Mary (MMM): Ealing

Medical Mission Sisters (Society of Catholic Medical Missionaries - SCMM): Acton, Hanwell, Northfields

Missionary Community of Divine Providence (MPS): Underwood Road

Missionaries of Charity (MC): Kensal New Town, Southall

Missionary Sisters of Christ the King (MChR): Willesden Green

SECTION 4

Missionary Sisters of the Immaculate (PIME): Chiswick

Missionary Sisters of Our Lady of Africa (White Sisters) (MSOLA): Ealing

Missionary Sisters of the Society of Mary (SMSM): French Church

Pallottine Missionary Sisters (SAC): Clerkenwell

Poor Clares (OSC): Barnet

Poor Handmaids of Jesus Christ (PHJC): Hendon

Poor Servants of the Mother of God (PSMG): Brentford, Hampton-on-Thames, Somers Town

Religious of the Assumption (RA): Bayswater, Kensington 2, Twickenham

Religious of Mary Immaculate (RMI): Kensington 2

Religious of the Sacred Heart of Mary (RSHM): Northfields

Religious Sisters of Charity (RSC): Acton, Hackney

School Sisters of Notre Dame (SSND): Copenhagen Street

Servants of Mary (OSM): Clapton, Stamford Hill

Sisters of Charity of Jesus and Mary (SCJM): Letchworth, Stevenage

Sisters of Charity of St Jeanne Antide (S de C); Sisters of St Martha: Ealing, Potters Bar

Sisters of Charity of St Paul (Selly Park) (SP): Hackney

Sisters of Christian Instruction (St Gildas) (SCI): Barnet, Stroud Green

Sisters of the Cross and Passion (CP) Fulham Road, Islington

Sisters of the Holy Cross (HC): Ealing

Sisters of the Holy Family of Bordeaux (HFB): Kilburn, Willesden Green

Sisters of the Holy Family of Nazareth (CSFN): Enfield

Sisters of the Holy Name of Jesus: Polish Church 3

Sisters Hospitallers of the Sacred Heart (HSC): Fulham Road

Sisters of the Infant Jesus (IJS): Acton East

Sisters of Jesus and Mary (rjm): Kensal Rise

Sisters of Jesus in the Temple (SJT): Notting Hill

Sisters of Mercy (RSM): Clapton Park, Commercial Road, Cricklewood, Feltham, Hillingdon, Kensal New Town, St John's Wood, Twickenham

Sisters of Notre Dame de Namur (SND): Pimlico

Sisters of Our Lady of the Missions: Wealdstone

Sisters of Our Lady of Sion (NDS): Bayswater

Sisters of Providence (of the Immaculate Conception): Royston

Sisters of Providence (Rosminian) (SPR): Lincoln's Inn Fields

Sisters of Providence (Ruille-sur-Loir): Stroud Green

Sisters of the Resurrection (CR): Ealing, Polish 3

Sisters of the Sacred Heart of Jesus (St Jacut) (SSCJ): Whetstone

Sisters of the Sacred Hearts of Jesus and Mary (Chigwell): Uxbridge

Sisters of St Dorothy (SSD): Hampstead

Sisters of St John of God (SSJG): West Green

Sisters of St Joseph of Peace (CSJ): Cricklewood, Hanwell

Sisters of St Louis (SSL): Cockfosters, Harrow South, New Southgate

Sisters of St Marcellina (IM) : Hampstead

Sisters of Saint Mary of Namur (SSMN): Harrow-on-the-Hill

Sisters of St Paul de Chartres (SPC): Highbury

Society of the Holy Child Jesus (SHCJ):
Brook Green

Society of Marie Auxiliatrice: Muswell Hill

Society of the Sacred Heart (RSCJ): Brook
Green

Ursulines of Jesus (UJ): Kingsland, Manor
House, Stamford Hill

Verbum Dei Missionary Fraternity (FMVD):
West Green

Wisdom (La Sagesse) Daughters of (DW):
Archbishop's House, Willesden Green

SECTION 4

Conference of Religious in England and Wales (COREW) - 'Providing Strength through Unity'

The Conference supports the leaders of the religious communities of England and Wales. COR aims to help men and women Religious face the challenges and needs of 21st century society. The aim is to focus on agreed initiatives and provide religious leaders with the support and educational resources that enable them to serve their individual communities better. Over the past 60 years the Conference has identified key needs for its members who themselves have worked tirelessly serving our communities to improve the lives of parishioners through their educational, healthcare and prayer roles, social justice and pastoral work.

Contacts

Valerie Nazareth **General Secretary**
Email: gensecvn@corew.org
Bernadette Kehoe **Communications & Development Lead**
Email: communications@corew.org
Administrative Co-ordinator
Email: admin@corew.org
St Philomena's Convent, 70-71 Euston Square NW1 1DJ
Web: www.corew.org Twitter: @OfReligious Instagram: religiouslifeleaders

Consecrated Hermit (Code c. 603) Sr Marianne **P.O. Box 14945 London W5 3ZZ**

Consecrated Women
See *Conscecrated Women* under Catholic Societies and Organisations, Section 6

The Grail A grant-making body, supporting activities consonant with the aims of the former Grail Secular Institute. See *Grail, The* under Catholic Societies and Organisations, Section 6

The Leaven A Carmelite way of life for single or widowed Catholic women
See *Carmelite Secular Institute* under Catholic Societies and Organisations, Section 6

St Boniface Secular Institute (English Region) 44 Exeter Road NW2 4SB
Tel: 020 8438 9628 Email: hostel@institut-st-bonifatius.de
Web: www.hostel-lioba-house.de
See *German Church* and *Willesden Green* parish entries

Servants of the Word (SW) An ecumenical congregation based in Acton at **31a Lynton Road W3 9HL Tel: 020 8993 8113**

Servite Secular Institute (SSI) A life of service through vows of chastity, poverty and obedience in union with others of like mind, remaining in their own circumstances. Women of prayer living in the world as Servants of Mary.
Email: vocations@ssi.org.uk Web: www.ssi.org.uk

Section 5

CATHOLIC SCHOOLS

All schools are listed under the local authority area in which they are situated, and, for primary schools, the name of the parish is also indicated. In the case of secondary schools and colleges the name of the deanery is only given where that is different from the local authority area in which the school or college is situated. The Parish Priest normally acts as Chaplain for primary schools. In secondary schools and colleges, the name of the Chaplain is given.

Unless stated otherwise, all schools are voluntary aided and co-educational, and all primary schools are junior and infant. (A) indicates that the school is an Academy. (+N) indicates that the school has a nursery. (RO) indicates that the school is in the trusteeship of a Religious Order. (R) indicates that it is recognised as Catholic by the Cardinal Archbishop; all other schools are in the trusteeship of the Diocese. All schools with websites are to be found listed at **www.rcdow.org.uk.**

Statistics

Primary (Aided & Academy)	154
Primary (Independent)	8
Secondary (Aided & Academy)	39
Secondary (Independent)	3
All-age (Non-maintained Special)	2
All-age (Independent)	3
VI Form Colleges	2
Total	**211**

CITY OF WESTMINSTER   (213)

PRIMARY SCHOOLS

Our Lady of Dolours: (+N) (3381) **19 Cirencester Street W2 5SR**
Tel: 020 7641 4326 Fax: 020 7641 4389 Email: head@ourladydolours.co.uk
Head Mrs Sarah Alley (Paddington)

St Edward: (+N) (3432) **Lisson Grove NW1 6LH**
Tel: 020 7723 5911 Fax: 020 7723 5250 Email: office@stedwardsprimary.co.uk
Executive Head Mr Martin Tissot **Head of School** Mrs Anne Thomas (St John's Wood) (RO)

St Joseph, Maida Vale: (+N) (3473) **Lanark Road W9 1DF**
Tel: 020 7286 3518 Fax: 020 7286 2303 Email: head@stjosephsschool.org.uk
Head Mrs Katharine Maria Husain **Acting Head** Dr Ninette Fernandes Viana (St John's Wood)

St Mary of the Angels: (+N) (3532) **Shrewsbury Road W2 5PR**
Tel: 020 7792 1883 Fax: 020 7641 4484 Email: head@stmaryangels.co.uk
Head Mrs Mary Wilson (Bayswater)

SECTION 5

St Vincent, Marylebone: (+N) (3610) St Vincent Street W1U 4DF
Tel: 020 7641 6110 Fax: 020 7641 6116 Email: head@stvincentsprimary.org.uk
Head Miss Marina Coleman (Spanish Place)

St Vincent de Paul: (+N) (3611) Morpeth Terrace SW1P 3EP
Tel: 020 7641 5990 Fax: 020 7641 5901 Email: head@svpschool.co.uk
Head Mr Nathaniel Scott Cree (Cathedral)

Westminster Cathedral: (3623) Bessborough Place SW1V 3SE
Tel: 020 7641 5915 Fax: 020 7821 9349 Email: office@westcathsch.co.uk
Head Mrs Alexandra Stacey (Pimlico)

Independent
St Christina (6225) (Girls) 25 St Edmund's Terrace NW8 7PY
Tel: 020 7722 8784 Fax: 020 7586 4961 Email: head@saintchristinas.org.uk
Head Mr Alistair Gloag (St John's Wood) (RO)

Westminster Cathedral Choir School: (6197) (Boys) Ambrosden Avenue SW1P 1QH
Tel: 020 7798 9081 Fax: 020 7798 9060 Email: office@choirschool.com
Head Mr Neil McLaughlan (Cathedral)

SECONDARY SCHOOL
St George: (A) (4809) Lanark Road W9 1RB
Tel: 020 7328 0904 Fax: 020 7624 6083 Email: s.williams@stgeorgesrc.org
Executive Head - Trust CEO Mr Martin Tissott **Acting Deputy Trust CEO** Mr James Martin
Acting Head of School Mrs Michelle Henderson
Chaplain Bernard Dadswell (Marylebone Deanery)

LONDON BOROUGH OF BARNET   (302)
PRIMARY SCHOOLS
The Annunciation: (Infants +N) (3500) Thirleby Road, Edgware HA8 0HQ
Tel: 020 8959 2325 Fax: 020 8906 4116 Email: head@annunciationinf.barnetmail.net
Head Miss Teresa Lynch BA (Burnt Oak)

The Annunciation: (Junior) (3514) The Meads, Edgware HA8 9HQ
Tel: 020 8906 0723 Fax: 020 8906 0377 Email: head@annunciationjnr.barnetmail.net
Head Miss Carol Minihan (Burnt Oak)

Blessed Dominic: (+N) (3511) Lanacre Avenue NW9 5FN
Tel: 020 8205 3790 Fax: 020 8205 9341 Email: office@blesseddominic.barnetmail.net
Head Mrs Geraldine Pears (Grahame Park)

Our Lady of Lourdes, Finchley: (+N) (3501) Bow Lane N12 0JP
Tel: 020 8346 1681 Fax: 020 8346 0579 Email: office@olol.barnetmail.net
Head Miss Barbara Costa (Finchley East)

Sacred Heart, Whetstone: (3510) 2 Oakleigh Park South N20 9JU
Tel: 020 8445 3854 Fax: 020 8445 0862 Email: office@sacredheart.barnetmail.net
Head Mrs Catherine McMahon (Whetstone)

St Agnes, Cricklewood: (+N) (3502) Thorverton Road NW2 1RG
Tel: 020 8452 4565 Fax: 020 8830 6709 Email: office@stagnes.barnetmail.net
Head Mrs Susan O'Reilly (Cricklewood)

St Catherine, Barnet: (+N) (3504) Vale Drive, Barnet EN5 2ED
Tel: 020 8440 4946 Fax: 020 8441 3436 Email: head@stcatherines.barnetmail.net
Head Miss Maureen Kelly (Barnet)

St Joseph, Hendon: (3509) Watford Way NW4 4TY
Tel: 020 8202 5229 Fax: 020 8202 5530 Email: head@stjosephs.barnet.sch.uk
Executive Head Dr James Lane (Hendon)

St Theresa: (3507) East End Road N3 2TD
Tel: 020 8346 8826 Fax: 020 8346 0215 Email: office@sttheresas.barnetmail.net
Head Mrs Linda O'Melia (Finchley Church End)

St Vincent, Mill Hill: (3506) The Ridgeway NW7 1EJ
Tel: 020 8959 3417 Fax: 020 8906 9733 Email: head@stvincents.barnet.sch.uk
Head Miss Marie Tuohy (Mill Hill)

Independent
St Anthony School for Girls: (6008) (Girls) Ivy House, 94-96 North End Road NW11 7SX
Tel: 020 3869 3070 Email: info@stanthonysgirls.co.uk
Head Mrs Laura Martin (Golders Green)

SECONDARY SCHOOLS
Bishop Douglass Catholic High: (A) (5408) Hamilton Road N2 0SQ
Tel: 020 8444 5211/3 Fax: 020 8444 0416 Email: head@bishopdouglass.barnet.sch.uk
Executive Head Mr Martin Tissot Associate Head Mrs D McLean-Boyd
Chaplain Fr Kevin Ryan SX

Finchley Catholic High: (5405) (Boys) Woodside Lane N12 8TA
Tel: 020 8445 0105 Fax: 020 8446 0691 Email: info@finchleycatholic.org.uk
Head Mrs Niamh Arnull Chaplain Rebecca Parsons

St James Catholic High: (5407) Great Strand NW9 5PE
Tel: 020 8358 2800 Fax: 020 8358 2801 Email: admin@st-james.barnet.sch.uk
Head Mrs Carolyn Laws Chaplains Jennifer Whelan and Mariella Signorini

St Michael Catholic Grammar: (5404) (Girls) Nether Street N12 7NJ
Tel: 020 8446 2256 Fax: 020 8343 9598 Email: office@st-michaels.barnet.sch.uk
Head Mr Michael Stimpson Chaplain Imelda Meehan(RO)

SECTION 5

Schools

LONDON BOROUGH OF BRENT   (304)

PRIMARY SCHOOLS

The Convent of Jesus & Mary: (Infants +N) (3507) 21 Park Avenue NW2 5AN
Tel: 020 8459 5890 Fax: 020 8451 9499 Email: admin@conventinf.brent.sch.uk
Head Mrs Teresa O'Higgins (Willesden Green)

Our Lady of Grace, Dollis Hill: (A) (Infants +N) (3510) Dollis Hill Avenue NW2 6EU
Tel: 020 8450 6757 Fax: 020 8452 1501 Email: philbourne@ologinfants.brent.sch.uk
Head Mrs Philomena Bourne (Dollis Hill)

Our Lady of Grace, Dollis Hill: (A) (Junior) (3500) Dollis Hill Lane NW2 6HS
Tel: 020 8450 6002 Fax: 020 8208 3430 Email: head@ologjuniors.brent.sch.uk
Head Mr Stephen McGrath (Dollis Hill)

Our Lady of Lourdes, Willesden: (+N) (3508) Wesley Road NW10 8PP
Tel: 020 8961 5037 Fax: 020 8963 1197 Email: mbickerstaff@lourdes.brent.sch.uk
Head Miss Mary Bickerstaff (Stonebridge)

Federation of St Joseph Infant and Junior Schools, Wembley:
St Joseph, Wembley: (Infants +N) (3509) Waverley Avenue, Wembley HA9 6TA
Tel: 020 8903 6032 Fax: 020 8903 5263 Email: mwhelan@sjinf.brent.sch.uk
Executive Head Mrs Amanda Whelan (Wembley 1)

St Joseph, Wembley: (Junior) (3501) Chatsworth Avenue, Wembley HA9 6BE
Tel: 020 8902 3438 Fax: 020 8903 5482 Email: admin@sjjnr.brent.sch.uk
Executive Head Mrs Amanda Whelan Associate Head Mr Mark Betts (Wembley 1)

St Joseph, Willesden: (+N) (5203) Goodson Road NW10 9LS
Tel: 020 8965 5651 Fax: 020 8961 9022 Email: dtitus@stjo.brent.sch.uk
Head Miss Dawn Titus (Willesden)

St Margaret Clitherow, Neasden: (A) (+N) (3511) Quainton Street NW10 0BG
Tel: 020 8450 3631 Fax: 020 8450 3729 Email: head@clitherow.brent.sch.uk
Head Mrs Ewa McSperrin BEd (Wembley 2)

St Mary, Kilburn: (+N) (3602) Canterbury Road NW6 5ST
Tel: 020 7624 3830 Fax: 7372 4932 Email: admin@marycps.brent.sch.uk
Head Mrs Bridget Pratley (Kilburn)

St Mary Magdalen: (Junior) (3505) Linacre Road NW2 5BB
Tel: 020 8459 3159 Fax: 020 8459 0108 Email: lmcswiggan@marymag.brent.sch.uk
Head Miss Lucy McSwiggan (Willesden Green)

St Robert Southwell: (+N) (3506) Slough Lane NW9 8YD
Tel: 020 8204 6148 Fax: 020 8905 0287 Email: admin@robsouth.brent.sch.uk
Head Miss Honor Beck (Kingsbury Green)

SECONDARY SCHOOLS

Convent of Jesus & Mary Language College: (A) (5404) (Girls) **Crownhill Road NW10 4EP**
Tel: 020 8965 2986 Fax: 020 8838 0071 Email: office@cjmlc.co.uk
Head Mrs Louise McGowan **Chaplain** Ann-Marie Sylvestercha

Newman Catholic College: (5407) (Boys) **Harlesden Road NW10 3RN**
Tel: 020 8965 3947 Fax: 020 8965 3430 Email: office@ncc.brent.sch.uk
Head Mr Daniel Coyle **Chaplain** John Roche

St Gregory Catholic Science College: (A) (5406) **Donnington Road, Harrow HA3 0NB**
Tel: 020 8907 8828 Fax: 020 8909 1161 Email: cryan@stgregorys.harrow.sch.uk
Head Mr Andrew Prindiville **Chaplain** Michael Coughlan

LONDON BOROUGH OF CAMDEN   (202)

PRIMARY SCHOOLS

Our Lady, Camden: (+N) (3655) **Pratt Street NW1 0DP**
Tel: 020 7485 7997 Fax: 020 7428 9426 Email: head@ourladys.camden.sch.uk
Executive Head Mrs Juliette Jackson **Associate Head** Ms Moya Richardson (Camden Town)

Rosary: (+N) (3391) **238 Haverstock Hill NW3 2AE**
Tel: 020 7794 6292 Fax: 020 7794 6292 Email: admin@rosary.camden.sch.uk
Head Miss Sophie Kennedy (Haverstock Hill)

St Aloysius: (+N) (3400) **Aldenham Street NW1 1PS** *(until 31/12/2019 only)*
Tel: 020 7387 3551 Email: executivehead@acps.camden.sch.uk
Executive Head Miss Clare McFlynn **Head of School** Mrs Bronagh McCann (Somers Town)

St Dominic, Camden: (+N) (3429) **Southampton Road NW5 4JS**
Tel: 020 7485 5918 Fax: 020 7284 0961 Email: head@stdominics.camden.sch.uk
Head Ms Jennifer O'Prey (Haverstock Hill)

St Eugene de Mazenod: (3649) **Mazenod Avenue, Quex Road NW6 4LS**
Tel: 020 7624 4837 Fax: 020 7328 2280 Email: head@steugene.camden.sch.uk
Executive Head Mrs Juliette Jackson (Kilburn)

St Joseph, Macklin Street: (+N) (3482) **Macklin Street, Drury Lane WC2B 5NA**
Tel: 020 7242 7712 Fax: 020 7430 1834 Email: head@stjosephs.camden.sch.uk
Head Miss Helen Tyler (Lincoln's Inn Fields)

St Patrick, Kentish Town: (+N) (3560) **Holmes Road NW5 3AH**
Tel: 020 7267 1200 Fax: 020 7485 4691 Email: head@stpatricks.camden.sch.uk
Head Mr Sean Cranitch (Kentish Town)

Independent

St Anthony's Preparatory: (6181) (Boys) **90 Fitzjohn's Avenue NW3 6AA**
Tel: 020 7431 1066 Fax: 020 7435 9223 Email: sadhna.halai@stanthonysprep.co.uk
Head Mr Paul Keyte (Hampstead) **Chaplain** Mgr Phelim Rowland (R)

SECTION 5

St Mary's, Hampstead: (6084) (Girls) **47 Fitzjohn's Avenue NW3 6PG**
Tel: 020 7435 1868 Fax: 020 7794 7922 Email: office@stmh.co.uk
Head Mrs Harriet Connor-Earl (Swiss Cottage) (R)

SECONDARY SCHOOLS
La Sainte Union: (5041) (Girls) **Highgate Road NW5 1RP**
Tel: 020 7428 4600 Fax: 020 7267 7647 Email: sfegan@lsu.camden.sch.uk
Head Mrs Sophie Fegan **Chaplain** Shirley Taylor (RO)

Maria Fidelis Catholic School FCJ: (4652 **1-39 Drummond Crescent NW1 1LY**
Tel: 020 7387 3856 Fax: 020 7388 9558 Email: office@mariafidelis.camden.sch.uk
Head Ms Helen Gill **Chaplain** Yasmin Mirza (RO)

LONDON BOROUGH OF EALING (307)
PRIMARY SCHOOLS
Holy Family School: (2000) **Vale Lane W3 0DY**
Tel: 020 8992 3980 Email: head@holyfamily.ealing.sch.uk
Head Mr Thomas Doherty (Acton West)

Mount Carmel: (+N) (3500) **Little Ealing Lane W5 4EA**
Tel: 020 8567 4646 Fax: 020 8579 5362 Email: admin@mountcarmel.ealing.sch.uk
Head Mrs Clare Walsh (Brentford)

Our Lady of the Visitation: (3503) **Greenford Road, Greenford UB6 9AN**
Tel: 020 8575 5344 Fax: 020 8575 6734 Email: admin@olovrc.com
Head Miss Kathleen Coll (Greenford)

St Anselm, Southall: (3505) **Church Avenue, Southall UB2 4BH**
Tel: 020 8574 3906 Fax: 020 8571 6308 Email: head@st-anselms.ealing.sch.uk
Head Mrs Ruth Sykes (Southall)

St Gregory, Ealing: (+N) (3506) **Woodfield Road W5 1SL**
Tel: 020 8997 7550 Fax: 020 8810 6506 Email: mkolanowska@st-gregorys.ealing.sch.uk
Head Ms Margaret Kolanowska (Ealing)

St John Fisher, Perivale: (+N) (3504) **Sarsfield Road, Perivale UB6 7AF**
Tel: 020 8799 0970 Fax: 020 8998 6618 Email: head@st-johnfisher.ealing.sch.uk
Head Mrs Tracey Brosnan (Perivale)

St Joseph, Hanwell: (+N) (3507) **York Avenue W7 3HU**
Tel: 020 8567 6293 Fax: 020 8840 0278 Email: jrakowski1.307@lgflmail.org
Head Mr Julian Rakowski (Hanwell)

St Raphael: (3508) **Hartfield Avenue, Northolt UB5 6NL**
Tel: 020 8841 0848 Fax: 020 8842 4617 Email: head@st-raphaels.ealing.sch.uk
Head Ms Evelyn Ward (Yeading)

St Vincent, Ealing: (3509) 1 Pierrepoint Road W3 9JR
Tel: **020 8992 6625** Fax: **020 8896 0623** Email: head@st-vincents.ealing.sch.uk
Head Mrs Monica McCarthy (Acton)

Independent
St Benedict Junior: (6606) **5 Montpelier Avenue W5 2XP**
Tel: **020 8862 2054** Fax: **020 8862 2058** Email: jssecretary@stbenedicts.org.uk
Head Mr Robert Simmons BA (Hons) **Chaplain** Dom Andrew Hughes OSB (R)

SECONDARY SCHOOL
The Cardinal Wiseman School: (4603) **Greenford Road, Greenford UB6 9AW**
Tel: **020 8575 8222** Fax: **020 8575 9963** Email: info@wiseman.ealing.sch.uk
Head Mr Michael Kiely **Chaplain** Jo Ahern

Independent
St Benedict Senior: (6006) **54 Eaton Rise W5 2ES**
Tel: **020 8862 2254** Fax: **020 8862 2199** Email: headmaster@stbenedicts.org.uk
Head Mr Andrew Johnson **Chaplain** Dom Alexander Bevan OSB (RO)

PRIMARY & SECONDARY SCHOOL
Independent
St Augustine Priory School: (6005) (Girls) **Hillcrest Road W5 2JL**
Tel: **020 8997 2022** Fax: **020 8810 6501** Email: head@sapriory.com
Head Mrs Sarah Raffray **Chaplain** Mari King (R)

LONDON BOROUGH OF ENFIELD   (308)

PRIMARY SCHOOLS
Our Lady of Lourdes: (3504) **The Limes Avenue N11 1RD**
Tel: **020 8361 0767** Fax: **020 8361 6682** Email: headteacher@ololschool.enfield.sch.uk
Head Mrs Gillian Hood (New Southgate)

St Edmund, Enfield: (3501) **Hertford Road N9 7HJ**
Tel: **020 8807 2664** Fax: **020 8807 8877** Email: mhanley3.308@lgflmail.org
Head Mrs Margaret Hanley (Edmonton)

St George, Enfield: (3502) **Gordon Road, Enfield EN2 0QA**
Tel: **020 8363 3729** Fax: **020 8367 2275** Email: headteacher@st-georges.enfield.sch.uk
Head Mr Paul O'Rourke (Enfield)

St Mary, Enfield: (+N) (5403) **Durants Road, Enfield EN3 7DE**
Tel: **020 8804 2396** Fax: **020 8805 8847** Email: office@stmarys.enfield.sch.uk
Head Miss Maeve Creed (Ponders End)

St Monica, Enfield: (3503) **Cannon Hill, Cannon Road N14 7HE**
Tel: **020 8886 4647** Fax: **020 8882 8424** Email: office@st-monicas.enfield.sch.uk
Head Mrs Kate Baptiste (Palmers Green)

SECTION 5

SECONDARY SCHOOLS

St Anne Catholic High for Girls: (4706) (Girls) Oakthorpe Road N13 5TY
Tel: 020 8886 2165 Fax: 020 8886 6552 Email: admin@st-annes.enfield.sch.uk
Head Ms Siobhan Gilling; *from 1/1/20* Mrs Emma Loveland **Chaplain** John Ravi

St Ignatius College: (3500) (Boys) Turkey Street, Enfield EN1 4NP
Tel: 01992 717835 / 760520 Fax: 01992 652070 Email: head@st-ignatius.enfield.sch.uk
Head Mrs Mary O'Keefe **Chaplain** John Dawson (RO)

LONDON BOROUGH BOROUGH OF HACKNEY   (204)

PRIMARY SCHOOLS

Our Lady and St Joseph: (+N) (3371) Buckingham Road N1 4DG
Tel: 020 7254 7353 Fax: 020 7249 3870 Email: seanjflood@yahoo.co.uk
Head Mr Sean Flood MA BEd (Hons) (Kingsland)

St Dominic, Hackney: (+N) (2900) Ballance Road E9 5SR
Tel: 020 8985 0995 Fax: 020 8985 2915 Email: dfinan@stdominics.hackney.sch.uk
Head Mrs Deirdre Finan BEd (Hons) MA (Homerton)

St Monica, Hackney: (+N) (3553) Hoxton Square N1 6NT
Tel: 020 7739 5824 Fax: 020 7613 4465 Email: office@st-monicas.hackney.sch.uk
Head Mrs Amanda Ruthven (Hoxton)

St Scholastica (+N) (3659) Kenninghall Road E5 8BS
Tel: 020 8985 3466 Fax: 020 8533 0014 Email: sbrierley@st-scholasticas.hackney.sch.uk
Head Mrs Sandra Brierley (Clapton)

SECONDARY SCHOOLS

Cardinal Pole: (4714) 205 Morning Lane E9 6LG
Tel: 020 8985 5150 Fax: 020 8533 7325 Email: tracymortimer@cardinalpole.co.uk
Head Ms Jane Heffernan **Chaplain** James Ryan

Our Lady's Catholic High School: (4641) (Girls) 6-16 Amhurst Park N16 5AF
Tel: 020 8800 2158 Fax: 020 8809 8898 Email: jmcdonald@ourladys.hackney.sch.uk
Head Ms Justine McDonald **Chaplain** Sr Dominico Savio (RO)

LONDON BOROUGH OF HAMMERSMITH & FULHAM   (205)

PRIMARY SCHOOLS

The Good Shepherd: (+N) (3602) Gayford Road W12 9BY
Tel: 020 8743 5060 Fax: 020 8740 1626 Email: head@goodshepherdrc.lbhf.sch.uk
Head Mrs Imogen Lavelle (Shepherds Bush)

Holy Cross, Fulham: (+N) (3354) Basuto Road SW6 4BL
Tel: 020 7736 1447 Fax: 020 7371 9954 Email: admin@holycross.lbhf.sch.uk
Executive Head Mrs Kathleen Williams **Associate Head** Mrs Catherine MacGonigal
(Parsons Green)

Larmenier & Sacred Heart: (+N) (3649) **41a Brook Green W6 8DH**
Tel: 020 8748 9444 Fax: 020 8748 2387 Email: head@larshrc.lbhf.sch.uk
Head Miss Jennifer McGinty (Brook Green)

St Augustine: (3378) **Disbrowe Road W6 8QE**
Tel: 020 7385 4333 Fax: 020 7386 7751 Email: admin@staugustinesrc.lbhf.sch.uk
Head Mr Martin Kincaid (Hammersmith)

St John XXIII: (+N) (3645) **1 India Way W12 7QT**
Tel: 020 8743 9428 Fax: 020 8749 7117 Email: head@stjohnxxiii.lbhf.sch.uk
Head Mrs Karen Cunningham (White City)

St Mary: (+N) (3529) **Masbro Road W14 0LT**
Tel: 020 7603 7717 Fax: 020 7602 7432 Email: head@stmarysrc.lbhf.sch.uk
Head Ms Robina Maher (Brook Green)

St Thomas of Canterbury: (3648) **Estcourt Road SW6 7HB**
Tel: 020 7385 8165 Fax: 020 7385 0918 Email: admin@stthomasrc.lbhf.sch.uk
Executive Head Mrs Karen Wyatt **Head of School** Miss Jo Breslin (Fulham 1)

SECONDARY SCHOOLS
The London Oratory: (A) (5400) (Boys) **Seagrave Road SW6 1RX**
Tel: 020 7385 0102 Fax: 020 7381 3836 Email: admin@los.ac
Head Mr Daniel Wright **Chaplain** Fr George Bowen (RO)

Sacred Heart High: (A) (3394) (Girls) **212 Hammersmith Road W6 7DG**
Tel: 020 8748 7600 Fax: 020 8748 0392 Email: mdoyle@sacredh.lbhf.sch.uk
Head Mrs Marian Doyle **Chaplain** Vicky Lorenzato (RO)

LONDON BOROUGH OF HARINGEY   (309)

PRIMARY SCHOOLS
Our Lady of Muswell: (+N) (3500) **Pages Lane N10 1PS**
Tel: 020 8444 6894 Fax: 020 8365 4620 Email: office@ourladymuswell.haringey.sch.uk
Head Mrs Angela McNicholas (Muswell Hill)

Federation of St Francis de Sales Infant and Junior Schools, Haringey:
St Francis de Sales: (Infants+N) (3507) **Brereton Road N17 8DA**
Tel: 020 8808 2923 Email: head.federation@sfds.haringey.sch.uk
Head Dr James Lane (Tottenham)

St Francis de Sales: (Junior) (3501) **Brereton Road N17 8DA**
Tel: 020 8808 2923 Email: admin.junior@sfds.haringey.sch.uk
Head Dr James Lane (Tottenham)

St Gildas: (Junior) (3509) **1 Oakington Way N8 9EP**
Tel: 020 8348 1902 Fax: 020 8340 7805 Email: admin@st-gildas.haringey.sch.uk
Executive Head Mrs Angela McNicholas (Stroud Green)

SECTION 5

St Ignatius: (+N) (3502) **St Ann's Road N15 6ND**
Tel: 020 8800 2771 Fax: 020 8802 7156 Email: head@st-igs.haringey.sch.uk
Head Mr Con Bonner (Stamford Hill)

St John Vianney: (+N) (3510) **Stanley Road N15 3HD**
Tel: 020 8889 8421 Fax: 020 8881 2528 Email: head@st-johnvianney.haringey.sch.uk
Head Mr Stephen McNicholas (West Green)

St Martin de Porres: (+N) (3508) **Blake Road N11 2AF**
Tel: 020 8361 1445 Fax: 020 8361 5849 Email: head@st-martinporres.haringey.sch.uk
Head Mrs Louise Fleming (Wood Green)

Federation of St Mary Priory Infant and Junior Schools:
St Mary Priory: (Infants +N) (3505) **Hermitage Road N15 5RE**
Tel: 020 8800 9305 Fax: 020 8800 1142 Email: admin@stmarysrcpriory.haringey.sch.uk
Executive Head Mr Stephen McNicholas (Stamford Hill) (RO)

St Mary Priory: (Junior) (3503) **Hermitage Road N15 5RE**
Tel: 020 8800 9305 Fax: 020 8880 1142 Email: admin@stmarysrcpriory.haringey.sch.uk
Executive Head Mr Stephen McNicholas (Stamford Hill) (RO)

St Paul: (3504) **Bradley Road N22 4SZ**
Tel: 020 8888 7081 Fax: 020 8889 1397 Email: headteacher@st-pauls.haringey.sch.uk
Executive Head Mrs Louise Fleming **Head of School** Mr Peter O'Shaughnessy (Wood Green)

St Peter-in-Chains: (Infants) (3506) **3 Elm Grove N8 9AJ**
Tel: 020 8340 6789 Fax: 020 8340 3653 Email: head@st-peter-in-chains-rc.haringey.sch.uk
Executive Head Mrs Angela McNicholas (Stroud Green)

SECONDARY SCHOOL
St Thomas More: (A) (4703) **Glendale Avenue N22 5HN**
Tel: 020 8888 7122 Fax: 020 8826 9370 Email: headteacher@stthomasmoreschool.org.uk
Executive Head Mr Martin Tissot **Head of School** Mr Mark Rowland
Chaplain Elaine Henry

LONDON BOROUGH OF HARROW   (310)
PRIMARY SCHOOLS
St Anselm, Harrow: (3501) **Roxborough Park, Harrow HA1 3BE**
Tel: 020 8422 1600 Fax: 020 8422 3564 Email: monahana@st-anselms.harrow.sch.uk
Head Mrs Anne Monahan (Harrow-on-the-Hill)

St Bernadette, Harrow: (A) (3500) **Clifton Road, Kenton, Harrow HA3 9NS**
Tel: 020 8204 8902 Fax: 020 8905 0738 Email: office@stbernadette.harrow.sch.uk
Head Mr David O'Farrell (Kenton)

St George, Harrow: (A) (3508) **Sudbury Hill, Harrow HA1 3SB**
Tel: 020 8422 1272 Fax: 020 8864 5540 Email: head@stgeorges.harrow.sch.uk
Head Mrs Deirdre Monaghan (Sudbury)

St John Fisher: (A) (3505) **Melrose Road, Pinner HA5 5RA**
Tel: 020 8868 2961 Fax: 020 8866 5882 Email: mconlon.310@lgflmail.org
Head Mrs Maria Conlon (Harrow North)

St Joseph, Harrow: (A) (3507) **Dobbin Close, Belmont, Harrow HA3 7LP**
Tel: 020 8863 8531 Fax: 020 8863 3341 Email: cbriggs21.310@lgflmail.org
Head Mr Christopher Briggs (Wealdstone)

St Teresa, Harrow: (+N) (3504) **Long Elmes, Harrow Weald HA3 6LE**
Tel: 020 8428 8640 Fax: 020 8420 1571 Email: llowney1.310@lgflmail.org
Head Miss Laura Lowney (Headstone Lane)

SECONDARY SCHOOLS

Sacred Heart Language College: (A) (4700) (Girls) **186 High Street, Wealdstone HA3 7AY**
Tel: 020 8863 9922 Fax: 020 8861 5051 Email: ghiggins@tshlc.harrow.sch.uk
Head Miss Geraldine Higgins **Chaplain** Marie Wright

Salvatorian College: (A) (5400) (Boys) **High Road, Harrow Weald HA3 5DY**
Tel: 020 8863 2706 Fax: 020 8863 3435 Email: admin@salvatorian.harrow.sch.uk
Executive Head Mr Martin Tissot **Chaplain** Sharma Henry (RO)

SIXTH FORM COLLEGE

St Dominic: (8600) **Mount Park Avenue, Harrow-on-the-Hill HA1 3HX**
Tel: 020 8422 8084 Fax: 020 8422 3759 Email: ap@stdoms.ac.uk
Principal Mr Andrew Parkin **Chaplain** Dominic Cunliffe

LONDON BOROUGH OF HILLINGDON (312)

PRIMARY SCHOOLS

Botwell House: (+N) (3401) **Botwell Lane, Hayes UB3 2AB**
Tel: 020 8573 2229 Fax: 020 8569 0286 Email: head@ibotwell.co.uk
Head Mr Kevin Oakley (Hayes)

Sacred Heart, Ruislip: (+N) (3405) **Herlwyn Avenue, Ruislip HA4 6EZ**
Tel: 01895 633240 Fax: 01895 625 772 Email: office@shpsruislip.org
Head Mrs Theresa McManus (Ruislip)

St Bernadette, Hillingdon: (+N) (3402) **160 Long Lane, Hillingdon UB10 0EH**
Tel: 01895 232298 Fax: 01895 230086 Email: office@stbernadetteschool.co.uk
Head Mrs Colette Acres (Hillingdon)

St Catherine, West Drayton: (+N) (3403) **Money Lane, West Drayton UB7 7NX**
Tel: 01895 442839 Fax: 01895 442631 Email: office@stcatherine.co.uk
Head Miss Elizabeth Doonan (West Drayton)

SECTION 5

St Mary, Uxbridge: (+N) (3404) Rockingham Close, Uxbridge UB8 2UA
Tel: 01895 232814 Fax: 01895 235403 Email: ashevlin@stmarysuxbridge.org.uk
Head Miss Ann Shevlin (Uxbridge)

St Swithun Wells: (+N) (3400) Hunters Hill, South Ruislip HA4 9HS
Tel: 01895 808194 Fax: 020 8845 1611 Email: kdavis@ssw.school
Head Mrs Kristy Davis (Ruislip South)

SECONDARY SCHOOL

The Douay Martyrs: (A) (5408) Edinburgh Drive, Ickenham, Uxbridge UB10 8QY
Tel: 01895 679400 Fax: 01895 679401 Email: tcorish@douaymartyrs.co.uk
Head Mr Anthony Joseph Corish **Chaplain** Luisa Foley

NON-MAINTAINED SPECIAL SCHOOL

Pield Heath House: (7006) Pield Heath Road, Hillingdon UB8 3NW
Tel: 01895 258507 Fax: 01895 256497 Email: admin@pieldheathschool.org.uk
Head Sr Julie Rose **Chaplain** Eryl D'Souza (RO)

LONDON BOROUGH OF HOUNSLOW   (313)

PRIMARY SCHOOLS

Our Lady & St John: (+N) (3502) Boston Park Road, Brentford TW8 9JF
Tel: 020 8560 7477 Fax: 020 8568 8806 Email: head@stjohnrc.hounslow.sch.uk
Head Mrs Susan Cunningham (Brentford)

The Rosary: (3941) 10 The Green, Heston TW5 0RL
Tel: 020 8570 4942
Email: head@rosary.hounslow.sch.uk
Acting Head Miss Fiona Bass (Heston)

St Lawrence: (+N) (3503) Victoria Road, Feltham TW13 4AF
Tel: 020 8890 3878 Fax: 020 8883 1885 Email: head@st-lawrence.hounslow.sch.uk
Head Mr Leo Duggan (Feltham)

St Mary, Chiswick: (+N) (3505) Duke Road W4 2DF
Tel: 020 8994 5606 Fax: 020 8742 7630 Email: head@stmarys.hounslow.sch.uk
Executive Head Miss Joan Harte (Chiswick)

St Mary, Isleworth: (+N) (3504) South Street, Isleworth TW7 7EE
Tel: 020 8560 7166 Fax: 020 8232 8820 Email: head@smi.hounslow.sch.uk
Head Mr Farley Marsh (Isleworth)

St Michael's and St Martin's: (+N) (3507) Belgrave Road, Hounslow TW4 7AG
Tel: 020 8572 9658 Fax: 020 8572 1982 Email: head@stmichaelrc.hounslow.sch.uk
Head Mrs Nicola Duggan (Hounslow)

SECONDARY SCHOOLS

Gumley House: (A) (5400) (Girls) **St John's Road, Isleworth TW7 6XF**
Tel: 020 8568 8692 Fax: 020 8758 2674 Email: cbraggs@gumleyhouse.com
Head Mrs Caroline Braggs **Chaplain** Celia Hannigan (RO)

Gunnersbury: (5401) (Boys) **The Ride, Boston Manor Road, Brentford TW8 9LB**
Tel: 020 8568 7281 Fax: 020 8569 7946 Email: headteacher@gunnersbury.hounslow.sch.uk
Head Mr Kevin Burke **Chaplain** Misha Koval

St Mark: (A) (4800) **106 Bath Road, Hounslow TW3 3EJ**
Tel: 020 8577 3600 Fax: 020 8577 0559 Email: waughlucasa@st-marks.hounslow.sch.uk
Head Mrs Andrea Waugh-Lucas **Chaplain** Ivan Cižmárik

LONDON BOROUGH OF ISLINGTON (206)

PRIMARY SCHOOLS

Blessed Sacrament: (+N) (3643) **Boadicea Street N1 0UF**
Tel: 020 7278 2187 Fax: 020 7278 0015
Email: norah.flatley@blessedsacrament.islington.sch.uk
Head Mrs Norah Flatley (Copenhagen Street)

Christ the King: (+N) (3633) **55 Tollington Park N4 3QW**
Tel: 020 7272 5987 Fax: 020 7272 7780 Email: admin@ctks.co.uk
Executive Head Mr John Lane (Tollington Park)

Sacred Heart, Islington: (3384) **68 George's Road N7 8JN**
Tel: 020 7607 3407 Fax: 020 7606 4906 Email: john.lane@sacredheart.islington.sch.uk
Head Mr John Lane (Holloway)

St Joan of Arc, Highbury: (+N) (3631) **Northolme Road N5 2UX**
Tel: 020 7226 3920 Fax: 020 7704 9220 Email: headteacher@st-joanofarc.islington.sch.uk
Head Miss Clare Campbell (Highbury)

St John the Evangelist: (+N) (3456) **Duncan Street N1 8BL**
Tel: 020 7226 1314 Fax: 020 7226 5563
Email: stephanie.day@stjohnevangelist.islington.sch.uk
Head Miss Stephanie Day (Islington)

St Joseph: (+N) (3483) **Highgate Hill N19 5NE**
Tel: 020 7272 1270 Fax: 020 7272 9728 Email: head@st-josephs.islington.sch.uk
Head Miss Clare McFlynn (Highgate) (RO)

St Peter and St Paul, Islington: (+N) (3575) **Compton Street EC1V 0EU**
Tel: 020 7253 0839 Fax: 020 7336 7226 Email: tpeters9.206@lgflmail.org
Head Miss Tracey Peters (Clerkenwell)

SECTION 5

SECONDARY SCHOOL

St Aloysius: (4651) (Boys) **Hornsey Lane N6 5LY**
Tel: 020 7561 7800 Fax: 020 7263 5963 Email: loderick.d@sta.islington.sch.uk
Executive Head Mrs Jane Heffernan **Chaplain** Helen Baly

ROYAL BOROUGH OF KENSINGTON AND CHELSEA   (207)

PRIMARY SCHOOLS

Oratory: (3379) **Bury Walk, Cale Street SW3 6QH**
Tel: 020 7589 5900 Fax: 020 7581 5220 Email: head@oratory.rbkc.sch.uk
Head Mrs Jane Griffiths (Oratory) (RO)

Our Lady of Victories: (+N) (5200) **Clareville Street SW7 5AQ**
Tel: 020 7373 4491 Fax: 020 7244 0591 Email: allyson.hodnett@olov.rbkc.sch.uk
Head Mr Christopher McPhilemy (Kensington 1)

St Charles: (+N) (5201) **83 St Charles Square W10 6EB**
Tel: 020 8969 5566 Fax: 020 8960 4338 Email: ann.slavin@st-charles.rbkc.sch.uk
Head Miss Ann Slavin (St Charles Square)

St Francis of Assisi: (+N) (3437) **Treadgold Street W11 4BJ**
Tel: 020 7727 8523 Fax: 020 7229 2174 Email: info@franassisi.rbkc.sch.uk
Executive Head Mrs Kathleen Williams (Notting Hill)

St Joseph, Chelsea: (+N) (3477) **Cadogan Street SW3 2QT**
Tel: 020 7589 2438 Fax: 020 7581 9489 Email: Karen.wyatt@stjosephs.rbkc.sch.uk
Executive Head Mrs Karen Wyatt (Chelsea 1)

St Mary, East Row: (+N) (3542) **East Row W10 5AW**
Tel: 020 8969 0321 Fax: 020 8964 3122 Email: joan.harte@st-marys.rbkc.sch.uk
Executive Head Mrs Joan Harte (Kensal New Town)

The Servite: (+N) (3613) **252 Fulham Road SW10 9NA**
Tel: 020 7352 2588 Fax: 020 7351 4024 Email: kathleen.williams@servite.rbkc.sch.uk
Head Mrs Kathleen Williams (Fulham Road) (RO)

Independent

St Philip's Preparatory School: (6104) (Boys) **6 Wetherby Place SW7 4NE**
Tel: 020 7373 3944 Fax: 020 7244 9766 Email: office@stpschool.co.uk
Head Mr Alexander Wulffen-Thomas (Kensington 2) (RO)

SECONDARY SCHOOLS

The Cardinal Vaughan Memorial School: (A) (5402) (Boys) **89 Addison Road W14 8BZ**
Tel: 020 7603 8478 Fax: 7602 3124 Email: StubbinP@cvms.co.uk
Head Mr Paul Stubbings **Chaplain** Fr Dominic Allain

All Saints Catholic College: (4801) St Charles Square W10 6EL
Tel: 020 8969 7111 Fax: 020 8969 5119 Email: a.oneill@allsaintscc.org.uk
Head Mr Andrew O'Neill Chaplain Cheryl Subban (North Kensington Deanery)

St Thomas More Language College, Chelsea: (4861) Cadogan Street SW3 2QS
Tel: 020 7589 9734 Fax: 020 7823 7868 Email: info@stm.rbkc.sch.uk
Head Dr Trevor Papworth Chaplain Fr Anthony Homer

Independent
More House School: (6202) (Girls) 22 Pont Street SW1X 0AA
Tel: 020 7235 2855 Fax: 020 7259 6782 Email: office@morehouse.org.uk
Co-Heads Mrs Amanda Leach and Mr Michael Keeley Chaplain Davina Reid (RO)

SIXTH FORM COLLEGE
St Charles Catholic Sixth Form College: (8600) 74 St Charles Square W10 6EY
Tel: 020 8968 7755 Fax: 020 8968 1061 Email: principal@stcharles.ac.uk
Principal Mr Martin Twist Chaplain Heather Jamieson (North Kensington Deanery)

LONDON BOROUGH OF RICHMOND   (318)

PRIMARY SCHOOLS
The Sacred Heart, Teddington: (3320) St Mark's Road, Teddington TW11 9DO
Tel: 020 8977 6591 Fax: 020 8943 2449 Email: bsmith@sacredheart.richmond.sch.uk
Head Mrs Bernadette Smith (Teddington)

St Edmund, Whitton: (3315) St Edmund's Lane, Nelson Road, Whitton TW2 7BB
Tel: 020 8894 7898 Fax: 020 8898 3032 Email: g.nicholl@st-edmunds.richmond.sch.uk
Head Mrs Carmel Moreland (Whitton)

St James, Twickenham: (+N) (3316) 260 Stanley Road, Twickenham TW2 5NP
Tel: 020 8898 4670 Fax: 020 8893 3032 Email: info@st-james.richmond.sch.uk
Head Mrs Louise Yarnell (Twickenham)

PRIMARY AND SECONDARY SCHOOL
St Richard Reynolds Catholic College Federation:
St Richard Reynolds (Primary): (2000) Clifden Road, Twickenham TW1 4LT
Tel: 020 8325 4630 Email: r.burke@srrcc.org.uk
Head Mr Richard Burke BSc MA (Twickenham)

St Richard Reynolds Catholic College: (4000) Clifden Road, Twickenham TW1 4LT
Tel: 020 8325 4630 Email: r.burke@srrcc.org.uk
Head Mr Richard Burke BSc MA Chaplain Molly Bayliss-Conway (Upper Thames Deanery)

Independent
St Catherine Catholic School: (6008) (Girls) Cross Deep, Twickenham TW1 4QJ
Tel: 020 8891 2898 Fax: 020 8744 9629 Email: headmistress@stcatherineschool.co.uk
Head Mrs Johneen McPherson Chaplain Mary Ryan (RO) (Upper Thames Deanery)

SECTION 5

LONDON BOROUGH OF TOWER HAMLETS   (211)

PRIMARY SCHOOLS

English Martyrs: (+N) (3619) **St Mark Street E1 8DJ**
Tel: 020 7709 0182 Fax: 020 7680 9395 Email: head@englishmartyrs.towerhamlets.sch.uk
Head Ms Bronagh Nugent (Tower Hill)

Guardian Angels: (3346) **Whitman Road E3 4RB**
Tel: 020 8980 3939 Fax: 020 8983 4210 Email: head@guardianangels.towerhamlets.sch.uk
Executive Head Mrs Sheila Mouna **Head of School** Ms Louise Nottage (Mile End)

Our Lady and St Joseph: (+N) (3667) **Wade's Place E14 0DE**
Tel: 020 3764 8860 Fax: 020 3764 8861 Email: patrick.devereux@olsj.co.uk
Head Mr Patrick Devereux (Poplar)

St Agnes, Bow: (+N) (3397) **Rainhill Way E3 3ES**
Tel: 020 8980 3076 Fax: 020 8983 1770 Email: admin@st-agnes.towerhamlets.sch.uk
Head Ms Brid McDaid (Bow)

St Anne, Whitechapel: (+N) (3411) **Underwood Road E1 5AW**
Tel: 020 7247 6327 Fax: 020 7377 5024 Email: head@st-annes.towerhamlets.sch.uk
Head Mrs Sheila Mouna (Underwood Road)

St Edmund, Millwall: (+N) (3431) **299 West Ferry Road E14 3RS**
Tel: 020 7987 2546 Fax: 020 7538 0332 Email: head@st-edmunds.towerhamlets.sch.uk
Head Ms Gail O'Flaherty (Millwall)

St Elizabeth: (+N) (2003) **Bonner Road E2 9JY**
Tel: 020 8980 3964 Fax: 020 8983 3377 Email: head@st-elizabeth.uk
Head Miss Angelina John (Bethnal Green)

St Mary and St Michael: (+N) (2002) **Sutton Street E1 0BD**
Tel: 020 7790 4986 Fax: 020 7790 9343
Email: admin@st-marymichael.towerhamlets.sch.uk
Head Mrs Rachel Mahon (Commercial Road)

SECONDARY SCHOOLS

Bishop Challoner Catholic Federation of Schools:
Bishop Challoner: (4726) (Girls) **352 Commercial Road E1 0LB**
Tel: 020 7791 9500 Fax: 020 7791 9589 Email: dwhelan@bishop.towerhamlets.sch.uk
Executive Head Mr Richard Fitzgerald **Chaplain** Rev Tony Flavin (Deacon)

Bishop Challoner: (4298) (Boys) **352 Commercial Road E1 0LB**
Tel: 020 7791 9500 Fax: 020 7791 9589 Email: dwhelan@bishop.towerhamlets.sch.uk
Executive Head Mr Richard Fitzgerald **Head of School** Mr Bryan Young
Chaplain Rev Tony Flavin (Deacon)

COUNTY OF HERTFORDSHIRE (919)

PRIMARY SCHOOL (ENFIELD DEANERY)

Pope Paul: (3975) Baker Street, Potters Bar EN6 2ES
Tel: 01707 659755 Fax: 01707 665431 Email: head@popepaul.herts.sch.uk
Head Mrs Elizabeth Heymoz (Potters Bar)

PRIMARY SCHOOLS (LEA VALLEY DEANERY)

Sacred Heart, Ware: (3424) Broadmeads, Ware SG12 9HY
Tel: 01920 461678 Fax: 01920 461418 Email: head@sacredheart312.herts.sch.uk
Head Mrs Michelle Fusi (Ware)

St Augustine, Hoddesdon: (+N) (3345) Riversmead, Hoddesdon EN11 8DP
Tel: 01992 463549 Email: head@staugustines.herts.sch.uk
Head Mrs Gillian Napier (Hoddesdon)

St Cross: (3408) Upper Marsh Lane, Hoddesdon EN11 8BN
Tel: 01992 467309 Fax: 01992 450362 Email: admin@stcross.herts.sch.uk
Head Mrs Kathryn Hall (Hoddesdon)

St Joseph, Bishop's Stortford: (+N) (3318) Great Hadham Road, Bishop's Stortford
CM23 2NL Tel: 01279 652576 Fax: 01279 466519 Email: head@stjosephs207.herts.sch.uk
Head Mr Peter Coldwell (Bishop's Stortford)

St Joseph, Hertford: (+N) (3341) North Road, Hertford SG14 2BY
Tel: 01992 583148 Fax: 01992 550503 Email: head@stjosephs255.herts.sch.uk
Head Mrs Justine Page (Hertford)

St Joseph, Waltham Cross: (+N) (3327) Royal Avenue, Waltham Cross EN8 7EN
Tel: 01992 629503 Fax: 01992 628824 Email: head@stjosephs351.herts.sch.uk
Head Mrs Barbara O'Connor (Waltham Cross)

St Paul, Cheshunt: (+N) (3423) Park Lane, Cheshunt EN7 6LR
Tel: 01992 635060 Fax: 01992 625215 Email: head@stpauls373.herts.sch.uk
Head Miss Gillian Chumbley (Cheshunt)

St Thomas of Canterbury: (3367) High Street, Puckeridge, near Ware SG11 1RZ
Tel: 01920 821450 Fax: 01920 822534 Email: head@stcanterbury.herts.sch.uk
Head Mrs Michelle Keating (Old Hall Green and Puckeridge)

PRIMARY SCHOOLS (ST ALBANS DEANERY)

St Adrian: (+N) (3389) Watling View, St Albans AL1 2PB
Tel: 01727 852687 Fax: 01727 850822 Email: head@stadrians.herts.sch.uk
Head Mr Dominic Bedford (St Albans South)

St Alban & St Stephen: (Infants +N) (3362) Vanda Crescent, St Albans AL1 5EX
Tel: 01727 854643 Email: head@ssasinfants.herts.sch.uk
Executive Head Miss Clare McFlynn (St Albans)

SECTION 5

St Alban & St Stephen: (Junior) (3421) Cecil Road, St Albans AL1 5EG
Tel: 01727 866668 Fax: 01727 810710 Email: head@ssasjm.herts.sch.uk
Executice Head Miss Clare McFlynn (St Albans)

St Albert the Great: (3391) Acorn Road, Rant Meadow, Hemel Hempstead HP3 8DW
Tel: 01442 264835 Fax: 01442 246418 Email: head@albertthegreat.herts.sch.uk
Head Mrs Kathryn Little (Hemel Hempstead East)

St Bernadette, London Colney: (+N) (3416) Walsingham Way, London Colney AL2 1NL
Tel: 01727 822489 Fax: 01727 823327 Email: head@stbernadette.herts.sch.uk
Head Mrs Sandra Lavelle-Murphy (London Colney)

St Cuthbert Mayne: (Junior) (3386) Clover Way, Gadebridge, Hemel Hempstead HP1 3EA
Tel: 01442 253347 Fax: 01442 230320 Email: head@cuthbertmayne.herts.sch.uk
Head Mrs Fionnuala Smith (Hemel Hempstead West)

St Dominic, Harpenden: (+N) (3401) Southdown Road, Harpenden AL5 1PF
Tel: 01582 760047 Fax: 01582 760047 Email: head@stdominic.herts.sch.uk
Head Miss Clare O'Sullivan (Harpenden)

St John Fisher, St Alban's: (3403) Hazelmere Road, Marshalwick, St Albans AL4 9RW
Tel: 01727 861077 Fax: 01727 831163 Email: head@sjfisher.herts.sch.uk
Head Miss Patricia O'Donnell (St Albans)

St Rose: (Infants +N) (3409) Green End Road, Boxmoor, Hemel Hempstead HP1 1QW
Tel: 01442 398855 Fax: 01442 398835 Email: head@stroses.herts.sch.uk
Head Mrs Ella Ryan (Hemel Hempstead West)

St Teresa, Borehamwood: (+N) (3384) Brook Road, Borehamwood WD6 5HL
Tel: 020 8953 3753 Fax: 020 8381 5273 Email: head@stteresas.herts.sch.uk
Head Mrs Teresa McBride (Borehamwood)

St Thomas More, Berkhamsted: (+N) (3402) Greenway, Berkhamsted HP4 3LF
Tel: 01442 385060 Fax: 01442 385061 Email: head@stmore.herts.sch.uk
Executive Head Mrs Kathryn Little (Berkhamsted)

Independent

St Columba's College: (6136) (Boys) Preparatory School, 8 King Harry Lane,
St Albans AL3 4AW
Tel: 01727 862616 Fax: 01727 892025 Email: Coakley.b@stcolumbascollege.org
Head Mrs Ruth Loveman (St Albans South) (RO)

PRIMARY SCHOOLS (STEVENAGE DEANERY)
Holy Family, Welwyn Garden City (+N) (3404) Crookhams, Welwyn Garden City AL7 1PG
Tel: 01707 375518 Email: head@holyfamily.herts.sch.uk
Head Mrs Kate Linnane (Welwyn Garden City Digswell)

Our Lady, Hitchin: (A) (3399) Old Hale Way, Hitchin SG5 1XT
Tel: 01462 622555 Fax: 01462 622777 Email: head@ourladys.herts.sch.uk
Head Mrs Ciara Nicholson (Hitchin)

Our Lady, Welwyn Garden City: (+N) (3382) Woodhall Lane, Welwyn Garden City AL7 3TF
Tel: 01707 324408 Fax: 01707 391005 Email: admin@ourladys527.herts.sch.uk
Head Mr Richard Curry (Welwyn Garden City East)

St John, Baldock: (A) (+N) (3413) Providence Way, Baldock SG7 6TT
Tel: 01462 892478 Fax: 01462 892683 Email: head@stjohns4.herts.sch.uk
Head Ms Alex Hanou (Baldock)

St Margaret Clitherow, Stevenage: (3397) Monkswood Lane SG2 8RH
Tel: 01438 352863 Fax: 01438 352553 Email: head@clitherow.herts.sch.uk
Head Miss Carmela Puccio (Stevenage Shephall)

St Mary, Royston: (A) (+N) (5200) Melbourn Road, Royston SG8 7DB
Tel: 01763 246021 Fax: 01763 248825 Email: head@st-marys-royston.herts.sch.uk
Head Mrs Julia Pearce (Royston)

St Philip Howard (3388) Woods Avenue, Hatfield AL10 8NN
Tel: 01707 263969 Fax: 01707 263969 Email: head@sphoward.herts.sch.uk
Head Mrs Mairead Ann Waugh (Hatfield)

St Thomas More, Letchworth: (A) (3400) Highfield, Letchworth Garden City SG6 3QB
Tel: 01462 620670 Fax: 01462 620670 Email: admin@strcjmi.herts.sch.uk
Head Mrs Jane Perry (Letchworth)

St Vincent de Paul, Stevenage: (+N) (3977) Bedwell Crescent, Stevenage SG1 1NJ
Tel: 01438 729555 Fax: 01438 358122 Email: head@stvincent.herts.sch.uk
Head Mr Jonathan White (Stevenage Bedwell)

PRIMARY SCHOOLS (WATFORD DEANERY)
Divine Saviour: (A) (+N) (3410) Broomfield Rise, Abbots Langley WD5 0HW
Tel: 01923 265607 Fax: 01923 291632 Email: head@divinesaviour.herts.sch.uk
Executive Head Mr Stephen Wheatley (Abbots Langley)

The Holy Rood: (A) (+N) (3985) Greenbank Road, Watford WD17 4FS
Tel: 01923 223785 Fax: 01923 481342 Email: head@holyrood.herts.sch.uk
Executive Head Mr Stephen Wheatley Head of School Mrs Emma Brand (Watford)

SECTION 5

Sacred Heart, Bushey: (3415) Merryhill Road, Bushey WD23 1SU
Tel: 01923 01923 901179 Fax: 01923 493041 Email: head@sacredheart682.herts.sch.uk
Executive Head Mrs Linda Payne (Bushey and Oxhey)

St Anthony: (+N) (3428) Croxley View, Watford WD18 6BW
Tel: 01923 226987 Fax: 01923 234645 Email: head@stanthonys.herts.sch.uk
Head Mrs Pauline Wilson MA (Watford)

St Catherine of Siena: (A) (5211) Horseshoe Lane, Garston, Watford WD25 7HP
Tel: 01923 676022 Fax: 01923 893497 Email: head@st-catherine.herts.sch.uk
Head Ms Nicola Kane (Garston)

St John, Rickmansworth: (A) (3398) Berry Lane, Mill End, Rickmansworth WD3 7HG
Tel: 01923 774004 Fax: 01923 710915 Email: head@stjohns705.herts.sch.uk
Head Mr Tony Hall (Mill End)

St Joseph, South Oxhey: (+N) (3383) Ainsdale Road, South Oxhey, Watford WD19 7DW
Tel: 020 8428 5371 Fax: 020 8421 0568 Email: head@stjosephs775.herts.sch.uk
Head Mrs Linda Payne (Carpenders Park)

SECONDARY SCHOOLS (HERTFORDSHIRE)
John F Kennedy: (4619) Hollybush Lane, Hemel Hempstead HP1 2PH
Tel: 01442 266150 Fax: 01442 200014 Email: admin@jfk.herts.sch.uk
Head Mr Paul Neves Chaplain Calum Moore (St Albans Deanery)

John Henry Newman: (A) (5413) Hitchin Road, Stevenage SG1 4AE
Tel: 01438 314643 Fax: 01438 747882 Email: admin@jhn.herts.sch.uk
Head Mr Clive Mathew MSc Chaplain Alison Bailiss
(Stevenage Deanery)

Loreto: (A) (4620) (Girls) Hatfield Road, St Albans AL1 3RQ
Tel: 01727 856206 Fax: 01727 833794 Email: admin@loreto.herts.sch.uk
Head Mrs Maire Lynch Chaplain Shane McCarthy (RO) (St Albans Deanery)

Nicholas Breakspear: (A) (5412) Colney Heath Lane, St Albans AL4 0TT
Tel: 01727 860079 Fax: 01727 848912 Email: admin@nbs.herts.sch.uk
Head Mr Declan Linnane Chaplain Barry O'Sullivan (St Albans Deanery)

St Joan of Arc: (A) (5418) High Street, Rickmansworth WD3 1HG
Tel: 01923 773881 Fax: 01923 897545 Email: admin@joa.herts.sch.uk
Head Mr Peter Sweeney BEd (Hons) MA NPQH Chaplain Liam Lynch (Watford Deanery)

St Mary, Bishop's Stortford: (5422) Windhill, Bishop's Stortford CM23 2NQ
Tel: 01279 654901 Fax: 01279 653889 Email: a.celano@stmarys.net
Head Mr Andrew Celano Chaplain Deirdre McHugh (Lea Valley Deanery)

St Michael: (A) (5417) High Elms Lane, Garston, Watford WD25 0SS
Tel: 01923 673760 Fax: 01923 680511 Email: admin@stmichaelscatholichighschool.co.uk
Head Mr Edward Conway STB MA BA(Psych) Chaplain Fr Terkura Igbe CSSp (Watford Deanery)

Independent
St Columba College: (6025) (Boys) King Harry Lane, St Albans AL3 4AW
Tel: 01727 855185 Fax: 01727 892024 Email: Coakley.b@stcolumbascollege.org
Head Mr David Buxton Chaplain Sarah Brooks (RO) (St Albans Deanery)

NON-MAINTAINED SPECIAL SCHOOL
St Elizabeth Centre: (7006) South End, Much Hadham SG10 6EW
Tel: 01279 843451 Fax: 01279 843903 Email: schooloffice@stelizabeths.org.uk
Director of Education and Skills Development Mr Alec Clark
Head of School Mrs Samantha Steinke-Sanderson Head of College Awaiting appointment
Chaplain Fr Paul Arnold (RO) (Lea Valley Deanery)

PRIMARY AND SECONDARY SCHOOL
Independent
St Edmund's College and Prep: (6115) Old Hall Green, Ware SG11 1DS
Tel: 01920 821504 Fax: 01920 823011 Email: head@stedmundscollege.org
Head Mr Matthew Mostyn
Priest-in-Residence Fr Peter Lyness Lay Chaplain Paula Peirce (Lea Valley Deanery)

COUNTY OF SURREY   (936)

PRIMARY SCHOOLS
Our Lady of the Rosary: (3461) Park Avenue, Staines-upon-Thames TW18 2EF
Tel: 01784 453539 Fax: 01784 449485 Email: handrews@ourlady.surrey.sch.uk
Executive Head Mrs Helen Andrews Head of School Mrs Taryn Hancock
 (Staines-upon-Thames)

St Ignatius, Sunbury: (3459) Green Street, Sunbury-on-Thames TW16 6QG
Tel: 01932 785396 Fax: 01932 771418 Email: handrews@st-ignatius.surrey.sch.uk
Head Mrs Helen Andrews (Sunbury)

St Michael, Ashford: (3915) Feltham Hill Road, Ashford TW15 2DG
Tel: 01784 253333 Fax: 01784 240834 Email: head@st-michaels.surrey.sch.uk
Head Mr John Anthony Lane (Ashford)

SECONDARY SCHOOL
St Paul College: (5411) Manor Lane, Sunbury-on-Thames TW16 6JE
Tel: 01932 783811 Fax: 01932 786485 Email: jmcnulty@st-pauls.surrey.sch.uk
Head Mr James McNulty Chaplain Rebecca Walker (Upper Thames Deanery)

Section 6

CATHOLIC SOCIETIES AND ORGANISATIONS

Organisations in this section have a membership widely distributed in the Diocese and a fundamental commitment to the teaching of the Catholic Church, particularly as expressed by the documents of the Second Vatican Council and the Catechism of the Catholic Church.

AID TO THE CHURCH IN NEED

ACN is a Pontifical Foundation directly under the Holy See. As a Catholic charity, it supports the faithful wherever they are persecuted, oppressed or in need, through information, prayer, and action. Founded in 1947 by Fr Werenfried van Straaten, whom Pope St John Paul II named 'an outstanding Apostle of Charity', the organisation is now at work in 140 countries throughout the world. Undertaking thousands of projects every year, the charity provides emergency support for people experiencing persecution, transport for clergy and lay Church workers, Children's Bibles, media and evangelisation projects, churches, Mass stipends and other support for priests and nuns, and training for seminarians.

Aid to the Church in Need UK is a registered charity in England and Wales [1097984] and Scotland [SC040748]. The UK office is in Sutton, Surrey and there is a Scottish office in Motherwell, near Glasgow and another office based in Lancaster that covers the North-West.

National Director Neville Kyrke-Smith **Aid to the Church in Need UK, 12-14 Benhill Avenue, Sutton SM1 4DA** Tel: 020 8662 8668 Email: acn@acnuk.org

ANSCOMBE BIOETHICS CENTRE

A national Catholic Research Centre, established by the Catholic Bishops of England and Wales in 1977. It seeks to promote understanding of Catholic teaching on healthcare and biotechnology issues through research and educational outreach. The Centre engages in scholarly dialogue with academics and practitioners of different traditions, and contributes to public policy debates and consultations. In addition to academic conferences and seminars, it also runs educational programmes for, and gives advice to, healthcare professionals, biomedical scientists, students and the wider Catholic community.

Director Prof David Albert Jones **17 Beaumont Street, Oxford OX1 2NA**
Tel: 01865 610212 Email: admin@bioethics.org.uk Web: www.bioethics.org.uk

ARCHCONFRATERNITY OF ST STEPHEN

The Archconfraternity of St Stephen exists to promote and encourage high standards of altar serving. Servers can be enrolled into the Guild with permission of their Parish Priest once they have been serving for at least six months and made their First Communion. Please contact the Hon Secretary or Diocesan Director for details on how a parish can be affiliated to the Guild.

National Director Fr Dennis F P Touw Tempelmans-Plat (Fulham I)
Diocesan Director Fr Keith Stoakes (Poplar / Limehouse)
Hon President to be confirmed
Hon Secretary Michael Malone **PO Box 568, London WC1A 1YT**
Email: secretary@guildofststephen.org

ASSOCIATION FOR LATIN LITURGY

(Under the patronage of the Bishops' Conference of England & Wales)
We promote the use of Latin in the Ordinary Form and the Church's inheritance of
Gregorian Chant, working especially to enable the faithful to participate fully in the Latin liturgy
in its contemporary form. We arrange meetings with sung Masses, Vespers and Benediction in
Latin, talks, chant days, publish our journal *Latin Liturgy*, engage in liturgical studies, liaise with the
hierarchy, and produce liturgical booklets for congregations. Our latest publication, the Introits
of the *Graduale Parvum*, provides simple but authentic settings for all Sundays of the year, in
Latin and English, suitable for small choirs and for congregations. The other chants of the
Propers will follow. **Contact** Membership Secretary **173 Davidson Road, Croydon CR0 6DP**
General enquiries: enquiries@latin-liturgy.org. Web: www.latin-liturgy.org /
www.facebook.com/latinliturgy twitter.com/latinliturgyuk

ASSOCIATION FOR THE PROPAGATION OF THE FAITH (APF)

Part of the Missio network, the Association for the Propagation of the Faith (APF) builds much
needed infrastructure in predominantly impoverished, remote areas – from chapels and
schools, to orphanages, clinics and dispensaries. Requested by the local community, our support
transforms lives and creates a hub from which the young Church can flourish and grow,
spreading the Good News of the Gospel, ministering to the faithful and delivering essential
services in health and education through the Red Mission boxes and the World Mission
Sunday annual collection.
Diocesan Director Fr Philip Knights **Email:** philipknights@rcdow.org.uk
Mill Hill Appealer for the Diocese Fr John Hemer MHM
Tel: 020 7349 5609 **Email:** johnhemer@gmail.com
National Office for Missio 23 Eccleston Square SW1V 1NU (Reg. Charity No. 1056651)
Tel: 020 7821 9755 **Email:** apf@missio.org.uk **Web:** www.missio.org.uk

ASSOCIATION OF MARY HELP OF CHRISTIANS

To promote personal devotion to, and public honour of Our Lady under the title 'Help of
Christians'. A prayer meeting is held on the fourth Saturday of each month at 3.30pm at
9 Henry Road N4 2LH Contact Rev Deacon Kassa Tsegaye **120 Seaford Road N15 5DT**
Tel: 07930 416927, Fr Hugh Preston SDB **Tel: 07806 803683**

ASSUMPTION VOLUNTEERS

Volunteer abroad for one year in India, the Philippines, Rwanda, Lithuania or Newcastle-upon-
Tyne, England, in educational and social projects connected with the Assumption Sisters
worldwide. There are 10 subsidised placements each year. Share your skills and your life with
the young in poor communities around the world and let them teach you a new way of living.
Contact Volunteer Co-ordinator **20 Kensington Square W8 5HH Tel: 020 7361 4752**
Email: vc@assumptionvolunteers.org.uk **Web:** www.assumptionvolunteers.org.uk
Facebook: AssumptionVolunteers

BANNEUX ND. INTERNATIONAL UNION OF PRAYER

Promulgates the message given by Our Lady at Banneux under the title 'Virgin of the Poor' by showing films and leading retreats and pilgrimages.

Secretary Lisa Pirie I Lines Road, Stevenage SG1 3DJ **Tel: 07500 288384**
Email: banneuxndgb@gmail.com

BEGINNING EXPERIENCE

A Catholic ministry for men and women who find themselves single again following divorce, separation or the death of a partner. It offers a weekend programme which seeks to encourage participants to close the door gently on the past and to approach life with more confidence and hope in the future.

Contact Freda Bacon **Tel: 01322 838415**, Maura Heaney **Tel: 01322 551503**, or John Brotherton **Email: johnabrotherton@hotmail.co.uk Web: www.beginningexperience.org**

CAFOD (CATHOLIC AGENCY FOR OVERSEAS DEVELOPMENT)

This international development and relief agency of the Church in England and Wales builds partnerships with local organisations in over 30 countries across Africa, Asia and Latin America, supporting them to build a better world for people living in extreme poverty. CAFOD focuses on sustainable livelihoods, clean water and sanitation, combating HIV/AIDS, and peace-building. In emergencies it provides immediate relief and long-term programmes to rebuild people's lives. Support can be offered through donations, prayer, volunteering and campaigning. CAFOD's Lent Family Fast Day is on 6 March and Harvest Fast Day is on 2 October and donation envelopes will be available in churches on the weekends before and after.

Contact Tony Sheen **CAFOD Westminster Volunteer Centre, 29 Bramley Road N14 4HE**
Tel: 020 8449 6970 Email: westminster@cafod.org.uk Web: cafod.org.uk
Blog: cafodwestminster.wordpress.com

CARITAS CHRISTI

International secular institute for women living a celibate life. For the single or widowed.
Web: www.ccinfo.org

CARITAS SOCIAL ACTION NETWORK

CSAN is the official agency of the Catholic Bishops' Conference of England and Wales for domestic social action. We support and facilitate our network of over 40 Catholic dioceses and independent charities. Our members provide help for families and children, the elderly, homeless people, refugees, the disabled, and prisoners. The national team strives to develop the network, to advance the education, training, practice and formation of those active in Catholic social action, and to offer a coherent Catholic voice on social justice in the public arena. CSAN is a member of *Caritas Internationalis*, within the *Caritas Europa* group.

Chairman of Trustees Rt Rev Terence Drainey **Vice-Chairman** Sr Lynda Dearlove
CEO Dr Philip McCarthy **Romero House, 55 Westminster Bridge Road SE1 7JB**
Tel: 020 7870 2210 Email: admin@csan.org.uk Web: www.csan.org.uk

SECTION 6

CARMELITES OF THE DISCALCED CARMELITE SECULAR ORDER

Carmelite Seculars, together with the friars and nuns, are sons and daughters of the Order of Our Lady of Mount Carmel and St Teresa of Jesus. They share the same charism. It is one family with the same spiritual possessions, the same call to holiness and the same apostolic mission. There are four groups that meet regularly within the Westminster diocese.
Contact Mark Courtney **Tel: 020 8288 0536 Email:** mark.courtney@oxon.org
Web: www.carmeldiscalcedsecular.org.uk

CARMELITE SECULAR INSTITUTE (THE LEAVEN)

The Leaven, the Secular Institute of Our Lady of Mount Carmel, is a secular institute for single women and widows founded in 1949. There are currently members in England, Scotland, Namibia and Australia. The individual apostolate of members is rooted in a life of prayer drawing on the rich heritage of the Carmelites and each member lives her everyday life wherever she finds herself: alone, with family or friends. The commitment to service and contemplation is shown in the vows they take of poverty, celibacy and obedience.
Contact Angela Kneale **8 Fulwell Court, St Leger Drive, Great Linford, Milton Keynes MK14 5HB Tel: 01908 231209 Email:** theleavensi@gmail.com

CARMELITE THIRD ORDER (ANCIENT OBSERVANCE)

Carmel-in-London offers laity and diocesan clergy the opportunity to deepen their following of Christ within one of the Church's most ancient spirituality traditions, combining contemplative reflection with prophetic service and action for justice. Drawing inspiration from the prophet Elijah, the Blessed Virgin Mary and the Saints of Carmel, we form praying communities in the heart of the Church at the service of all God's people, through formal Carmelite Third Order gatherings and more diverse Carmelite Spirituality Groups. A Carmelite Third Order Group of the Ancient Observance (O.Carm) meets regularly in Westminster Diocese, alongside the monthly Carmel-in-the-City Spirituality Group. **Contact** Sylvia Lucas
Email: sylvia_lucas@btinternet.com **Web:** www.carmelinthecity.org.uk

CATENIAN ASSOCIATION

International Association of Catholic men, with over 250 local groups in the UK including 20+ in Westminster diocese. Catenians support each other, their families and friends, their clergy and parishes, vocations, young people, and many charities each year. We share our faith as friends and meet monthly to renew friendships, share a meal, organise events, and unload the daily stresses and strains of modern living.
Contact Declan O'Farrell (Director) **Tel: 07866 523092 Email:** declanofarrell@hotmail.com

CATHOLIC ARCHIVES SOCIETY

The Catholic Archives Society promotes and advises on listing, management and preservation of records of dioceses, religious foundations and institutions of the Catholic Church. It does not collect or store archives.
Secretary Sarah Maspero **38 Crawford Drive, Fareham PO16 7RW**
Email: sarah.maspero@gmail.com **Web:** www.catholicarchivesociety.org

CATHOLIC ASSOCIATION FOR RACIAL JUSTICE

The Catholic Association for Racial Justice is an independent charity, and a membership organisation. CARJ works with people of diverse backgrounds, in Church and society, to create a more just, more equal, more co-operative community. We do this through education, advocacy and facilitating mutual support among:
· schools, families and young people in marginalised communities
· Gypsies, Roma and Traveller communities
· those working in poor urban communities
· those suffering discrimination based on race, caste, religion and social class.
Wherever possible, CARJ works in formal or informal partnership with members, friends and fellow citizens who share our basic values.
Chair Mrs Yogi Sutton **Catholic Association for Racial Justice, 9 Henry Road N4 2LH**
Tel: 020 8802 8080 Fax: 020 8211 0808 Email: info@carj.org.uk Web: www.carj.org.uk

CATHOLIC ASSOCIATION OF PERFORMING ARTS (FORMERLY CATHOLIC STAGE GUILD)

Open to everyone with an interest in the performing arts, enabling them to use their talents to help others, work with like-minded professionals, enjoy social and networking opportunities and explore and develop their spiritual side.
Chaplain Fr Alan Robinson **Secretary** Molly Steele **1 Maiden Lane WC2E 7NB**
Email: secretary@caapa.org.uk Web: www.caapa.org.uk

CATHOLIC CHARISMATIC RENEWAL

Information Centre on behalf of the National Service Committee (NSC) about Catholic Charismatic Renewal, with contacts for prayer groups and communities, and details of Goodnews, our quarterly magazine. **Contact** Goodnews, **CCR Centre, PO Box 67138 London SW11 9FD Tel: 07932 457767**
Email: ccrcentre.goodnews@gmail.com Web: www.ccr.org.uk

CATHOLIC CONCERN FOR ANIMALS

(Registered Charity 231022) CCA is the principal animal welfare organisation within the Catholic Church worldwide and we exist to promote and care for the well-being and protection of all of God's creation and work within the spirit of *Laudato Si'*, the Encyclical on the Environment by Pope Francis.
Contact Chris Fegan **Tel: 07817 730472 Email: chrisfegancca@gmail.com**
Web: www.catholic-animals.com

CATHOLIC EDUCATION SERVICE

CES is the education agency of the Bishops' Conference. Founded by the Vicars-Apostolic in 1847, its principal aim remains to represent the collective view of the bishops to central government and other national agencies in the field of education. It also supports the work of diocesan education services and religious orders who are trustees of schools. In the Catholic sector across England and Wales there are 2,204 schools and colleges educating over 853,000 students. There are also 4 Catholic universities and 8 other Catholic higher education institutions.

Chair The Rt Rev Marcus Stock, Bishop of Leeds **Director** Paul Barber
39 Eccleston Square SW1V 1BX Tel: 020 7901 1900 Fax: 020 7901 1939
Email: general@catholiceducation.org.uk Web: www.catholiceducation.org.uk

CATHOLIC EVANGELISATION SERVICES

Produce Catholic teaching resources on DVD to equip parishes, schools and colleges. A wide
range of CaFE (Catholic Faith Exploration) resources are available for sacramental preparation,
parish renewal, chaplaincy groups and to support the RE curriculum in secondary schools.
Director David Payne **PO Box 333, St Albans AL2 1EL** Tel: 0845 050 9428
Email: resources@faithcafe.org Web: www.faithcafe.org www.youthcafe.org

CATHOLIC EVIDENCE GUILD

For the training and provision of public speakers on the Catholic Faith.
Enquiries Mr Phil Gough **Tel: 07590 035522**

CATHOLIC FAMILY HISTORY SOCIETY

The Society exists to help and encourage those who have Catholic ancestry in England, Wales
and Scotland to research their family history. Details of membership, publications and resources
are obtainable through the website or by email.
Email: cfhsrecords@gmail.com Web: http://catholicfhs.online

CATHOLIC GRANDPARENTS ASSOCIATION

The Catholic Grandparents Association is a global organisation of the faithful. An integral part
of the Catholic Grandparents Association is setting up branches at the parish level. These act as
prayer and support groups for grandparents. Grandparents have a unique vocation that must
be fostered and cherished in the spirit of St Joachim and St Anne, the grandparents of Jesus
and parents of Mary. **PO Box 90, Walsingham, Norfolk NR21 1AQ** Tel: 01328 560333

CATHOLICS IN FUNDRAISING

A network to share best practice amongst Catholics working in fundraising for charities. Meets
twice a year in London for a topical presentation, discussion and networking. There is also a
LinkedIn group 'Catholics in Fundraising, UK'
Contact John Green **Email: brixtongreens@hotmail.co.uk**

CATHOLIC MEDICAL ASSOCIATION

For Catholic members of the medical and healthcare professions
39 Eccleston Square SW1V 1BX Tel: 020 7901 4895 Fax: 020 7901 4819
Chairman of Westminster Branch Rev Dr Michael Jarmulowicz **337 Harrow Road W9 3RB**
Tel: 020 7286 2170 Email: secretary@catholicmedicalassociation.org.uk
Web: www. catholicmedicalassociation.org.uk

CATHOLIC MISSIONARY UNION OF ENGLAND AND WALES

The national forum and information centre of the missionary societies and congregations - lay and religious - working in mission and human development projects overseas. It promotes mission, coordinates the annual parish mission appeals by the member societies and is a consultative body to the Bishops' Conference.

Secretary Richard Owens **CMU, 37-39 Shakespeare Street, Southport PR8 5AB**
Tel: 01704 533708 Email: secretariat@cmu.org.uk Web: www.cmu.org.uk

CATHOLIC PEOPLE'S WEEKS

Established in 1945, CPW runs educational, residential events which provide the opportunity for people to combine study of their faith with thoughtful joyous liturgy, time to reflect and relax, community experience and a holiday for young and old. New programme each January.
Email: secretarycpw@gmail.com Web: www.catholicpeoplesweeks.org

CATHOLIC RECORD SOCIETY

Founded in 1904 to make available material for study of the Catholic history of England and Wales since the Reformation, publishing transcripts of diaries; letters and biographies; legal, court and official papers; and records of old Catholic missions, seminaries, colleges and convents. Since then its purview has broadened considerably; it hosts an annual conference and its peer-reviewed academic journal, *British Catholic History*, is published twice a year by Cambridge University Press.

Contact Hon Secretary Dr Serenhedd James **Oriel College, Oxford, OX1 4EW**
Email: secretary@crs.org.uk Web: www.crs.org.uk

CATHOLIC TRUTH SOCIETY

We believe in helping people to discover, nurture and share their faith, by providing honest and compelling answers to life's deepest questions. Everything we do is authentic, accessible, and authoritative. You can rely on us to tackle the important issues of life and faith, to make the complicated easy to understand, and that the works we publish are in line with the teachings of the Catholic Church.

Chair Rt Rev Paul Hendricks MA PhL VG, Auxiliary Bishop in Southwark Archdiocese
General Secretary Pierpaolo Finaldi **Publishing Office 42-46 Harleyford Road SE11 5AY**
Tel: 020 7640 0042 Fax: 020 7640 0046 Email: orders@CTSbooks.org
Web: www.CTSbooks.org

CATHOLIC UNION OF GREAT BRITAIN AND C.U. CHARITABLE TRUST

CUGB, founded in 1870, is the voice of the Catholic laity which works to represent Catholic interests in Parliament and public life by working with the Bishops' Conferences and members of both Houses of Parliament. This is to ensure that our values and interests are presented to key decision makers who determine legislation and social policy. We liaise with the wider Christian community on issues of common interest. The funding of CUGB is by annual or life individual membership subscription or donation. **President** Rt Hon Sir Edward Leigh MP
Director Nigel Parker **St Maximilian Kolbe House, 63 Jeddo Road W12 9EE**
Tel: 020 8749 1321 Email: info@catholicunion.org.uk Web: catholicunion.org.uk

The Charitable Trust (CUCT) was launched in 2015. Its principal aim is to advance Catholic moral, social and spiritual teaching by means of conferences, lectures, training and seminars. Its funding is by donations which are eligible for gift aid. Registered at Companies House (no. 07333172) and with the Charity Commission (no. 1137317).

Chairman James Bogle **Secretary** Tom Martin

Address & telephone as above Email: info@cuct.org **Web:** cuct.org

CATHOLIC VOICES

An Apologetics project that has spread to 22 countries. Set up to train spokespersons for radio and TV interviews, it now also offers speakers to parishes, chaplaincies, and schools. It holds topical briefings when the Church is in the news, runs a blog (www.cvcomment.org) and has led to publications, including 'How to Defend the Faith Without Raising Your Voice'. It offers bespoke media trainings for dioceses and Catholic organisations in the UK and abroad. Independent of the Bishops' Conference, it is supported as part of their 'Confidently Catholic' agenda, encouraging lay people 'to know and live their faith with courage and give witness to it with confidence'.

Lead Co-ordinator Brenden Thompson **Email:** info@catholicvoices.org.uk
Web: www.catholicvoices.org.uk **Twitter:** @CatholicVoices.

CATHOLIC WOMEN'S LEAGUE

The Catholic Women's League was founded in 1906. It is a Catholic agency uniting Catholic women in a bond of friendship and encouraging them to use their talents in the service of the Church and the community, reaching out to every area of concern.

Contact Veronica Comparini, President Westminster Branch **Tel:** 01442 258684
Email: veedotcomp@gmail.com, Jean Clarke, National Secretary **Email:** natsec@cwlhq.org.uk
Web: catholicwomensleaguecio.org.uk

CHRISTIAN LIFE COMMUNITY

Small groups of Christians who meet regularly to help each other deepen their life of prayer. CLC's special characteristic is the spirituality of St Ignatius, helping members to integrate prayer with action in their daily lives.

National Chaplain Br Alan Harrison SJ **Diocesan Representative** Jackie Gill **(Administrator)**
114 Mount Street W1K 3AH **Email:** president@clcew.org.uk

COMMUNITY OF SANT'EGIDIO

The Community of Sant'Egidio is a 'Church Public Lay Association' which began in Rome in 1968. The different communities, spread across 73 countries, share the same spirituality and principles which characterise the way of Sant'Egidio: Prayer, Communicating the Gospel, Solidarity with the Poor, Ecumenism, and Dialogue. The Community regularly gathers for common prayer, as a pathway to becoming familiar with Jesus' words, presenting to the Lord the needs of poor people, our own needs and the needs of the whole world.

Sant'Egidio, in London as elsewhere, lives in service to the poor in friendship and familiarity, considering them as brothers and sisters, especially the homeless and the elderly. Feel free to contact us for details regarding our services throughout the year and at Christmastime.

Email: info@santegidio.org.uk Web: www.santegidio.org.uk Facebook: @santegidiolondon
Twitter: @santegidiouk Instagram: @santegidiouk

COMMUNITY OF THE RISEN LORD

The mission of the Community of the Risen Lord (CRL) UK is to bring life-transforming renewal both to parishes and dioceses, with outreach and pastoral activities based on the teaching of the Catholic Church. Meetings are held at St. Joseph's Pastoral Centre, Hendon, from 3.30-5.30 pm on 2nd and 4th Sundays.

Contact: Sonia Tissera **(UK Co-ordinator),** Niru Fernando **and** Eric Jeevaraj **(Co-Group Team)** 70 Roxeth Green Avenue, South Harrow HA2 8AG Tel: 07957 117928
Email: ericc2210@gmail.com Web: www.crlmain.org

CONSECRATED WOMEN

Vatican II restored the Order of Virgins, which dates from the early Church. Canon 604 speaks of this form of consecrated life, mentioned in the Catechism (paras 922-4). We are consecrated publicly by the Bishop to live an independent life within the local church community. Each woman is autonomous, and her pattern of life is planned by herself and approved by the Bishop. She is responsible for her own finances. Other women are consecrated as widows; our vow is for life. Those who wish meet annually for a week at Hyning monastery. This kind of religious life combines freedom with commitment.

Contact: Gosia Brykczynska OCV **148 Carlyle Road** W5 4BJ Tel: 020 8560 0120
Email: gosia.brykczynska@talktalk.net

CONSTANTINIAN ORDER OF ST GEORGE

Internationally recognised ancient and charitable Catholic Order of Knighthood under the custodianship of the Royal House of Bourbon Two Sicilies.

Grand Master HRH The Duke of Castro **Prior** HE Vincent Cardinal Nichols, Archbishop of Westminster **Sub-Prior** Most Rev George Stack, Archbishop of Cardiff; **Chief Chaplain for Ireland** Most Rev Dr Raymond Field, Auxiliary to the Archbishop of Dublin; **Delegate for Britain and Ireland** HE Mr Anthony Bailey;

Vice-Delegates HE Mr John Bruton **(Ireland),** The Rt Hon Lord Murphy of Torfaen **(Great Britain),** The Hon Sir Peter Caruana **(Gibraltar)**

Contact Sacred Military Constantinian Order of St George
12 Queen's Gate Gardens SW7 5LY Tel: 020 7594 0275 Fax: 020 7594 0265
Email: chancery@constantinian.org.uk Web: www.constantinian.org.uk

COUPLES FOR CHRIST (CFC)

Renewing the face of the earth, moved by the Holy Spirit, one with the Catholic Church, and blessed to witness to Christ's love and service, Couples for Christ is a united global community of family evangelizers that sets the world on fire with the fullness of God's transforming love.
Web: https://www.couplesforchristuk.org/

SECTION 6

DOMINICAN LAITY

For those called to spread the Gospel in the tradition of St Dominic. The Fraternity meets monthly at St Dominic's Priory, Southampton Road NW5 4LB.
Secretary Alison Fincham **5 New Street, Canterbury CT2 8AU**
Email: alison_fincham@yahoo.co.uk

EMMANUEL COMMUNITY

A Public Association of the Faithful, recognised by the Holy See, for lay people, priests, deacons and consecrated men and women. **Web: www.emmanuel.info**

ENGLISH CATHOLIC HISTORY ASSOCIATION

To promote interest and encourage research into English and Welsh Catholic history. Helps preserve relevant documents. Arranges regular meetings/visits. Members' quarterly newsletter.
Secretary Mrs Angela Hodges **45 High Street, Stoke sub Hamdon, Somerset TA14 6PR**
Tel: 01935 823928 Email: secretary@echa.org.uk Web: www.echa.org.uk

FOCOLARE MOVEMENT

An international ecclesial movement started by Chiara Lubich in 1943 at Trent in N. Italy. Its principal aim is to help bring about the fulfilment of the prayer of Jesus :'That all may be one'.
Focolare Centre for Unity, 69 Parkway, Welwyn Garden City AL8 6JG
Tel: 01707 323620 Email: cfu@focolare.org.uk Web: www.focolare.org/gb

FRIENDS OF THE HOLY FATHER

To pray for the Holy Father's intentions, study and promote his teaching. Supports a fund assisting in defraying expenses of his Apostolic Ministry. **Chair** John Dean DipLaw, DipLP
Secretary Dr Michael Straiton MB, KCSG **23a Vincent House, Vincent Square SW1P 2NB**
Email: fhfenquiries@gmail.com Web: www.thefriendsoftheholyfather.org

FRIENDS OF THE HOLY LAND

FHL, an ecumenical charity (registered no. 1130054 and established in 2009), fosters resilience and hope among Christians. Our efforts flow from Christians through Christians to Christians. We are non-political and have the backing and blessing of the Catholic and Anglican Bishops of England and Wales. We seek to raise awareness of the daily challenges faced by Christians living in the Holy Land, supporting them with our prayers and fund-raising, and encouraging Christians to visit the Holy Land and meet local Christian communities. In the Holy Land we provide funding to meet the emergency needs of the most vulnerable, and support small sustainable projects mainly in education, employment, health and housing, which ultimately make a difference to individual Christians and their families. Cardinal Nichols is one of the Charity's patrons.
Contact Office Manager **Friends of the Holy Land, Farmer Ward Road, Kenilworth CV8 2DH** Tel: 01926 512980 Email: office@friendsoftheholyland.org.uk
Web: www.friendsoftheholyland facebook@friendsoftheholyland twitter@Social_FHL

FRIENDS OF THE ORDINARIATE OF OUR LADY OF WALSINGHAM

The aim of the Friends is to raise money from across the Catholic community to support the work and mission of the Ordinariate. In particular we assist with the training and support of priests and invest in churches owned or used by the Ordinariate..
Contact Peter Sefton-Williams **c/o 24 Golden Square W1F 9JR**
Email: peter@seftonwilliams.com Web: http://friendsoftheordinariate.org.uk/

FRIENDS OF THE *VENERABILE* (THE ENGLISH COLLEGE IN ROME)

The Friends (Charity no. 1075141) support students of the College, who will be our future priests, with prayers, encouragement and financial help. **Contact** Mike Lang **Tel: 01364 644811**
Email: mikelang537@btinternet.com Web: www.friendsofenglishcollegerome.org.uk

GOOD COUNSEL NETWORK

A Catholic, pro-life pregnancy centre in central London providing friendship and practical help and ongoing support of all kinds to assist pregnant women to choose life for their children. We have Daily Mass and Adoration in our Centre. We provide speakers and run a monthly day of prayer and fasting for the end of abortion. We provide post-abortion counselling, too. We welcome volunteers who wish to help us in our work.
Director Clare McCullough **The Good Counsel Network, PO Box 46679 NW9 8ZT**
Tel: 020 7723 1740 Email: info@goodcounselnetwork.com
Web: www.goodcounselnetwork.com Blog: mariastopsabortion.blogspot.com

GRAIL, THE

The Grail has always worked to share its Christian inspiration and values with the world by encouraging awareness of God's presence in the individual, communities and creation, in the belief that to help one person to grow is to help to build the world. Today this work is being continued through the making of small grants to other charities or groups whose work embodies these values. For full details of eligibility and application forms **contact**
Email: president@grailsociety.org.uk Web: www.grailsociety.org.uk

GUILD OF OUR LADY OF RANSOM

Founded 29th November 1887 with a threefold mission: 1. The conversion of England and Wales; 2. The restoration of the lapsed; and 3. Praying for the forgotten dead.
The Guild has moved its administration to Walsingham. To support its work, **contact**
The Guild of Our Lady of Ransom **Catholic National Shrine of Our Lady, Pilgrim Bureau, Friday Market Place, Walsingham, Norfolk NR22 6EG** Tel: 01328 801007
E-mail: info@guild-ransom.co.uk Web: www.guild-ransom.co.uk

GUILD OF OUR LADY OF WILLESDEN

The Guild is open to all and meets every Tuesday at **Our Lady of Willesden, Nicoll Road NW10 9AX** after the 7pm Mass. Its purpose is to pray for the intentions and protection of London through the intercession of Our Lady of Willesden.
Guild Master Fr Stephen Willis

SECTION 6

GUILD OF ST AGATHA

Catholic Association of Bellringers. **Guild Office, I Albert Road, Bournemouth BH1 1BZ**
Diocesan Representative Canon Shaun Lennard **243 Mutton Lane, Potters Bar EN6 2AT**
Tel: 01707 654359

HOLY SEPULCHRE, EQUESTRIAN ORDER OF THE

To strengthen in its members the Christian life, in fidelity to the Pope and the teachings of the
Church, observing the principles of charity for assistance to the Holy Land; to aid the
charitable, cultural and social works and institutions of the Church in the Holy Land, particularly
those of and in the Latin Patriarchate of Jerusalem, with which the Order maintains ties; to
support the propagation of the Faith there, involving in this work Catholics scattered
throughout the world, united in charity by the symbol of the Order; and also all brother
Christians; and to sustain the rights of the Catholic Church in the Holy Land.
Contact Roland Hayes **Email:** khswestminsterpres@gmail.com **Web:** www.khs.org.uk

HOME MISSION OFFICE

CBCEW's Department of Evangelisation and Catechesis helps the local Church to make the
joy of the Gospel a reality in England and Wales. The priorities of the Department are:
• to inspire the Faithful to deepen and share their faith;
• to support those involved in Evangelisation by promoting their efforts and providing ongoing
training; and
• to develop outreach to people who do not ascribe to any faith.
To achieve these priorities, the Home Mission Office works with Diocesan evangelisation
personnel, leaders of New Movements, CYMFed and Catholic resource providers who
support evangelisation and catechesis in a parish context. It is also responsible for producing
resources for Home Mission Sunday.
Bishop Mark O'Toole chairs the Department, and the day to day work is done by the
Development Officer, Teresa Carvalho, with Executive Assistant Sylvia Ideh. Victoria Seed is the
Catechetical Development Officer.
Tel: 020 7901 4818 Email: Homemission@cbcew.org.uk **Web:** www.homemission.org.uk
The National Office for Vocation (NOV) works to help people hear God's Call. It aims:
• to build a culture of vocation within the Church in England & Wales
• to work with youth and youth organisations to nurture young people into leadership and
responsibility in the Church
• to work with the department of Evangelisation and other ecclesial bodies to help people
grow in their baptismal calling as disciples of Jesus Christ.
Sr Elaine Penrice is the Director of NOV, assisted by Juliet Chiosso, the Vocations Administrator.
Tel: 020 7901 4829 Email: enquiries@ukvocation.org **Web:** www.ukvocation.org

HOUSING JUSTICE

Through national membership we offer advice and training on delivering services to people
who are homeless or in housing need; facilitate and co-ordinate frontline services, including a
London-wide winter shelters forum; and campaign for better legislation. We support the
development of services nationwide and champion alternative solutions, notably housing co-

operatives and community land trusts. Members are available to speak to groups or after Masses about homelessness and housing. We also co-ordinate the annual Homeless Sunday in October.

Chief Executive Kathy Mohan **256 Bermondsey Street SE1 3UJ** Tel: **020 3544 8094** Email: info@housingjustice.org.uk Web: www.housingjustice.org.uk

IMPACT

Young people making a difference (13-17 year-olds) trains young people to become leaders in life using the 'See, Judge, Act' method. See '**Young Christian Workers**' for more details.

JOHN PAUL II FOUNDATION FOR SPORT (JP2F4S)

Launched by Pope Benedict XVI during his visit to Britain, to honour the memory of St John Paul II and his vision for sport, this charity enables the setting up of clubs in parishes and schools, supports clubs in need of advice and guidance and produces educational materials for schools and parishes. Catholic in inspiration, working with all and for all, its purpose is summed up in its strapline: 'Educating young people through sport'.

Contact Mgr Vladimir Felzmann CEO **John Paul II Foundation for Sport, Vaughan House, 46 Francis Street SW1P 1QN** Email: info@jp2f4s.org

KNIGHTS OF ST COLUMBA

Fraternal order of Catholic men supporting the mission of the Church and the spiritual, intellectual and material welfare of its members and their families.

Head Office, 75 Hillington Road South, Glasgow G52 2AE Tel: **0141 883 5700** Email: headoffice@ksc.org.uk

Provincial Grand Knights: Province 11 Roger Khan, **Province 29** Benjamin Agwunobi **Province 30** Rosario Fichardo

LATIN MASS SOCIETY

Founded in 1965, LMS is an association of Catholic faithful and a registered charity with around 2,000 members, predominantly lay, drawn from every age, group and walk of life. It is dedicated to promoting the use and wider provision of the Traditional Latin Mass (the Extraordinary Form) and other Sacraments. Working with its network of local representatives, the Society organises pilgrimages, retreats, days of recollection, training conferences for priests and servers, conferences for the general public, research and campaigning. It is a supporter of the Gregorian Chant Network (**www.gregorianchantnetwork.org**). Details of its sodality for altar servers, the Society of St Tarcisius (**www.lms.org.uk/society-st-tarcisius**), and family and youth affiliates can be obtained from the London office. It also publishes a quarterly magazine, Mass of Ages. Its online shop offers books and DVDs on the Traditional Mass and devotions.

Contact National Office **130 Old Street EC1V 9BD** Tel: **020 7404 7284** Email: info@lms.org.uk Web: lms.org.uk

LAY MISSION AND VOLUNTEER NETWORK

An informal group of Catholic missionary and volunteer organisations which offer faith-based volunteering overseas. Co-ordinators meet to share ideas and resources and each summer run a residential week-long pre-departure training course for volunteers. This training course is also open to those going to volunteer abroad with religious orders who may not have access to training.

Each organisation has its own charism and sending practice (opportunities, countries, length of service, age range). If you'd like to volunteer with one of us contact details for each website can be found on **Facebook page LMVN**

LIFE ASCENDING MOVEMENT (FORMERLY THE ASCENT)

For Christians in middle and later life helping them grow spiritually and to take up their responsibilities as members of the Church through friendship, spirituality and mission, with parish-based regular meeings.

National President Mr Ross Roberts **77 Bingham Road, Addiscombe, Croydon CRO 7EJ** Tel: **020 8656 6873** Email: rosscharlesroberts@yahoo.com Web: www.lifeascending.org.uk **National Secretary** Mrs Dulcie Jacob **35 Capri Road, Croydon CR0 6LG** Tel: **020 8406 4783** / **07305 779202** Email: dalroti@hotmail.com

LONDON CATHOLIC WORKER

LCW is part of the international Catholic Worker movement founded in 1933 by Dorothy Day and Peter Maurin. CW communities are houses of hospitality for the poor as well as places to perform the works of mercy and organise resistance to the works of war, injustice and violence. The movement practises hospitality, active non-violence, gentle personalism and voluntary poverty. Each community is independent, with no HQ. We need full-time live-in community members and volunteers, as well as part-time volunteers and donations in cash or in kind. **Contact** London Catholic Worker **49 Mattison Road N4 1BG** Tel: **020 8348 8212** Email: londoncatholicworker@yahoo.co.uk Web: www.londoncatholicworker.org

MALTA, ORDER OF (BRITISH ASSOCIATION)

A British charity and a religious order of the Church, supporting in the UK, inter alia, The Orders of St John Care Trust, soup kitchens in London, Oxford, Cambridge, Colchester and St Andrews and pilgrimages for the sick to Lourdes and Walsingham.

British Association Sovereign Military Order of Malta, Craigmyle House, 13 Deodar Road SW15 2NP Tel: **020 7286 1414** Email: basmom@btconnect.com.

MARIST WAY

The Marist Way is the lay branch of the Marist Congregation, bringing together people who wish to participate in the life and mission of the Church in the `Spirit of Mary', a way envisaged by Jean-Claude Colin, founder of the Marists, who are Priests, Sisters, Brothers and Laity.

Marists endeavour to think, feel, judge and act as Mary did, at Nazareth and at Pentecost All Marists believe that Mary maintains a special interest in bringing the women and men of our time into contact with her Son, Jesus. They feel called to share in this concern of Mary's and to become part of her family to work on her behalf. The term `the work of Mary' describes this essentially missionary spirit.

Contact Mrs Pat O'Connor 12 Harrow Road, Linthorpe, Middlesbrough TS5 5PD
Tel: 01642 814486 Email: patriciaoconnor@ntlworld.com Facebook: Marist Way England

MARRIAGE CARE

We provide marriage preparation and relationship counselling to thousands of couples each year through a network of centres and professionally accredited volunteers. Visit our website to book a place on a marriage preparation course for those marrying in the Catholic Church or for a counselling appointment. If you are interested in helping us support couples in your community, we'd love to hear from you; please visit the website also.

Registered office (Charity number 218159): Marriage Care, Huntingdon House, 278 Huntingdon Street, Nottingham NG1 3LY Tel: 0800 389 3801
Email: info@marriagecare.org.uk Web: www.marriagecare.org.uk

MARRIAGE ENCOUNTER

Provides weekends for couples and those who are engaged, in association with priests and religious, to enrich their lives through improving communication.
Web: http://wwme.org.uk/

MARY POTTER CENTRE

Offering counselling, coaching, spiritual direction, talks, courses, and workshops to build self-understanding, confidence, deal with stress, difficult relationships, loss, bereavement, anxiety and distress; also psychometric testing. EFT, Tips for prevention of age-related memory loss.
Director Sr Josephine Bugeja LCM, MA, RGN, RMN **Flat 10 Berkeley Court, 33 Gordon Road W5 2AE** Tel: 020 8810 4432 Email: jbugeja@aol.com

MING-AI (LONDON) INSTITUTE

A lifelong education centre having close links with Caritas-Hong Kong, providing MA in Chinese Cultural Heritage Management and a wide range of leisure, cookery, health, business, oriental language classes, as well as community projects. It promotes links between our Diocese and the Church in Hong Kong and China. **Chairman** Professor Jonathan Liu
Dean Ms Chungwen Li **Ming-Ai (London) Institute, 1 Cline Road N11 2LX**
Tel: 020 8361 7161 Email: enquiry@ming-ai.org.uk Web: www.ming-ai.org.uk

MISSIO

The Pope's official charity for overseas mission, with 120 offices worldwide under the co-ordination of the Pontifical Mission Societies in Rome. We are the Holy Father's chosen instrument for sharing the Gospel and building the Church throughout the world. Together, the Missio offices globally support 1,069 dioceses in 157 countries. It is the only Catholic charity which supports the 40% of the Universal Church that is too new, young or poor to support itself. We aim to follow Christ's example by helping everyone in need, regardless of background or belief.

SECTION 6

Missio comprises four branches which work together: the Association for the Propagation of the Faith (APF), the Society of St Peter the Apostle (SPA), Mission Together (MT), and the Pontifical Missionary Union (PMU).

National Director Fr Anthony Chantry MHM

National Office for Missio 23 Eccleston Square SW1V 1NU (Reg. Charity No. 1056651)
Tel: 020 7821 9755 Email: info@missio.org.uk Web: www.missio.org.uk

MISSION TOGETHER (HOLY CHILDHOOD)

Part of the Missio network, Mission Together (MT) provides such things as healthcare and education for the world's poorest children, regardless of background or belief. It supports vulnerable children via educational, medical and welfare projects through schools, orphanages, health centres, children's homes and nutrition programmes. The food, education, medications, shelter, and formation that MT provides fulfil both the children's spiritual and practical needs.

National Office for Missio 23 Eccleston Square SW1V 1NU (Reg. Charity No. 1056651)
Tel: 020 7821 9755 Email: missiontogether@missio.org.uk Web: www.missio.org.uk

NATIONAL BOARD OF CATHOLIC WOMEN

A consultative body to the Bishops' Conference of England & Wales with consultative status within the United Nations, with representatives from 32 Catholic organisations and the dioceses. A forum in which women are enabled to share their views and concerns and make recommendations at all levels.

Tel: 07724 685780 Email: nbcwpres@gmail.com Web: nbcw.co.uk

NATIONAL COUNCIL FOR LAY ASSOCIATIONS (ENGLAND AND WALES)

A consultative body to the Bishops' Conference, consisting of lay apostolic national organisations, 8 liaison representatives, advisors & executive. **Adviser** Bishop Tom Williams
President John Smartt Tel: 07711 148907 Email: john.smartt45@gmail.com
Secretary Debbie Cottam Tel: 07778 266059 Email: deborahcottam@blueyonder.co.uk

NEOCATECHUMENAL WAY

The Neocatechumenal Way is an itinerary of Catholic formation lived in small communities within the parish. It helps people different in age, social background, mentality and culture, to rediscover and to live the immense riches of their baptism. They meet on a regular basis to celebrate the Liturgy of the Word and the Eucharist, going through various stages similar to those of the 'catechumenate' of the Early Church. The Neocatechumenal Way is governed by a Statute approved by the Holy See. **Email: ncway.gb@gmail.com**
Web: www.camminoneocatecumenale.it

NEWMAN ASSOCIATION

National association of Catholic laity and clergy, with local circles in London and Hertfordshire
Web: http://www.newman.org.uk/

OUR LADY'S CATECHISTS (SPECIAL COMMITTEE OF THE CATHOLIC WOMEN'S LEAGUE)

An association of men and women who are qualified to give religious instruction. We work in parishes and also by distance learning. Postal and online courses include our Foundation Course, leading to a qualification certificate for training parish catechists or as a personal development course only; our Diploma Course, which provides more academic training enabling catechists to lead parish programmes; the Catholicism Made Simple Course, which is a basic introduction to the faith for adults and youth; and the Children's Section, which provides courses and lesson leaflets for parents or catechists working with children attending non-Catholic schools and in preparation for the first Sacraments. Our latest course is Mysteries of the Christian Life, based on the 20 decades of the Rosary.

Contact Charmaine Jayasuriya **Tel: 01442 267035 Email:** dcharmainej@gmail.com
Web: www.ourladyscatechists.wordpress.com

PAX CHRISTI

Pax Christi is a gospel-based international movement for peace, open to all. We strive to help the Church and wider community to proclaim and make peace through its work for reconciliation and the promotion of a culture of peace and non-violence. We offer a wide range of materials for education, reflection and campaigning for peace. Pax Christi also produces material for parishes each year to encourage support for Peace Sunday (the Pope's World Peace Message), celebrated on the 2nd Sunday in Ordinary Time.

National President Archbishop Malcolm McMahon OP **Director** Theresa Alessandro
St Joseph's, Watford Way NW4 4TY Tel: 020 8203 4884 Email: info@paxchristi.org.uk
Web: www.paxchristi.org.uk

PONTIFICAL MISSIONARY UNION (PMU)

Part of the Missio network, the Pontifical Mission Union (PMU) is responsible for encouraging all the faithful to have passion for mission and evangelisation. As Catholics we are encouraged to share the love of God through our words and actions with our global family.

National Office for Missio 23 Eccleston Square SW1V 1NU (Reg. Charity No. 1056651)
Tel: 020 7821 9755 Email: info@missio.org.uk **Web:** www.missio.org.uk

POPE'S WORLDWIDE PRAYER NETWORK

The Network (formerly the Apostleship of Prayer) is based with the Jesuit Community at St Ignatius church in Stamford Hill, where the National Director, Fr David Stewart SJ, is resident. Its renewal was mandated by Pope Benedict, then by Pope Francis. The 175 year-old ministry is active in almost 100 countries, inviting the faithful to pray the Monthly Intentions of the Holy Father. It offers the Daily Prayer Pathway, expanding the traditional Morning Offering, whilst the new 'Way of the Heart' renews the much-loved devotion to the Sacred Heart. All parishes are invited and encouraged to pray with the Pope. Office hours: Monday and Tuesday only.

PWPN National Office, 27 High Road N15 6ND Tel: 020 8442 5232 / 07432 591117
Email: prayernetwork@jesuit.org.uk **Twitter:** @PraywiththePope **Skype:** jdstewartsj

SECTION 6

PRAY AS YOU GO

Pray As You Go is a daily prayer session produced by Jesuits in Britain, designed to go with you wherever you go, to help you pray whenever you find time, but particularly whilst travelling to and from work, study, etc. Pray As You Go also provides audio retreats and extra Ignatian resources. Available as an app for iOS and Android, as a podcast, or online at **www.pray-as-you-go.org.**

PRISON ADVICE & CARE TRUST (FORMERLY THE BOURNE TRUST)

Pact is the national Catholic charity working to support prisoners, people with convictions and their families. We work in courts, prisons and in the community to support people to make a fresh start, and to minimise the harm that can be caused by imprisonment to people who have committed offences, on families and on communities. If you or someone you know needs support, call free, confidential helpline **0808 808 3444**, email **helpline@prisonadvice.org.uk** or fill in the webform at **prisonadvice.org.uk/forms/contact-our-helpline**. If interested in the criminal justice system, please get in touch for information about volunteer opportunities.
29 Peckham Road SE5 8UA Tel: 020 7735 9535 Email: ParishAction@prisonadvice. org.uk Web: www.prisonadvice.org.uk

PROJECT 2030

Our group enables Catholics in their 40s to get together at a social and spiritual level. Events include Masses, retreats, walks, meals, museum visits, pilgrimages, holidays, and other opportunities to meet up together.
National office: St John's, 266 Wellington Road North, Heaton Chapel SK4 2QR Contact Rev Hugh Hanley SCJ **Email: project2030@btinternet.com**

RETROUVAILLE

A lifeline for troubled marriages, helping heal and renew marriages in distress. For couples who are finding it difficult to communicate; who argue about everything or live in silence; who feel alone, lonely and distant; who may think separation and divorce are their only options.
Tel: 07887 296983 / 07973 380443 Email: info@retrouvaille.org.uk Web: www.retrouvaille.org.uk

ST BARNABAS SOCIETY (SUCCESSOR TO THE CONVERTS' AID SOCIETY)

For the assistance of needy former clergy and religious received into the Catholic Church.
Secretary Fr Paul Martin **Windsor House, Heritage Gate, East Point Business Park, Sandy Lane West, Oxford OX4 6L Tel: 01865 513377 Email: directorstbarnabas@gmail.com Web: www.StBarnabasSociety.org.uk**

ST FRANCIS LEPROSY GUILD

The Guild was founded in 1895 to help those suffering from leprosy. It supports leprosy hospitals, treatment centres, rehabilitation centres and residential care for people suffering from or affected by leprosy in 23 countries, as well as projects to eradicate leprosy one community at a time. **President** Michael Forbes Smith **Hon. Secretary** Sr Helen McMahon FMM

73 St Charles Square W10 6EJ Tel: 020 8969 1345 Email: enquiries@stfrancisleprosy.org.
Web: www.stfrancisleprosy.org.

ST FRANCIS OF ASSISI CATHOLIC RAMBLERS CLUB

Organises Sunday walks in London and the Home Counties throughout the year. Rambles on additional days and further afield are occasionally provided, plus other social activities. **Contact** Antoinette Adkins **Tel: 020 8769 3643** or **Email: antoinette_adkins2000@yahoo.co.uk** for an information pack or for further details go to **www.stfrancisramblers.ukwalkers.com**

ST JOSEPH'S SOCIETY (FORMERLY THE AGED POOR SOCIETY)

Provides accommodation for elderly Catholics in need and of limited means.
Secretary S Dolan **St Joseph's Almshouse, 42 Brook Green W6 7BW**
Tel: 020 7603 9817 Email: stjosephssociety@yahoo.co.uk

ST VINCENT DE PAUL SOCIETY

The St Vincent de Paul Society (SVP) is an international Christian society, Catholic in character and origin. The Society's mission is to bear witness to Christ's love and to put his teaching into practice. With mutual support, friendship and encouragement, members seek to reach out and extend their commitment through person-to-person care for those disadvantaged, neglected or in need. They seek to identify the causes of need, provide items of furniture, clothing and food where appropriate and offer the hand of friendship. In these ways members aim to develop their own spiritual lives, strengthening their own faith and deepening their love of God and their neighbour.
Contact St Vincent de Paul Society **Romero House, 55 Westminster Bridge Road SE1 7JB**
Tel: 020 7703 3030 Email: info@svp.org.uk Web: www.svp.org.uk

ST VINCENT'S FAMILY PROJECT

The Project provides direct support to families in Westminster and beyond. Family Space supports 130+ families, offering free accredited parenting programmes, Drop-In, Crèche, Speech & Language assessment, Specialised Advice & Healthy Living classes. In addition, Creative Arts Therapy, via Art, Drama and Dance & Movement provides for 28+ local children experiencing emotional difficulties. Our 40+ Volunteering and Student Intern opportunities are via the Volunteer Space programme. Our six Vincentian values are: being respectful, inspired, travellers together, professional, holistic and compassionate.
St Vincent's Family Project, Methodist Central Hall, Storey's Gate
SW1H 9NH Tel: 020 7654 5351 Email: info@svfp.org.uk Web: www.svfp.org.uk

SECULAR CLERGY COMMON FUND

Secretary Michael O'Shea **St Mary's Cemetery, 679-681 Harrow Road NW10 5NU**
Tel: 020 8969 1145

SECULAR CLERGY NEW COMMON FUND

Chief Administrator Mgr Canon Nicholas Rothon **Tel: 020 8852 5420**
Diocesan Representative Fr Graham Stokes **Tel: 020 8868 7531**

SECTION 6

SECULAR FRANCISCAN ORDER

St Francis of Assisi left us 'a Dream to dream and a Journey to challenge everyone'. All Franciscans are inspired by him to follow Christ. The Secular Franciscan Order belongs to this family. In their secular state, members permanently commit themselves to live the Gospel as Francis did, following his Rule approved by the Pope. The OFS is open to the laity and diocesan clergy. There are more than 850 Secular Franciscans in Great Britain. Gathering in fraternities, they strive to grow in the love of God and in peace with each other. In this way, they aspire to be faithful disciples of Christ.
Web: ofsgb.org

SION CENTRE FOR DIALOGUE & ENCOUNTER

A centre for study and growth in mutual understanding between Christians and Jews, as well as other faiths and cultures. As a place to listen, learn, reflect and respect we offer a regular programme of courses and lectures, as well as times for reflection and prayer. Our specialist library has staff available to assist with research. Outside groups also use our facilities for their own seminars, training and meetings. The Centre is run by the Sisters of Our Lady of Sion.
34 Chepstow Villas W11 2QZ Tel: 020 7313 8286
Email: sioncentrefordialogue@gmail.com Web: https://sioncentre.org/

SOCIETY OF CATHOLIC ARTISTS

Aims to encourage high standards in Church art, to assist prospective patrons in the selection of suitable artists and craftsmen and to provide fellowship to those who have the arts and Catholicism in common.
Email: mj.sibtain@virgin.net Web: www.catholicartists.co.uk

SOCIETY OF OUR LADY OF LOURDES

To promote devotion to Our Lady, organise services and pilgrimages and assist sick pilgrims, financially and otherwise, to go to Lourdes. c/o Church of the Immaculate Heart of Mary, Botwell Lane, Hayes UB3 2AB Tel: 020 8848 9833 Fax: 020 8848 9844
Email: enquiries@soll-lourdes.com Web: www.soll-lourdes.com

SOCIETY OF ST AUGUSTINE OF CANTERBURY

Promotion and advancement of the Roman Catholic religion in England and Wales, principally through assistance in the maintenance of Archbishop's House, Westminster.
Secretary Richard Collyer-Hamlin 77 Gibbon Road, Kingston upon Thames, Surrey KT2 6AE
Tel: 07970 401731 Email: richardcollyerhamlin@hotmail.com
Web: www.staugustineofcanterbury.org.uk

SOCIETY OF ST GREGORY

The national Catholic society promoting understanding, active participation and good practice in the celebration of the liturgy. It organises summer schools, lectures and study for all who are engaged in liturgy and music. The journal Music and Liturgy (available by subscription) contains articles, news, reviews and a practical liturgy planner.

Diocesan representative John Ainslie **76 Great Bushey Drive N20 8QL Tel: 020 8445 5724**
Email: john.ainslie@ssg.org.uk **Web:** www.ssg.org.uk

SOCIETY OF ST JOHN CHRYSOSTOM

Founded in 1926 to encourage greater knowledge, understanding and appreciation of the tradition of the Eastern Churches, to promote Catholic-Orthodox unity and to support the Eastern Catholic Churches. Publishes *Chrysostom* three times a year.
Email: johnchrysostom@btinternet.com **Web:** www.orientalelumen.org.uk
President Cardinal Vincent Nichols, Archbishop of Westminster
Chair Fr Mark Woodruff **Tel: 07710 024505 Email: as above**
Membership & General Enquiries Mrs Ola Stayne **22 Esher Avenue, Walton on Thames KT12 2TA** Email: miss_ola0127@yahoo.pl

SOCIETY OF ST PETER THE APOSTLE (SPA)

Part of the Missio network, the Society of St Peter the Apostle trains the Church leaders of tomorrow, bringing the love of Christ to vulnerable communities, and passing on the gift of faith to future generations in over 157 countries around the world. Every year Missio's SPA supports the training of 30,000 future priests and 11,000 religious sisters in the mission dioceses. Only SPA, as the Pope's own charity, has this unique role throughout the world.
Diocesan Director for Missio Fr Philip Knights **Email:** philipknights@rcdow.org.uk
National Office for Missio 23 Eccleston Square SW1V 1NU (Reg. Charity No. 1056651)
Tel: 020 7821 9755 Email: spa@missio.org.uk **Web:** www.missio.org.uk

STELLA MARIS (APOSTLESHIP OF THE SEA)

Stella Maris (Apostleship of the Sea) is the official maritime agency of the Catholic Church in Great Britain. It is a registered charity (no. 1069833) reliant on the annual Sea Sunday appeal and donations to sustain its ministry. Ninety percent of world trade is carried by ship; however, seafarers often work in dangerous conditions suffering loneliness, deprivation and even exploitation. Stella Maris (AoS) deploys chaplains and ship visitors who welcome merchant seafarers to our shores and provides for their pastoral and practical needs – regardless of creed or nationality. Catholic seafarers are also given the opportunity to receive the sacraments. In addition, we provide chaplains on board cruise ships, work to maintain seafarers' centres inside ports, and collaborate with industry bodies to speak up for seafarers' rights. Stella Maris (AoS) relies on a network of valued contacts and volunteers to sustain its development.
Director Martin Foley **Stella Maris (AoS), 39 Eccleston Square W1V 1BX**
Email: info@apostleshipofthesea.org.uk **Web:** www.apostleshipofthesea.org.uk

TEAMS (EQUIPES NOTRE-DAME)

International movement for married couples of all ages whose purpose is to help couples live fully the Sacrament of Marriage. Groups of 4-6 couples, with a chaplain or spiritual advisor, meet monthly in each others' homes to support, pray and discuss Scripture. There are over 13,500 such Teams around the world.
Email: info@teamsgb.org.uk **Web:** www.teamsgb.org.uk

SECTION 6

THINKING FAITH

The online journal of the Jesuits in Britain. Articles, film reviews and book reviews to help you think about your faith and think, through your faith, about the world. Visit **www.thinkingfaith.org** to see latest content, search the archive and subscribe to regular email alerts.

114 Mount Street W1K 3AH Tel: 020 7499 0285 Email: editor@thinkingfaith.org

UNION OF CATHOLIC MOTHERS

National organisation for the preservation of the family and sanctification of the home.
Diocesan President Mrs Iona De Souza **47 Redfern Avenue, Whitton TW4 5NA**
Tel: 020 8894 2366 Email: ionadesouza@aol.com
Spiritual Director Fr Michael Johnston **Email: michaeljohnston@rcdow.org.uk**

VINCENTIAN VOLUNTEERS

A challenging and fulfilling Gap Year in the UK for 18-35 year olds of any nationality, living in small communities serving people who are vulnerable, in the spirit of St Vincent de Paul.
Contact Marion Osuide **St Matthew's Presbytery, Worsley Road, Eccles, Manchester M30 8BL Tel: 07708 314996 Email: marion@vincentianvolunteers.org.uk**
Web: www.vincentianvolunteers.org.uk

YOUNG CHRISTIAN WORKERS & IMPACT

A movement of apostolic formation, for young people between 13 and 30. Through a programme of enquiry in small groups in parishes and schools, YCW educates and trains young people for their mission of Christian service in everyday life. It enables them to become apostles to other young people and prepares them for the responsibilities of adult Christian life. YCW also produces educative enquiry discussion material and arranges numerous training events, including residential weekends.
Contact YCW HQ **St Anthony's Presbytery, Eleventh Street, Trafford Park, Manchester M17 1JF Tel: 0161 872 6017 Email: info@ycwimpact.com**
Web: www.ycwimpact.com

YOUTH 2000

Seeks to enable young people to encounter Jesus Christ, at the heart of the Catholic Church. This is primarily through weekend Prayer Festivals, where young people are introduced to the essentials of the Catholic faith: Mass, Eucharistic Adoration, Confession, Scripture and Devotion to Our Lady. These are opportunities to build friendships, experience God's love, receive the grace of conversion and begin living anew the christian life. **Charity No. 1000371**
Contact Youth 2000 **Pilgrim Bureau, Friday Market Place, Walsingham NR22 6EG**
Email: info@youth2000.org Web: http://youth2000.org

WORLD APOSTOLATE OF FATIMA

A Public Association of the Faithful with Pontifical Right, which promotes Our Lady's call to live the gospel more profoundly through prayer (daily Holy Rosary), penance, sanctification of one's daily duties in a spirit of sacrifice, reparation through the Five First Saturdays devotion and consecration by wearing the Brown Scapular. Every year (mostly in July), a week-long National Pilgrimage to Fatima is organised. **National President** Jerry Rivera
42 Blenheim Gardens, Kingston upon Thames KT2 7BW Tel: 07786 487557
Email: rivers72uk@gmail.com Web: www.worldfatima-englandwales.org.uk
Diocesan Spiritual Director Fr Richard Nesbitt **The Catholic Presbytery, Our Lady of Fatima Church, Commonwealth Avenue W12 7QR Email: whitecity@rcdow.org.uk**

WORLD COMMUNITY FOR CHRISTIAN MEDITATION

Promotes the prayer of Christian meditation as taught by John Main, monk of Ealing Abbey, simple practical wisdom that brings the truths of faith alive in our own experience.
Lido Centre, 63 Mattock Lane W13 9LA Tel: 020 8280 2283
Email: uk@wccm.org Web: www.wccm.org / www.christianmeditation.org.uk

OTHER USEFUL ADDRESSES

Catholic Communications Network
39 Eccleston Square SW1V 1BX Tel: 020 7901 4800 Email: ccn@cbcew.org.uk

Catholic Safeguarding Advisory Service (CSAS)
39 Eccleston Square SW1V 1BX Tel: 020 7901 1920 Email: admin@csas.uk.net
Web: www.csas.uk.net

Catholic Spirituality Network (CSN, formerly CNRS, NRM)
A national network of individuals and groups including prayer guides, spiritual companions, chaplains, Retreat Centre teams, pastoral workers and clergy. We are the Catholic member group of the Ecumenical Retreat Association. We produce two newsletters a year and organize an annual conference, open to all, and day events around the country.
Catholic Spirituality Network (CSN), c/o St George's Cathedral, Westminster Bridge Road SE1 7HY Tel: 07756 864754
Email: catholicspiritualitynetwork@gmail.com Web: www.csn.retreats.org.uk

Churches Together in England
27 Tavistock Square WC1H 9HH Tel: 020 7529 8131

Independent Catholic News - the UK's daily on-line Catholic news service
Tel: 020 7267 3616 Web: www.indcatholicnews.com

Jesuit Refugee Service [JRS-UK]
Hurtado Jesuit Centre, 2 Chandler Street E1W 2QT Tel: 020 7488 7310
Fax: 020 7488 7329 Email: uk@jrs.net

Mary's Meals
Sets up school feeding programmes in some of the world's poorest communities where poverty and hunger prevent children from gaining an education. Currently 1,504,571 children are fed one good nutritious meal every school day in countries such as Malawi, Liberia, Haiti, India, South Sudan, Lebanon and Syria.
13 Hippodrome Place W11 4SF Tel: 020 7221 5745
Email: London.admin@marysmeals.org   Web: www.marysmeals.org.uk

National Catholic Safeguarding Commission (NCSC)
39 Eccleston Square SW1V 1BX Tel: 07779 984942
Email: admin@catholicsafeguarding.org.uk Web: www.catholicsafeguarding.org.uk

The Retreat Association
PO Box 1130, Princes Risborough, Bucks HP22 9RP
Tel: 01494 569056 Email: info@retreats.org.uk Web: www.retreats.org.uk

Society for the Protection of Unborn Children (SPUC)
Our principal aims and objectives are:
· To affirm, defend and promote the existence and value of human life from the moment of conception until natural death;
· To defend and protect human life generally and in particular, whether born or unborn;
· To defend, assist and promote the life and welfare of mothers during pregnancy and of their children from the time of conception up to, during and after birth.
SPUC pursues these aims through engaging in political lobbying and campaigns, educating young people and the public, publishing academic research, fighting legal battles, and through other forms pro-life work.
SPUC, Unit B, 3 Whitacre Mews, Stannary Street SE11 4AB
Tel: 020 7091 7091 Email: information@spuc.org.uk

women@thewell
Provides services for the most vulnerable women caught up in multiple cycles of abuse, particularly those involved in street-based prostitution and those who struggle with substance abuse.
54/55 Birkenhead Street WC1H 8BB Tel: 020 7520 1710
Email: info@watw.org.uk Web: www.watw.org.uk

Section 7

THE CYCLE OF PRAYER

The liturgical year has been divided into six periods. We are asked to use the intentions during the current period, both corporately and in personal prayer, as well as on specific Days of Prayer. Parish Priests are asked to make the Cycle known by displaying and distributing copies in their churches, and to issue a reminder when a new period of the Cycle begins. When a Day of Special Prayer occurs on a Sunday, it is sufficient to announce the Day at the beginning of Mass and to include a suitable petition in the Universal Prayer. An introductory leaflet and leaflets for the seasons as well as model intercessions are available on the Bishops' Conference Liturgy Office website: **www.liturgyoffice.org.uk** .

ADVENT/CHRISTMAS 2019

Intentions: Openness to the Word of God; Expectant Mothers.

Bible Sunday	Sunday 8 December	2nd Sunday of Advent
Expectant Mothers	especially on 22 December	4th Sunday of Advent

ORDINARY TIME: TO SPRING 2020

Intentions: Peace on Earth; Christian Unity; The Sick and Those who care for them; Victims of Trafficking and Those who work to combat it; Racial Justice; The Unemployed.

Octave of Prayer for Christian Unity		18 – 25 January
Peace Day	Sunday 19 January	2nd Sunday in O.T.
Day for Victims of Trafficking	Saturday 8 February	St Josephine Bakhita
World Day for the Sick	Tuesday 11 February	Our Lady of Lourdes
Racial Justice Day	Sunday 9 February	3 Sundays before Lent 1
Europe	Friday 14 February	Ss Cyril and Methodius
Day for the Unemployed	Sunday 23 February	Sunday before Lent 1

LENT 2020

Intentions: Candidates for the Sacraments (especially on the Sundays of Lent); Women; The Needy and Hungry of the World; Penitents and Wanderers.

World Day of Prayer	Friday 6 March	1st Friday in March
Lent Fast Day	Friday 6 March	Friday, 1st Week of Lent
Day of Prayer for Victims and Survivors of Sexual Abuse	Friday 3 April	Friday, 5th Week of Lent

EASTER 2020

Intentions: New Members of the Church; Vocations; The Right Use of the Media; The Church; Human Work.

Europe	Monday 29 April	St Catherine of Siena
Human Work	Friday 1 May	St Joseph the Worker
World Day of Prayer for Vocations	Sunday 3 May	4th Sunday of Easter
World Communications Day	Sunday 24 May	7th Sunday of Easter
The Church	Sunday 31 May	Pentecost

SECTION 7: CYCLE OF PRAYER

ORDINARY TIME: SUMMER 2020 (until September)

Intentions: A Deeper Understanding between Christians and Jews; Those who suffer Persecution, Oppression and Denial of Human Rights; Europe; Human Life; Seafarers.

Day for Life	Sunday 21 June	3rd Sunday in June
Those who suffer persecution	Monday 22 June	Ss John Fisher and Thomas More
Europe	Saturday 11 July	St Benedict
Sea Sunday	Sunday 12 July	2nd Sunday in July
Europe	Thursday 23 July	St Bridget of Sweden
Europe	Sunday 9 August	St Teresa Benedicta of the Cross

ORDINARY TIME: AUTUMN 2020 (September to OLJC, King of the Universe)

Intentions: Migrants and Refugees; Students and Teachers; The Spread of the Gospel; The Harvest; The Fruits of Human Work, and the Reverent Use of Creation; Justice and Peace in the World; All Victims of War; Young People; Prisoners and their Families.

The Care of Creation	Tuesday 1 September	1 September
Education Day	Sunday 13 September	2nd Sunday in September
Home Mission Day	Sunday 20 September	3rd Sunday in September
The Harvest	Sunday 27 September, or whenever harvest festivals are held	Sunday 22–28 September,
Migrants and Refugees	Sunday 27 September	Last Sunday in September
Harvest Fast Day	Friday 2 October	1st Friday in October
Prisons Week	11-17 October	2nd Week in October
World Mission Day	Sunday 18 October	penultimate Sunday in October
Remembrance Day	Sunday 8 November	2nd Sunday in November
World Day of the Poor	Sunday 15 November	33rd Sunday in O.T.
Youth Day	Sunday 22 November	Christ the King

ADVENT/CHRISTMAS 2020

Intentions: Openness to the Word of God; Migrants and Refugees; Expectant Mothers.

Migrants' Day	Thursday 3 December	St Francis Xavier
Bible Sunday	Sunday 6 December	2nd Sunday of Advent
Expectant Mothers	especially on 20 December	4th Sunday of Advent

Dated Days of Prayer are also repeated against the relevant date; the symbol § indicates a reference to the Cycle of Prayer.

THE HOLY FATHER'S PRAYER INTENTIONS 2019/20

DECEMBER 2019
Evangelisation - That every country determine to take the necessary measures to make the future of the very young, especially those who suffer, a priority.

JANUARY 2020
Evangelisation - Promotion of World Peace: We pray that Christians, followers of other religions, and all people of goodwill may promote peace and justice in the world.

FEBRUARY 2020
Universal - Listen to the Migrants' Cries: We pray that the cries of our migrant brothers and sisters, victims of criminal trafficking, may be heard and considered.

MARCH 2020
Evangelisation - Catholics in China: We pray that the Church in China may persevere in its faithfulness to the Gospel and grow in unity.

APRIL 2020
Universal - Freedom from Addiction: We pray that those suffering from addiction may be helped and accompanied.

MAY 2020
Evangelisation - For Deacons: We pray that deacons, faithful in their service to the Word and the poor, may be an invigorating symbol for the entire Church.

JUNE 2020
Evangelisation - The Way of the Heart: We pray that all those who suffer may find their way in life, allowing themselves to be touched by the Heart of Jesus.

JULY 2020
Universal - Our Families: We pray that today's families may be accompanied with love, respect and guidance.

AUGUST 2020
Universal - The Maritime World: We pray for all those who work and live from the sea, among them sailors, fishermen and their families.

SEPTEMBER 2020
Universal - Respect for the Planet's Resources: We pray that the planet's resources will not be plundered, but shared in a just and respectful manner.

SECTION 7: HOLY FATHER'S PRAYER INTENTIONS

Special Collections

OCTOBER 2020

Evangelisation - The Laity's Mission in the Church: We pray that by the virtue of baptism, the laity, especially women, may participate more in areas of responsibility in the Church.

NOVEMBER 2020

Universal - Artificial Intelligence: We pray that the progress of robotics and artificial intelligence may always serve humankind.

DECEMBER 2020

Evangelisation - For a life of prayer: We pray that our personal relationship with Jesus Christ be nourished by the Word of God and a life of prayer.

SPECIAL COLLECTIONS 2020

Collection	Announce	Collect	Send to
Racial Justice *	2 Feb	9 Feb	CaTEW via Finance, Vaughan House
Cardinal's Lenten Appeal ****	23 Feb	During Lent	Finance, Vaughan House
CAFOD Family Fast Day * (Friday 6 Mar)	1 Mar	8 Mar	CAFOD, Romero House, 55 Westminster Bridge Road SE1 7JB
Holy Places ** (Good Friday)	5 Apr	10 Apr	Finance, Vaughan House
Priest Training Fund ****	26 Apr	3 May	Finance, Vaughan House
Catholic Communications Network **	17 May	24 May	CaTEW via Finance, Vaughan House
Day for Life ***	14 Jun	21 Jun	CaTEW Finance Department, CBCEW, 39 Eccleston Square SW1V 1BX
Peter's Pence **	21 Jun	28 Jun	Finance, Vaughan House
Apostleship of the Sea ***	5 Jul	12 Jul	Apostleship of the Sea, 39 Eccleston Square SW1V 1PX
Catholic Education Service *	6 Sep	13 Sep	Finance, Vaughan House
Home Mission Appeal ***	13 Sep	20 Sep	CaTEW via Finance, Vaughan House
CAFOD Harvest Fast Day * (Friday 2 Oct)	27 Sep	4 Oct	CAFOD, Romero House, 55 Westminster Bridge Road SE1 7JB
World Mission Sunday **	11 Oct	18 Oct	Missio, 23 Eccleston Square SW1V 1NU
Sick & Retired Priests ****	1 Nov	8 Nov	Finance, Vaughan House
Missionary Orders Annual Appeal *		Any time	Society of African Missions

* Optional
** Mandatory, Holy See
*** Mandatory, CBCEW
****Mandatory, Diocesan

LITURGICAL INFORMATION

Universal Calendar

Announcements from the Congregation for Divine Worship:

(1) The celebrations of St John XXIII, Pope, and St John Paul II, Pope, (http://www.liturgyoffice.org.uk/Calendar/National/JPII-E.pdf) become Optional Memorials on 11 October and 22 October respectively. St John Paul II therefore appears no longer in the list for the National Calendar.

(2) St Mary Magdalene, hitherto celebrated as an Obligatory Memorial, is now kept as a Feast. Texts for Mass and the Office remain as hitherto, except for a new Preface, which will receive *Confirmatio* in English translation in due course.

(3) The Obligatory Memorial of the Blessed Virgin Mary, Mother of the Church, with Proper Readings (http://www.liturgyoffice.org.uk/Calendar/Sanctoral/May.shtml#MMC), is now celebrated on the Monday after Pentecost.

(4) The Optional Memorial of St Paul VI, Pope, is celebrated on 29 May (http://www.liturgyoffice.org.uk/Calendar/Sanctoral/May.shtml#May29).

Variations from the Universal Calendar

Where no indication of rank is given, the celebration is an Optional Memorial.

(1) National

Proper prayers are found in the Proper of Saints in the Roman Missal; readings are taken from the appropriate Common in the Lectionary.

12 January	St Aelred of Rievaulx	
19 January	St Wulstan, Bishop	
14 February	**Ss Cyril, Monk and Methodius, Bishop, Patrons of Europe**	Feast
1 March	**St David, Bishop, Patron of Wales**	Feast
17 March	**St Patrick, Bishop, Patron of Ireland**	Feast
21 April	St Anselm, Bishop & Doctor	
23 April	**St George, Martyr, Patron of England**	Solemnity
24 April	St Adalbert, Bishop & Martyr	
	St Fidelis of Sigmaringen, Priest & Martyr	
29 April	**St Catherine of Siena, Virgin & Doctor, Patron of Europe**	Feast
4 May	**The English Martyrs**	Feast
19 May	St Dunstan, Bishop *(in Westminster, observed on 3 February)*	
25 May	St Bede the Venerable, Priest & Doctor	Memorial
27 May	**St Augustine of Canterbury**	Feast
5 June	St Boniface, Bishop & Martyr	Memorial
9 June	St Columba, Abbot	
16 June	St Richard of Chichester, Bishop	
20 June	St Alban, Protomartyr	

22 June	Ss John Fisher, Bishop,	
	and Thomas More, Martyrs	Feast
23 June	St Etheldreda (Audrey), Abbess	
1 July	St Oliver Plunkett, Bishop & Martyr	
11 July	**St Benedict, Abbot, Patron of Europe**	Feast
23 July	**St Bridget, Religious, Patron of Europe**	Feast
9 August	**St Teresa Benedicta of the Cross**	
	(Edith Stein), Virgin & Martyr,	
	Patron of Europe	Feast
26 August	Blessed Dominic of the Mother	
	of God, Priest	
30 August	Ss Margaret Clitherow, Anne Line	
	and Margaret Ward, Martyrs	
31 August	St Aidan, Bishop, and the Saints of Lindisfarne	
3 September	**St Gregory the Great, Pope & Doctor**	Feast
4 September	St Cuthbert, Bishop	
19 September	St Theodore of Canterbury, Bishop *(in Westminster, observed on 3 February)*	
24 September	Our Lady of Walsingham	Memorial
9 October	St John Henry Newman	
10 October	St Paulinus of York, Bishop	
12 October	St Wilfrid, Bishop	
13 October	St Edward the Confessor	
26 October	Ss Chad and Cedd, Bishops	
3 November	St Winifride, Virgin	
7 November	St Willibrord, Bishop	
16 November	St Edmund of Abingdon, Bishop	
	St Margaret of Scotland	
17 November	St Hilda, Abbess	
	St Hugh of Lincoln, Bishop	
	St Elizabeth of Hungary, Religious	
30 November	**St Andrew, Apostle, Patron of Scotland**	Feast
29 December	**St Thomas Becket, Bishop & Martyr**	
	Patron of the Parish Clergy	Feast

Thursday after Pentecost		
	Our Lord Jesus Christ, the Eternal High Priest	Feast
	(see www.liturgyoffice.org.uk/Calendar/Sanctoral/May.shtml#OLJC)	

(2) Diocesan

Proper prayers are found in the Diocesan Proper (either in booklet form or available online) or National Proper in the Missal; readings are taken from the appropriate Lectionary Common.

| 3 February | Ss Laurence, Dunstan, Theodore, Archbishops of Canterbury | Memorial |
| 19 April | St Alphege, Bishop | Memorial |

24 April	Ss Erkenwald and Mellitus, Bishops	Memorial
20 June	St Alban, Protomartyr	Memorial
27 June	St John Southworth, Priest & Martyr	Memorial
	(Solemnity in the Cathedral)	
1 July	Dedication of the Cathedral	Feast
	(Solemnity in the Cathedral)	
13 October	St Edward the Confessor	Feast
	(Solemnity in the City of Westminster)	
29 October	Blessed Martyrs of Douai College	Memorial
16 November	St Edmund of Abingdon, Bishop	Memorial

(3) Local

Each church celebrates as a Solemnity its Feast of Title, and, if it is consecrated, the Anniversary of Dedication. Falling on a Sunday of Ordinary Time or Sunday in the octave of Christmas they may replace the liturgy of that Sunday. On Sundays of Advent, Lent or Easter or on another Solemnity they are transferred to the following day. These celebrations may also, for pastoral reasons, be transferred to an ordinary Sunday or other suitable day.

(4) Holy Days of Obligation for England and Wales in 2020

By Prot. N.180/17 of 4 August 2017, the Congregation for Divine Worship approved the Bishops' Conference's request that the Epiphany be henceforth celebrated on 6 January, unless this falls on a Saturday or Monday, in which case it is celebrated on the Sunday. The Ascension of the Lord will henceforth be celebrated on the Thursday in Week 6 of Eastertide.

Epiphany of the Lord	Sunday 5 January
Ascension of the Lord	Thursday 21 May
Corpus Christi	Sunday 14 June
Ss Peter and Paul	Sunday 28 June
Assumption BVM	Sunday 16 August
All Saints	Sunday 1 November
Christmas	Friday 25 December

(5) Calendar for the Extraordinary Form

The basic Calendar for the Extraordinary Form according to the Missale Romanum 1962 is given on the website of the Liturgy Office for England and Wales.

Following a request for information, the Bishops' Conference of England and Wales submitted a *dubium* to the Pontifical Commission *Ecclesia Dei*, which confirmed that in the Roman Rite, whichever Form of the liturgy is being celebrated, the Holy Days of Obligation are held in common. When the Holy Day is transferred to the Sunday, this is to be followed in both Ordinary and Extraordinary Form celebrations of Mass.

(6) Additional Days of Prayer

(1) The World Day of Prayer for the Care of Creation is kept on 1 September. Liturgical resources are available at www.liturgyoffice.org.uk/Calendar/Cycle/AutumnCP.shtml#Harvest.

(2) The Day of Prayer for Victims and Survivors of Abuse is kept on Friday of the 5th Week of Lent. The Pontifical Commission has produced resources on its website: http://www.protectionofminors.va/content/tuteladeiminori/en.html .

Choice of Mass to be celebrated

(1) Mass *ad libitum* in Ordinary Time

Where a Mass is to be celebrated *ad libitum*, the priest may choose:

from the Mass formula of the preceding Sunday or any one of the Sundays in Ordinary Time, even with some of the prayers taken from any another Sunday in Ordinary Time or from the prayers for Various Needs and Occasions; or

from the Mass of a Saint noted in the calendar as an optional memorial, or of a saint noted in the Martyrology for that day; or

from any Mass for the dead, although the formulas of the daily Mass for the dead may only be used if the Mass is actually said for the dead; or

a Mass for Various Needs; or

a Votive Mass.

(2) Occasions when Mass texts of the day may be replaced

	V1	V2	V3	D1	D2	D3
1. Solemnities of precept						
2. Sundays in the seasons of Advent, Lent and Easter	X	X	X	X	X	X
3. Holy Thursday, Easter Triduum						
4. Solemnities not of precept, All Souls						
5. Ash Wednesday, weekdays of Holy Week	X	X	X	✓	X	X
6. Days in the octave of Easter						
7. Sundays of Christmas and Sundays in Ordinary Time	✓	X	X	✓	X	X
8. Feasts						
9. Weekdays in the season of Advent from 17 to 24 December	✓	X	X	✓	✓	X
10. Days in the octave of Christmas						
11. Weekdays in the season of Lent						
12. Obligatory memorials						
13. Weekdays in the season of Advent to 16 December	✓	✓	X	✓	✓	X
14. Weekdays in the season of Christmas from 2 January						
15. Weekdays in the season of Easter						
16. Weekdays in Ordinary Time	✓	✓	✓	✓	✓	✓

✓ = permitted.

X = not permitted.

The table of rubrics inserted here governs when celebrations using the formularies from Ritual Masses, Masses for Various Needs and Occasions, Votive Masses, and Masses for the Dead are permitted within the liturgical year.

VI = Ritual Masses (General Instruction of the Roman Missal [hereafter, GIRM], no. 372). Masses for various needs and occasions and votive Masses, in cases of serious need or pastoral advantage, at the direction of the local Ordinary or with his permission (GIRM, no. 374).

V2 = Masses for various needs and occasions and votive Masses, in cases of serious need or pastoral advantage, at the discretion of the rector of the church or the priest celebrant (GIRM, no. 376).

V3 = Masses for various needs and occasions and votive Masses chosen by the priest celebrant in favour of the devotion of the people (GIRM, nn. 373, 375).

D1 = Funeral Mass (GIRM, no. 380).

D2 = Mass on the occasion of news of a death, final burial, or the first anniversary (GIRM, no. 381).

D3 = Daily Mass for the dead (GIRM, no. 381). When D1 and D2 are not permitted, neither is D3.

(3) Funeral Mass

A Funeral Mass may be celebrated on any day, except solemnities which are Holy Days of Obligation, Maundy Thursday, the Triduum, and the Sundays of Advent, Lent, and Eastertide.

(4) Prefaces of the Eucharistic Prayer

Solemnities, Feasts and certain other days are provided with Prefaces (either Proper or Common). These are indicated in the Calendar and are always used.

On Memorials either a seasonal Preface or an appropriate Preface of Saints may be used, according to the desire of the priest.

Prayers I and II for Reconciliation have their own Prefaces, but may be used with other appropriate Prefaces that refer to penance, e.g. the Prefaces of Lent.

Prayers I-IV for Use in Masses for Various Needs have their own Prefaces which may not be replaced.

(5) Choice of Eucharistic Prayer

Prayer I (The Roman Canon) may always be used, and particularly on days for which proper texts or insertions are provided; the feasts of apostles and saints mentioned in the Prayer; and on Sundays.

Prayer II is more appropriately used on weekdays and in special circumstances. Its own Preface may always be replaced by another. It is also suitable for a Mass for the Dead, with the optional formula for naming the deceased.

Prayer III is preferred for Sundays and feasts of the saints, who may be named within it. It also offers a formula for the dead, making it appropriate for occasions commemorating Christian Death.

Prayer IV is an integral text, with an invariable preface. It may only be used on Sundays and ferial days of Ordinary Time, when a Mass has no Proper Preface of its own.

Prayers I and II for Reconciliation and Prayers I-IV for Use in Masses for Various Needs may be used in association with the Votive and other Masses noted in the rubrics for each Prayer.

SECTION 7: LITURGICAL INFORMATION

Fulfilment of Obligation

The obligation of participating in the Mass is satisfied by assisting at Mass wherever it is celebrated in a Catholic rite, either on the Sunday or Holy Day itself or on the evening of the previous day. (Canon 1248.1)

Reception of the Eucharist a Second Time on the Same Day

It is permitted to receive Holy Communion twice on one day, provided this takes place during the celebration of Mass (Canon 917). This provision is to be observed, except in the case of Viaticum for the dying.

Eucharistic Fast

Whoever is to receive the blessed Eucharist is to abstain for at least one hour before Holy Communion from all food and drink, with the sole exception of water and medicine (Canon 919.1).

A priest who, on the same day, celebrates Mass twice or three times may consume something before the second or third celebration, even though there is not an hour's interval (Canon 919.2).

The elderly, and those who are suffering from some illness, as well as those who care for them, may receive the blessed Eucharist even if within the preceding hour they have consumed something (Canon 919.3).

Abstinence

(1) The Bishops of England and Wales recognise that simple acts of witness, accompanied by sincere prayer, can be a powerful call to faith. Traditional Catholic devotions such as making the sign of the cross with care and reverence, praying the Angelus and saying a prayer before and after meals, are straightforward actions which both dedicate certain moments in our daily lives to Almighty God and demonstrate our love and trust in His goodness and providence. If these devotions have been lost or even forgotten, particularly in our homes and schools, we have much to gain from learning and living them again.

(2) Every Friday is set aside as a special day of penitence, as it is the day of the suffering and death of the Lord. It is important that all the faithful again be united in a common, identifiable act of Friday penance since the virtue of penitence is best acquired as part of a common resolve and witness. The law of the Church requires Catholics on Fridays to abstain from meat, or some other form of food, or to observe some other form of penance laid down by the Bishops' Conference. The Bishops have decided that this penance be fulfilled simply by abstaining from meat and by uniting this to prayer. Those who cannot or choose not to eat meat as part of their normal diet should abstain from some other food of which they regularly partake. This decision came into effect on Friday 16 September 2011.

(3) Re-emphasising the importance of penitence is but one of the responses the Bishops wish to make to the growing desire of people to deepen and give identity to the spiritual aspects of their lives. It is also clear that many of us forget our obligation to do penance on a Friday. On a Sunday our prayer is in thanksgiving to God for the new and eternal life brought to us by Christ's resurrection from the dead. On a Friday our prayer is in thanksgiving for the gift of the mortal life that we have been given; a life which Christ willingly sacrificed on the cross for our sake. A fitting prayer then, as part of our Friday penance, would be to ask Almighty God to turn

away all threats to mortal life. The act of abstinence itself can be offered consciously as a prayer for life and in reparation for sins against life. It can also be put at the service of others if we make a sacrifice and give the financial savings made from our abstention (or fasting) to charities which assist those who are poor or suffering. If we are unable to make that financial sacrifice, we can still perform a 'work of charity', an act of kindness and love to another person who is in need or suffering in some way.

(4) Canon 1251 states: 'Abstinence from eating meat or another food according to the prescriptions of the Conference of Bishops is to be observed on Fridays throughout the year unless they are solemnities; abstinence and fast are to be observed on Ash Wednesday and on the Friday of the Passion and Death of Our Lord Jesus Christ'.

Canon 1252 states: 'The law of abstinence binds those who have completed their fourteenth year. The law of fasting binds those who have attained their majority, until the beginning of their sixtieth year. Pastors of souls and parents are to ensure that even those who by reason of their age are not bound by the law of fasting and abstinence, are taught the true meaning of penance'.

Those under fourteen years of age, the sick, the elderly and frail, pregnant women, seafarers, manual workers according to need, guests at a meal who cannot excuse themselves without giving great offence to their hosts or causing friction, and those in other situations of moral or physical impossibility are not required to observe abstention from meat; in other words, we should act prudently.

(5) The Holy See has noted that the 'gravity' of the obligation applies to our intention to observe penance as a regular and necessary part of our spiritual lives as a whole. Therefore, the 'gravity' of the obligation does not relate to observing the specific act of penance (abstaining from meat) prescribed by the Conference of Bishops. The 'gravity' of the obligation applies to the intention to do penance during the prescribed penitential days and seasons of the Church's year. Failure to abstain from meat on a particular Friday then would not constitute a sin.

KEY TO THE CALENDAR

RANKS OF CELEBRATION
There are three ranks of celebration: Solemnity, Feast, Memorial. These are indicated in the calendar by the typeface used, thus:

SOLEMNITY   FEAST   Memorial

ABBREVIATIONS
+ indicates that attendance at Mass fulfils the Sunday or Holy Day obligation
Ps on the right of the page indicates the Week of the Psalter
§ indicates a reference to the Cycle of Prayer

CELEBRATION OF FIRST VESPERS
These are noted for Vigil Masses which have proper readings and/or prayers, for Solemnities and for Feasts falling on Sundays, which would otherwise not have First Vespers.
Solemnities and all Sundays other than Easter Day have First Vespers, unless these are impeded by Second Vespers of a higher-ranking Solemnity.

LITURGICAL COLOURS

B   Black
G   Green
P   Purple
R   Red
RP   Rose Pink
W   White

When the Saturday Mass of the Blessed Virgin Mary is celebrated in Ordinary Time, either White or Green vestments may be used.
When vestments of the appropriate colour are not available, White may always be substituted.

TABLE OF MOVEABLE FEASTS

	2020	2021	2022
Lectionary (Sunday/Weekday)	A/2	B/1	C/2
First Sunday of Advent	1 December 2019	29 November 2020	28 November 2021
Nativity of the Lord	25 December	25 December	25 December
Epiphany	5 January	6 January	6 January
Ash Wednesday	26 February	17 February	2 March
Easter Sunday	12 April	4 April	17 April
Ascension	21 May	13 May	26 May
Pentecost	31 May	23 May	5 June
Corpus Christi	14 June	6 June	19 June
Ss Peter and Paul	28 June	29 June	29 June
Assumption BVM	16 August	15 August	14 August
All Saints	1 November	31 October	1 November
First Sunday of Advent	29 November	28 November	27 November

- **Bold entries** denote Holydays of Obligation in England and Wales. The Epiphany, Ss Peter & Paul, the Assumption BVM and All Saints, falling on Saturday or Monday are transferred to the Sunday.
- Table supplied by CBCEW Liturgy Office for England and Wales: **www.liturgyoffice.org.uk**

DECEMBER 2019

LECTIONARY FOR SUNDAYS: YEAR A

ADVENT

Advent has a twofold character: as a season to prepare for Christmas, when Christ's first coming to us is remembered; and as a season when that remembrance directs the mind and heart to await Christ's Second Coming at the end of time. Advent is thus a period for devout and joyful expectation.

The playing of the organ and other musical instruments, and the decoration of the altar with flowers should be done in a moderate manner, as is consonant with the character of the season, without anticipating the full joy of the Nativity of the Lord. The same moderation should be observed in the celebration of Matrimony.

Eucharistic Prayer 4 is not used in this season.

NOVEMBER 2019

30 Sat evening	P	First Vespers (Divine Office Volume I)

DECEMBER 2019

1 Sun	P	+ 1st SUNDAY OF ADVENT *Ps Week 1* *Creed, Advent Preface 1 (and on following days)* Mass & Office of the day
2 Mon	P	Advent feria, First Week of Advent: Mass & Office of the day *The Alternative 1st Reading is used*
3 Tue	W	St Francis Xavier, Priest: Mass & Office of the Memorial
4 Wed	P W	Advent feria: Mass & Office of the day *or* St John Damascene, Priest & Doctor: Mass & Office of the Memorial
5 Thu	P	Advent feria: Mass & Office of the day
6 Fri	P W	Advent feria: Mass & Office of the day *or* *Friday abstinence* St Nicholas, Bishop: Mass & Office of the Memorial
7 Sat	W	St Ambrose, Bishop & Doctor: Mass & Office of the Memorial
evening	P	First Vespers

DECEMBER 2019

8 Sun	P	+ 2nd SUNDAY OF ADVENT Ps Week 2

8 Sun — P — + 2nd SUNDAY OF ADVENT   *Ps Week 2*
Creed, Advent Preface I
Mass & Office of the day, 2nd Vespers and
+ Evening Mass
§ Bible Sunday

9 Mon — W — **THE IMMACULATE CONCEPTION OF THE BLESSED VIRGIN MARY, Patron of the Diocese**
Gloria, Creed, Proper Preface
Mass & Office of the Solemnity

10 Tue — P / W — Advent feria, Second Week of Advent: Mass & Office of the Day *or*
Blessed Virgin Mary of Loreto: Mass & Office of the Memorial

11 Wed — P / W — Advent feria: Mass & Office of the day *or*
St Damasus I, Pope: Mass & Office of the Memorial

12 Thu — P / W — Advent feria: Mass & Office of the day *or*
Our Lady of Guadalupe: Mass & Office of the Memorial

13 Fri — R — St Lucy, Virgin & Martyr: Mass & Office of the Memorial   *Friday abstinence*

14 Sat — W — St John of the Cross, Priest & Doctor: Mass & Office of the Memorial   *Friday abstinence*

evening — RP or P — First Vespers

15 Sun — RP or P — + 3rd SUNDAY OF ADVENT (Gaudete Sunday)   *Ps Week 3*
Creed, Advent Preface I
Mass & Office of the day

16 Mon — P — Advent feria, Third Week of Advent: Mass & Office of the day

Memorials which occur on days between 17 and 31 December may be commemorated at Mass by using the collect of the saint in place of the collect of the day. In the Office of Readings the proper hagiographical reading and responsory may be added after the Patristic reading and responsory; the collect of the saint concludes the office. At Lauds and Vespers the antiphon (proper or common) and collect of the saint may be added after the collect of the day.

At Mass, proper texts and readings are given for the weekdays from 17-24 December, and these should be used instead of those indicated for the weekdays of the third or fourth week of Advent.

DECEMBER 2019

17 Tue	P	Advent feria: Mass & Office of 17 December	
		Advent Preface II (and on following days)	
18 Wed	P	Advent feria: Mass & Office of 18 December	
19 Thu	P	Advent feria: Mass & Office of 19 December	
20 Fri	P	Advent feria: Mass & Office of 20 December	*Friday abstinence*
21 Sat	P	Advent feria: Mass & Office of 21 December	
		(Alternative 1st Reading)	
		(St Peter Canisius, Priest & Doctor)	
evening	P	First Vespers: Magnificat antiphon of 21 December	

22 Sun   P   **+ 4th SUNDAY OF ADVENT**   *Ps Week 4*
Creed, Advent Preface II
Mass of the day; Office of the day, with readings, also Benedictus
& Magnificat antiphons of 22 December
(see Divine Office Vol I, page 154 ff)
§ Expectant Mothers
Announce Holy Day of Obligation

23 Mon	P	Advent feria: Mass & Office of 23 December	
		(St John of Kanty, Priest)	
24 Tue	P	Advent feria: Mass & Office of 24 December	

CHRISTMAS SEASON
After the annual celebration of the Paschal Mystery there is no more ancient feast day for the Church than the recalling of the memory of the Nativity of the Lord and of the mysteries of his first appearing. Eucharistic Prayer 4 is not used in this season.

evening   W / W   **First Vespers**
+ Proper Vigil Mass of Christmas precedes or follows
Gloria, Proper Readings (Short form Gospel), Creed, (kneel at Incarnatus), a Preface of the Nativity & Communicantes in the Roman Canon

For pastoral reasons, readings at the following Christmas Masses may be chosen from among all those provided for the Solemnity. It is appropriate that a Solemn Vigil be kept by celebrating the Office of Readings before the Mass during the Night. Compline is omitted by those attending that Mass.

DECEMBER 2019

	W	**+ Mass during the Night** *Gloria, Proper Readings, Creed (kneel at* Incarnatus), *a Preface of the Nativity & Communicantes in the Roman Canon*
25 Wed	W	**+ THE NATIVITY OF THE LORD (CHRISTMAS)** *Gloria, Proper Readings (Short form Gospel), Creed (kneel at* Incarnatus), *a Preface of the Nativity & Communicantes in the Roman Canon* **Mass & Office of the Solemnity** All priests may celebrate or concelebrate three Masses today, provided that they are celebrated at their proper time.
26 Thu	R	ST STEPHEN, The First Martyr *Gloria, Proper Readings, a Preface of the Nativity & Communicantes in the Roman Canon* **Mass, Lauds & Lesser Hours of St Stephen; Vespers of the Octave**
	R	*(In parishes dedicated to ST STEPHEN, The First Martyr, his Solemnity is observed:* *Gloria, 1st Reading Proper, 2nd Reading from the Common of Martyrs, Gospel Proper, Creed, a Preface of the Nativity & Communicantes in the Roman Canon,* **Second Vespers of the Solemnity)**
27 Fri	W	ST JOHN, Apostle & Evangelist *No Friday* *Gloria, Proper Readings, a Preface of the Nativity* *abstinence* *& Communicantes in the Roman Canon* **Mass, Lauds & Lesser Hours of St John; Vespers of the Octave**
	W	*(In parishes dedicated to ST JOHN, Apostle & Evangelist, his Solemnity is observed:* *Gloria, 1st Reading from the Proper of All Saints, 2nd Reading & Gospel Proper, Creed, a Preface of the Nativity & Communicantes in the Roman Canon,* **First & Second Vespers of the Solemnity)**
28 Sat	R	THE HOLY INNOCENTS, Martyrs *Gloria, Proper Readings, a Preface of the Nativity & Communicantes in the Roman Canon* **Mass, Lauds & Lesser Hours of the Holy Innocents**
	W	First Vespers
29 Sun	W	**+ THE HOLY FAMILY OF JESUS, MARY AND JOSEPH** *Ps Week 1* *Gloria, 1st and 2nd Readings, Gospel of Year A, Creed, a Preface of the Nativity & Communicantes in the Roman Canon* **Mass & Office of the Feast**
	R	*(In parishes dedicated to ST THOMAS BECKET, Bishop & Martyr, his Solemnity is observed:* *Gloria, 1st Reading from the Common of Martyrs, 2nd reading & Gospel proper, a Preface of the Nativity & Communicantes in the Roman Canon* **1st Vespers, Mass & Office of the Solemnity)**

DECEMBER 2019/JANUARY 2020

Announce Holy Day of Obligation

30 Mon	W	**6th DAY IN THE OCTAVE OF CHRISTMAS** *Gloria, a Preface of the Nativity & Communicantes in the Roman Canon* Mass & Office of the Octave
31 Tue	W	**7th DAY IN THE OCTAVE OF CHRISTMAS** *Gloria, a Preface of the Nativity & Communicantes in the Roman Canon* Mass & Office of the Octave (St Sylvester I, Pope)
evening	W	First Vespers

JANUARY 2020

1 Wed	W	**SOLEMNITY OF MARY, THE HOLY MOTHER OF GOD** THE OCTAVE DAY OF THE NATIVITY OF THE LORD *Gloria, Creed, Preface 1 of Blessed Virgin Mary & Communicantes in the Roman Canon* Mass & Office of the Solemnity

A Preface of the Nativity is used on weekdays of the Christmas season, unless other provision is made.

2 Thu	W	Ss Basil the Great and Gregory Nazianzen, Bishops & Doctors *Readings of 2 January* Mass & Office of the Memorial
3 Fri	W	Christmas feria *Friday abstinence* *First Collect, Readings of 3 January* Mass & Office of the Day *or*
	W	The Most Holy Name of Jesus: Mass & Office of the Memorial
4 Sat	W	Christmas feria *First Collect, Readings of 4 January* Mass & Office of the Day
evening	W W	First Vespers + Proper Vigil Mass of the Epiphany precedes or follows *Gloria, Epiphany Readings, Creed, Proper Preface & Communicantes of the Epiphany in the Roman Canon*

JANUARY 2020

5 Sun	W	**+ THE EPIPHANY OF THE LORD**

Gloria, Creed, Proper Preface & Communicantes of the Epiphany in the Roman Canon; an increased display of lights is recommended.
At today's Mass, after the Gospel, the announcement may be made of moveable feasts according to the formula given in the Roman Pontifical, on page 1247 of the Missale Romanum, editio typica tertia and page 1505 of the Roman Missal.
Mass & Office of the Solemnity

A Preface of the Nativity or of the Epiphany is used until the Christmas season ends, unless other provision is made.

6 Mon	W	Christmas feria	*Ps Week 2*
		Second Collect, Readings of 6 January	
		Mass & Office of the day	

7 Tue	W	Christmas feria
		Second Collect, Readings of 7 January
		Mass & Office of the day *or*
	W	St Raymond of Penyafort, Priest: **Mass & Office of the Memorial**

8 Wed	W	Christmas feria
		Second Collect, Readings of 8 January
		Mass & Office of the day

9 Thu	W	Christmas feria
		Second Collect, Readings of 9 January
		Mass & Office of the day

10 Fri	W	Christmas feria	*Friday abstinence*
		Second Collect, Readings of 10 January	
		Mass & Office of the day	

11 Sat	W	Christmas feria	*Friday abstinence*
		Second Collect, Readings of 11 January	
		Mass & Office of the day	

evening	W	First Vespers

12 Sun	W	**+ THE BAPTISM OF THE LORD**

Gloria, (Alternative Collect), 1st and 2nd Reading, Gospel of Year A, Creed, Proper Preface
Mass & Office of the Feast

Christmas Time ends.
LECTIONARY FOR SUNDAYS: YEAR A
WEEKDAY LECTIONARY: YEAR 2

Eucharistic Prayer 4 may be used in this Season
The choice of Masses which may be celebrated *ad libitum* is shown in the Liturgical Information on page 294.
On ferial days in Ordinary Time the Office of a saint included for that day in the Roman Martyrology may be celebrated. Occasional Votive Offices are permitted, although care to observe the four-week cycle of the Office should be maintained.

13 Mon	G	feria, First Week of Year 2:	Ps Week 1
		Mass ad lib; Office of the day *or*	
	W	St Hilary, Bishop & Doctor: Mass & Office of the Memorial	
14 Tue	G	feria: Mass ad lib; Office of the day	
15 Wed	G	feria: Mass ad lib; Office of the day	
16 Thu	G	feria: Mass ad lib; Office of the day	
17 Fri	W	St Anthony, Abbot:	*Friday abstinence*
		Mass & Office of the Memorial	

From 18-25 January the Octave of Prayer for Christian Unity takes place. A Mass for the Unity of Christians may be celebrated on any ferial day during the Octave.

18 Sat	G	feria: Mass ad lib; Office of the day *or*	
	W	Blessed Virgin Mary on Saturday: Mass & Office of the Memorial	
evening	G	First Vespers	
19 Sun	G	+ 2nd SUNDAY IN ORDINARY TIME	Ps Week 2
		Gloria, Creed, a Preface of Sundays in O.T.	
		Mass & Office of the day	
		§ Peace Day	
20 Mon	G	feria, Second Week of Year 2: Mass ad lib; Office of the day *or*	
	R	St Fabian, Pope & Martyr: Mass & Office of the Memorial *or*	
	R	St Sebastian, Martyr: Mass & Office of the Memorial	
21 Tue	R	St Agnes, Virgin & Martyr: Mass & Office of the Memorial	
22 Wed	G	feria: Mass ad lib; Office of the day *or*	
	R	St Vincent, Deacon & Martyr: Mass & Office of the Memorial	
23 Thu	G	feria: Mass ad lib; Office of the day	

JANUARY/FEBRUARY 2020

24 Fri	W	St Francis de Sales, Bishop & Doctor: *Friday abstinence* Mass & Office of the Memorial Anniversary of the Episcopal Ordination of Cardinal Vincent Nichols (1992). An intention may be included in the Universal Prayer and the Mass 'For the Bishop' (Roman Missal page 1306) may be celebrated.
25 Sat	W	THE CONVERSION OF ST PAUL THE APOSTLE *Gloria, (Alternative 1st Reading), Preface I of Apostles* Mass, Lauds & Lesser Hours of the Feast
evening	G	First Vespers
26 Sun	G	+ 3rd SUNDAY IN ORDINARY TIME (OF THE WORD OF GOD) *Ps Week 3* *Gloria, (Short form Gospel), Creed, a Preface of Sundays in O.T.* Mass & Office of the day
27 Mon	G W	feria, Third Week of Year 2: Mass ad lib; Office of the day *or* St Angela Merici, Virgin: Mass & Office of the Memorial
28 Tue	W	St Thomas Aquinas, Priest & Doctor: Mass & Office of the Memorial
29 Wed	G	feria: Mass ad lib; Office of the day
30 Thu	G	feria: Mass ad lib; Office of the day
31 Fri	W	St John Bosco, Priest: *Friday abstinence* Mass & Office of the Memorial

FEBRUARY 2020

1 Sat	G W	feria: Mass ad lib; Office of the day *or* Blessed Virgin Mary on Saturday: Mass & Office of the Memorial
evening	W	First Vespers
2 Sun	W	+ THE PRESENTATION OF THE LORD *Blessing of candles with Procession or Solemn Entry, no Penitential Act,* *Gloria, 1st and 2nd Reading, (Short form Gospel), Creed, Proper Preface* Mass & Office of the Feast Announce Optional Racial Justice Collection

FEBRUARY 2020

3 Mon	W	Ss Laurence, Dunstan and Theodore, Archbishops of Canterbury	Ps Week 4

3 Mon — **W** — Ss Laurence, Dunstan and Theodore, Archbishops of Canterbury *Ps Week 4 Diocesan*
see Diocesan Supplement Book or online
The blessing of St Blaise on throats may be given today.
Mass & Office of the Memorial

4 Tue — **G** — feria, Fourth Week of Year 2: Mass ad lib; office of the day

5 Wed — **R** — St Agatha, Virgin & Martyr: Mass & Office of the Memorial

6 Thu — **R** — St Paul Miki and Companions, Martyrs: Mass & Office of the Memorial

7 Fri — **G** — feria: Mass ad lib; Office of the day *Friday abstinence*

8 Sat — **G / W / W / W** — feria: Mass ad lib; office of the day *or*
St Jerome Emiliani: Mass & Office of the Memorial *or*
St Josephine Bakhita: Mass & Office of the Memorial *or*
Blessed Virgin Mary on Saturday: Mass & Office of the Memorial
§ Day for Victims of Trafficking and those who work to combat it

evening — **G** — First Vespers

9 Sun — **G** — + 5th SUNDAY IN ORDINARY TIME *Ps Week 1*
Gloria, Creed, a Preface of Sundays in O.T.
Mass & Office of the day
§ Racial Justice
Collection for Racial Justice

10 Mon — **W** — St Scholastica, Virgin: Mass & Office of the Memorial

11 Tue — **G** — feria, Fifth Week of Year 1: Mass ad lib; Office of the day *or*
Our Lady of Lourdes: Mass & Office of the Memorial
§ World Day for the Sick

12 Wed — **G** — feria: Mass ad lib; Office of the day

13 Thu — **G** — feria: Mass ad lib; Office of the day

14 Fri — **W** — Ss CYRIL, Monk & METHODIUS, Bishop, Patrons of Europe *Friday abstinence National*
Gloria, Proper Readings, Preface of Holy Pastors
Mass & Office of the Feast
§ Europe

15 Sat — **G / W** — feria: Mass ad lib; Office of the day *or*
Blessed Virgin Mary on Saturday: Mass & Office of the Memorial

FEBRUARY 2020

evening	G	First Vespers
16 Sun	G	**+ 6th SUNDAY IN ORDINARY TIME** *Ps Week 2* *Gloria, (Short form Gospel), Creed, a Preface of Sundays in O.T.* Mass & Office of the day
17 Mon	G W	feria, Sixth Week of Year 2: Mass & Office of the day *or* The Seven Holy Founders of the Servite Order: Mass & Office of the Memorial
18 Tue	G	feria: Mass ad lib; Office of the day
19 Wed	G	feria: Mass ad lib; Office of the day
20 Thu	G	feria: Mass ad lib; Office of the day
21 Fri	G W	feria: Mass ad lib; Office of the day *or* *Friday abstinence* St Peter Damian, Bishop & Doctor: Mass & Office of the Memorial
22 Sat	W	**THE CHAIR OF ST PETER THE APOSTLE** *Gloria, Preface I of Apostles* Mass, Lauds & Lesser Hours of the Feast
evening	G	First Vespers
23 Sun	G	**+ 7th SUNDAY IN ORDINARY TIME** *Ps Week 3* *Gloria, Creed, a Preface of Sundays in O.T.* Mass & Office of the day § Day for the Unemployed Announce Ash Wednesday, Day of Fast and Abstinence Announce Mandatory Diocesan Lenten Alms Appeal
24 Mon	G	feria, Seventh Week of Year 2: Mass ad lib; Office of the day
25 Tue	G	feria: Mass ad lib; Office of the day

LENT

The season of Lent is a preparation for the celebration of Easter. The liturgy prepares the catechumens for the celebration of the Paschal Mystery by the various stages of Christian initiation; it also prepares the faithful, who recall their baptism and do penance in preparation for Easter.

Memorials which occur on a weekday may only be commemorated at Mass by using the collect of the saint in place of the collect of the day. In the Office of Readings the proper hagiographical reading and responsory may be added after the Patristic reading and responsory; the collect of the saint concludes the office.

At Lauds and Vespers the antiphon (proper or common) and collect of the saint may be added after the collect of the day.

The *Alleluia* is always omitted, both in the Office and in Mass.

It is not permitted to adorn the altar with flowers, and the organ and other instruments may only be played for the purpose of sustaining the singing. An exception is made for *Laetare* Sunday, and for Solemnities and Feasts.

During the Lenten season the Apostles' Creed may suitably be used as an alternative when the Creed is appointed to be said.

For the celebration of marriage, the parish priest should alert spouses to the need to take account of the particular penitential character of this season.

Eucharistic Prayer 4 is not used in this Season; Eucharistic Prayers for Reconciliation may appropriately be used during Lent.
(Divine Office Volume II)

26 Wed	P	**ASH WEDNESDAY** *Penitential Act omitted, Blessing and distribution of ashes after the homily, Preface III or IV of Lent* *The ashes, according to custom, are from branches blessed the previous year. The blessing and distribution of ashes may take place outside Mass, in a Liturgy of the Word after the homily; the celebration then concludes with the Universal Prayer, Blessing and Dismissal.* **Mass & Office of the day; at Lauds, Pss and Canticle of Friday, Week 3 may be used**	*Fast &* *Abstinence* *Ps Week 4*

On ferial days of the Lenten season one of the four Lenten prefaces is used, unless other provision is made.

27 Thu	P	Lent feria: Mass & Office of the day	
28 Fri	P	Lent feria: Mass & Office of the day	*Friday abstinence*
29 Sat	P	Lent feria: Mass & Office of the day	
in Cathedral evening	P	3 pm Rite of Election (First Service) First Vespers	

MARCH 2020

1 Sun	P	+ 1st SUNDAY OF LENT *(Short form 2nd Reading), Creed, Preface of First Sunday of Lent* Mass & Office of the day	*Ps Week 1*
in Cathedral		3pm Rite of Election (Second Service) § Candidates for the Sacraments Announce Optional CAFOD Family Fast Day	

MARCH 2020

2 Mon	P	Lent feria: Mass & Office of the day
3 Tue	P	Lent feria: Mass & Office of the day
4 Wed	P	Lent feria: Mass & Office of the day (St Casimir)
5 Thu	P	Lent feria: Mass & Office of the day
6 Fri	P	Lent feria: Mass & Office of the day *Friday abstinence* § Family Fast Day § World Day of Prayer
7 Sat	P	Lent feria: Mass & Office of the day (Ss Perpetua & Felicity, Martyrs)
evening	P	First Vespers
8 Sun	P	+ 2nd SUNDAY OF LENT *Ps Week 2* *Creed, Preface of Second Sunday of Lent* Mass & Office of the day § Candidates for the Sacraments Collect Family Fast Day Offerings for CAFOD
9 Mon	P	Lent feria, Second Week of Lent: Mass & Office of the day (St Frances of Rome)
10 Tue	P	Lent feria: Mass & Office of the day
11 Wed	P	Lent feria: Mass & Office of the day
12 Thu	P	Lent feria: Mass & Office of the day
13 Fri	P	Lent feria: Mass & Office of the day *Friday abstinence* Anniversary of the Election of Pope Francis (2013). In England and Wales, by decision of the Bishops' Conference, this is observed on the Solemnity of Ss Peter and Paul, Sunday 28 June.
14 Sat	P	Lent feria: Mass & Office of the day
evening	P	First Vespers
15 Sun	P	+ 3rd SUNDAY OF LENT *Ps Week 3* *(Short form Gospel), Creed, Proper Preface* Mass & Office of the day

MARCH 2020		RCIA - First Scrutiny: the Ritual Mass (pages 1177-9), (Short form Gospel), Proper Preface (pages 260-1) and Insertions in the Eucharistic Prayer. § Candidates for the Sacraments
		The Gospel of the Samaritan Woman may be repeated on a ferial weekday, with 1st Reading and Psalm as in Year A of the Lectionary. The matching Preface and Communion Antiphon should also be used.
16 Mon	P	Lent feria, Third Week of Lent: Mass & Office of the day
17 Tue	W	ST PATRICK, Bishop, Patron of Ireland *National* *Gloria, Proper National Readings, Preface of Holy Pastors* Mass & Office of the Feast
18 Wed	P	Lent feria, Third Week of Lent: Mass & Office of the day (St Cyril of Jerusalem, Bishop & Doctor)
	W	First Vespers
19 Thu	W	**ST JOSEPH, Spouse of the Blessed Virgin Mary, Patron of the Diocese** *Gloria, Proper Readings (Alternative Gospel Reading), Creed, Preface of St Joseph* Mass & Office of the Solemnity
20 Fri	P	Lent feria: Mass & Office of the day *Friday abstinence*
21 Sat	P	Lent feria: Mass & Office of the day
		The Lenten discipline in the use of organ, other musical instruments and flowers does not apply to *Laetare* Sunday.
evening	RP or P	First Vespers
22 Sun	RP or P	+ 4th SUNDAY OF LENT (*Laetare* Sunday) *Ps Week 4* *(Short form Gospel), Creed, Proper Preface* Mass & Office of the day RCIA - Second Scrutiny: the Ritual Mass (pages 1179-80) with Year A Readings (Short form Gospel), Proper Preface (pages 270-1) and Insertions in the Eucharistic Prayer. § Candidates for the Sacraments

SECTION 7: LITURGICAL CALENDAR

MARCH 2020

The Gospel of the Man born Blind may be repeated on a ferial weekday, with 1st Reading and Psalm as in Year A of the Lectionary. The matching Preface and Communion Antiphon should also be used.

23 Mon	P	Lent feria, Fourth Week of Lent: Mass & Office of the day (St Turibius of Mogrovejo, Bishop)
24 Tue	P	Lent feria: Mass & Office of the day
	W	First Vespers

25 Wed	W	**THE ANNUNCIATION OF THE LORD** *Gloria, Proper Readings, Creed (kneel at Incarnatus), Proper Preface* Mass & Office of the Solemnity
26 Thu	P	Lent feria: Mass & Office of the day
27 Fri	P	Lent feria: Mass & Office of the day — *Friday abstinence*
28 Sat	P	Lent feria: Mass & Office of the day

The practice of covering crosses and images in the church may be observed. Crosses remain covered until the end of the celebration of the Lord's Passion on Good Friday; images until the beginning of the Easter Vigil.

evening	P	First Vespers

29 Sun	P	+ 5th SUNDAY OF LENT — *Ps Week 1* *(Short form Gospel), Creed, Proper Preface* Mass & Office of the day RCIA - Third Scrutiny: the Ritual Mass (pages 1180-1) with Year A Readings (Short form Gospel), Proper Preface (pages 281-2) and Insertions in the Eucharistic Prayer. § Candidates for the Sacraments

The Gospel of Lazarus may be repeated on a ferial weekday, with 1st Reading and Psalm as in Year A of the Lectionary. The matching Preface and Communion Antiphon should also be used.

30 Mon	P	Lent feria, Fifth Week of Lent: Mass & Office of the day *(Short form 1st Reading), Preface 1 of the Passion of the Lord (and on following days)*

MARCH/APRIL 2020

| 31 Tue | P | Lent feria: Mass & Office of the day |

APRIL 2020

| 1 Wed | P | Lent feria: Mass & Office of the day |

| 2 Thu | P | Lent feria: Mass & Office of the day |
| | | (St Francis of Paola, Hermit) |

3 Fri	P	Lent feria *Friday abstinence*
		Alternative Collect
		Mass & Office of the day
		§ Day of Prayer for the Victims and Survivors of Abuse

| 4 Sat | P | Lent feria |
| | | (St Isidore, Bishop & Doctor) |

HOLY WEEK

In Holy Week the Church celebrates the mysteries of salvation accomplished by Christ in the last days of his earthly life, from his messianic entry into Jerusalem, until his blessed Passion and glorious Resurrection. Lent continues until Maundy Thursday.

| evening | R | First Vespers |

| 5 Sun | R | **+ PALM SUNDAY OF THE PASSION OF THE LORD** |
| | | *Ps Week 2* |

Blessing of Palms and Procession or Solemn Entrance before the Principal Mass; the latter may be repeated or the Simple Entrance used before other Masses, Narrative of the Lord's Passion (Short form), Creed, Proper Preface
Mass & Office of the day
§ Candidates for the Sacraments
Announce Good Friday, Day of Fast and Abstinence
Announce Mandatory Holy See Good Friday collection

| 6 Mon | P | MONDAY OF HOLY WEEK: Mass & Office of the day |
| | | *Preface II of the Passion of the Lord* |

7 Tue	P	TUESDAY OF HOLY WEEK: Mass & Office of the day
		Preface II of the Passion of the Lord
	W	Chrism Mass in the Cathedral

| 8 Wed | P | WEDNESDAY OF HOLY WEEK: Mass & Office of the day |
| | | *Preface II of the Passion of the Lord* |

APRIL 2020

THE PASCHAL TRIDUUM

In the Sacred Triduum, the Church solemnly celebrates the greatest mysteries of our redemption, keeping by means of special celebrations the memorial of her Lord, crucified, buried and risen.

The Paschal Fast should also be kept sacred. It is to be celebrated everywhere on the Friday of the Lord's Passion and, where appropriate, prolonged also through Holy Saturday as a way of coming, with spirit uplifted, to the joys of the Lord's Resurrection.

9 Thu   **P**

MAUNDY THURSDAY: Office of the day

Vespers are not said by those attending the Evening Mass.

Holy Communion may be distributed to the faithful only during the Mass of the Lord's Supper. The sick, however, may receive Communion at any hour. The celebration of Mass without a congregation is prohibited.

W

Evening Mass of the Lord's Supper

Gloria, during which bells are rung; the Washing of Feet may be carried out; Preface I of the Most Holy Eucharist and insertions in the Roman Canon. Procession & Reposition of the Blessed Sacrament take place if the Celebration of the Lord's Passion is to take place in the Church; watching before the Altar of Repose then follows with solemnity until midnight and may conclude with Compline II of Sunday.

10 Fri   **R**

GOOD FRIDAY: Office of the Day   *Fast &*

It is highly appropriate that the Office of Readings   *Abstinence* and Lauds be celebrated solemnly with the people.

Vespers are not said by those attending the Afternoon Liturgy.

Compline II of Sunday may conclude the day.

Holy Communion is distributed to the faithful only during the Celebration of the Lord's Passion, but may be taken at any time to the sick who are unable to take part in this liturgy. Only the Sacraments of Penance and of the Anointing of the Sick may be celebrated.

R

The Celebration of the Passion of the Lord

This takes place in the afternoon, at about 3pm (or at least not before noon and not after 9pm).

Collection for the Holy Places

11 Sat   **P**

HOLY SATURDAY: Office of the day   *Fast as desired*

It is highly appropriate that the Office of Readings and Lauds be celebrated solemnly with the people. Vespers are of Holy Saturday. Compline (II of Sunday) is not said by those attending the Easter Vigil.

The Church today abstains completely from the celebration of Mass. Holy Communion may only be given as Viaticum. Only the Sacraments of Penance and of the Anointing of the Sick may be celebrated.

EASTER SEASON

Throughout the Easter season, the *Angelus* is replaced by *Regina Caeli*. The Apostles' Creed may suitably be used as an alternative on days when the Creed is appointed to be said.

Eucharistic Prayer 4 is not used in this Season.

at night	W	**+ The Easter Vigil in the Holy Night**

The entire celebration of the Easter Vigil must take place during the night, so that it begins after nightfall and ends before daybreak. The celebration of a Mass without the rites of the Easter Vigil is not permitted.
Gloria, Year A Gospel, Preface I of Easter, Proper Insertions in the Roman Canon, Commemoration of the Baptised in the Eucharistic Prayer (pages 1183-4), double Alleluia *added to* Ite, missa est
The Office of Readings is omitted by those who attend the Vigil.
The Paschal candle should be placed near the ambo or altar, and kept there for the whole Easter season until the end of Pentecost Sunday. It is lit for the more solemn liturgical celebrations during this time.

12 Sun	W	**+ EASTER SUNDAY OF THE RESURRECTION**

Either: In place of the Penitential Act, Vidi aquam *is sung and all are sprinkled with water blessed at the Vigil to recall their Baptism; in this case the Creed is used.*
Or: If the Renewal of Baptismal Promises is desired, this takes place after the homily and the Creed is omitted.
Gloria, (Alternative 2nd Reading, Alternative Gospel Readings of the Vigil or Easter Wednesday [latter Evening Mass only]*), Sequence, Creed or Renewal of Baptismal Promises, Preface I of Easter, Proper Insertions in the Roman Canon, Commemoration of the Baptised in the Eucharistic Prayer (pages 1183-4), double* Alleluia *added to* Ite, missa est .
Mass & Office of the Solemnity

13 Mon	W	**MONDAY WITHIN THE OCTAVE OF EASTER**

Gloria, Sequence ad lib, Preface I of Easter, Proper Insertions in the Roman Canon, double Alleluia *added to* Ite, missa est
Mass & Office of the Solemnity

14 Tue	W	**TUESDAY WITHIN THE OCTAVE OF EASTER**

Gloria, Sequence ad lib, Preface I of Easter, Proper Insertions in the Roman Canon, double Alleluia *added to* Ite, missa est
Mass & Office of the Solemnity

SECTION 7: LITURGICAL CALENDAR

APRIL 2020		

15 Wed — W — **WEDNESDAY WITHIN THE OCTAVE OF EASTER**
Gloria, Sequence ad lib, Preface 1 of Easter, Proper Insertions in the Roman Canon, double Alleluia added to Ite, missa est
Mass & Office of the Solemnity

16 Thu — W — **THURSDAY WITHIN THE OCTAVE OF EASTER**
Gloria, Sequence ad lib, Preface 1 of Easter, Proper Insertions in the Roman Canon, double Alleluia added to Ite, missa est
Mass & Office of the Solemnity

17 Fri — W — **FRIDAY WITHIN THE OCTAVE OF EASTER**
Gloria, Sequence ad lib, Preface 1 of Easter, Proper Insertions in the Roman Canon, double Alleluia added to Ite, missa est   *No Friday*
Mass & Office of the Solemnity   *abstinence*

18 Sat — W — **SATURDAY WITHIN THE OCTAVE OF EASTER**
Gloria, Sequence ad lib, Preface 1 of Easter, Proper Insertions in the Roman Canon, double Alleluia added to Ite, missa est
Mass & Office of the Solemnity

evening — W — First Vespers

19 Sun — W — **+ SECOND SUNDAY OF EASTER** (or of DIVINE MERCY)
Gloria, Sequence ad lib, Creed, Preface 1 of Easter, Proper Insertions in the Roman Canon, double Alleluia added to Ite, missa est
Mass & Office of the Solemnity

Throughout the Easter season, particular attention should be paid to the mystagogical formation of the newly baptised.
On ferial days of the Easter season one of the five Easter prefaces is said, unless other provision is made.

20 Mon — W — Easter feria, Second Week of Easter   *Ps Week 2*
Mass & Office of the day

21 Tue — W — Easter feria: Mass & Office of the day *or*
W — St Anselm, Bishop & Doctor   *National*
Mass & Office of the Memorial

22 Wed — W — Easter feria: Mass & Office of the day

— R — First Vespers

23 Thu — R — **ST GEORGE, Martyr,**   *National*
Patron of England
Gloria, 1st Reading from Common 2nd Reading & Gospel from National Proper, (Alternative Gospel Reading), Creed, Preface I or II of

		Holy Martyrs **Mass & Office of the Solemnity**	
24 Fri	W	**Ss Erkenwald & Mellitus, Bishops** see *Diocesan Supplement Book or online* **Mass & Office of the Memorial**	*Diocesan*
25 Sat	R	**ST MARK, Evangelist** *Gloria, Proper Readings, Preface II of Apostles* **Mass, Lauds & Lesser Hours of the Feast**	
	W	First Vespers	
26 Sun	W	**+ 3rd SUNDAY OF EASTER** *Gloria, Creed, a Preface of Easter* **Mass & Office of the day** Announce Mandatory Diocesan PTF Collection	*Ps Week 3*
27 Mon	W	Easter feria, Third Week of Easter: **Mass & Office of the day**	
28 Tue	W R W	Easter feria: **Mass & Office of the day** *or* St Peter Chanel, Priest & Martyr **Mass & Office of the Memorial** *or* St Louis M Grignion de Montfort, Priest **Mass & Office of the Memorial**	
29 Wed	W	**ST CATHERINE OF SIENA, Virgin & Doctor,** **Patron of Europe** *Gloria, Proper Readings, Preface of Holy Virgins & Religious* **Mass & Office of the Feast** § Europe	*National*
30 Thu	W W	Easter feria: **Mass & Office of the day** *or* St Pius V, Pope: **Mass & Office of the Memorial**	
MAY 2020			
1 Fri	W W	Easter feria: **Mass & Office of the day** *or* **Mass & Office of the day** *or* St Joseph the Worker: **Mass & Office of the Memorial** *Proper Gospel Reading, Preface of St Joseph* § Human Work	*Friday abstinence*
2 Sat	W	St Athanasius, Bishop & Doctor: **Mass & Office of the Memorial**	
evening	W	First Vespers	

MAY 2020

3 Sun	W	**+ 4th SUNDAY OF EASTER**	*Ps Week 4*
		Gloria, Creed, a Preface of Easter	
		Mass & Office of the Day	
		§ World Day of Prayer for Vocations	
		Collection for Priests' Training Fund	

4 Mon	R	**THE ENGLISH MARTYRS**	*National*
		Gloria, Either the Readings for today's former Feast of the Beatified	
		Martyrs or those for the former Feast of the Forty Martyrs on 25	
		October, given in the current editions of the Lectionary, may be used,	
		Preface I or II of Holy Martyrs	
		Mass & Office of the Feast	

5 Tue	W	Easter feria, Fourth Week of Easter: Mass & Office of the day	

6 Wed	W	Easter feria: Mass & Office of the day	

7 Thu	W	Easter feria: Mass & Office of the day	

8 Fri	W	Easter feria: Mass & Office of the day	*Friday abstinence*

9 Sat	W	Easter feria: Mass & Office of the day	

evening	W	First Vespers	

10 Sun	W	**+ 5th SUNDAY OF EASTER**	*Ps Week 1*
		Gloria, Creed, a Preface of Easter	
		Mass & Office of the day	

11 Mon	W	Easter feria, Fifth Week of Easter: Mass & Office of the day	

12 Tue	W	Easter feria, Fifth Week of Easter: Mass & Office of the day *or*	
	R	Ss Nereus and Achilleus, Martyrs	
		Mass & Office of the Memorial *or*	
	R	St Pancras, Martyr: Mass & Office of the Memorial	

13 Wed	W	Easter feria, Fourth Week of Easter: Mass & Office of the day *or*	
	W	Our Lady of Fatima: Mass & Office of the Memorial	

14 Thu	R	**ST MATTHIAS, Apostle**	
		Gloria, Proper Readings, Preface I or II of Apostles	
		Mass & Office of the Feast	

15 Fri	W	Easter feria: Mass & Office of the day	*Friday abstinence*

16 Sat	W	Easter feria: Mass & Office of the day	

MAY 2020			
evening	W	First Vespers	
17 Sun	W	+ 6th SUNDAY OF EASTER *Gloria, Creed, a Preface of Easter* Mass & Office of the day Announce Mandatory Holy See CCN Collection Announce Holy Day of Obligation	*Ps Week 2*
18 Mon	W R	Easter feria, Sixth Week of Easter: Mass & Offfice of the day *or* St John I, Pope & Martyr: Mass & Office of the Memorial	
19 Tue	W	Easter feria: Mass & Office of the day	
20 Wed	W W	Easter feria: Mass & Office of the day *or* St Bernadine of Siena, Priest: Mass & Office of the Memorial	
evening	W W	First Vespers + Proper Vigil Mass of the Ascension precedes or follows *Gloria, Ascension Readings, Creed, Preface I or II of the Ascension &* *Communicantes in the Roman Canon*	
21 Thu	W	+ **THE ASCENSION OF THE LORD** *Gloria, (Alternative Collect), Creed, Preface I or II of the Ascension &* *Communicantes in the Roman Canon* Mass & Office of the Solemnity Anniversary of the Installation of Cardinal Vincent Nichols, Eleventh Archbishop of Westminster (2009). An intention may be included in the Universal Prayer.	
		On ferial days until Pentecost a preface of Easter or of the Ascension is used, unless other provision is made.	
22 Fri	W W	Easter feria: Mass & Office of the day *or* St Rita of Cascia, Religious: Mass & Office of the Memorial	*Friday abstinence*
23 Sat	W	Easter feria: Mass & Office of the day	
24 Sun	W W	First Vespers + 7th SUNDAY OF EASTER *Gloria, Creed, a Preface of Easter or of the Ascension* Mass & Office of the day § World Communications Day Collection for Catholic Communications Network	*Ps Week 3*
25 Mon	W	St Bede the Venerable, Priest & Doctor Mass & Office of the Memorial	*National*

MAY 2020

26 Tue	W	St Philip Neri, Priest: Mass & Office of the Memorial
27 Wed	W	**ST AUGUSTINE OF CANTERBURY,** Bishop *National* *Gloria, Proper National Readings, Preface of Holy Pastors* **Mass & Office of the Feast**
28 Thu	W	Easter feria, Seventh Week of Easter: Mass & Office of the day
29 Fri	W W	Easter feria: Mass & Office of the day *or* *Friday abstinence* St Paul VI, Pope: Mass & Office of the Memorial *[see page 291]*
30 Sat	W	Easter feria: Mass & Office of the day

The fifty days of the sacred season of Easter conclude with Pentecost Sunday, when the Church recalls the gift of the Holy Spirit to the Apostles, the beginnings of the Church, and the start of her mission to all tongues and peoples and nations.

It is appropriate that the Vigil Mass of Pentecost be celebrated in the extended form, using the readings and prayers to be found in the liturgical books. This Mass, however, does not have a baptismal character, as does the Easter Vigil, but instead is a celebration of more intense prayer, after the example of the Apostles and disciples, who together with Mary, the Mother of Jesus, were one in persevering prayer, as they awaited the outpouring of the Holy Spirit.

| evening | R
R | **First Vespers**
+ Proper Vigil Mass of Pentecost precedes, follows or incorporates
Gloria, (Two Alternative Collects), (Choice of Old Testament Readings), Creed, Proper Preface & Communicantes *in the Roman Canon, double* Alleluia *added to* Ite, missa est |
| 31 Sun | R | **+ PENTECOST SUNDAY**
Gloria, Sequence, Creed, Proper Preface & Communicantes *in the Roman Canon, double* Alleluia *added to* Ite, missa est
Mass & Office of the Solemnity
§ The Church |

The Easter season ends. After today, the Paschal Candle is no longer kept in the sanctuary, but moved to the baptistry, where it is lit at baptisms. At funerals it is placed and lit near the coffin, to signify that Christian death is a true Passover.

From tomorrow, the recitation of the *Angelus* is resumed.

[R]   When Monday or Tuesday after Pentecost are days on which it is customary for the faithful to attend Mass, the Mass of Pentecost Sunday or the Votive Mass of the Holy Spirit may be used.

ORDINARY TIME - AFTER THE EASTER SEASON

JUNE 2020

The weeks of Ordinary Time celebrate no particular aspect of Christ. Instead, celebration is made of the mystery of Christ in all its fullness.

LECTIONARY FOR SUNDAYS: YEAR A
WEEKDAY LECTIONARY: YEAR 2
ORDINARY TIME: WEEK 9
(Divine Office Volume III)
Eucharistic Prayer 4 may be used in this Season.
The choice of Masses which may be celebrated *ad libitum* is shown in the Liturgical Information on page 294.
On ferial days in Ordinary Time the Office of a saint included for that day in the Roman Martyrology may be celebrated. Occasional Votive Offices are permitted, although care to observe the four-week cycle of the Office should be maintained.

JUNE 2020

1 Mon	W	The Blessed Virgin Mary, Mother of the Church *Ps Week 1* *Readings of the ferial day or from the Common of the BVM* Mass & Office of the Memorial (Roman Missal, Votive Mass 10 B, page 1411 ff; Office *ad interim* from the Common of the BVM)	
2 Tue	G R	feria, Ninth Week of Year 2: Mass ad lib; Office of the day *or* Ss Marcellinus and Peter, Martyrs: Mass & Office of the Memorial	
3 Wed	R	Ss Charles Lwanga and Companions, Martyrs Mass & Office of the Memorial	
4 Thu	W	OUR LORD JESUS CHRIST, THE ETERNAL HIGH PRIEST *Gloria, Proper Year A Readings (Alternative 1st Reading), Preface of the Priesthood of Christ and of the Church [see Chrism Mass, page 324 ff]* Mass and Office of the Feast *[see Liturgical information, National Calendar, page 292]*	*National*
5 Fri	R	St Boniface, Bishop & Martyr Mass & Office of the Memorial	*Friday abstinence* *National*
6 Sat	G W W	feria: Mass ad lib; Office of the day *or* St Norbert, Bishop: Mass & Office of the Memorial *or* Blessed Virgin Mary on Saturday: Mass & Office of the Memorial	
evening	W	First Vespers	
7 Sun	W	**+ THE MOST HOLY TRINITY** *Gloria, Creed, Proper Preface* Mass & Office of the Solemnity	

JUNE 2020

8 Mon	G	feria, Tenth Week of Year 2 *Ps Week 2* Mass ad lib; Office of the day
9 Tue	G W W	feria: Mass ad lib; Office of the day *or* St Ephrem, Deacon & Doctor: Mass & Office of the Memorial *or* St Columba, Abbot: Mass & Office of the Memorial *National*
10 Wed	G	feria: Mass ad lib; Office of the day
11 Thu	R	St Barnabas, Apostle *Proper 1st Reading, Preface I or II of Apostles* Mass & Office of the Memorial
12 Fri	G	feria: Mass ad lib; Office of the day *Friday abstinence*
13 Sat	W	St Anthony of Padua, Priest & Doctor Mass & Office of the Memorial
evening	W	First Vespers
14 Sun	W	**+ THE MOST HOLY BODY AND BLOOD OF CHRIST (CORPUS ET SANGUIS CHRISTI)** *Gloria, Sequence ad lib, Creed, Preface II of the Most Holy Eucharist (Preface I may be used)* Mass & Office of the Solemnity Announce Mandatory CBCEW Day for Life Collection
15 Mon	G	feria, Eleventh Week of Year 2 *Ps Week 3* Mass ad lib; Office of the day
16 Tue	G W	feria: Mass ad lib; Office of the day *or* St Richard of Chichester, Bishop *National* Mass & Office of the Memorial
17 Wed	G	feria: Mass ad lib; Office of the day
18 Thu	G	feria: Mass ad lib; Office of the day
evening	W	First Vespers
19 Fri	W	**THE MOST SACRED HEART OF JESUS (Diocese consecrated to the Sacred Heart, 17 June 1873)** *No Friday abstinence* *Gloria, Creed, Proper Preface* Mass & Office of the Solemnity

JUNE 2020			
20 Sat	W	The Immaculate Heart of the Blessed Virgin Mary *Proper Gospel, Preface I of the Blessed Virgin Mary* Mass & Office of the Memorial	
evening	G	First Vespers	
21 Sun	G	+ 12th SUNDAY IN ORDINARY TIME *Gloria, Creed, a Preface of Sundays in O.T.* Mass & Office of the day § Day for Life Collection for Life Announce Mandatory Holy See Collection for Peter's Pence	*Ps Week 4*
22 Mon	R	Ss JOHN FISHER, Bishop and THOMAS MORE, Martyrs *Gloria, Proper National Readings, Preface I or II of Holy Martyrs* Mass & Office of the Feast § Those who suffer persecution	*National*
23 Tue	G W	feria, Twelfth Week of Year 2: Mass ad lib; Office of the day *or* St Etheldreda (Audrey), Virgin Mass & Office of the Memorial	*National*
evening	W W	First Vespers Proper Vigil Mass of the Nativity of St John the Baptist precedes or follows *Gloria, Proper Readings, Creed, Preface of St John the Baptist*	
24 Wed	W	**THE NATIVITY OF ST JOHN THE BAPTIST** *Gloria, Creed, Preface of St John the Baptist* Mass & Office of the Solemnity	
25 Thu	G	feria Mass ad lib; Office of the day	
26 Fri	G	feria: Mass ad lib; Office of the day	*Friday abstinence*
in Cathedral	R	First Vespers	*No abstinence*
27 Sat	R	St John Southworth, Priest & Martyr *see Diocesan Supplement Book or online, (Short form 1st Reading)* Mass, Lauds & Lesser Hours of the Memorial	*Diocesan*

JUNE/JULY 2020

in Cathedral	R	**ST JOHN SOUTHWORTH,** *Diocesan* **Priest & Martyr** *Gloria, 1st, 2nd & Gospel Readings all from the Common, Creed,* *Preface I or II of Holy Martyrs; see Diocesan Supplement Book or* *online* Mass, Lauds & Lesser Hours of the Solemnity
evening	R R	First Vespers + Proper Vigil Mass of Ss Peter and Paul precedes or follows *Gloria, Proper Readings, Creed, Preface of Ss Peter and Paul*
28 Sun	R	**+ Ss PETER and PAUL, Apostles** **St Peter, Prince of Apostles, Patron of the Diocese** *Gloria, Creed, Preface of Ss Peter & Paul* Mass & Office of the Solemnity The anniversary of the election of Pope Francis is observed today, by decision of the Bishops' Conference. A special intention for the Holy Father should be included in the Universal Prayer. Collection for Peter's Pence
29 Mon	G	feria, Thirteenth Week of Year 2 *Ps Week I* Mass ad lib; Office of the day
30 Tue	G R	feria: Mass ad lib; Office of the day *or* The First Martyrs of Holy Roman Church Mass & Office of the Memorial
in Cathedral	W	First Vespers

JULY 2020

1 Wed	W	DEDICATION OF THE CATHEDRAL *Diocesan* *Gloria, Readings Lectionary Vol. 2, page 1392, Common of the* *Dedication of a Church II, page 1095* Mass & Office of the Feast
in Cathedral	W	**DEDICATION OF THE CATHEDRAL** *Diocesan* **(1910)** *Mass in the Dedicated Church: Gloria, 1st & 2nd Readings and Gospel* *from Lectionary Vol. 2, page 1392, Creed, Common of the Dedication* *of a Church I, page 1091* Mass & Office of the Solemnity
2 Thu	G	feria: Mass ad lib; Office of the day

JULY 2020

3 Fri	R	**ST THOMAS, Apostle** *Friday abstinence*
		Gloria, Proper Readings, Preface I or II of Apostles
		Mass & Office of the Feast

4 Sat	G	feria: Mass ad lib; Office of the day *or*
	W	St Elizabeth of Portugal: Mass & Office of the Memorial *or*
	W	Blessed Virgin Mary on Saturday: Mass & Office of the Memorial

| evening | G | First Vespers |

5 Sun	G	**+ 14th SUNDAY IN ORDINARY TIME** *Ps Week 2*
		Gloria, (Short form Gospel), Creed, a Preface of Sundays in O.T.
		Mass & Office of the day
		Announce Mandatory CBCEW Collection for AoS

6 Mon	G	feria Fourteenth Week of Year 2: Mass ad lib; Office of the day *or*
	R	St Maria Goretti, Virgin & Martyr:
		Mass & Office of the Memorial

| 7 Tue | G | feria: Mass ad lib; Office of the day |

| 8 Wed | G | feria: Mass ad lib; Office of the day |

9 Thu	G	feria: Mass ad lib; Office of the day *or*
	R	St Augustine Zhao Rong, Priest, and Companions, Martyrs:
		Mass & Office of the Memorial

| 10 Fri | G | feria: Mass ad lib; Office of the day *Friday abstinence* |

11 Sat	W	**ST BENEDICT, Abbot, Patron of Europe** *National*
		Gloria, Proper Readings, Preface of Holy Pastors or
		Holy Virgins and Religious
		Mass & Office of the Feast
		§ Europe

| evening | G | First Vespers |

12 Sun	G	**+ 15th SUNDAY IN ORDINARY TIME** *Ps Week 3*
		Gloria, (Short form Gospel), Creed, a Preface of Sundays in O.T.
		Mass & Office of the day
		§ Sea Sunday
		Collection for Apostleship of the Sea

| 13 Mon | G | feria, Fifteenth Week of Year 2 : Mass ad lib; Office of the day *or* |
| | W | St Henry: Mass & Office of the Memorial |

| 14 Tue | G | feria: Mass ad lib; Office of the day *or* |
| | W | St Camillus de Lellis, Priest: Mass & Office of the Memorial |

JULY 2020		
15 Wed	W	St Bonaventure, Bishop & Doctor: Mass & Office of the Memorial
16 Thu	G W	feria: Mass ad lib; Office of the day *or* Our Lady of Mount Carmel: Mass & Office of the Memorial
17 Fri	G	feria: Mass ad lib; Office of the day *Friday abstinence*
18 Sat	G W	feria: Mass ad lib; Office of the day *or* Blessed Virgin Mary on Saturday: Mass & Office of the Memorial
evening	G	First Vespers
19 Sun	G	+16th SUNDAY IN ORDINARY TIME *Ps Week 4* *Gloria, (Short form Gospel), Creed, a Preface of Sundays in O.T.* Mass & Office of the day
20 Mon	G R	feria, Sixteenth Week of Year 2: Mass ad lib; Office of the day *or* St Apollinaris, Bishop & Martyr: Mass & Office of the Memorial
21 Tue	G W	feria: Mass ad lib; Office of the day *or* St Lawrence of Brindisi, Priest & Doctor Mass & Office of the Memorial
22 Wed	W	ST MARY MAGDALENE *Gloria, Proper Readings (Alternative First Reading), Proper Preface* *(presently Latin only)* Mass & Office of the Feast
23 Thu	W	ST BRIDGET OF SWEDEN, Patron of Europe *National* *Gloria, Proper Readings, Preface of Holy Virgins and Religious* Mass & Office of the Feast § Europe
24 Fri	G W	feria: Mass ad lib; Office of the day *or* *Friday abstinence* St Sharbel Makhluf, Priest: Mass & Office of the Memorial
25 Sat	R	ST JAMES, Apostle *Gloria, Proper Readings, Preface I or II of Apostles* Mass, Lauds and Lesser Hours of the Feast
evening	G	First Vespers
26 Sun	G	+ 17th SUNDAY IN ORDINARY TIME *Ps Week 1* *Gloria, (Short form Gospel), Creed, a Preface of Sundays in O.T.* Mass & Office of the day
27 Mon	G	feria, Seventeenth Week of Year 2: Mass ad lib; Office of the day

JULY/AUGUST 2020

28 Tue	G	feria: Mass ad lib; Office of the day
29 Wed	W	St Martha *Proper Alternative Gospels* Mass & Office of the Memorial
30 Thu	G W	feria: Mass ad lib; Office of the day *or* St Peter Chrysologus, Bishop & Doctor: Mass & Office of the Memorial
31 Fri	W	St Ignatius of Loyola, Priest *Friday abstinence* Mass & Office of the Memorial

AUGUST 2020

1 Sat	W	St Alphonsus Liguori, Bishop & Doctor: Mass & Office of the Memorial

On 2nd August the plenary indulgence ('the Portiuncula') may be acquired in minor basilicas, shrines and parish churches. Requirements: a devout visit to a church and the recitation there of the Lord's Prayer and Creed, in addition to sacramental confession, Holy Communion and prayer for the intentions of the Holy Father. This indulgence may be gained only once. The visit may be made from noon the previous day to midnight on the day itself.

evening	G	First Vespers
2 Sun	G	+18th SUNDAY IN ORDINARY TIME *Ps Week 2* *Gloria, Creed, a Preface of Sundays in O.T.* Mass & Office of the day
3 Mon	G	feria, Eighteenth Week of Year 2 *Alternative Gospel is used* Mass ad lib; Office of the day
4 Tue	W	St John Vianney, Priest *Alternative Gospel is used* Mass & Office of the Memorial
5 Wed	G W	feria: Mass ad lib; Office of the day *or* The Dedication of the Basilica of St Mary Major Mass & Office of the Memorial
6 Thu	W	THE TRANSFIGURATION OF THE LORD *Gloria, 1st or 2nd Reading, Year A Gospel, Proper Preface* Mass & Office of the Feast

SECTION 7: LITURGICAL CALENDAR

AUGUST 2020

7 Fri	G	feria: Mass ad lib; Office of the day *or*	*Friday abstinence*
	R	Ss Sixtus II, Pope, and Companions, Martyrs: Mass & Office of the Memorial *or*	
	W	St Cajetan, Priest: Mass & Office of the Memorial	
8 Sat	W	St Dominic, Priest: Mass & Office of the Memorial	
evening	G	First Vespers	
9 Sun	G	+ 19th SUNDAY IN ORDINARY TIME	*Ps Week 3*
		Gloria, Creed, a Preface of Sundays in O.T.	
		Mass & Office of the day	
10 Mon	R	ST LAWRENCE, Deacon & Martyr	
		Gloria, Proper Readings, Preface I or II of Holy Martyrs	
		Mass & Office of the Feast	
11 Tue	W	St Clare, Virgin: Mass & Office of the Memorial	
12 Wed	G	feria, Nineteenth Week of Year 2: Mass ad lib; Office of the day *or*	
	W	St Jane Frances de Chantal, Religious: Mass & Office of the Memorial	
		[see Divine Office for 12 December, Vol I, p 33* ff]	
13 Thu	G	feria: Mass ad lib; Office of the day *or*	
	R	Ss Pontian, Pope, & Hippolytus, Priest, Martyrs: Mass & Office of the Memorial	
14 Fri	R	St Maximilian Mary Kolbe, Priest & Martyr:	*Friday abstinence*
		(Alternative 1st Reading)	
		Mass & Office of the Memorial	
15 Sat	G	feria: Mass ad lib; Office of the day *or*	
	W	Blessed Virgin Mary on Saturday: Mass & Office of the Memorial	
evening	W	First Vespers	
	W	+ Proper Vigil Mass of the Assumption precedes or follows	
		Gloria, Proper Readings, Creed, Proper Preface	
16 Sun	W	**+ THE ASSUMPTION OF THE BLESSED VIRGIN MARY**	
		Gloria, Creed, Proper Preface	
		Mass & Office of the Solemnity	
17 Mon	G	feria, Twentieth Week of Year 2	*Ps Week 4*
		Mass ad lib; Office of the day	

AUGUST 2020

18 Tue	G	feria: Mass ad lib; Office of the day
19 Wed	G W	feria: Mass ad lib; Office of the day *or* St John Eudes, Priest: Mass & Office of the Memorial
20 Thu	W	St Bernard, Abbot & Doctor: Mass & Office of the Memorial
21 Fri	W	St Pius X, Pope: Mass & Office of the Memorial *Friday abstinence*
22 Sat	W	The Queenship of the Blessed Virgin Mary *Preface I or II of the Blessed Virgin Mary* Mass & Office of the Memorial
evening	G	First Vespers
23 Sun	G	+ 21st SUNDAY IN ORDINARY TIME *Ps Week 1* *Gloria, Creed, a Preface of Sundays in O.T.* Mass & Office of the day
24 Mon	R	ST BARTHOLOMEW, Apostle *Gloria, Proper Readings, Preface I or II of Apostles* Mass & Office of the Feast
25 Tue	G W W	feria, Twenty-First Week of Year 2: Mass ad lib; office of the day *or* St Louis: Mass & Office of the Memorial *or* St Joseph Calasanz, Priest: Mass & Office of the Memorial
26 Wed	G W	feria: Mass ad lib; Office of the day *or* Blessed Dominic of the Mother of God, Priest *National* Mass & Office of the Memorial
27 Thu	W	St Monica: Mass & Office of the Memorial
28 Fri	W	St Augustine, Bishop & Doctor *Friday abstinence* Mass & Office of the Memorial
29 Sat	R	The Passion of St John the Baptist *Proper Gospel, Preface of St John the Baptist* Mass & Office of the Memorial
evening	G	First Vespers
30 Sun	G	+ 22nd SUNDAY IN ORDINARY TIME *Ps Week 2* *Gloria, Creed, a Preface of Sundays in O.T.* Mass & Office of the day

SECTION 7: LITURGICAL CALENDAR

AUGUST/SEPTEMBER 2020

31 Mon   G   feria, Twenty-Second Week of Year 2
Mass ad lib; Office of the day *or*

           W   St Aidan, Bishop, and the Saints of Lindisfarne: *National*
Mass & Office of the Memorial

SEPTEMBER 2020

1 Tue   G   feria: Mass ad lib; Office of the day
Anniversary of the Death of Cardinal Cormac Murphy O'Connor,
Tenth Archbishop of Westminster (2017)
§ World Day of Prayer for the Care of Creation

2 Wed   G   feria: Mass ad lib; Office of the day

3 Thu   W   ST GREGORY THE GREAT, Pope & Doctor   *National*
Gloria, Proper National Readings, Preface of Holy Pastors
Mass & Office of the Feast

4 Fri   G   feria: Mass ad lib; Office of the day *or*   *Friday abstinence*
       W   St Cuthbert, Bishop: *National*
Mass & Office of the Memorial

5 Sat   G   feria: Mass ad lib; Office of the day

evening   G   First Vespers

6 Sun   G   + 23rd SUNDAY IN ORDINARY TIME   *Ps Week 3*
Gloria, Creed, a Preface of Sundays in O.T.
Mass & Office of the day
Announce Optional Catholic Education Service Collection

7 Mon   G   feria, Twenty-Third Week of Year 2: Mass ad lib; Office of the day

8 Tue   W   THE NATIVITY OF THE BLESSED VIRGIN MARY
Gloria, Proper Readings (Alternative 1st Reading, also Short form Gospel), Preface I or II of the Blessed Virgin Mary
Mass & Office of the Feast

9 Wed   G   feria: Mass ad lib; Office of the day *or*
       W   St Peter Claver, Priest: Mass & Office of the Memorial

10 Thu   G   feria: Mass ad lib; Office of the day

11 Fri   G   feria: Mass ad lib; Office of the day   *Friday abstinence*

SEPTEMBER 2020

12 Sat	G	feria: Mass ad lib; Office of the day *or*
	W	The Most Holy Name of Mary: Mass & Office of the Memorial *or*
	W	Blessed Virgin Mary on Saturday: Mass & Office of the Memorial
evening	G	First Vespers
13 Sun	G	+ 24th SUNDAY IN ORDINARY TIME *Ps Week 4* *Gloria, Creed, a Preface of Sundays in O.T.* Mass & Office of the day § Education Sunday Collection for Catholic Education Service Announce Mandatory CBCEW Home Mission Appeal collection
14 Mon	R	THE EXALTATION OF THE HOLY CROSS *Gloria, 1st or 2nd Reading, Preface of the Holy Cross (Preface I of the Passion of the Lord may be used)* Mass & Office of the Feast
15 Tue	W	Our Lady of Sorrows *Sequence ad lib, (Alternative Gospel Reading), Preface I or II of the Blessed Virgin Mary* Mass & Office of the Memorial
16 Wed	R	Ss Cornelius, Pope, and Cyprian, Bishop, Martyrs: Mass & Office of the Memorial
17 Thu	G	feria, Twenty-Fourth Week of Year 2: Mass ad lib; Office of the day *or*
	W	St Robert Bellarmine, Bishop & Doctor: Mass & Office of the Memorial
18 Fri	G	feria: Mass ad lib; Office of the day
19 Sat	G	feria: Mass ad lib; Office of the day *or*
	R	St Januarius, Bishop & Martyr: Mass & Office of the Memorial *or*
	W	Blessed Virgin Mary on Saturday: Mass & Office of the Memorial
evening	G	First Vespers
20 Sun	G	+ 25th SUNDAY IN ORDINARY TIME *Ps Week 1* *Gloria, Creed, a Preface of Sundays in O.T.* Mass & Office of the day Annual Mass Count - 1 § Home Mission Day Collection for Home Mission Appeal

SEPTEMBER/OCTOBER 2020

21 Mon	R	**ST MATTHEW, Apostle & Evangelist** *Gloria, Proper Readings, Preface I or II of Apostles* Mass & Office of the Feast
22 Tue	G	feria, Twenty-Fifth Week of Year 2: Mass ad lib; Office of the day
23 Wed	W	St Pius of Pietrelcina, Priest: Mass & Office of the Memorial
24 Thu	W	Our Lady of Walsingham: *National* Mass & Office of the Memorial
25 Fri	G	feria: Mass ad lib; Office of the day *Friday abstinence*
26 Sat	G R W	feria: Mass ad lib; Office of the day *or* Ss Cosmas and Damian, Martyrs Mass & Office of the Memorial *or* Blessed Virgin Mary on Saturday: Mass & Office of the Memorial
evening	G	First Vespers
27 Sun	G	**+ 26th SUNDAY IN ORDINARY TIME** *Ps Week 2* *Gloria, (Short form 2nd Reading), Creed, a Preface of Sundays in O.T.* Mass & Office of the day Annual Mass Count – 2 § Migrants and Refugees Announce Optional CAFOD Harvest Fast Day collection
28 Mon	G R R	feria, Twenty-Sixth Week of Year 2 Mass ad lib; Office of the day *or* St Wenceslaus, Martyr: Mass & Office of the Memorial *or* St Lawrence Ruiz and Companions, Martyrs: Mass & Office of the Memorial
29 Tue	W	**Ss MICHAEL, GABRIEL and RAPHAEL, Archangels** *Gloria, Proper Readings (Alternative 1st Reading), Preface of the Angels* Mass & Office of the Feast
30 Wed	W	St Jerome, Priest & Doctor: Mass & Office of the Memorial

OCTOBER 2020

The Rosary should be recommended to the faithful, and its nature and importance explained. A plenary indulgence may be gained by reciting five decades of the Rosary in church, as a family at home, as a religious community, or as a pious fraternity, or in general whenever several persons have gathered for a good purpose; in other circumstances a partial indulgence may be gained.

OCTOBER 2020

1 Thu	W	St Thérèse of the Child Jesus, Virgin & Doctor: Mass & Office of the Memorial

2 Fri	W	The Holy Guardian Angels	*Friday abstinence*
		Proper Gospel Reading, Preface of the Angels	
		Mass & Office of the Memorial	
		§ Harvest Fast Day	

3 Sat	G	feria: Mass ad lib; Office of the day *or*
	W	Blessed Virgin Mary on Saturday: Mass & Office of the Memorial
evening	G	First Vespers

4 Sun	G	+ 27th SUNDAY IN ORDINARY TIME	*Ps Week 3*
		Gloria, Creed, a Preface of Sundays in O.T.	
		Mass & Office of the day	
		Annual Mass Count – 3	
		§ The Harvest	
		Collect Harvest Fast Day Offerings for CAFOD	

5 Mon	G	feria, Twenty-Seventh Week of Year 2 Mass ad lib; Office of the day

6 Tue	G	feria: Mass ad lib; Office of the day *or*
	W	St Bruno, Priest: Mass & Office of the Memorial

7 Wed	W	Our Lady of the Rosary: Mass & Office of the Memorial

8 Thu	G	feria: Mass ad lib; Office of the day

9 Fri	G	feria: Mass ad lib; Office of the day *or*	*Friday abstinence*
	R	St Denis, Bishop, and Companions, Martyrs: Mass & Office of the Memorial *or*	
	W	St John Leonardi, Priest: Mass & Office of the Memorial *or*	
	W	St John Henry Newman, Priest: Mass & Office of the Memorial	*National*

10 Sat	G	feria: Mass ad lib; Office of the day *or*	
	W	St Paulinus of York, Bishop: Mass & Office of the Memorial *or*	*National*
	W	Blessed Virgin Mary on Saturday: Mass & Office of the Memorial	
evening	G	First Vespers	

SECTION 7: LITURGICAL CALENDAR

OCTOBER 2020

11 Sun — G

+ 28th SUNDAY IN ORDINARY TIME   *Ps Week 4*
Gloria, (Short form Gospel), Creed, a Preface of Sundays in O.T.
Mass & Office of the day
Annual Mass Count – 4
§ Week of Prayer for Prisoners and their Families
Announce Mandatory Holy See World Mission Sunday collection

12 Mon — G / W

feria, Twenty-Eighth Week of Year 2: Mass ad lib; Office of the day *or*
St Wilfrid, Bishop: Mass & Office of the Memorial   *National*

in City of Westminster — W

First Vespers

13 Tue — W

ST EDWARD THE CONFESSOR,   *Diocesan*
Patron of the Diocese
Gloria, Proper National Readings, Preface I or II of Saints; see Diocesan Supplement Book or online
Mass & Office of the Feast

in City of Westminster — W

ST EDWARD THE CONFESSOR,   *Diocesan*
Patron of the Diocese and of the City of Westminster
Gloria, Proper National Readings (1st from Common), Creed, Preface I or II of Saints; see Diocesan Supplement Book or online [also National Collect]
Mass & Office of the Solemnity

14 Wed — G / R

feria: Mass ad lib; Office of the day *or*
St Callistus I, Pope & Martyr: Mass & Office of the Memorial

15 Thu — W

St Teresa of Jesus, Virgin & Doctor: Mass & Office of the Memorial

16 Fri — G / W / W

feria: Mass ad lib; Office of the day *or*   *Friday abstinence*
St Hedwig, Religious: Mass & Office of the Memorial *or*
St Margaret Mary Alacoque, Virgin: Mass & Office of the Memorial

17 Sat — R

St Ignatius of Antioch, Bishop & Martyr:
Mass & Office of the Memorial

evening — G

First Vespers

18 Sun — G

+ 29th SUNDAY IN ORDINARY TIME   *Ps Week 1*
Gloria, Creed, a Preface of Sundays in O.T.
Mass & Office of the day
§ World Mission Day (One Mass for the Evangelisation of Peoples is permitted today or on a subsequent ferial day)
Collection for World Mission Sunday

OCTOBER 2020

19 Mon	G	feria, Twenty-Ninth Week of Year 2: Mass ad lib; Office of the day *or*
	R	Ss John de Brébeuf and Isaac Jogues, Priests, and Companions, Martyrs: Mass & Office of the Memorial *or*
	W	St Paul of the Cross, Priest: Mass & Office of the Memorial
20 Tue	G	feria: Mass ad lib; Office of the day
21 Wed	G	feria: Mass ad lib; Office of the day
22 Thu	G	feria: Mass ad lib; Office of the day *or*
	W	St John Paul II, Pope *Common of Pastors: For a Pope* Mass & Office of the Memorial
23 Fri	G	feria: Mass ad lib, Office of the day *or* *Friday abstinence*
	W	St John of Capistrano, Priest: Mass & Office of the Memorial
24 Sat	G	feria: Mass ad lib; Office of the day *or*
	W	St Anthony Mary Claret, Bishop: Mass & Office of the Memorial *or*
	W	Blessed Virgin Mary on Saturday: Mass & Office of the Memorial
evening	G	First Vespers
25 Sun	G	+ 30th SUNDAY IN ORDINARY TIME *Ps Week 2* *Gloria, Creed, a Preface of Sundays in O.T.* Mass & Office of the day
26 Mon	G	feria, Thirtieth Week of Year 2; Mass ad lib; Office of the day *or*
	W	Ss Chad and Cedd, Bishops: *National* Mass & Office of the Memorial
27 Tue	G	feria: Mass ad lib; Office of the day
28 Wed	R	Ss SIMON and JUDE, Apostles *Gloria, Proper Readings, Preface I or II of Apostles* Mass & Office of the Feast
29 Thu	R	Blessed Martyrs of Douai College *Diocesan* *see Diocesan Supplement Book or online* Mass & Office of the Memorial
30 Fri	G	feria: Mass ad lib; Office of the day *Friday abstinence*

OCTOBER/NOVEMBER 2020

31 Sat	G	feria: Mass ad lib; Office of the day *or*
	W	Blessed Virgin Mary on Saturday: Mass & Office of the Memorial
evening	W	First Vespers

NOVEMBER 2020

A plenary indulgence, applicable only to the souls in Purgatory, is granted to any of the faithful who (1) on one of the days from 1-8 November visit devoutly a cemetery or simply pray mentally for the dead; (2) on All Souls' Day visit a church or chapel with devotion and there recite the Our Father and the Creed.

A partial indulgence, applicable only to the souls in Purgatory, is granted to any of the faithful who (1) visit devoutly a cemetery or who simply pray mentally for the dead; (2) recite devoutly Lauds or Vespers of the Office of the Dead, or the invocation *'Eternal rest grant unto them, O Lord...'*

1 Sun	W	**+ ALL SAINTS**
		Gloria, Creed, Proper Preface
		Mass & Office of the Solemnity
		Announce Mandatory Diocesan Sick & Retired Priests collection

| 2 Mon | P or B | THE COMMEMORATION OF ALL THE FAITHFUL DEPARTED (ALL SOULS' DAY) |

The altar is not decorated with flowers and the organ is used only to sustain the singing.
Readings selected from Masses for the Dead, a Preface for the Dead
Mass & Office of the Dead

All priests are permitted to say three Masses today, with an interval of time between one Mass and the next, and on condition that while one of the Masses may be applied in favour of any person, the second Mass should be applied for all the faithful departed, and the third for the intentions of the Holy Father.

3 Tue	G	feria, Thirty-First Week of Year 2: Ps Week 3
		Mass ad lib; Office of the day *or*
	W	St Martin de Porres, Religious: Mass & Office of the Memorial *or*
	W	St Winifride, Virgin: Mass & Office of the Memorial *National*
4 Wed	W	St Charles Borromeo, Bishop: Mass & Office of the Memorial
5 Thu	G	feria: Mass ad lib; Office of the day
6 Fri	G	feria: Mass ad lib; Office of the day *Friday abstinence*

NOVEMBER 2020		
7 Sat	G	feria: Mass ad lib; Office of the day *or*
	W	St Willibrord, Bishop: Mass & Office of the Memorial *or* *National*
	W	Blessed Virgin Mary on Saturday: Mass & Office of the Memorial
evening	G	First Vespers
8 Sun	G	+ 32nd SUNDAY IN ORDINARY TIME *Ps Week 4*
		Gloria, (Short form 2nd Reading), Creed, a Preface of Sundays in O.T.
		Mass & Office of the day
	P	+ One Requiem Mass permitted (REMEMBRANCE SUNDAY)
	or B	*1st, 2nd & Gospel Readings from Masses for the Dead, Creed, a Preface for the Dead*
		Collection for Sick and Retired Priests
9 Mon	W	THE DEDICATION OF THE LATERAN BASILICA
		Gloria, 1st or 2nd Reading, Proper Preface
		Mass & Office of the Feast
10 Tue	W	St Leo the Great, Pope and Doctor: Mass & Office of the Memorial
11 Wed	W	St Martin of Tours, Bishop: Mass & Office of the Memorial
12 Thu	R	St Josaphat, Bishop & Martyr: Mass & Office of the Memorial
13 Fri	G	feria, Thirty-Second Week of Year 2 *Friday abstinence*
		Mass ad lib; Office of the day
14 Sat	G	feria: Mass ad lib; Office of the day *or*
	W	Blessed Virgin Mary on Saturday: Mass & Office of the Memorial
evening	G	First Vespers
15 Sun	G	+ 33rd SUNDAY IN ORDINARY TIME *Ps Week 1*
		Gloria, (Short form Gospel), Creed, a Preface of Sundays in O.T.
		Mass & Office of the day
		§ World Day of the Poor
16 Mon	W	St Edmund of Abingdon, Bishop *Diocesan*
		see Diocesan Supplement Book or online [also National Collect]
		Mass & Office of the Memorial

NOVEMBER 2020

17 Tue	G	feria, Thirty-Third Week of Year 2: Mass & Office of the day *or*	
	W	St Hilda, Abbess	*National*
		Mass & Office of the Memorial *or*	
	W	St Hugh of Lincoln, Bishop	*National*
		Mass & Office of the Memorial *or*	
	W	St Elizabeth of Hungary, Religious	*National*
		Mass & Office of the Memorial	
18 Wed	G	feria: Mass ad lib; Office of the day *or*	
	W	The Dedication of the Basilicas of Ss Peter and Paul, Apostles	
		Proper Readings	
		Mass & Office of the Memorial	
19 Thu	G	feria: Mass ad lib; Office of the day	
20 Fri	G	feria: Mass ad lib; Office of the day	*Friday abstinence*
21 Sat	W	The Presentation of the Blessed Virgin Mary	
		Preface I or II of the Blessed Virgin Mary	
		Mass and Office of the Memorial	
evening	W	First Vespers	
22 Sun	W	**+ OUR LORD JESUS CHRIST, King of the Universe**	
		Gloria, Creed, Proper Preface	
		Mass & Office of the Solemnity	
		§ Youth Day	
23 Mon	G	feria, Thirty-Fourth Week of Year 2	*Ps Week 2*
		Mass ad lib; Office of the day *or*	
	R	St Clement I, Pope & Martyr: Mass & Office of the Memorial *or*	
	W	St Columban, Abbot: Mass & Office of the Memorial	
24 Tue	R	St Andrew Dũng-Lạc, Priest, and Companions, Martyrs	
		Mass & Office of the Memorial	
25 Wed	G	feria: Mass ad lib; Office of the day *or*	
	R	St Catherine of Alexandria, Virgin & Martyr:	
		Mass & Office of the Memorial	
26 Thu	G	feria: Mass ad lib, Office of the day	
27 Fri	G	feria: Mass ad lib; office of the day	*Friday abstinence*
28 Sat	G	feria: Mass ad lib; Office of the day *or*	
	W	Blessed Virgin Mary on Saturday: Mass & Office of the Memorial	

NOVEMBER/DECEMBER 2020

LECTIONARY FOR SUNDAYS: YEAR B

ADVENT

Advent has a two-fold character: as a season to prepare for Christmas, when Christ's first coming to us is remembered; and as a season when that remembrance directs the mind and heart to await Christ's coming at the end of time. Advent is thus a period for devout and joyful expectation.

The playing of the organ and other musical instruments, and the decoration of the altar with flowers should be done in a moderate manner, as is consonant with the character of the season, without anticipating the full joy of the Nativity of the Lord. The same moderation should be observed in the celebration of marriage. **Eucharistic Prayer 4 is not used in this Season.**

evening	P	First Vespers (Divine Office Volume I)	
29 Sun	P	**+ 1st SUNDAY OF ADVENT** *Creed, Advent Preface I (and on following days)* Mass & Office of the day	*Ps Week I*
30 Mon	R	**ST ANDREW, Apostle, Patron of Scotland** *Gloria, Preface I or II of Apostles* Mass & Office of the Feast	*National*

DECEMBER 2020

1 Tue	P	Advent feria, First Week of Advent: Mass & Office of the day	
2 Wed	P	Advent feria: Mass & Office of the day	
3 Thu	W	St Francis Xavier, Priest: Mass & Office of the Memorial	
4 Fri	P W	Advent feria: Mass & Office of the day *or* St John Damascene, Priest & Doctor: Mass & Office of the Memorial	*Friday abstinence*
5 Sat	P	Advent feria: Mass & Office of the day	
evening	P	First Vespers	
6 Sun	P	**+ 2nd SUNDAY OF ADVENT** *Creed, Advent Preface I* Mass & Office of the day § Bible Sunday	*Ps Week 2*
7 Mon	W	St Ambrose, Bishop & Doctor: Mass & Office of the Memorial	

DECEMBER 2020

evening	W	First Vespers
8 Tue	W	**THE IMMACULATE CONCEPTION OF THE BLESSED VIRGIN MARY, Patron of the Diocese** *Gloria, Creed, Proper Preface* Mass & Office of the Solemnity
9 Wed	P W	Advent feria, Second Week of Advent: Mass & Office of the day *or* St Juan Diego Cuauhtlatoatzin: Mass & Office of the Memorial
10 Thu	P	Advent feria: Mass & Office of the day
11 Fri	P W	Advent feria: Mass & Office of the day *or* *Friday abstinence* St Damasus I, Pope: Mass & Office of the Memorial
12 Sat	P W	Advent feria: Mass & Office of the day *or* Our Lady of Guadalupe: Mass & Office of the Memorial
evening	RP or P	First Vespers
13 Sun	RP or P	+ 3rd SUNDAY OF ADVENT (Gaudete Sunday) *Ps Week 3* *Creed, Advent Preface I* Mass & Office of the day
14 Mon	W	St John of the Cross, Priest & Doctor: Mass & Office of the Memorial
15 Tue	P	Advent feria, Third Week of Advent: Mass & Office of the day
16 Wed	P	Advent feria: Mass & Office of the day
		Memorials which occur on days between 17 and 31 December may be commemorated at Mass by using the collect of the saint in place of the collect of the day. In the Office of Readings the proper hagiographical reading and responsory may be added after the Patristic reading and responsory; the collect of the saint concludes the office. At Lauds and Vespers the antiphon (proper or common) and collect of the saint may be added after the collect of the day. At Mass, proper texts and readings are given for the weekdays from 17-24 December, and these should be used instead of those indicated for the weekdays of the third or fourth week of Advent.
17 Thu	P	Advent feria *Advent Preface II (and on following days)* Mass & Office of 17 December

DECEMBER 2020

18 Fri	P	Advent feria: Mass & Office of 18 December	*Friday abstinence*
19 Sat	P	Advent feria: Mass & Office of 19 December	
evening	P	First Vespers: Magnificat antiphon of 19 December	

20 Sun — P

+ 4th SUNDAY OF ADVENT   *Ps Week 4*
Creed, Advent Preface II
Mass of the day; Office of the day, with readings, also Benedictus &
Magnificat antiphons of 20 December
(see Divine Office Vol I, page 139 ff)
§ Expectant Mothers
Announce Holy Day of Obligation

21 Mon — P

Advent feria: Mass & Office of 21 December
(Alternative 1st Reading)
(St Peter Canisius, Priest and Doctor)

22 Tue — P

Advent feria: Mass & Office of 22 December

23 Wed — P

Advent feria: Mass & Office of 23 December
(St John of Kanty, Priest)

24 Thu — P

Advent feria: Mass & Office of 24 December

CHRISTMAS SEASON
After the annual celebration of the Paschal Mystery there is no more
ancient feast day for the Church than the recalling of the memory of
the Nativity of the Lord and of the mysteries of his first appearing.
Eucharistic Prayer 4 is not used in this season.

evening — W / W

First Vespers
+ Proper Vigil Mass of Christmas precedes or follows
Gloria, Proper Readings (Short form Gospel), Creed, (kneel at Incarnatus)*, a
Preface of the Nativity & Communicantes in the Roman Canon*

For pastoral reasons, readings at the following Christmas Masses
may be chosen from among all those provided for the Solemnity.
It is appropriate that a Solemn Vigil be kept by celebrating the Office
of Readings before the Mass during the Night. Compline is omitted by
those attending that Mass.

W

+ Mass during the Night
Gloria, Proper Readings, Creed (kneel at Incarnatus)*, a Preface of the
Nativity & Communicantes in the Roman Canon*

SECTION 7: LITURGICAL CALENDAR

DECEMBER 2020

25 Fri	W	**+ THE NATIVITY OF THE LORD (CHRISTMAS)**

Gloria, Proper Readings (Short form Gospel), *No Friday*
Creed (kneel at Incarnatus), *a Preface of the Nativity* *abstinence*
& Communicantes in the Roman Canon
Mass & Office of the Solemnity
All priests may celebrate or concelebrate three Masses today,
provided that they are celebrated at their proper time.

26 Sat	R	ST STEPHEN, The First Martyr

*Gloria, Proper Readings, a Preface of the Nativity & Communicantes in
the Roman Canon*
Mass, Lauds & Lesser Hours of St Stephen

	R	*(In parishes dedicated to ST STEPHEN, The First Martyr, his*

Solemnity is observed:
*Gloria, 1st Reading Proper, 2nd Reading from the Common of Martyrs,
Proper Gospel, Creed, a Preface of the Nativity & Communicantes in
the Roman Canon,* **Second Vespers of the Solemnity**

evening	W	First Vespers

27 Sun	W	+ THE HOLY FAMILY OF JESUS, MARY AND JOSEPH

*Gloria, 1st and 2nd Readings, Gospel of Year B or ad lib Year B Readings,
Creed, a Preface of the Nativity & Communicantes in the Roman Canon*
Mass & Office of the Feast

	W	*(+ In parishes dedicated to ST JOHN, Apostle & Evangelist, his*

Solemnity is observed:
*Gloria, 1st Reading from the Proper of All Saints, Other Readings Proper,
Creed, a Preface of the Nativity & Communicantes in the Roman
Canon* **First and Second Vespers of the Solemnity)**

28 Mon	R	THE HOLY INNOCENTS, Martyrs

*Gloria, Proper Readings, a Preface of the Nativity
& Communicantes in the Roman Canon*
**Mass, Lauds & Lesser Hours of the Holy Innocents; Vespers of the
Octave**

29 Tue	R	ST THOMAS BECKET, Bishop and Martyr *National*

Patron of the Parish Clergy
*Gloria, Proper National Readings, a Preface of the Nativity &
Communicantes in the Roman Canon*
**Mass, Lauds & Lesser Hours of St Thomas Becket; Vespers of the
Octave**

	R	*(In parishes dedicated to ST THOMAS BECKET, Bishop & Martyr, his*

Solemnity is observed:
*Gloria, 1st Reading from the Common of Martyrs, 2nd Reading & Gospel
Proper, Creed, a Preface of the Nativity & Communicantes in the Roman
Canon,* **1st and 2nd Vespers of the Solemnity)**

DECEMBER 2020/JANUARY 2021

30 Wed	W	**6th DAY IN THE OCTAVE OF CHRISTMAS**
		Gloria, a Preface of the Nativity & Communicantes in the Roman Canon
		Mass & Office of the Octave

31 Thu	W	**7th DAY IN THE OCTAVE OF CHRISTMAS**
		Gloria, a Preface of the Nativity & Communicantes in the Roman Canon
		Mass & Office of the Octave
		(St Sylvester 1, Pope)

evening	W	First Vespers

JANUARY 2021

1 Fri	W	**SOLEMNITY OF MARY,** *No Friday*
		THE HOLY MOTHER OF GOD *abstinence*
		THE OCTAVE DAY OF THE NATIVITY OF THE LORD
		Gloria, Creed, Preface 1 of Blessed Virgin Mary & Communicantes in the Roman Canon
		Mass & Office of the Solemnity

A Preface of the Nativity is used on weekdays of the Christmas season, unless other provision is made.

2 Sat	W	Ss Basil the Great and Gregory Nazianzen, *Ps Week 1*
		Bishops & Doctors
		Readings of 2 January
		Mass & Office of the Memorial

evening	W	First Vespers

3 Sun	W	SECOND SUNDAY AFTER THE NATIVITY *Ps Week 2*
		Gloria, (Short form Gospel), Creed, a Preface of the Nativity
		Mass & Office of the day
		Announce Holy Day of Obligation

4 Mon	W	Christmas feria
		First Collect, Readings of 4 January
		Mass & Office of the day

5 Tue	W	Christmas feria
		First Collect, Readings of 5 January
		Mass & Office of the day

evening	W	First Vespers
	W	+ Proper Vigil Mass of the Epiphany precedes or follows
		Gloria, Epiphany Readings, Creed, Proper Preface & Communicantes of the Epiphany in the Roman Canon

SECTION 7: LITURGICAL CALENDAR

JANUARY 2021

6 Wed	W	**+ THE EPIPHANY OF THE LORD**

Gloria, Creed, Proper Preface & Communicantes *of the Epiphany in the Roman Canon; an increased display of lights is recommended.*

At today's Mass, after the Gospel, the announcement may be made of moveable feasts according to the formula given in the Roman Pontifical, on page 1247 of the Missale Romanum, editio typica tertia *and page 1505 of the Roman Missal.*

Mass & Office of the Solemnity

A Preface of the Nativity or of the Epiphany is used until the Christmas season ends, unless other provision is made.

7 Thu	W	Christmas feria *or*

St Raymond of Penyafort
Second Collect, Readings of Thursday after Epiphany
Mass & Office of the day *or*
Mass & Office of the Memorial

8 Fri	W	Christmas feria	*Friday abstinence*

Second Collect, Readings of Friday after Epiphany
Mass & Office of the day

9 Sat	W	Christmas feria

Second Collect, Readings of Saturday after Epiphany
Mass & Office of the day

evening	W	First Vespers

10 Sun	W	+ THE BAPTISM OF THE LORD

Gloria, (Alternative Collect), 1st and 2nd Reading, Gospel of Year B, or ad lib *Year B Readings, Creed, Proper Preface*
Mass & Office of the Feast

Christmas Time ends.

INDEX OF ADVERTISEMENTS

Further advertisements which may be helpful can be found in the **Westminster Record.**

INDEX

NOTES

NOTES

Calendar 2020

JANUARY

S	M	T	W	T	F	S
			1	2	3	4
5	6	7	8	9	10	11
12	13	14	15	16	17	18
19	20	21	22	23	24	25
26	27	28	29	30	31	

FEBRUARY

S	M	T	W	T	F	S
						1
2	3	4	5	6	7	8
9	10	11	12	13	14	15
16	17	18	19	20	21	22
23	24	25	26	27	28	29

MARCH

S	M	T	W	T	F	S
1	2	3	4	5	6	7
8	9	10	11	12	13	14
15	16	17	18	19	20	21
22	23	24	25	26	27	28
29	30	31				

APRIL

S	M	T	W	T	F	S
			1	2	3	4
5	6	7	8	9	10	11
12	13	14	15	16	17	18
19	20	21	22	23	24	25
26	27	28	29	30		

MAY

S	M	T	W	T	F	S
					1	2
3	4	5	6	7	8	9
10	11	12	13	14	15	16
17	18	19	20	21	22	23
24	25	26	27	28	29	30
31						

JUNE

S	M	T	W	T	F	S
	1	2	3	4	5	6
7	8	9	10	11	12	13
14	15	16	17	18	19	20
21	22	23	24	25	26	27
28	29	30				

JULY

S	M	T	W	T	F	S
			1	2	3	4
5	6	7	8	9	10	11
12	13	14	15	16	17	18
19	20	21	22	23	24	25
26	27	28	29	30	31	

AUGUST

S	M	T	W	T	F	S
						1
2	3	4	5	6	7	8
9	10	11	12	13	14	15
16	17	18	19	20	21	22
23	24	25	26	27	28	29
30	31					

SEPTEMBER

S	M	T	W	T	F	S
		1	2	3	4	5
6	7	8	9	10	11	12
13	14	15	16	17	18	19
20	21	22	23	24	25	26
27	28	29	30			

OCTOBER

S	M	T	W	T	F	S
				1	2	3
4	5	6	7	8	9	10
11	12	13	14	15	16	17
18	19	20	21	22	23	24
25	26	27	28	29	30	31

NOVEMBER

S	M	T	W	T	F	S
1	2	3	4	5	6	7
8	9	10	11	12	13	14
15	16	17	18	19	20	21
22	23	24	25	26	27	28
29	30					

DECEMBER

S	M	T	W	T	F	S
		1	2	3	4	5
6	7	8	9	10	11	12
13	14	15	16	17	18	19
20	21	22	23	24	25	26
27	28	29	30	31		

NOTES